Ghazālī and the Poetics of Imagination

Islamic Civilization and Muslim Networks

Carl W. Ernst and Bruce B. Lawrence, editors

GHAZĀLĪ

and the Poetics of Imagination

EBRAHIM MOOSA

The University of North Carolina Press

Chapel Hill and London

Manufactured in the United States of America

Designed by April Leidig-Higgins
Set in Monotype Garamond by Tseng Information Systems, Inc.

The paper in this book meets the guidelines for permanence and durability of the Committee on Production Guidelines for Book Longevity of the Council on Library Resources.

Library of Congress Cataloging-in-Publication Data
Moosa, Ebrahim.
Ghazālī and the poetics of imagination /
Ebrahim Moosa.
p. cm. — (Islamic civilization and Muslim networks)
Includes bibliographical references and index.
ISBN 0-8078-2952-8 (cloth : alk. paper) —
ISBN 0-8078-5612-6 (pbk.)
1. Ghazālī, 1058–1111. 2. Philosophy, Islamic.
3. Imagination—Religious aspects—Islam.
4. Creative ability—Religious aspects—Islam.
I. Title. II. Islamic civilization & Muslim networks.
B753.G34M66 2005
181'.5—dc22 2005043094

cloth 09 08 07 06 05 5 4 3 2 1
paper 09 08 07 06 05 5 4 3 2 1

To Nisa, Lamya, and Shibli
With love and gratitude

As the end approaches, wrote Cartaphilus, *there are no longer any images from memory—there are only words*. Words, words, words taken out of place and mutilated, words from other men—those were the alms left him by the hours and the centuries.—Jorge Luis Borges, "The Immortal"

As for the rest of us, we cannot transform completely. Not even myths can change those invisible roots, ingrained like ancient fossil in rock. We do not metamorphose. We merely crumble into dust. That is my triumph. . . .
I have broken the cycle of remembrance.—Achmat Dangor, *Kafka's Curse*

Contents

Acknowledgments

No acknowledgment can do justice to the many people—family, friends, close colleagues, loved ones, and strangers—I have known over many years. If it takes a village to raise a child, then it takes much more to nurture one who aspires to scholarship. One learns from all of life's facets, the pleasant and unpleasant. You learn from friends and foes, from intimates and strangers. To all of them, I owe a debt of gratitude.

I want to thank my parents for their nurture and support over the years. I want to thank all my siblings, my extended family from both the paternal and the maternal sides, as well as my extended family of in-laws, for their warm and generous support over the years. Without you all, I would be the poorer. I want to thank my many teachers and instructors, some of whom have passed on, for all their efforts and labors over time.

The support, friendship, and collegiality of friends have sustained me over the years, and I have learned a great deal from them. I will forever remember the late Ayesha Valley-Omar, whom I called "Naa." There could not be a more tender soul; she lovingly cared for and nurtured me—and all of us Moosa kids—in my early childhood and youth. She was our role model of compassion, integrity, and the finer points of etiquette (*adab*). I shall forever mourn the loss of three close friends—Soraya Bosch, Shamima Shaikh, and Yakoub Vawda—whose lives have enriched me immensely. I would like to personally thank some of my friends and colleagues, even at the risk of knowing that I am excluding many. Each one of those I list has enriched me in a specific way, and I want to thank them all: Naṣr Ḥāmid Abū Zayd, Abdullahi An-Naim, Talal Asad, Ahmad Dallal, Farid Esack, Khaled Abou El Fadl, Muneer Fareed, Muhammad Fadel, Lenn Goodman, Bob Gregg, Ḥasan Ḥanafī, Abdul Hakim Sherman Jackson, Shamil Jeppie, Naᶜeem Jeenah, Mahmood Mamdani, the Manjras—Ismail, Ahmad, and Shuaib—Muhammad Khalid Masud, Ahmad Musaddequrrahman, Abdul Rashied Omar, Abdulaziz Sachedina, Saᶜdiyya

Shaikh, Tahir Fuzile Sitoto, Abdulkader Tayob, Richard C. Martin, and Amina Wadud. My colleagues in the Department of Religion and at the John Hope Franklin Center at Duke University have all been supportive. In particular, I want to thank the departmental chair, Wesley Kort, as well as Kalman Bland, Richard Jaffe, Melvin Peters, Leela Prasad, and Lucas von Rompay for their support and collegiality, just as I must thank the administrative staff—Nancy Hurtgen, Sandra Woods, Gay Trotter, and Katherine Duke—for making our lives easier. Deans William Chafe and Karla Holloway have been supportive in every way, as have Gilbert W. Merkx, vice provost for international affairs and development, and Rob Sikorski, executive director of the Center for International Studies. I want to thank my colleagues in the Department of Religious Studies at Stanford University, who were supportive in every way during my extended visit there. During my decade in the Department of Religious Studies at the University of Cape Town, my colleagues and the university administrators provided me with extraordinary support during the early and formative part of my academic career, which I acknowledge with deep appreciation.

During the preparation of this manuscript, several people read early drafts, made suggestions, and assisted with bibliographical research and preparation. I want to thank Hina Azam, Usep Matin, Youshaa Patel, and Mareike Winkelmann, who read very early drafts of this manuscript and made valuable suggestions. Librarians have been immensely helpful and supportive to me. I want to thank Asia Brey, formerly at the Jagger Library at the University of Cape Town, Kavous Barghai at the Hoover Library at Stanford, and Christoff Galli at Duke University. Abdul Aleem Somers has been a wonderful supplier of books, wisdom, and friendship over the years. My thanks to my editor at the University of North Carolina Press, Elaine Maisner, for her immense support and dedication in this venture. It has been a privilege to work with her. Paula Wald at UNC Press conducted the entire editing process professionally, efficiently, and caringly, for which I am grateful. I owe special gratitude to Ruth Homrighaus, whose rigorous editorial skills and sensitive editing of this manuscript have not only saved me from several embarrassing infelicities but also helped to bring clarity and focus to the text that I could not have achieved unaided.

Carl Ernst kindly read the entire manuscript and gave me the benefit of his valuable insights, while miriam cooke, my colleague at Duke, read sections of the manuscript at various stages of the project and made helpful editorial suggestions; I wish to thank her for her support. Walter Mignolo, Nelson

Maldonando-Torres, and my colleagues in the Dialogical Ethics and Critical Cosmopolitanism working group at Duke University were regular interlocutors. There are few words that can describe my debt to Bruce B. Lawrence for his selfless friendship and passionate collegiality. Bruce was a constant sounding board for ideas, a counselor, and a friend who read my many drafts. I am deeply in his debt. Needless to say, all errors and shortcomings are mine alone.

Finally, I owe a great debt and gratitude to my family. Nisa, my wife, has stood steadfastly by my side through the many twists of our lives that have taken us over continents and shores, and she has been a tower of support. Our children, Lamya and Shibli, have graciously, if sometimes reluctantly, understood the demands of scholarship and academic service on my time. Their support and encouragement have always been my source of comfort and have given me strength to continue.

Chronology

450/1058–59	Ghazālī is born in Ṭūs near what is today the city of Mashhad, Iran.
465/1073	Begins studies in Ṭūs with Muḥammad al-Rādhkānī around age fifteen.
465–70/1073–78	Travels to Jurjān to study law with Ismāʿīl b. Masʿada al-Ismāʿīlī for at least two years.
470/1077–78	Returns to Ṭūs; famous encounter with thieves takes place.
473/1080	Goes to Nisapūr to study with al-Juwaynī.
478–84/1085–91	Remains in the entourage of the *wazīr*, Niẓām al-Mulk.
484/1091	Appointed professor in Baghdād Niẓāmīya.
488/1095	Leaves Baghdād on pretext of pilgrimage.
488–93/1095–1100	Commutes between Damascus, Jerusalem, Makka, and Madīna, with possible visits to Baghdād and Hamadhān.
493/1099–1100	Returns to Ṭūs in semiretirement, teaching selected students and establishing a ṣūfī retreat center.
499/1106	Recalled to teach at the Niẓāmīya in Nisapūr by the *wazīr*, Fakhr al-Mulk, the son of Niẓām al-Mulk.
503/1109–10	Ends his teaching in Nisapūr and returns to Ṭūs.
505/1111	Dies in Ṭūs Monday, 14 Jamādi al-ākhira; buried at the cemetery in the nearby village of Sanābād.

Ghazālī and the Poetics of Imagination

An unexamined life is not worth living. —Socrates

Introduction

In many ways, this book is a dialogical encounter with perhaps the most influential intellectual in the Muslim tradition: Abū Ḥāmid al-Ghazālī.[1] It is a dialogue with many voices, one that fosters motion, discovery, playfulness, and invention. It is a dialogue that serendipitously began some three decades ago, when on a busy street in what was then Bombay, now Mumbai, as a shell-shocked but aspiring student ready to study in one of India's many seminaries (called *madrasas* or *dār al-ʿulūms*), I bought my first book on the history of Islamic thought. I purchased it from a secondhand bookseller on the cluttered pavement of Mumbai's Mohammed Ali Road. I still vividly recall the garish red vinyl cover of the book; it was a translation of a few selected chapters from Ghazālī's influential and well-known text *Resuscitation of the Sciences of Religion* (*Iḥyāʾ ʿulūm al-dīn*).

For some years, this red book adorned the shelves of my student residence rooms. I remember that the translator was someone of South Asian descent. However, there is a reason why I impulsively purchased the book: the name

"Imām al-Ghazālī" resonated with me. My religious and cultural education in South Africa had made me aware that Ghazālī was a major figure in the history of the Muslim tradition, but I did not know why he was considered so important.

To be brutally honest, at the time of purchasing the red book at age seventeen I could barely understand what this author was saying. And, like so many well-intentioned book acquisitions, this one never came off the shelf for serious reading during my student days. I made perhaps one or two attempts to make sense of its contents only to be frustrated by my inability to grasp its purpose. So I jealously guarded this book like one would revere the pages of a talisman. Eventually, however, I either lent this precious acquisition to someone who never returned it, or, as is the custom with unused books, it vanished mysteriously when neglected by its owner!

Whatever the fate of that red-covered book, Ghazālī never left me entirely. Over the years, haltingly and hesitatingly, I started to read selected pages of the *Resuscitation*, often mining it in search of inspiration or ideas in preparation for a talk. And gradually, even surreptitiously, this author became an indispensable companion in my intellectual and existential journey. I offer what follows as but one installment—the distance of one way station—in my journey with Ghazālī.

My own intellectual journey ranges from early studies in the scholastic Muslim tradition with grounding in the classical texts of Arabic grammar, literature, law, legal theory, theology, philosophy, and logic, among other subjects, to an encounter with modern disciplines of the humanities and the social sciences. In trying to make sense of two intellectual traditions while existentially battling racism, colonialism, and imperialism in my own South African community, I have had to struggle with several issues and questions. In more than one way, this book also maps the way I negotiate these questions in the company of Ghazālī.

Brief Biography

Known as "al-Gazel" in the Christian West, Ghazālī is by far one of the most influential thinkers in the world. His enduring legacy has guaranteed his eminence as an intellectual not only for Islamdom but also beyond it: his relevance surpasses the limitations of cultures and creeds. His critical interventions in religious thought gave the Muslim intellectual tradition an unprecedented vitality and depth for which he has been canonized over the centuries, even though some Muslim intellectuals have viewed—and continue to view—him as a contested figure.

Near the modern city of Mashhad in northern Iran, Abū Ḥāmid Muḥammad al-Ghazālī was born in 450 A.H./1058–59 A.D. This was some seven years before the Battle of Hastings and the Norman Conquest of England. Ṭūs, the city of his birth, was particularly poor; it had been ravaged by severe drought and consequent famine for several years.[2] Ghazālī was born to a modest household; his father probably derived his income from vending wool, which may explain the attribution *ghazzāl* (wool spinner or vendor) in his family name. Others speculate that the attribution refers to an unidentified village of the same name.

There have been as many Ghazālīs as there have been readers of this major figure. The popular version of Ghazālī as the man who encounters doubt and dramatically changes the direction of his life is a thrilling account, immortalizing his ideas and his sterling contributions to religious thought. In many parts of today's Muslim world, Ghazālī is a household name, while in some other locations people have only a vague recollection or memory of him as an renowned scholar or a pious figure. By his critics, Ghazālī is also viewed as formidable, but formidable for the harm that he has done. They charge that it was he who sowed the seeds for some of the most interminable discursive aporias in Muslim thought.

I concur with the well-attested-to view that one can identify at least two major phases in the life of Ghazālī. The first encompasses his student years in Ṭūs, Jurjān, and later in Nisapūr. His formative education took place in each of these three cities with teachers such as Aḥmad b. Muḥammad al-Rādhkānī (d. ca. 475/1082) in Ṭūs and Abū al-Qāsim Ismāʿīl b. Masʿada al-Ismāʿīlī (d. 477/1084), who was the leading jurist and scholar among the Shāfiʿīs in Jurjān.[3] There is a good chance that Ghazālī either encountered ʿAbd al-Qāhir al-Jurjānī (d. 471/1078 or 474/1081), a literary critic and an influential language theorist of his time, in that city or at least became familiar with Jurjānī's ideas, since there are unmistakable traces of them in Ghazālī's writing. At the Nisapūr branch of the Niẓāmīya, Ghazālī studied with one of the leading scholars of the time, Imām al-Ḥaramayn ʿAbd al-Malik b. ʿAbd Allāh al-Juwaynī (d. 478/1085), better known as Abū al-Maʿālī al-Juwaynī, who held the celebrated chair in Shāfiʿī law for thirty years.

Between 478/1085 and 484/1091, a period of roughly seven years, it is not

Iraq and Iran in the Tenth and Eleventh Centuries. Based on Hugh Kennedy, ed., *An Historical Atlas of Islam* (Leiden: Brill, 2002).

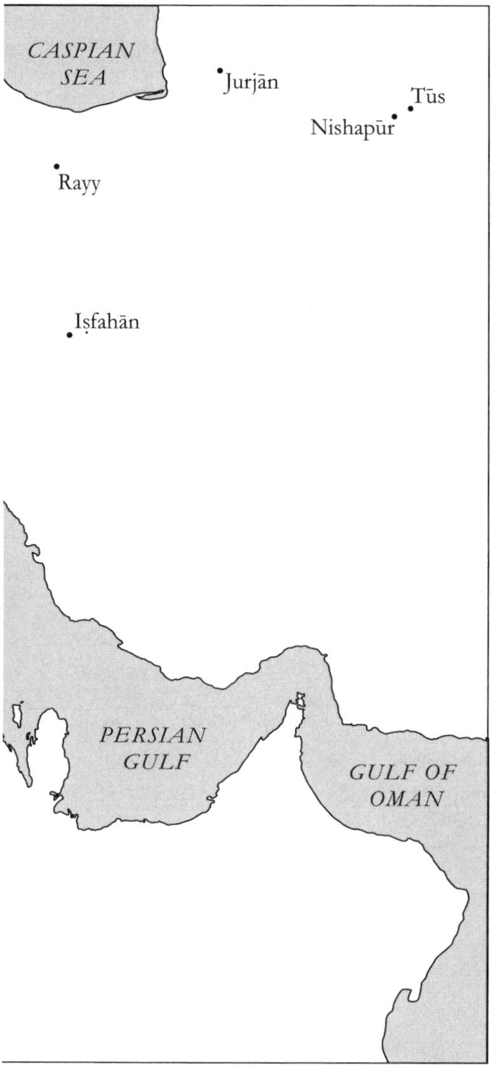
CASPIAN SEA
Jurjān
Ṭūs
Nishapūr
Rayy
Iṣfahān
PERSIAN GULF
GULF OF OMAN

clear what Ghazālī was doing. The most reliable accounts suggest that he spent these years in the retinue of scholars associated with the leading Saljūq *wazīr*, Niẓām al-Mulk Abū ʿAlī al-Ḥasan b. ʿAlī al-Ṭūsī (d. 485/1092). This extensive period of apprenticeship culminated in his appointment to a professorship in Shāfiʿī law at the Niẓāmīya College in Baghdād, which was founded by and named after the same *wazīr*. During this period, Ghazālī was extremely productive in his scholarship, achieving almost celebrity status from around 484/1091. It was during this time that he wrote some of his most influential texts on Muslim law, political theology, and logic, as well as especially significant critiques of the views of the Muslim philosophers.

The year 488/1095 turns out to have been Ghazālī's annus horribilis. The causes of his setback still remain a contentious area in scholarship. The result, however, was a debilitating illness during which he exhibited signs of depression and intellectual fatigue. He cryptically mentioned some of these symptoms in his spiritual testimony, appropriately titled *Rescuer from Misguidance* (*Al-munqidh min al-ḍalāl*).

When, in the same year, he abruptly abandoned his prestigious professorship, much to the chagrin of his friends and students, he set out traveling in the Islamic East. The second major phase of his career began with these life-transforming travels to the cities of Jerusalem, Damascus, and then later Makka and Madīna in Arabia. During this stage, Ghazālī developed an intense craving for the mystical realm and identified spiritual experience as the only path through which he could slake his thirst for certainty and inner peace. Throughout this intense struggle with his self, Ghazālī continued to write large and small treatises on a range of topics. The achievement that crowned Ghazālī's ṣūfī phase was the writing of his magnum opus, *Resuscitation of the Sciences of Religion*; he also wrote notable texts on gnostic piety, legal theory, and theology.

Around 493/1099–1100, he returned to his native Ṭūs, where he established a ṣūfī lodge and gave tuition to selected students. But much of his time was spent in prodigious writing, especially of the *Resuscitation*. With the exception of short trips to Baghdād or nearby regions for meetings with authorities, Ghazālī during this period had no major distractions except one. That was when the *wazīr*, Fakhr al-Mulk (d. 500/1106–7), with the endorsement of the Saljūq *sulṭān*, invited him to resume teaching at the Niẓāmīya in Nisapūr in 499/1106. That turned out to be for a very short spell, not longer than three years, since by 503/1109–10 he was back in Ṭūs, where he died in 505/1111.

Context

Ghazālī entered an eleventh-century Irano-Semitic, or Persianate, world that had already undergone momentous changes. Some sections of his native Persian society had been converted to Islam from the middle of the seventh century, in the very first century of the rise of Islam. By the time he arrived on the scene, Persia had been under substantial Islamic influence for at least three centuries, since large numbers of Persians converted to Islam in the ninth century.[4] The Arabicity of Islam gradually displaced Zoroastrianism and Manicheanism, once the dominant religions of Persia. It was sign of high culture during Ghazālī's time to be knowledgeable in Arabic and about the teachings of the Arab Prophet, while to be knowledgeable in the laws of Cyrus was less important. Yet Persianate culture was not totally effaced; it insinuated its way back into Islamic thought, as Ghazālī's work on occasion demonstrates.

Innumerable converts from China and India, of the Turkic races of the Mongolian steppes, from Africa, and even some from the Iberian Peninsula of Europe made up the mélange of the new faces of Islam. Each one of these groups brought with it its peculiar and particular articulations of the rapidly growing faith. The Pax Islamica had by then truly created an empire covering diverse parts of the globe and different nations, ethnicities, cultures, language groups, and economic and political environments. Those who articulated and explained Islam were no longer only Arabs; non-Arabs like Ghazālī also played a prominent role. No less an authority than the Tunis-born historian and sociologist ʿAbd al-Raḥmān Ibn Khaldūn (d. 784/1382) credits non-Arab intelligentsia with making up the largest number of those who shaped and determined the intellectual legacy of Islam.[5]

Ghazālī came on the stage about five centuries after the Prophet Muḥammad had proclaimed his message of monotheism to the world from the desert sands of Arabia. As such, he was born at the midpoint of Islam's march to a millennium—a fact that did not go unnoticed by Ghazālī and his admirers, who kept an eye on charismatic figures, casting them as those who renewed the faith at the beginning of every hundred years of the Muslim calendar. Furthermore, not only had the intellectual tradition of Islam undergone profound changes over the intervening five centuries, but Ghazālī too became a changed man within a few decades in his life.

His portrait is multifaceted. He was a person committed to many political and intellectual causes. But his embrace of law, politics, mysticism, and philosophy did not follow a uniform path. His was a complex psychology, a life pattern that did not yield to the Homeric orderly succession and alteration of emotions. It was more akin to the "simultaneous existence of various layers of consciousness and the conflict between them."[6] If the unpredictability of life shapes the career of a great person, then it is significant that Ghazālī's life was radically unpredictable and followed no logical pattern. Above all, one would be hard pressed to argue, as some have tried to do, that Ghazālī followed a middle-of-the-road position in his several ventures.[7]

A Milieu of Scholars and Intellectuals

Ghazālī was severely critical of the scholars of his day, whom he charged with abdicating their responsibility to perform their role as "heirs of the prophets."[8] As his own life turned toward the austere and mystical, his judgment of the scholars became increasingly critical, even entirely deprecatory. Despite their bias, Ghazālī's observations of the scholarly milieu provide us with some clues about the intellectual environment and how he saw it. It is worth citing some of his more passionate jeremiads: "The guides for the road [to salvation] are the learned," he notes, "who are the heirs of the prophets." But, he adds, the "times are devoid of them." With oracular force, he laments:

> Only the superficial among them remain, and those too, Satan has overcome and lured to iniquity. Each one of them is preoccupied with his own immediate interests, to the point that he views the good to be evil and the evil to be good. The result is that knowledge of religion has disappeared, extinguishing therewith the torch of guidance in all parts of the globe. They duped the people into believing that there was no knowledge except government decrees,[9] on which judges rely in order to settle disputes when the mobs riot. [What remains, are those scholars] who through polemics seek to attain glory by way of triumph in debate or in refuting [an opponent] or in producing flowery prose, with which the preacher gradually tries to win favor with the populace. Without these three goals, they can find no other means to attain illegal profit and earthly wealth.[10]

Ghazālī paints a corrosive picture of the scholars of his day. Intellectuals, he argues, are motivated by self-interest (*aghrāḍ*), yet they continue to delude themselves into believing that their nefarious motives are consistent with religion and religiosity.[11] "Among those engaged in delivering sermons and lectures, in performing the duties of judgeship and acting as official preachers, as well as among those occupying different levels of leadership," he continues relentlessly, "one will surely find those who follow their lusts." Reflecting on their motives, he adds: "They will pretend nevertheless, that their true motive is religious, claiming that they are motivated by the desire to earn rewards [in the hereafter] and that they truly wish to vie with one another in matters of religion. But, [in fact,] this is nothing but the height of idiocy and vanity."[12]

Ghazālī was not the only respectable figure to hold such unflattering views about scholar-jurists. If we read his opinion together with the comments of two prominent predecessors, we get a better commentary on the spirit of the intellectual milieu. The first writer preceded Ghazālī by more than a century, and the second died when Ghazālī was only an infant. Abū al-Ḥasan al-ʿĀmirī (d. 381/992), in a political treatise, *Publicizing the Virtues of Islam* (*Al-iʿlām bi manāqib al-Islām*), says something almost akin to what Ghazālī later said about his fellow scholar-jurists. "The jurists have now made it their purpose to lord over the common people to curry favor with the authorities," observes ʿĀmirī, "in order to gain control over the property of the powerless, and to invalidate at will the rights of others." He continues ruefully: "Therefore, their craft, which once deserved praise, now attracts blame, in fulfillment with the word of God: 'Woe to those who pray, but who do not care for it, who make a show [of loyalty], but refuse to support [it].'"[13]

But it is the breathtaking humanist poet Abū al-ʿAlāʾ al-Maʿarrī (d. 449/1057) who writes with a certain chastity when he does parody the religious scholars of his day in his *Luzūmiyāt*:

They recite their sacred books, although [the fact informs me]
  that these are fiction from first to last
O Reason, thou [alone] speakest the truth. Then perish the fools
  Who forged the [religious] traditions or interpreted them!
A rabbi is no heretic among his disciples,
  If he sets a high price on stories which he invented
He only desired to marry women
  And amass riches by his lies.
Softly! Thou has been deceived, honest man as thou art,
  By a cunning knave who preaches to the women.
Amongst you in the morning he says that wine is forbidden, but
  He makes a point of drinking it himself in the evening.[14]

Flaunting his skepticism, Maʿarrī diagnoses a moral weakness among public preachers and scholars of religion, a point of view that Ghazālī later endorsed. Ghazālī makes a similar complaint: that the jurists and scholars gave disproportionate attention to the texts of the law, expediently seeking financial rewards at the expense of spiritual commitment.

Ghazālī did not condemn all the scholars. In fact, he acknowledged those who were "truly learned" and who espoused the nobility that knowledge brings, praising those who comprehended the true meaning of the word "discernment" (*fiqh*), a term usually used to refer to positive law.[15] He went on to say that proper discernment means seeking the path to salvation and success in the hereafter. The "prattling wearers of flowing robes" (as he mockingly refers to the pretentious scholar-jurists in his savage broadsides) and the preachers of his day were too obsessed, he thought, with the minutiae of the law and legal controversies.[16] It was not surprising, given their misplaced interest, that they failed to grasp the deeper meaning of the Qur'ān and piety, unlike the scholars of early Islam. Ghazālī designates the comprehension of these meanings as a form of enlightened discernment (*tafaqquh*).[17]

Ghazālī laments the lack of intellectual independence and integrity on the part of the scholars. They cannot meet the demands of their calling as torchbearers of prophetic knowledge. Ultimately, only prophetic knowledge can illuminate the path to true emancipation. Most scholars, he notes, are sycophants, groveling at the feet of political leaders, displaying egotistical behavior, driven by insatiable materialism. The passion with which Ghazālī speaks about his peers gives one the impression that he based his writing on personal observation.

However, there was something subtle lurking behind his jeremiads against those entrusted with the guardianship of the intellectual legacy of religion. Despite his negativity toward the scholars of religion, he nevertheless recognized the important place of religion in the engineering of society. In this sense, the intellectual functionaries of religion did indeed serve as a crucial index of the moral pulse and well-being of society. His dim view of the scholarly classes and jurists must be seen in the light of his own conversion and his deep disenchantment with their intellectual orientation, which he had in part abandoned; in more than one sense, he was both an insider of and an outsider to the institutions of his time. His condemnation of the scholars of his day should not be taken to mean that all intellectuals were utterly remiss in their social functions. None other than his own professor, Juwaynī, had to flee persecution in Khurāsān and seek exile in Makka for several years for speaking truth to power. Juwaynī's ostensible offense was his refusal to give obeisance to certain authority figures within the Saljūq administration.

Similarly, it would be improper to issue a blanket dismissal of the political classes as essentially corrupt, proffering these selective snapshots as evidence. For, despite their autocratic style of governance and their insatiable desire for power, the expedient Saljūqs did have a sense of respect for the rule of law. Even on those occasions when the Saljūqs intended to manipulate political institutions to their advantage, they did so using legal means. To this end, they would mobilize and secure a legal opinion (*fatwā*) in order to justify a particular change. Or they would co-opt the educated classes by bestowing honorifics on judges and scholars or commissioning them to perform certain public functions as advisors, envoys, and mediators. Ghazālī's disparaging remarks that some scholars were predisposed to issuing rulings that conformed to the wishes of authority may have referred to these legitimating activities. Indirectly, the remarks suggest that the Saljūqs adhered to the rule of law and recognized that the legal system and its functionaries carried weight, affirming that it was essential to the proper functioning of society for the scholar-jurists to have a modicum of authority.

For instance, during the bitter rivalry between the sons of the Saljūq *sulṭān* Malikshāh (d. 485/1092) over the *sulṭanate*, one son, Barkyāruq (d. 498/1105), dispatched two *qāḍīs*, Abū al-Muẓaffar al-Jurjānī and Abū al-Faraj Aḥmad al-Hamadhānī (d. 525/1131), in 497/1104 to negotiate a truce with his brother Muḥammad.[18] As occupants of a high office and persons of prestige and authority, the *qāḍīs* were often seen as interlocutors and defenders of the people's rights when invading armies were about to plunder or assault cities. In Wāsiṭ, the *qāḍī* requested that Barkyāruq's army be restrained. A few years earlier, in 495/1101, when there was a conflict between Il-Ghāzī, the military governor (*shiḥna*) of Baghdād, and the people of Baghdād, the caliph, Mustaẓhir, delegated a classmate and friend of Ghazālī's, Ilkiyā al-Harrāsī, a professor at the Baghdād Niẓāmīya College, to resolve the conflict between the disputing parties.

The world in which Ghazālī moved was indeed in a great deal of political ferment. Together with the intellectual movements, the rise of religious colleges, sectarian divisions, and the repeated change of the political guard around the caliphate from the Buwayhids to the Saljūqs made up the disparate elements of the spirit of the times. Life in the main cities of Khurāsān and Baghdād was swathed in a cosmopolitan air: diverse ethnic groups lived side by side under the influence of an Arabizing political culture, while Persianate culture also flourished, with its own inevitable rhythms of change. Colleges and institutions of learning played an important role in these societies, as they produced the core of the bureaucracy and intelligentsia. Despite the political despotism that was commonplace at the time, the Buwayhids, who were precursors to the Saljūqs, fostered an intellectual culture that reached a new high water mark. Under their rule, the arts, sciences, theology, and philosophy flourished. That era produced stellar figures, among them poets such as Mutanabbī and Maʿarrī and the philosopher Abū ʿAlī Ibn Sīnā (d. 428/1037).

The intellectual "renaissance" that took place under the Buwayhids, as Adam Mez characterized that period, set the scene for a great deal of intellectual ferment and creativity to have developed by the time that the Saljūqs became active in the late fifth/eleventh century.[19] Compared to the Buwayhids, the Saljūqs were on the whole less sympathetic to the philosophical sciences; nevertheless, they still patronized learning.[20] The Saljūqs made vast financial investments and endowments that entrenched and institutionalized a cosmopolitan intellectual culture. The educational institutions they sponsored offered career paths to teaching, scholarship, the judiciary, the bureaucracy, and preaching. Given the diversity of roles of the learned scholars (*ʿulamāʾ*), it is difficult to treat them as a class and offer a uniform description.

Traces of Ghazālī

A cursory survey will show that the Muslim tradition is saturated with Ghazālī's traces. His influence is to be found in many expressions of Muslim thought as a result of the breadth of his scholarship. From the very foundational texts of the legal tradition to theology, philosophy, mysticism, and ethics, Ghazālī's footprint is legible on some of the major documents that constitute the intellectual record. Few scholars can transcend their immediate ideological and contextual limitations as he did. It is a tribute to Ghazālī that even ideological and sectarian groups outside his own have taken him seriously. Ghazālī's intellectual output not only influences and shapes a variety of intellectual trends within the broad tapestry of Muslim thought, it also influences thinkers outside the Muslim sphere.

Despite the gulf between Sunnī and Shīʿī theological claims, Ghazālī's legacy has transcended sectarian boundaries. One of the leading Shīʿī scholars of Ṣafawid Persia, Muḥsin al-Kāshānī (d. 1090/1679), also known as Muḥsin-i Fayḍ-i Kāshānī, a student of the famous Mullā Ṣadrā (d. 1050/1640), adapted Ghazālī's opus *Resuscitation* and translated it so that it resonated with Shīʿī sensibilities. In a multivolume redaction called *The Bright Destination* (*Al-maḥajja al-bayḍāʾ*), Kāshānī made Ghazālī's ideas amenable to Shīʿī intellectual purposes, and this text is still used by scholars in Iran today.[21] While he followed the structure of the *Resuscitation* with minor amendments, Kāshānī found authentic Shīʿī sources for the prophetic reports (*ḥadīth*, pl. *aḥādīth*) and replaced the weak ones with more appropriate materials from Shīʿī sources.[22]

Even some of Ghazālī's fiercest critics, like the fastidious Ḥanbalī moralist and chronicler ʿAbd al-Raḥmān Ibn al-Jawzī (d. 597/1200) of the Ayyūbid period, who could barely tolerate Ghazālī's broad-gauged epistemology, conceded the value of his scholarship. For all his vehemence, Ibn al-Jawzī actually took the trouble to summarize elements of the *Resuscitation* into an epitome, which he titled *Path of the Truth-Seekers* (*Minhāj al-qāṣidīn*).[23] Likewise, the polemical Ibn Taymīya (d. 728/1328), who excoriated Ghazālī for his excessive infatuation with Hellenic thought, admitted that the underlying message of his work is consistent with the canons of Muslim teachings, namely the Qur'ān and *Sunna*. It is precisely the intellectual gravitas of Ghazālī's work that compels people to engage him even when they hold contradictory opinions about the value of his voluminous output.

Outside Muslim circles, the impact of Ghazālī's ideas on other intellectual traditions still awaits a more nuanced and critical assessment. However, one of the first people in Europe to acknowledge his debt to Ghazālī was the Majorcan theologian and philosopher Ramon Lull (1232–1316). This extraordinary nobleman-turned-evangelist wrote almost three hundred works, large and small, in Latin, Arabic, and Catalan in pursuit of his life's goal of promoting the Christian faith.[24] Lull's scholastic thirst has earned him a contentious reputation as a broad-gauged scholar. His interest in logic and Aristotelian demonstration in particular led him to Ghazālī.[25] Indeed, his first writing on logic, which accents its popular, natural, and moralizing themes, was titled *Compendium Logicae Algazelis*, a book he probably wrote around 1275.[26]

In fact, the *Compendium* has more than a titular link to Ghazālī. It is an adaptation of Ghazālī's *Goals of the Philosophers* (*Maqāṣid al-falāsifa*). The *Goals* was translated into Latin, probably as early as 1151, certainly between 1151 and 1166, by Dominicus Gundissalinus and a group of other scholars working in Toledo. Intellectual contact between Baghdād and the non-Muslim scholars of Toledo must have been remarkably brisk and efficient for such a work to have been translated within less than fifty years of the death of Ghazālī. What Lull found attractive in Ghazālī was the common intellectual passion each of them pursued in his own way.

For even though Ghazālī studied logic and philosophy in a combative mode, his main purpose was to integrate the methodology of the logicians into the study of theology in order to support religious doctrines as a means to illuminate the discourse of religion. Lull had a similar agenda. He was searching for a unique dialectical system known as the Great Universal Art, which was "neither material nor formal in any recognized logical sense, but rather spiritual in a broadly theological sense of 'speaking about God.'"[27] It is therefore not surprising that Lull felt an affinity for Ghazālī's work, since the latter was in search of every intellectual artifice that could fortify the Muslim discursive tradition in a grand and coherent epistemic framework.

A growing scholarship suggests that Ghazālī may have had a larger influence in European scholastic circles than our current knowledge of intellectual history acknowledges. There are suggestions that Saint Thomas Aquinas may have known of Ghazālī's works and studied them.[28] The Egyptian scholar Maḥmūd Ḥamdī Zaqzūq points out that there is a remarkable similarity and coincidence in the approach of Ghazālī and that of the French philosopher René Descartes (1596–1650), especially in the way in which philosophical questions tortured both men. Both took recourse to doubt at first but then followed different paths to ascertain what knowledge is and how we come to "know" with certainty.[29]

However, in the modern period, there has been an equal fascination with Ghazālī on the part of Western scholars ranging from serious students of culture and philosophy to orientalists and Christian missionaries who found him compelling for a variety of reasons and motives. Duncan B. Macdonald (1863–1943), once a professor at Hartford Theological Seminary in Connecticut, was one of a handful of American scholars who took an interest in Islam, with a specific focus on Ghazālī. In 1899, he published an essay on Ghazālī that had a particular resonance with occidental scholars of Islam.[30] Refining the orientalist approach of making backhanded insults, Macdonald confidently noted: "The difference in the Oriental is not essentially religiosity, but the lack of the sense of law. For him, there is no immovable order of nature."[31] Understanding Macdonald's approach to Ghazālī requires that one grasp his Manichean dichotomy of being and existence, which posits an unbridgeable distance between self and other, occidental and oriental, and Christian and Muslim.

For Macdonald, the distinctions were marked by an essential difference between the oriental and the occidental mind. The way in which the occidental mind is superior to the oriental mind—whatever that essential mind in either case might be—is not conceived of in terms of how each perceives faith and imagines the divine. Rather, it is premised on the preposterous generalization that two polar civilizations, namely Islamicate and Christian/Western, have different attitudes toward knowledge and law. Macdonald triumphantly asserts that "it is not really faith that is in question here, but knowledge; it is not the attitude to God, but the attitude to law." He continues: "The essential difference in the oriental mind is not credulity as to the unseen things, but inability to construct a system as to seen things."[32] With such unsubstantiated, magisterial wisdom, all orientals are dispatched to perpetual doom in an atomistic universe, and more: they are cast as congenitally and culturally predisposed to such flaws, so that they are believed to be unable to conjugate an empirical system based on observation. It is only, in Macdonald's view, the occidentals, by dint of their intellectual superiority, who have the capacity to apprehend complexity.

What really troubled Macdonald was that ethical and legal knowledge in Islam is rigidly construed. Of course, in his view, the overall weakness lay in Muslim epistemology. He believed that Muslim constructions of knowledge lacked the tenacity of a natural law—in other words, that they were bereft of a rational law. This, in turn, implied that Muslim dialectical theology (*kalām*) was based on the irrational, a proposition that is as preposterous as it is false. Surprisingly, he failed to recall that earlier he had acknowledged that Ghazālī in particular made a tenacious defense of natural law and admitted to notions of causality even though many of his critics claimed he subscribed to a notion of probable causes, not necessary causes.[33]

The bulk of Macdonald's work blends documentation with a torrent of condescending ad hominem remarks, and in the whole of Muslim history he found that only one person could have saved Islam or come close to it, namely, Ghazālī. With a penchant for hyperbole, he said that it was Ghazālī who once again built up the "breaches in the Muslim Zion, and that Islām exists still is largely due to him."[34] Just as it is necessary in all colonial projects to differentiate between the good native and the bad native, such too is the case in the contestation for knowledge. Therefore, the "good" Muslim is the colonized one, who is represented in heroic terms; Ghazālī is no doubt a victim of colonial historiography.

Macdonald even erroneously insisted that in Ghazālī's hands "theology took its final form," adding that "the Church of Muḥammad owes it to his strange experiences in personal religion." Macdonald was relentless in his single-minded pursuit: "What rigidity of grasp the hand of Islam would have exercised but for the influence of al-Ghazzālī might be hard to tell." With an air of relief, he observed that Ghazālī saved Islam "from scholastic decrepitude, and opened before the orthodox Muslim the possibility of a life hid in God."[35]

Reductionist analyses anticipate even more reductive solutions: one scholar can fix Islam, or one savior redeem an entire "civilization" called Islam. It is hard to imagine that orientalists like Macdonald could conceive of the Muslim discursive tradition as anything but a fetish. Regrettably, he was not the last scholar to make a fetish of an intellectual tradition; several contemporary "insiders" also do the same.

With what deafening frequency does one hear claims that the fastidious adherence to the most literal mutation of Islamic law (*sharīʿa*) is the panacea for all ills in Muslim society? And what Edward Said has identified as the bane of orientalism—its inability to view its discipline critically and engage in self-critique—applies equally to certain sections of doctrinaire Muslim traditionalism. Beyond self-critique, there is a need to pose and seek answers to the all-important questions that help us explain the production of human labor, the role of power, and the roles of men and women in society in different ages and under variable material conditions.[36]

Some of Ghazālī's occidental admirers frequently construed him either as a crypto-Christian or as a Muslim who had deep sympathies for Christianity. What they found particularly gratifying is this parallel: Ghazālī interrogated the purposes of the law just as Jesus of Nazareth questioned the salience of Jewish law. Christian missionaries, orientalists, and colonial administrators alike found the Muslim commitment to law (*sharīʿa*) and ritual almost incomprehensible. For surely, they believed, this commitment was different from Protestant and secular perceptions of religion. Obviously, it did not occur to them that orthodox Judaism, like Islam, also requires a commitment to law (*halakha*). Part of what makes Ghazālī an attractive candidate for study by orientalists and missionaries is that he at one level appeared to question the formalistic application of the law at the cost of suffocating the ethical purpose of law. This emanated from Ghazālī's stinging criticism of his contemporaries' attitudes toward the law. However, his solution was not to abandon the law—much to the disappointment of his orientalist admirers—but to transform the disposition of the adherent toward the law. Macdonald was obviously disappointed that Ghazālī, in the end, did not reform the law to the point of entirely reducing it to esoteric and interior sentiment.

Macdonald's consuming interest in Muslim thought inspired an early-twentieth-century American missionary, Samuel M. Zwemer, to study Ghazālī. Zwemer was a renowned figure in international and Middle Eastern

Christian missionary circles. Relying primarily on Macdonald's fundamental assumptions while making some rudimentary additional remarks, he wrote a book titled *A Moslem Seeker after God*. Most curious indeed is the subtitle of this book: *Showing Islam at Its Best in the Life and Teaching of al-Ghazali, Mystic and Theologian of the Eleventh Century*. Let us not forget, Zwemer reminded his readers, that "Islam is the prodigal son, the Ishmael, among the non-Christian religions."[37] Elaborating his motives for studying Ghazālī, who in his view represented "Islam at its best," Zwemer explained why this Muslim figure has pure instrumental value:

> There is a real sense in which al-Ghazali may be used as a schoolmaster to lead Moslems to Christ. His books were full of references to the teaching of Christ. He was a true seeker after God. . . . No one can read the story of al-Ghazali's life, so near and yet so far from the Kingdom of God, eager to enter and yet always groping for the doorway, without fervently wishing that al-Ghazali could have met a true ambassador of Christ. Then surely this great champion of the Moslem faith would have become an apostle of Christianity in his own day and generation. By striving to understand al-Ghazali we may at least better fit ourselves to help those who, like him, are earnest seekers after God amid the twilight shadows of Islam. His life also has a lesson for us all in its devout Theism and in its call to the practice of the Presence of God.[38]

Reticence was certainly not one of Zwemer's weaknesses! He candidly tells us what Ghazālī means to his missionary cause: Ghazālī was a theist, but not saved; he enjoyed the experience of the divine while only groping for the doorway; he reached some mini-kingdom yet was deprived of the imperial kingdom. Unspoken, though, is the feeling that Ghazālī is not relevant in his own right; instead, he serves as a heuristic category of Muslim who can be proselytized and delivered from the "twilight shadows of Islam" to the imperial kingdom of Christ. In short, Zwemer's missionary cause resonates with the imperial and colonial tropes: the Other has no intrinsic value. The Other is a utilitarian means for achieving the higher ends of the colonial and missionary self or selves. For this reason, Ghazālī was crassly colonized for Zwemer's higher ends.

There is no gainsaying that Ghazālī did carefully and frequently cite and elaborate on the teachings of Jesus. In fact, if his insights are properly articulated, they can serve as an ecumenical bridge between Islam and Christianity, one that could lead to a more productive understanding between the two Abrahamic traditions. But it is precisely this potential that eluded the missionary, for such an inclusive approach was antithetical to the exclusivist notions of religion held by Zwemer.

A later generation of historians and scholars of Arabic in the orientalist tradition attempted to deepen our understanding of Ghazālī. Foremost among them was Miguel Asín Palacios (1871–1944), a Spanish scholar who wrote a monumental work, *La espiritualidad de Algazel y su sentido Cristiano* (*Ghazālī's Spirituality and Its Christian Meaning*). Like his predecessors, Asín Palacios was obsessed to point out the Christian roots of Ghazālī's thinking. In so doing, he gave less attention to Ghazālī's original contributions. Asín Palacios was oblivious to the fact that cosmopolitan cultural environments of the kind that Ghazālī inhabited actively promote reciprocal influences that prompt new beginnings without detracting from intellectual originality. Farid Jabre is certainly right to point out that Asín Palacios's repeated attempts to find Christian equivalents for Ghazālī's thought have been singularly unhelpful.[39] Asín Palacios's work illustrates the preoccupation of a generation of orientalist scholars for whom Ghazālī's relevance only made sense when his ideas resonated with Christian sensibilities.

The Dutch scholar Arent J. Wensinck claimed that he would break the pattern of attitudes toward Ghazālī created by some of his Euro-American predecessors. He declared that his goal was to go beyond inquiries that only focused on borrowings by Muslim scholars from other cultural traditions and on the search for "origins" and "influences" on Muslim scholarship. Wensinck then placed Ghazālī within the context of the three major theological and philosophical systems of the oriental Middle Age, namely, Islam, Christianity, and Neoplatonism.

Despite his noble intentions, Wensinck's study ended up reiterating what several of his predecessors had already said, namely, that Ghazālī was unmistakably influenced by Christian and Neoplatonic thought.[40] However, Wensinck went a little further and made the astonishing claim that as a theologian Ghazālī was a Muslim, as a thinker and a man of science he was Neoplatonic, and as a moralist and mystic he was a Christian.[41] Whether this conclusion suggests that Ghazālī was a multifaceted genius or a charlatan is unclear, but what is certain is that the analogies are indeed limiting, even apart from their unspoken subtext.

The American historian of Islamicate civilization Marshall Hodgson has been extremely judicious and helpful in unveiling the underlying flaw that marks the kinds of analyses I have highlighted above. He draws our attention to what he calls the "precommitments" that scholars bring to their subject matter.[42] Those scholars who are Christian or who come from a Christian background, like Macdonald and Zwemer, think they are eminently qualified to judge a rival tradition. When they do pass judgment, then Islam is always viewed as Christianity manqué. Islam, for such scholars, remains a truncated version of Christian truth.

Furthermore, Hodgson points out, such scholars bring a value judgment to their scholarship and implicitly suggest that Muslims cannot grasp the whole or essential truth of Christianity.[43] This characterization by Hodgson is almost tailor-made to rebut the propositions made by Macdonald and Zwemer. Even the French orientalist Louis Massignon, renowned for his sophistication and dedication to scholarship on Muslim topics, could not see Islam, Hodgson points out, except as "a spiritual exile, veiled from divine presence, yet through that very exile charged with a special witness to bear."[44] Hodgson's sober prosecution is damning.

Meticulous investigation in modern scholarship has advanced our understanding of certain works attributed to Ghazālī. Studies by R. Gosche, Maurice Bouyges, and Farid Jabre have been followed by those of William Montgomery Watt, George F. Hourani, Kojiro Nakamura, and Nasrullah Pourjawadi.[45] There have also been useful systematic studies such as those by J. Obermann, Henri Laoust, and Hava Lazarus-Yafeh, to mention but a few.[46] More recent studies by Eric Ormsby, I. Bello, Kevin Reinhart, Richard Frank, David Burrell, Mustafa Abu Sway, Mustafa Hogga, Farouk Mitha, Timothy J. Gianotti, and Daniel Shaw have taken Ghazālian scholarship several steps further through comparative studies or more critical readings of specific themes.[47] In many respects, Watt together with Laoust and, to a lesser extent, Wensinck made the first efforts to place Ghazālian scholarship within the realm of intellectual history and the sociology of religion.

Extensive and highly differentiated contributions have been made to Ghazālian studies in a number of non-European languages ranging from Arabic, Persian, and Turkish to Urdu, Malay, and Hausa, to mention but a few. As these works are too numerous to document here, suffice it to say that they have grown into a monumental archive.[48] Shiblī Nuʿmānī, Zakī Mubārak, Sulaymān Dunyā, and, more recently, ʿAbd al-Ḥusayn Zarrinkūb, followed by the impressive Nasrullah Pourjawadi, have all made unique contributions to advance our understanding of Ghazālī in the annals of Muslim thought.[49]

Zakī Mubārak's *Ethics according to al-Ghazālī* (*Al-akhlāq ʿinda al-Ghazālī*) is a somewhat polemical and provocative work that had a very controversial reception in Egypt. Written in the first quarter of the twentieth century as a doctoral dissertation, it caused major controversy and outrage. Mubārak raised several critical questions about Ghazālī's intellectual project, questioned his motives for challenging the philosophers, lamented his silence regarding the Crusader attacks on Muslim lands, and disapproved of his unqualified commitment to ṣūfism. He was not reluctant to pass judgment on Ghazālī's intentions, and at times he stridently dismissed both Ghazālī's asceticism and his aesthetics. For Mubārak, twentieth-century Enlightenment rationalism was the standard by which every statement of Ghazālī was to be evaluated. In doing so, he demonstrated a complete inability to register the tonality of the different narrative strategies employed in Muslim literature over the ages. The entire debate then took an unfortunate turn when some zealous religious figures in Egypt issued accusations of heresy and anathema (*takfīr*) in order to excommunicate and silence Mubārak for daring to air his views. The zealots, unfortunately, did Ghazālī no favors and perhaps only harmed the legacy of a figure who tried to prevent accusations of heresy in intra-Muslim discourse.

Someone who does not hesitate to dethrone Ghazālī's reputation, even employing scurrilous charges to do so, is the Egyptian scholar ʿAbd al-Dā'im al-Anṣārī. In *Confessions of Ghazālī* (*Iʿtirāfāt al-Ghazālī*), Anṣārī almost literally adopts the Orwellian idea that saints should be judged guilty until they are proved innocent. He vehemently rejects the standard account of Ghazālī's conversion to mysticism. Anṣārī presents the strangest of arguments, accusing Ghazālī of bad faith, and he charges him with inventing his identity as a pietist. Arguing from very atomistic readings of *Rescuer from Misguidance*, Anṣārī boldly claims that Ghazālī never experienced a personal transformation. He offers a number of explanations as to why he thinks Ghazālī invented false identities and concocted lies about himself. Desperate to attain piety and wisdom that eluded him, an aging Ghazālī, alleges Anṣārī, faked his desires and compiled *Rescuer* as a heuristic and voyeuristic statement about religiosity. A confident Anṣārī says that he can substantiate his contrarian views by means of rigorous logic.

By contrast, the Iranian scholar ʿAbd al-Ḥusayn Zarrinkūb used his finely honed analytical skills to write a landmark biography of Ghazālī that is both elegant and comprehensive. The author meticulously consulted a variety of sources and integrated the materials with a historian's sophistication into a flowing narrative. *The Escape from the Madrasa* (*Al-firār min al-madrasa*) is a serious and critical study. It does not suffer from excessive adoration for Ghazālī, nor does the author indulge in a relentless hermeneutic of suspicion without evidence to substantiate his doubts. The main feature of Zarrinkūb's book is its value as an epitome. It gracefully consolidates the insights generated in Ghazālian scholarship during the past half a century and tells the story in a lucid and engaging style.

Reception of Ghazālī in Contemporary Islam

Ghazālī has as many admirers as he has opponents. In the broad spectrum of traditionalist scholarship, he occupies a reverential, almost iconic status. The outrage expressed by the mandarins of Egyptian orthodoxy about Zakī Mubārak's critique of Ghazālī in the early part of the twentieth century is perhaps the best illustration that some admirers esteem him to the point of believing him infallible. This occurs notwithstanding the fact that the legacy of Ghazālī is incontestably caught in the crosshairs of competing notions of orthodoxies as well as of competing reformist religious, cultural, and political agendas.

The other intellectual trend with which the Ghazālian legacy has to contend within contemporary Islam is the puritan outlook, broadly characterized as *salafism*. *Salafism* is in large part the inspiration behind nineteenth- and twentieth-century Islamic revivalism. *Salafism* is a generic term, depicting a school of thought that takes the pious ancestors (*al-salaf al-ṣāliḥ*) of the patristic period of early Islam as exemplary models. Often, *salafism* is accompanied by shades of literalism, though one cannot generalize this to be a universal feature of all *salafī* thought.

Modern iterations of *salafism* draw largely from the fourteenth-century intellectual giant Taqī al-Dīn Ibn Taymīya and his student Ibn Qayyim al-Jawzīya (d. 751/1350). Needless to say, each of these figures has cast a long shadow on the Muslim intellectual tradition. The Arab reformist figure Muḥammad ibn ʿAbd al-Wahhāb (d. 1206/1792), whose teachings, known as Wahhābism, are current in today's Saudi Arabia, also claimed to have been inspired by the teachings of Ibn Taymīya.

If Ghazālī ever had a trenchant early critic, it was Ibn Taymīya. He and Ibn Qayyim al-Jawzīya had major epistemic and methodological differences with Ghazālī. For them, knowledge and identity were inseparable. In radical *salafī* quarters in the modern period, there is little appreciation, let alone admiration, for the intellectual labors of Ghazālī. This is despite the fact that Ghazālī, too, ironically, evoked the memory of the pious ancestors as his models of authority from time to time.[50] However, moderate and more savvy *salafīs* maintain a prudent silence and distance from Ghazālī without offering vituperative criticism.[51]

Not all reformist intellectuals who identify themselves with certain shades of *salafism* have failed to engage constructively with Ghazālī's legacy. Nineteenth- and twentieth-century Muslim reformers from Jamāl al-Dīn al-Afghānī (d. 1897) and Muḥammad ʿAbduh (d. 1905) to Jamāl al-Din al-Qāsimī al-Dimashqī (d. 1914) and Rashīd Riḍā (d. 1935) included Ghazālī as one of their reference points and authorities despite his differences with Ibn Taymīya, one of their heroes. Many of their followers and counterparts in Asia, as well as elements within revivalist Muslim social movements ranging from the Muslim Brotherhood in Egypt to the Jamāt-e Islāmī in the Indian subcontinent, have acknowledged Ghazālī's legacy.[52]

Among traditionalists who espouse Islamic mysticism (*taṣawwuf*), Ghazālī is an indispensable advocate and ally. His teachings make piety and the perfection of the inner life a central element of Muslim religious practice and thus synchronize well with traditions that take ṣūfism seriously. Thus, Ghazālī receives wide recognition in the religious institutions of contemporary South Asia, Southeast Asia, and Africa. In the Indian subcontinent, Ghazālī enjoys a distinguished reputation. Among the Deoband school as well as among its archrival, the Barelwi school, Ghazālī's legacy is put to extensive use. Among traditionalists, Ghazālī is renowned for his teachings on self-formation, piety, and ethics. Since pious inculcation is such a crucial component of the educational curricula in seminaries in several regions of the Muslim world, his writings continue to be significant. Even when his texts are not used in official syllabi, one can detect his indirect influence, perhaps because his works are popular and readily available in vernacular translation.

In West Africa, Aḥmad b. Muḥammad b. Ḥabīb Allāh (d. 1927), better known as Shaykh Aḥmadu (Amadu) Bamba, the spiritual father of the Murīdīya ṣūfīs of Senegal, borrowed energetically from Ghazālī's teachings. Much later, in the middle of the twentieth century, Shaykh ʿAbd al-Ḥalīm Maḥmūd (d. 1978), the rector of al-Azhar, the leading Islamic university in Egypt, ardently advocated the Ghazālian intellectual legacy and modes of piety.[53]

With the rise of Arab nationalism and the accompanying critical introspection as to why Arabs and Muslims suffered setbacks before the collapse of the Ottoman Empire and especially after the European colonization of Muslim lands, Ghazālī's legacy has come under critical scrutiny. This introspective mood was best captured in the famous treatise of Amīr Shakīb Arsalān (d. 1946), *Our Decline and Its Causes*. Before him, similar questions were posed by the nineteenth-century reformer Jamāl al-Dīn al-Afghānī.

Linear analyses by ideologues and political activists have produced the analytical cant that a triumphant Muslim civilization was gradually undone by grotesque manifestations of mysticism. Mysticism, they claim, particularly affected the popular psyche, which effectively turned Arab societies into hotbeds of irrationality and superstition. Among the most recent Arab nationalist intellectual historians and thinkers to repeat this line of thinking is the Moroccan thinker Muḥammad ʿĀbid al-Jābirī, whose otherwise impressive, sober thinking is occasionally skewed by analytical reductionism.

In a fairly complex analysis of Muslim intellectual history, Jābirī observes that the Arabo-Islamic rational discursive tradition, which he calls "conspicuous elucidation" (*bayān*), suffered acutely from the intrusion of Hermetic gnosticism. This trend, Jābirī points out, was spearheaded by none other than the influential thinker and mystic Ḥārith al-Muḥāsibī (d. 243/857), who cultivated a new epistemology in a bid to reconcile rational discursivity with mystical cognition. In so doing, Muḥāsibī ushered in a defunct Hermetic rationalism that can be identified as the cause for the stunting of the Muslim intellectual tradition over time.[54]

Even more damaging than Muḥāsibī, and building on his legacy, claims Jābirī, were the intrusive intellectual interventions made by Ghazālī. The latter not only further embedded gnostic thought, he charges, but also celebrated the defunct Hermetic rationality. Jābirī adds that Ghazālī irreparably wounded the rational and philosophical tradition in eastern Islam, though not necessarily in the Islamic West.[55] Due to the intellectual labors of Ghazālī, Jābirī believes, dialectical theology (*kalām*) became the counterweight to philosophy. And it was Ghazālī who inscribed mysticism onto juristic and ethical thought (*fiqh*).[56]

If philosophy fails to recover, predicts Jābirī, it will be due to Ghazālī's critique. By declaring the views of the philosophers to be anathema to Muslim doctrines, Ghazālī made it impossible for even the Herculean efforts of Ibn Rushd (also called Averroës, d. 595/1198) to resuscitate the Muslim philosophical tradition. After making this dim assessment, Jābirī poses the hypothetical questions: "What do you think Arabo-Islamic thought would have been like, after Ghazālī, if Ghazālī had not existed? . . . What would Arabo-Islamic civilization have lost, if Ghazālī had not written anything?"[57] Jābirī does not directly respond to his own question. He does hint, however, that perhaps Ibn Rushd would have provided a greater service to Arabo-Islamic thought than did Ghazālī.

Jābirī is correct when he observes, "The past, by which I mean ideological and political struggles, continues to govern our Arabo-Islamic thought, at least to the extent that Ghazālī is present in this legacy."[58] Arab nationalist historiographers identify Ghazālī as the one responsible for two detrimental developments in Muslim intellectual history. First, he is seen as the theorist who provided the most eloquent justification for a mysticism that reaches into a *sharīʿa*-based discourse. Second, Ghazālī critiqued the philosophers and replaced a naturalistic ontology with a theistic theory of being (onto-theology), a move that is viewed as the ultimate coup de grâce to the adherents of a rationalist Muslim epistemology.

The Egyptian thinker Ḥasan Ḥanafī continues this line of critique. He holds Ghazālī responsible for the defeat of reason in the Muslim intellectual tradition. Ḥanafī believes that Ghazālī's ideas are now so hegemonic that they serve as an obstacle for reform and transformation. In Ḥanafī's words, Ghazālī is at the "heart of the bulwark against the free and healthy use of reason."[59] Ḥanafī's remedy is to combat what he believes to be Ghazālī's relentless attack on the rational sciences—philosophy and rationalism. He is particularly opposed to Ghazālī's preference for an intuitive transcendental sensibility, or a transcendent aesthetic sensibility (*dhawq*), over reason in matters of religion.[60] Richard Khuri agrees. He asserts that Ḥanafī's call to confront what he alleges to be Ghazālī's retrogressive legacy is intended to provoke a "triumphant new critique [that] would awaken a moribund orthodoxy to a modernist outlook that affirms the sovereignty of reason and personal or individual freedom."[61]

It is indeed baffling that some strands of Arab historiography can hold one person, Ghazālī, responsible for initiating the decline of the complex edifice known as Muslim civilization. While the overgeneralizations and flaws in such analyses and conclusions cannot be addressed here, they are most distinctive in their stunning reductionism. "The sound analysis of an ignorant person does not deserve much praise," the writer-philosopher Abū Ḥayyān al-Tawḥīdī (d. 414/1024) reminds us, "while the blunder of an intelligent person deserves to be seriously deplored."[62] Skeptical as one may be about the Manichean distinctions the analysts make, they also apportion undeserving credit to Ghazālī in a way that is characteristic of one-man-changes-history syndrome. In the Promethean contestation for the soul of Islam in the modern period, there are many other elements and many other actors than Ghazālī.

But his legacy, far from being settled, remains at the center of contestation and debate.

Ghazālī as Exemplar

The central question that must occupy both his admirers and his critics is this: What does a twelfth-century Muslim thinker like Abū Ḥāmid al-Ghazālī have to do with poetics and imagination, subjectivity and citizenship? My own response to this central heuristic question is "Everything." Even though Ghazālī is related to the past, he is equally related to the present and the emergent Muslim subjectivity. There are faint indications that Muslim thinkers are seeking new intellectual paradigms as well as forms of knowledge appropriate to this emergent subjectivity. Of course, it is a subjectivity that is shaped in the shadow of both long-standing Muslim traditions and different iterations of modernity. The challenge to any alternate paradigm and emergent subjectivity is to both retain a fidelity to the past and engage with the present without slavishly succumbing to any one—and without ignoring each—reality. Responses to this challenge should include a discussion of seminal issues such as values and modes of thinking, especially about the way that poetics construes knowledge as heterogeneous. Each of these issues, among others, and in more than one way, relates to both Ghazālī and the modern Muslim subject.

The relevance of Ghazālī's insights to contemporary Muslim intellectual struggles becomes even more crucial if one considers the context of knowledge production and creativity in the religious imagination. In a nutshell, the issues that preoccupy Muslim communities in the twenty-first century relate, among other things, to questions centered on knowledge—otherwise described as the revolution in knowledge—questions of identity, and the place and role of ethics. New forms of knowledge are a direct result of the hegemony of modernity. And, in significant ways, the different narratives and practices of modernity, wherever and however they reach Muslim societies, also rewrite the Muslim self and radically alter the subjectivities of adherents. And yet there can be no universal repudiation of modernity and its effects. For this reason, it is difficult to issue a value judgment without it being tempered by the dialogical relationship between the multiple traditions that communities inhabit.

One of the issues related to change that has exercised me for some time is an observation that stems from my reading of classical Islamic texts, whether they be law, theology, history, mysticism, or philosophy. When studying the ancients, I am struck by the epistemic openness and the liberty with which many thinkers and authors energetically engaged with a wide variety of knowledge traditions. They did so without allowing the provenance of knowledge to be a decisive veto factor. Hence, a good portion of early Muslim intellectuals were open to the spirit of knowledge, whether it came from Greek, Indian, Biblical, or other philosophical traditions. Some strains of thought did resist this intellectual orientation, but they were hardly successful in dampening it.

This picture contrasts radically with many strains of contemporary Muslim intellectual thought, especially religious discourse. The provenance of an idea or a practice is more significant in contemporary thought than the substance of the idea. The prevalence of this condition has not only resulted in the atrophy of knowledge, but the process of knowledge production itself has suffocated. Knowledge related to religious discourse, such as ethics, law, theology, and philosophy, is quarantined from intercourse with ideas that have a non-Islamic genealogy. Only in the realm of science and technology is knowledge of a non-Islamic provenance tolerated, since these are viewed as secular discourses. This symptomatic response, of course, is partly explicable in the light of the harsh aftermath of colonialism and the consequent loss of self-confidence among Muslim societies. But any antidote that is prepared exclusively to cope with the apparent symptoms would indeed be shortsighted and might amount to no remedy. In contemporary Muslim discourses, knowledge and identity questions have become so undifferentiated that the critical distance required between an idea and its historical unfolding is collapsed. The Muslim subject—in all its varieties—is significantly denied agency to appropriate ideas by some modes of maximalist (fundamentalist) thinking in its modernist, secularist, revivalist, and orthodox guises within contemporary Muslim societies. The effect is that the Muslim subject is reduced to being an automaton of authoritarianism.[63]

But this rewriting of the self does not occur passively. The self is rewritten in the cauldron of intense struggles within Muslim societies. The inherited Muslim knowledge traditions encounter newer traditions of modernity, producing complex, overlapping, and heterogeneous modes of knowledge. Some of these struggles for the recuperation of the self, society, and history have become visible in highly dramatized spectacles. However, it is well known that most of the critical issues facing Muslim societies are disguised by epiphenomena that do not readily reveal the underlying causes and unresolved tensions.

Many of these questions and concerns form the backdrop of my reading of the archeology of Ghazālī's thought. I argue that Ghazālī's legacy is a imaginative work of tradition. In his own complex space, or the *dihlīz*, the intermediate space or the threshold space that Ghazālī identified—one with intersecting boundaries and heterogeneous notions of practices and time—he forged different narratives of religion. These narratives were the outcome of his encounter with both inherited and contemporary forms of knowledge.[64]

Indispensable to Ghazālī's project was the notion of a dialogical imagination: a sense that all meaning is part of a greater whole and that the different parts of meaning constantly interact with each other irrespective of whether those meanings are held by believer or unbeliever, agnostic or mystic, male or female, friend or foe. In fact, it would not be incorrect to say that to a large extent Ghazālī partially resisted Parmenides' insistence on the unity of thought and being, or the unity of knowledge and identity. In so doing, he dented the Platonic link between ontology and epistemology. But he was also, in my view, a courageous bricoleur, one who creatively managed to put to work different ideas in a coherent framework for himself, for his society, and for the community that he served.

Ghazālī did his creative work on the eve of the most catastrophic onslaught experienced in the late-eleventh-century Muslim world: the beginning of the European Crusades against Muslim territories in the Islamic East. The parallels between his world and our twenty-first-century universe provide the ingredients for painful but sobering irony. Just as Ghazālī was dealing with formidable intellectual and political challenges, so too do postcolonial Muslims, whether they are resident in Jakarta or Jersey City, Calcutta or Casablanca, face enormous challenges. Some of these challenges include questions of identity, poverty, and governance, compounded by fears of domination by globalizing, late-capitalist economies that shore up the fortunes of Atlantic powers. These challenges exist separately from and in addition to the momentous military and economic standoffs that we witness between the United States and its European allies on the one side and political groups and nations in the Muslim world on the other.

Keeping in mind a snapshot of our immediate realities in a cosmopolitan world with ambiguous globalizing tendencies, I believe there is something we can learn from Ghazālī's ideas and experiences. He left for posterity a legacy that has for nearly nine centuries inspired millions of Muslim adherents but that also left a mark on the Jewish and Christian scholastic traditions of the medieval world. Ghazālī's relevance is not so much in the substance of his ideas, since we recognize that our world and his are so distant as to be almost irreconcilable in some crucial aspects. His relevance primarily lies in the architecture of his ideas. He was essentially a builder and creator of intellectual edifices and thought structures that produced practices for himself and societies over time.

If there is any concrete lesson to be learned from Ghazālī's experience, then it is this: the end to the enduring search for solutions to humanity's existential crises can be found in the creativity of the human spirit. Ghazālī is a sterling example of someone who conquered the odds and found a path out of depressing personal despair and social anomie. In the triumph of the spirit, Ghazālī stands out as a beacon of hope in times of anguish: he led with imagination in order to overcome ignorance; he preferred originality to imitation and favored renewal over complacency. With will, determination, discipline, and self-criticism, Ghazālī overcame both his personal struggles about the meaning of life and the weight of history that surrounded him. Surely, perfection is not what we seek from any exemplary figure, least of all from Ghazālī. However, what we do seek in our heroes and models is a depth of humanity, vision, and compassion in which we can find echoes of our own hopes and aspirations, our own various communities and societies.

Particularly during the last three centuries, Muslim societies the world over have experienced cataclysmic changes and transformations, including the long night of colonization and the mixed fortunes of the various postcolonies after independence. Those colonies and postcolonies have witnessed the dissipation of historical knowledge traditions, which were rapidly replaced or turned into hybrids by the addition of newer strands of knowledge and technology. In some instances, the death of knowledge traditions—epistemicide—has indeed occurred.

Muslim reformers and critical thinkers have long called for the reinvigoration of the intellectual traditions among Muslims. Central to their concerns is the need to update the knowledge component of Muslim religious and cultural discursive traditions. We are all too familiar with the rhetoric of "Islam and modernity," "Islamic reform," "revivalism," "fundamentalism," "Islamic orthodoxy," "Islamic modernism," and the need for independent thinking (*ijtihād*), to mention but a few categories. Huge intellectual labors and costly experiments in social engineering have been undertaken in order to stimulate or provoke a renaissance in Muslim religious thought. Many such initiatives remain stillborn. Some are still in progress, while newer ones have yet to see the light of day. Each makes a contribution to a complex tapestry of ideas and experiences: they form part of the endless work in progress of Muslim discursive traditions.

It would be a distortion to claim that this is the first time a civilization as complex as Islamicate civilization has faced serious internal upheavals. To know how Muslim thinkers in the past dealt with their challenges would be most edificatory. In the interest of making a modest contribution to excavating this knowledge of the past, I felt that it would be helpful to share some dimensions of Ghazālī's ideas, navigating those thoughts with him from my own location, rather than to tabulate a list of problems and crises contemporary Muslims face. In exploring some of Ghazālī's ideas, we may be in a position to see how past Muslim communities countenanced the critical issues that contemporary Muslims struggle with, namely, creativity and change in the discourse of religion. It is hard to think of a better figure than Abū Ḥāmid al-Ghazālī to illustrate the creative unfolding of tradition amid multiple challenges.

To me, this book is a journey: a journey of engaged friendship with Ghazālī in the hope that as we dialogue across the centuries we can come to a better understanding of his self, history, and society and what lessons these hold for ours in order that we may proceed into the future with a modicum of confidence and hope.

The Argument

This book pursues a line of thought about the aesthetics of imagining religion. It is an encounter between Ghazālī and a contemporary reader of his writings. It is an encounter that crisscrosses many temporal zones, subjectivities, and shared as well as different intellectual traditions. The key issue that animates this dialogue is the relationship between knowledge and subjectivity—the modes of creativity and innovation in ideas as a form of poetics. But, more importantly, I seek to know how a knowledge tradition coheres while also generating subjects with divergent and overlapping subjectivities.

I also excavate and rehabilitate a metaphor used by Ghazālī himself: the idea of the *dihlīz* in Arabic and Persian, meaning the threshold position. In some sense, this is a liminal space between the inside and the outside, a space that sublimated his own location and thinking. Far from being a middle-of-the-road kind of thinker, Ghazālī actually straddled, agonized over, and negotiated antinomies. In other words, he entered the force field of ideas, where antithetical currents are powerful, providing equally binding mandates for the ethical subject. This *dihlīz*-ian metaphor, I believe, is the key to interpreting Ghazālī's location in a world of heterogeneous knowledge and subjectivities. It is this Ghazālian signature that I appropriate in order to explore the in between-ness of being and the torn-ness of human existence. Only cross-pollination has the potential to bring about a paradigmatic shift in our thinking. As a consequence, it will also produce emergent knowledge in our desire to live in a polycentric world. Chapter 1, titled "Agonistics of the Self," adumbrates some of these themes. In addition, the chapter maps the key interpretive tools and concepts that I employ in trying to read and imagine Ghazālī. In short, it may provide an idea of my theoretical tool kit without being exhaustive.

Examining how Ghazālī thought about the self as well as how he narrated the self is my project in chapter 2, "Narrativity of the Self." I show how he negotiated the force field of the *dihlīz* by taking recourse to narrative. For in the skeins of narration, Ghazālī was able to renarrate ideas, concepts, and norms in an effortless and creative manner that only someone who combined the skills of an engineer and a bricoleur could accomplish as successfully as he did.

In chapter 3, "Poetics of Memory and Writing," I show that Ghazālī oscillated between the importance of memory and writing, shifting subtly and unobtrusively between the two and then finally settling on writing. He did adhere to forms of logocentric doxology, but he also embraced aspects of heterology via ṣūfism.

Chapter 4 deals with "Liminality and Exile" in Ghazālī's thought. Following a characteristic Abrahamic logic, Ghazālī heard the command to obey the norms of law and society. However, during liminal phases, he began to understand that the inward reality of belief is more forceful than the outward appearance. Thus, he came perilously close to suggesting that the willingness of conscience to respond to a deep voice might, in theory, violate the apparent norm. The notion of exile—to be a stranger in this world—as a spiritual motif is much more visible in Ghazālī's thinking than I was at first inclined to concede.

Cognitive certainty is a necessity, but it cannot be the only source of attaining certainty. In chapter 5, "Grammar of the Self," I show how Ghazālī imagined knowledge. He grappled with knowledge and its provenance and how all knowledge can become an instrument that leads to the truth. Dialectical theology is one means of arriving at some doxological certainty, but he showed ultimately how ambivalent such knowledge is and how fractious it can become.

Chapter 6, "Metaphysics of Belief," sheds some light on Ghazālī's quarrels with philosophy and the philosophers. Contrary to the suggestion that Ghazālī was against philosophy, I argue that he did see merit in it as a means to expound the truth. His criticism of philosophy was intended to demonstrate its limitations. But, more importantly, he thought that the hubris of the philosophers limited their openness to the truth. The crucial move that Ghazālī made was to subtly link ontology and epistemology. Ghazālī subscribed to an ontology of divine grace: everything rests not on the laws of nature or some potentiality but on an inexhaustible divine grace that can in theory make anything possible. The denial of such sovereignty to the divine by means of human constructs was what Ghazālī found offensive in the views of the philosophers.

Navigating the ambiguity of language by means of interpretation is one of the only accessible ways whereby one can stabilize meanings and *doxa* for communities. Chapter 7, "Dilemmas of Anathema and Heresy," demonstrates how Ghazālī tried to intervene in the vexatious heresiology of his time. He proposed a hermeneutic of reconciliation aimed at creating an intra-Muslim pluralism of views. However, at the same time, he was also blinded by his own political animus toward certain sects and contradicted himself by advocating unrestrained violence against specific political foes.

Knowledge of the self and the divine is acquired in order to serve specific ends, namely, to constitute virtuous individuals and subjects. These are the themes addressed in chapter 8, "Hermeneutics of the Self and Subjectivity." Here, I explore how a heteronomous ethics, one that has its origins outside the self, subjects the self to discipline. I show that heteronomy does not mean an end to autonomy but in fact facilitates autonomy through the aesthetic sensibilities of the self.

Chapter 9, "Technologies of the Self and Self-Knowledge," elaborates how Ghazālī articulated self-fashioning and the acquisition of ethical knowledge. Taking a position very different from those adopted by the majority of jurists, Ghazālī reconstructed *fiqh*, normally described as positive law, to mean the discovery of knowledge that identifies the path to salvation in the afterlife. In other words, *fiqh* constitutes certain ethical practices that are preceded by the inculcation of virtues and character traits (*ādāb* and *akhlāq*). Once these virtues and traits are internalized, or traced onto the habitus of the ethical subject, one ceases to think of *fiqh* as positive law and begins to think of its function as a juridical ethics. The chapter pursues certain insights that may pave the way for a dialogical relationship between the subjectivity (*fiqh al-bāṭin*) of the ethical subject and the external pronouncements of the legal form or ethics (*fiqh al-ẓāhir*). In other words, to what extent does the changed and altered subjectivity of the ethical subject impact the external, or legal, form of the ethical objectives?

These nine chapters are followed by a conclusion, "Knowledge of the Strangers," that reiterates the role of poiesis, the threshold position, and the location of the stranger or exile in the exploration and reconstruction of the self in Muslim ethics. My attempt has been to recapture for the present the most volatile of essences, traits, outlooks, trains of thought, and concepts as they are embodied in the thinking of a twelfth-century Muslim bricoleur, Abū Ḥāmid al-Ghazālī. While one has to avoid the temptation to write the history of the past solely in terms of the present, we cannot escape the paradox evoked by Michel Foucault: no matter how hard we try to unlock the unfathomable remoteness of the past, our writing of history will always be a history of writing the present.[65] Against Foucault, one has to immediately caution that history cannot be reduced to a realm of impenetrable otherness and that we can only grasp at the cost of brutally colonizing the past. It is because of the burden of history under which we stagger that the past cannot neatly fit into the present, not so much due to the restrictions of the present, but because of the enormity of the past. The challenge, of course, lies in carefully navigating the threshold of each horizon with fidelity to the texture of both the past and the present, which will in the end parent the future.

Social life . . . even its apparently quietest moments, is characteristically "pregnant" with social dramas. It is as though each of us has a "peace" face and a "war" face, that we are programmed for cooperation, but prepared for conflict. The primordial and perennial agonistic mode is the social drama.
—Victor Turner, *From Ritual to Theatre*

1 Agonistics of the Self

Imagination

The Syrian-born writer ʿAlī Aḥmad Saʿīd, better known by his pen name, Adonis, startles his readers with the subtitle "Journey in the Cities of al-Ghazālī" in a long poem titled "Eighth Sky."[1] It is startling because Adonis is a secularist, even a self-declared atheist. Why would someone with his secular predispositions show an interest in Ghazālī? What kind of inspiration can a modern poet derive by reaching into the twelfth century to a deeply religious figure like Ghazālī? Written in complex mystical verse and full of allegorical illusions, Adonis's poem unmistakably plays off the past against the present and prefigures the future. It is a captivating and brilliant poem punctured by lamentation about the perils facing the "Cities of al-Ghazālī." Poetic visions have to be inclusive, and Adonis must have kept alive in his imagination the past glory of Baghdād as one of the cities of al-Ghazālī, the miseries unleashed periodically on that city notwithstanding.

Utopian thought, even if it turns to the past, the exiled Russian writer Joseph Brodsky reminds us, "usually implies the unbearable character of the present."[2] Therefore, it would be erroneous to read Adonis's poem in a linear fashion and to unequivocally conclude, as some have done, that the poem is an attack on Ghazālī.[3] It contains the possibility of being both a critique and an appreciation of Ghazālī, since "ambiguity is an inevitable by-product of the struggle for objectivity."[4] Indeed, in the sequel to "Eighth Sky," in which the poet continues to refer to the "planet of al-Ghazālī," Adonis's mystical figure, Mihyār, makes an appearance. Mihyār personifies the poet's ideas, hopes, and dreams as a life symbol in continuous movement.[5]

By juxtaposing Ghazālī and Mihyār, is it possible that Adonis is suggesting that they are both on the side of continuous movement, creativity, and imagination? Yes, I think this is a reasonable conclusion. Do not both Ghazālī and Mihyār personify dreams? Dreams can be frightening and nightmarish; they scare us with the grotesque and ugly. Yet dreams can also inspire hope; they can offer us visions of the future and provide energy so that we may live out our desires and fantasies. Adonis, of course, realizes as much, despite the differences between his own life trajectory and Ghazālī's. And, interestingly for the modern poet, Ghazālī as an intellectual and a pious figure is not outside the range of resources indispensable to the poet's craft—the craft of imagination and inventive making and creating known as poiesis.

Here, I have chosen Ghazālī as my locus of enunciation, fully aware that I bring to the enterprise at least two epistemic languages: the conceptual tools and interpretive frameworks derived from a multiplicity of Muslim traditions as well as those of Western traditions. They reflect my own multiple locations and experiences of living in a *dihlīz*, an interspace, negotiating and struggling with the hegemonic and colonial knowledge traditions as well as the subalternized Islamicate knowledge systems to gain a modicum of emancipation and ultimately liberation from totalizing ways of existence.[6] In large part, I try to understand Ghazālī with the multiple cultural resources of the present. At the same time, I must also acknowledge that we cannot understand the present without taking account of how Ghazālī, his universe, and his pivotal role in the formation of ideas impact ours. Not to be aware of this critical tension brought about by dialogical thinking is to fall prey to the grossest forms of the colonization of knowledge.

In this chapter, I ground and elaborate the interpretive keystrokes that I will be using in subsequent chapters of this book. I explain how I use notions and concepts such as bricolage, poiesis, teleiopoiesis, the in-between space (*dihlīz*), tradition, orthodoxy, and history, all elements that underpin much of this book. Here, I also demonstrate the dialogical conversation that takes place in the heterogeneous disciplines that draw inspiration from nonsecular and non-Western contexts as well as from knowledge traditions that are broadly conceived of as Western humanities.

This attempt to foster a conversation among iterations of different intellectual traditions aims to advance an emancipatory and humane discursive tradition, one to which the Muslim intellectual legacy can make a meaningful contribution despite the double marginalization that Muslim thought suffers. Western humanities and modern philosophical traditions intentionally overlook Muslim thought as a sustainable inspiration for knowledge; this is one form of marginalization. And certain contemporary Muslim knowledge practices often consciously refrain from articulating Muslim thought in an accessible idiom or engaging with the historical Muslim tradition in an empowering manner from their multiple locations in the present. This is a form of surrender to the hegemonic discursivity of modernity, even though Islamist proponents would claim to resist modernity by means of such actions. For, indeed, those who choose isolation and absence unconsciously endorse the dominant knowledge practices as normative while reducing the knowledge of their own tradition to a subaltern status, veiled in its alleged purity and suffocating in its isolation.

Bricolage

To return to Adonis, it is apparent that he succeeds in casting Ghazālī as an enigma in his tantalizing poem. Many scholars agree that Ghazālī is an enigmatic and agonistic figure. It is perhaps due to his enigmatic personality and equally complex legacy that he has become such a pervasive force in the Muslim intellectual tradition. What is appealing about Ghazālī is that he left behind a nontotalizing intellectual legacy. While to some of his critics this is a weakness, for the modern Muslim subject he provides a treasure of resources with which one can construct a plausible trajectory for reimagining the religious tradition of Islam.

Ghazālī combined the skills of both an architect and a bricoleur. In one sense, he was an architect engaged in the creation of new art forms, the architecture of the imagination. In another sense, he was a bricoleur, busy with the indigenous art of making new things from quotidian objects and fashioning new meanings from fragments of myths. Being an architect as well as a bricoleur was by no means exceptional in the world that Ghazālī inhabited, but it takes a certain genius to make it work.

French anthropologist Claude Lévi-Strauss, from whom I borrow the concept of "bricolage," points out that the "difference" between an engineer and a bricoleur "is less absolute than it might appear."[7] An engineer, says Lévi-Strauss, always attempts to go beyond the constraints imposed by a particular moment in civilization. A bricoleur, on the other hand, is always inclined to remain within those limitations and constraints. Ghazālī combined the roles of both an engineer and a bricoleur: at times, he was prepared to transgress the boundaries drawn by civilization, and on other occasions he was ready to work within the constraints of his time.

Lévi-Strauss uses the expression "bricoleur" in order to describe the sort of worker who mends and maintains machinery or takes old materials and improvises new uses for them. He deploys this engaging metaphor with reference to two main processes: first, the appropriation of cultural elements from the dominant culture; and second, the transformation of meanings through ironic juxtaposition and innovative use in order to challenge and subvert existing meanings. Thus, the result of a series of improvisations might be that a multiplicity of very culture-specific meanings and norms is refashioned into a coherent unity.[8]

Even those of us who take ideas from many different sources and experiences in order to contemplate how their underlying and interlinking meanings make sense in a larger pattern of ideas and worldviews can be called bricoleurs. Being a bricoleur is different from being an eclectic. The crucial difference is this: in order for any performance or idea to be deemed eclectic, the provenance of the borrowed artifact must still be very much visible to the observer in the composite product. In fact, the borrowed idea does not develop a life of its own within the new setting. Lacking coherence, it sits uncomfortably in its new habitat as if it had been mechanically inserted into the new setting. By contrast, a bricoleur relocates artifacts in such a way that they form an integral part of the new environment. A bricoleur adds originality to a process or an artifact and in this crucial respect is different from an eclectic. A bricoleur demonstrates originality in the process of refinement and adaptation, making the borrowed artifact synthetically fit in with the new surroundings as if it had been there all the time and belonged there in the first place.

"Bricoleur" is an appropriate descriptor for Ghazālī. Extensive research has shown that he derived inspiration from a broad spectrum of thinkers who preceded him, including Miskawayh (d. 421/1030), Rāghib al-Iṣfahānī (d. ca. fifth/eleventh century), and Muḥāsibī, among others. Not only did he reconstruct ideas, but he did so with an originality that was secreted into his innovative interpretations. Of course, Ghazālī's reconstructed coherence did constitute a rift from the past; however, such a shift is in itself an event. It is a change that marks the end of one system of simultaneity and inaugurates a new one. "The same words and the same ideas are often reused," notes Michel de Certeau in another context, "but they no longer have the same meaning, [and] they are no longer thought and organized in the same way." He concludes, "It is upon this 'fact' that the project of an all-encompassing and unitary interpretation runs aground."[9]

Perhaps nature precedes humans in bricolage. "Your Lord inspired [*awḥā*] the bee," a delightful parable in the Qur'ān begins. It describes the labor of one of nature's most productive bricoleurs—the bee. Addressing the bee, the passage continues: "Prepare for thyself dwellings in mountains and in trees, and in what [humans] may build [for you by way of hives]. And then eat of all the fruits and follow humbly in the paths ordained by thy Sustainer. Then, from the bee's innards a drink of many hues pours forth; in it is a remedy for all humanity. In all this, behold, there is a message indeed for people who think."[10]

The parable of the bee is instructive. As a matter of habit, this insect draws from a diverse variety of sources—pollen and nectars—in order to produce a synthetic product that reflects all the colors and fruits of its immediate habitat. While the honey produced is in some way the aggregate of many diverse types of nectar, it is simultaneously something very new and unparalleled. In the end, the bee not only produces a delectable substance but also furthers reproduction through cross-pollination that in turn generates new flowers and restarts the cycle for the future production of honey.

Similarly, in the reconstruction of ideas from fragments, it is often the case that ideas that were once the end products of a constellation of thoughts are now deployed in the reconstructive process as means for different ends. In fact, bricolage has metalepsis as its equivalent in language. An embodied metaphorical process performs in similar ways to bricolage: one action is replaced by another action just as one metonym replaces another metonym in the figurative metaphor of metalepsis.

The other significant observation made by Lévi-Strauss, equally applicable to Ghazālī, is that a bricoleur "speaks" not only with things but also through the medium of things.[11] Thus, when bricoleurs make choices among a limited number of possibilities, in doing so they reveal their personalities and put something of themselves into the purposes behind their performances or deeds.

Poiesis

I couch my reading of Ghazālī within an understanding of the Aristotelian notion of poiesis. "Poiesis," or *shiʿrīya* in Arabic, is the making or construction of something by means of poetics, which involves imitation or representation, also called mimesis. For Aristotle, "poiesis" does not designate the finished poem; on the contrary, it signifies the act of poetic creation. Mimesis, or representation, has its own duality. As a form of action, it is a doing. But the making of a representation involves something more: standing back from one's actions and engaging in reflection requires one to actively consider how knowledge is made instead of viewing knowledge passively.[12] This is exactly how the brilliant Italian thinker and jurist Giambattista Vico (d. 1744) formulates humanity's immense debt to poetic wisdom (*sapientia poetica*), which he considers to be a way of knowing the ongoing process of history and the making of knowledge.[13]

Bolstering and reformulating his interpretations, Ghazālī did several things along the lines of poetics. He constructed a narrative by weaving a plethora of ideas and insights into a coherent but profoundly refigured whole. On some occasions, he reflected as to the reasons and justifications behind his viewpoints. In doing so, he demonstrated that thoughts and ideas are not given, but made and constructed. His narration is an account of doing, as well as an account of reflection as to what he achieved. At the same time, he elucidated a cosmology for Muslim thought that simultaneously imitated what came before it and innovated and provided something additional, something of what might be: the conditions of possibility.

Ghazālī, like a good bricoleur, employed the very materials used by his predecessors, such as verses of the Qur'ān; prophetic reports (*aḥādīth*); philosophical, legal, and theological discourses; and the narratives of mystics. But he did so with a crucial difference. He combined a variety of genres so that they constituted an organic unity. Not only was the whole of the new narrative very different from the sum of its parts, but the narrative also transformed the whole.

The renowned philosopher and jurist Abū al-Walīd Ibn Rushd singled out for opprobrium Ghazālī's use of poiesis (*shiʿrīya*) as well as his strategies of discursivity (*khiṭābīya*) and his dialectical polemics (*jadalīya*). What Ghazālī viewed to be constructive, Ibn Rushd deemed to be intellectually offensive. He lost patience with Ghazālī's intellectual promiscuity, pointing out that Ghazālī intentionally wished to signal his break with the established intellectual tradition by becoming a nonconformist. In a moment of irascibility, Ibn Rushd mocked Ghazālī as a man for all seasons—one who pretended to be an Ashʿarī when he was with theologians of that stripe, a mystic with the ṣūfīs, and a philosopher with philosophers.[14]

With their touch of infantine geniality, Ibn Rushd's observations, of course, say more about him than they do about his target of criticism. If anything, he blissfully skirted the process of self-reflection and avoided the essence of all knowledge: invention. For if he had looked inward, he might have acknowledged that a commitment to formalism and an uncritical repose in Aristotelianism can be limiting. Ghazālī, in turn, was a frontier thinker, working hard on the threshold (*dihlīz*) of multiple narratives of thought. Paradoxically, Ghazālī's commitment to poetics and bricolage could not have obtained a more eloquent endorsement than Ibn Rushd's intransigent but accurate description of his project.

However, it is because Ghazālī's intellectual taste was firmly rooted in a frontier scholarship, one that drew on the force field of poetics and bricolage, that it provided such an extravagantly rich texture to his ideas and thoughts. One of the most explicit effects of poiesis and bricolage is the development of multiple notions of time, or heterotemporality, which is lavishly inscribed onto the Ghazālian narrative.

The line of poiesis, the art of doing and reflecting, in Ghazālī's thought demonstrates the working of a rationally creative state of mind. It reveals how this pivotal thinker shaped new landscapes of the imagination from older ones. The rationally active state of mind, the consequence of doing and acting that relates to its ethical import, is different from the rationally creative state of mind.[15] But Ghazālī was as passionate about ethics as he was about poetics. Thus, it is very difficult to carefully separate Ghazālī's poetics from his ethics. And it may well be that his poetics served as an inspiration for his ethics.

So while I acknowledge that Ghazālī's ethics are at times inseparable from his poetics, I often try to delineate the poetics at work. For it was in his poetics that Ghazālī asked questions and sought to provide answers to his dilemmas and challenges as to what kind of Muslim subjectivity was required in order to create a new knowledge for his time. And it is precisely the archeology and structure of the questions and answers that I wish to capture, an archeology that has sustained generations of Muslims in their scholarship and inspired their practices.

There is another, possibly more compelling, reason to examine the scholars of the Islamic past, especially figures like Ghazālī. A number of modern

Muslim thinkers have explored a myriad of possible ways to imagine Islam and have attempted to rethink it as a religious tradition. The Indian poet-philosopher Muhammad Iqbal (d. 1938) was extremely perceptive about the enormous challenge and burden placed on the shoulders of the modern Muslim intellectual. He recognized that nothing less than radical ways of re-imagining Islam were required. "The task before the modern Muslim," Iqbal observed, "is therefore, immense." Iqbal continued: "He has to rethink the whole system of Islam without completely breaking with the past. The only course open to us is to approach modern knowledge with a respectful but independent attitude and to appreciate the teachings of Islam in the light of that knowledge, even though we may be led to differ from those who have gone before us."[16]

Not only is this an Herculean task—to rethink the Muslim tradition—but it is an equally daunting challenge. It requires the renewed Muslim subject to be different from the past due to temporal change, yet there remains a demand that subjectivity be simultaneously continuous with the past. We see glimpses of this creative tension throughout the work of Ghazālī. Perhaps the twenty-first-century challenge—greater even than the challenge of the Ghazālian, or post-Ghazālī, intellectual project—anticipates an even more radical solution: to discover a subjectivity that is competent to will a paradigmatic transition within Islam. What this emergent knowledge will look like is difficult to conceive in definitive terms, but one thing is sure. It will require critical and agonizing intellectual labor to make the discovery.

Future Friendships

If the contours of the Ghazālian/post-Ghazālī project I envisage remain difficult to discern, one can at least begin to imagine the kinds of friendships and alliances that any such rethinking will involve. With whom from the past will the coming generations of thinkers commune? If we look at Ghazālī's alliances, we clearly see that he had an ambivalent relationship with Manṣūr al-Ḥallāj (d. 309/922), the influential mystic and martyr whose anguished cry burst onto the tenth-century stage of Baghdād and the Muslim world. More than a century later, the scholar and judge ʿAyn al-Quḍāt al-Hamadhānī (d. 525/1131) looked in the direction of Ghazālī as a critical admirer. He questioned the hegemonic political thinking of his time and bequeathed a new vision and legacy for future generations to contemplate.[17] The actions of each one of these figures—Ḥallāj, Ghazālī, Hamadhānī—signaled a mutation in the field of the community (*umma*) and the political (*siyāsa*). Each one of these figures refused to yield to the hegemonic discourses of his day.[18] Sometimes, they willingly or unwillingly entered into unholy alliances with absolutist political forces or confronted such foes. Each one of them was nevertheless exposed to varying degrees of suffering and dangers within the confessional community. Two were expelled and executed on charges of heresy: such was the fate of both Ḥallaj and Hamadhānī. Ghazālī died a natural death, but during his lifetime his books were burned by intolerant foes in Muslim Spain and in the Maghrib.[19]

In modern history, the German thinker Friedrich Nietzsche, too, was such a "tortured" spirit, one who signaled a mutation in community and politics. It is extremely significant that a figure of the stature of the Indian poet-philosopher Muhammad Iqbal could desire that a radical occultation or mutation occur in Muslim thinking. The statement may well demonstrate Nietzsche's influence on him. The French thinker Jacques Derrida described Nietzsche as an "event of the text." This phrase is equally applicable to Ḥallāj, Ghazālī, and Hamadhānī: as "events," they signaled a mutation in the field of the political and the community in general.[20]

By engaging with the thinkers of the past, we anticipate the intellectual communities of the future. Derrida believes that when we do so, we imagine "an alliance without an institution"[21] in which the thinkers and philosophers of the future already exist. The reason that the thinkers of the future already exist is that we visualize them, address them here and now as a possible future hope and desire. In all these fictive acts, we are already declaring our friendship with the philosophers of the future, and in this gesture we become their heralds and precursors.[22] There is a compelling reason why we declare our friendship with some figures more than others. It is because, to use Dipesh Chakrabarty's appropriate words, they "refer us to the plurality of the 'now.'"[23]

It is in the context of friendship with Ḥallāj, Ghazālī, Hamadhānī, and many others, from my perspective, or Nietzsche, from Derrida's viewpoint, that Derrida launches a neologism, the idea of "teleiopoiós," or "teleiopoiesis." Derived from the Greek *teleios*, meaning "to perfect" and "to complete," *teleiosis* signifies perfection, completion, and consummation.[24] Derrida is aware of these iterations of meaning but beseeches us to play with the other *tele*, "the one that speaks to distance and the far removed."[25]

In other words, "teleiopoiesis" here means to speak to a future community. Derrida then asks the question: Can the future be measured by knowledge? If we knew the answer to that question, he points out, then things would not be different, and change would be unthinkable. Therefore, we cannot *totally* know the answer to this question. It is thus desirable to confess humility, a humility of ignorance, to admit to a certain non-knowledge. This confession of ignorance is not a pretentious claim to ignorance, or non-knowledge, but an admission that one knows that we do not know. An exemplary instance of such humble ignorance is the statement of the leading jurist of Madīna, Mālik bin Anas (d. 179/796), who, in reply to forty-eight questions posed to him, confidently said "I do not know" (*Lā adrī*) in response to thirty-two of them.[26]

The wish to say something in the future in a nontotalitarian way is what Derrida names in a single word the "teleiopoetic." Teleiopoiesis is an event of chance occurrence, the Nietzschean "perhaps" that signifies the only possible thought of a future event. This is what Derrida writes about as the longing for "a friendship to come and friendship for the future."[27] Teleiopoiesis is one of those ideas that destabilizes our sense of belonging to an actualized collectivity. More than that, it forces us into a constant risk-taking stance, as Gayatri Spivak elaborates, in order to influence the "distant in a poiesis or imaginative remaking without guarantees."[28] We need to hear what Nietzsche says:

> *Perhaps* to each of us will come the more joyful hour when we exclaim:
> Friends, there are no friends! thus said the dying sage;
> Foes, there are no foes! say I, the living fool.[29]

The single word "perhaps" encapsulates the only possible thought of the future event, of friendship to come and friendship for the future. For this reason, friendship is not enough; one must also love the future. For Derrida, this future is deliberately ambiguous. However, within Islamicate contexts, one would be compelled to ask: Is this a worldly or afterworldly future—namely, *dunyā* or *ākhira*—or does it refer to futures in both realms? Whatever perspective one chooses, the future can have no better category than "perhaps," where friendship and the future conjoin in a regime of a "possible whose possibilization," says Derrida, "must prevail over the impossible."[30] Then he adds: "The possibilization of the impossible must remain at one and the same time as undecideable—and therefore as decisive—as the future itself . . . teleiopoetics . . . but not without suggesting that friendship is implied in advance therein: friendship for oneself, for the friend and for the enemy."[31]

For, indeed, just as the future exists, so too do the future thinkers and philosophers already exist in our imaginations. The poetics of the future that we desire is, of course, messianic in its structure, like the Messiah about whom people (some Jews, Christians, and Muslims in their respective ways) ask, in the here and now, when *he* will come. The philosophers of the future are part of a messianic future. "We are not yet among these philosophers of the future," Derrida reminds us, "we who are calling them and calling them the philosophers of the future, but we are in advance their friends and, in this gesture of the call, we establish ourselves as their heralds and precursors [*ihre Herolde und Vorläufer*]. . . . This is perhaps the 'community of those without community.'"[32]

Imagined friendship and "community without community" are highly developed tropes in Arabo-Islamic literary traditions. Indeed, early Muslims spoke about archetypal *ʿuwaysī* relationships in which one seeks instructions or inspiration from someone who is physically absent.[33] The term itself derives its name from a long-distance admirer and disciple of the Prophet Muḥammad, one ʿUways al-Qaranī (d. 37/657), who hailed from Yemen but reportedly lived in Mesopotamia, where there is mausoleum built to his memory at Ar Raqqah in modern Syria. And, over time, there have been successive spiritual movements and intellectual networks that have been viewed as long-distance affiliations, as archetypes of *ʿuwaysī* relations across time and space in Muslim history.

In part, these liminal and romantic communities are inspired by teachings that reach back to Islam's earliest impulse. A saying by the Prophet Muḥammad welcoming the exiles is a central motif. "Islam began as a stranger/exile [*gharīb*]," a tradition attributed to the Prophet states, "and [Islam] will return to an exilic/estranged [state]; so blessed are the strangers/exiles."[34] Here, the idea of being a stranger or exile is idealized in manifold ways. It evokes a certain tyranny of the world and of time. Under such anticipated conditions, those who seek the truth become exiled and marginalized by the tyranny of the majority. The marginalized are exiles in their suffering and give solidarity to each other. Exile here has many permutations ranging from the physical and spiritual to the political and to other conceivable forms of suffering and marginalization.

If there is solidarity among exiles, then friendship can transform and reconcile the "self" with the "other." The Qur'ān urges us to repel wrong and iniquity with that which is "infinitely more beautiful" (*aḥsan*, the superlative for *ḥusn*, meaning "beauty"). The passage animates a belief that exemplary deeds and acts will turn an enemy into a bosom friend. Surely, the Qur'ān cautiously puts it, this gift of turning an enemy into a friend is a capacity one has to earn and acquire. By engaging in supreme acts of perseverance (*alladhīna ṣabarū*) coupled with a dose of good fortune (*dhū ḥaẓẓin ʿaẓīm*), one can hope to become deserving of the capacity to transform the self and the other.[35] In the end, it comes down to the project of the self. While the themes of exile, friendship, and imagined communities over time and space are extensively treated in discussions of Muslim mysticism, poetry, and literature, they are seldom related to the narrative of retelling, philosophy, and history. One of the purposes of this book is to make a modest attempt to reread the past so that the Muslim subject will be able to project the hope of teleiopoiesis—the hope of a future marked by friendship and just coexistence—as a real possibility among a plurality of discursive communities.

But the question remains: How does this friendship and future community manifest itself? To answer this question, one needs to revisit Edward Said's compelling and inspiring meditations on this very subject, thoughts that he encountered during his reading of the French orientalist Louis Massignon. Said's words also serve as a reply to my question posed above as to how one displays friendship and coexistence. Said observes:

> The importance of the spoken language is that it is a testimony (*shahāda*), and carried to its ultimate grammatical form (*shahīd*) it means martyr. To testify is to speak, and to speak is to move from yourself toward another, to displace self in order to accommodate another, your opposite and your guest, and also someone absent whose absence opposes your own presence. The irony of this is that you can never directly come together with another: your testimony can at best accommodate the other, and this of course is what language does and is, antithetically—presence and absence, unless in the case of the *shahīd* (martyr) the self is obliterated for the sake of the other, who because of the martyr's love is more distant, more an Other than ever.[36]

The maturation of the potential friendship and the act of bearing witness cannot occur without being preceded by something essential: the art of listening. Whether it be Ghazālī or any figure who captures our imagination as a potential friend, hearing requires a moment of listening, and only by listening can we bear witness. The culture to which Ghazālī was allied placed a great store on listening, an idea captured in the verse of the Qur'ān commenting on the reception of history.[37] It is only if histories are "heard" with the ear or the heart or both that they serve as "reminders," or something "worth mentioning" (*dhikrā*). The end point of history is to be a witness—a *shahīd*. Yet history, narrative, and events cannot serve as reminders, or as heuristic points, if they are unaccompanied by a proper form of listening (*samāʿ*).

Another way of listening and witnessing is to do so with the pectoral imagery of the "heart" (*qalb*), which in the Muslim tradition is the most powerful apparatus of affective cognition. To be a witness or even a martyr requires the act to be preceded—with due apologies for the neologisms—by an act of either "heart-listening" or "ear-throwing." "Indeed, in this [history]," says the verse of the Qur'ān, "there is a reminder for anyone who has a heart or lends an ear and stands witness."[38]

Thus, in large part, this book is about listening to Ghazālī in very specific ways, bearing in mind that the ear can be uncanny. It is only when the receiving ear engages in listening that the reader/listener *signs* the text, even if posthumously; only then is the contract of future friendship sealed. In other words, the reader/listener/investigator must be able to see his or her own present, no matter how faintly, as continuous with the object of investigation. Otherwise, as both Talal Asad and Dipesh Chakrabarty caution, the possibility is dramatically enhanced that the observation and investigation might only produce an unwanted incoherence in the presentation of the data or an anachronism in consciousness.[39] I am mindful of these concerns as I offer some readings of an exegetical and interpretative sort. The reading techniques employed are interventions in the Ghazālian text made by exploring the possible destinations of his interpretation under different thematics.[40] In this sense, one must take seriously both the corpus of Ghazālī's work and the body of Ghazālī as the subject. In particular, one has to critically examine the space from which he launched his interventions.

Archeology of the Threshold

How did Ghazālī imagine the space from which he engendered his new "texts"? If one listens carefully to Ghazālī in the dual role of a witness and an observer, it can lead to new possibilities. There is an interesting twist in how I detected the *dihlīz*, that in-between space that is imbricated in the Ghazālian imagination. It is a story that in part centers on translation but that also relates to the dialogical relationship between the multiple facets and influences of the present *in conjunction with* the multiple narratives of the past that shape us. That *conjunction*, or *junction*, is spatially represented by the *dihlīz*.

The *dihlīz* encompasses, in my view, the key to the Ghazālian secret, for it is the precursor to "the various feelings of the individual pinch of destiny," to use the words of psychologist of religion William James.[41] Yet even witnessing and observing occur under conditions of continuous play "between the excess of thought over language and the excess of language over thought," so that what may appear as commentary actually "translates" the residual latent meanings into new formulations.[42]

Trying to configure what Ghazālī's work and legacy means to us can be a daunting task, especially since his oeuvre has been the subject of so many specialized studies. Beyond that, the hegemony of a colonizing Western epistemology renders the knowledge systems of subaltern traditions either invisible or unsustainable. In fact, as is the case for many postcolonial subjects, indigenous traditions get rediscovered through different forms of translation. It is thus of consequence that the play between the excess of language over thought and vice versa loosens up earlier iterations of meaning and subtly questions settled dogmas. We know that Ghazālī scrupulously and with the use of knowledge did succeed in refashioning the way he looked at himself. Does he, in turn, dominate the way we look at ourselves in the mirror of his work? In what space did Ghazālī do this work? While I did locate that space to be the *dihlīz*, it is crucial to show how translation is critical to the discovery.

Conversation with colleagues working on Latin America exposed me to the work of the Chicana writer Gloria Anzaldúa.[43] Her work has inspired many thinkers to explore notions of border thinking. Anzaldúa points out that working and practicing at the diaphanous borders of intersecting cultures creates certain ambivalences arising from the clash of voices that result in mental and emotional states of complexity. Her insights suggest that postcolonial societies especially, and possibly also postcolonial subjects, live in a constant state of *nepantilism*, an Aztec word meaning "torn between ways," or *mestiza*. But that state of *nepantilism* is not entirely innocent; rather, it transfers the cultural and spiritual values of one group to another.

This line of inquiry prompted me to ask what kind of cross-pollination of ideas took place in early Muslim societies and how this cross-pollination occurs in contemporary Muslim societies. To ask this question is not to engage in the futile search for the origins of ideas but to explore the beginnings of intellectual trends and patterns of thought. It struck me that the early Muslim societies of the Near East developed overlapping and shared cultural traditions, yet hardly anyone describes them as having been torn between ways, or *mestiza*. In fact, distinct cultural traditions were simultaneously part of a larger pluriversal commonwealth, or empire. It is unlikely that people in the past imagined or used the idea of a border in the way we moderns do. If border thinking did take place, then such borders were not national boundaries but other kinds of demarcations. It is likely that when knowledge was transmitted from one culture to another it was mediated by some-*thing* or some-*body*.

The idea of a border works very successfully in contexts marked by the nation-state. In these contexts, a border serves as a territorial demarcation between sovereign territories and criminalizes improper crossing without authorization. But it also compels one to choose. A person invariably falls on one side of the border or the other—unless, of course, that person is prepared to straddle a no-man's-land. It became apparent to me that, despite all its merits, the use of border thinking in trying to configure Ghazālī's location in terms of the multiple currents and threads of his day has its limitations and that I needed to find a more appropriate metaphor.

Most scholars are aware that the hidden question is always an enticement and seduction to the investigator. The investigator is obliged to ask: What is the balance between research and search? One is reminded of the insightful remark of the writer Cynthia Ozick, who suggests "that the quarry is all the time in the pursuer."[44] Reading Clifford Geertz's shining essay on William James prodded me to reach for James's *The Varieties of Religious Experience*. I wanted to have a better grasp of the thought buried under the seductive phrase "the individual pinch of destiny," which was cited by Geertz.[45] As I read James's comments on Ghazālī's mystical experiences, his translation of the word "threshold," which he took from a French translation of Ghazālī's *Rescuer*, caught my attention. On consulting the Arabic text—and to my utter delight—the word to which I had not been attentive in the original, *dihlīz*, became enormously significant in "translation."

This brought me back to the *Rescuer*; or, to put it differently, Ghazālī came to my rescue. In the *Rescuer*, there is a single line—almost an orphaned line—that is tantalizingly intriguing, like a reply from a Delphic oracle. It occurs in a fragment of a sentence in which Ghazālī makes a most revealing statement. It reads: "And whatever precedes it is like a threshold/antechamber/vestibule [*dihlīz*] for the seeker of it [God]."[46] Translators have focused on the expression "seeker of it" (*li al-sālik ilayhi*), unsure whether "it" refers to the preceding discussion, which contains several possible referents, such as spiritual "annihilation" (*fanā'*) and the mystical "way," or whether "it" refers to "God." Without wishing to truncate the argument, I am convinced, as are several translators, that "it" in this fragment refers to the divine.[47]

However, the thrust of the sentence is not the referent but something else:

the unconscious dissemination of the spatial metaphor into Ghazālī's narrative through the word *dihlīz*. *Dihlīz* is a Persian word that has been Arabized. It means "that space between the door and the house."[48] The meaning of the passage without the *dihlīz* rider already made eminent sense: that the purification of the heart is the first step on the mystical path. There must have been a particular reason why Ghazālī felt so compelled to add the sentence: "And whatever precedes it is like a threshold for the seeker of God [*Wa mā qabla dhālika ka al-dihlīz li al-sālik ilayhi*]." So why did Ghazālī liken the space in which the seeker of God stands to the threshold space? Why was the liminal courtyard, or in-between space that one crisscrosses daily, so crucial to his thinking?

We must ask: Why did the *dihlīz*, out of all the images that may have occurred to him, make a bigger impression than the others? "A writer's biography," Brodsky reminds us, "is in his twists of language."[49] Here, in the purposefully deployed simile and its wondrous imagery of the *dihlīz*, Ghazālī ushers us into one of the deepest recesses of his imaginative psyche. The spatial metaphor signifies a multitude of meanings when Ghazālī's readers begin to ponder its interpretive possibilities. One is, of course, reticent to state categorically that Ghazālī's mental geography coagulated and mimicked the spatial geography of the *dihlīz*, even if one is inclined to state it emphatically.

What one slowly begins to fathom is that the *dihlīz*, or the *dihlīz*-ian space, is a liminal space. The *dihlīz* signifies the space as well as the action of two entries: entry from the *outside* and entry into the *inside*. It is the critical intermediate space between outside and inside, between exoteric (*ẓāhir*) and esoteric (*bāṭin*).[50] And it is also the space that one has to traverse in order to enter or exit, which is the real function of a threshold area. That *dihlīz*-ian space constitutes a bounded space, a threshold between door (*bāb*) and house (*dār*). It is not a useless space, but one that can be used for multiple purposes. Viewed from the house proper, the *dihlīz* is located on the outside. But viewed from the door leading to the street, the *dihlīz* is on the inside. A courtyard, a passage, a porch, or a vestibule can constitute the *dihlīz* in strict architectural terms. While it is the space into which smells and odors from inside the house waft and mix with those produced outside it, it is also more.

Unlike a border that serves as a territorial demarcation between sovereign territories and criminalizes improper crossing without authorization, the *dihlīz* is not a criminalizing space but a welcoming space. Furthermore, it ensures that one enters by the door in a disciplined manner while maintaining the decorum appropriate to the integrity of the occupants of the house and the people in the street. It is neither entirely private nor totally public, but something in between. However, the crucial dimension is the fact that without the *dihlīz* one cannot speak about an embodied "door" and a "house," nor can one speak of an "outside" and an "inside." Even though it is located in between spaces, the *dihlīz* frames all other spaces. And, for my purposes, the *dihlīz* becomes a new locus of epistemic and political enunciation.

In my view, Ghazālī celebrated this space as the space of beginnings and endings, as a locus of enunciation. It is in the *dihlīz*-ian space, I would argue, that one can optimally place Ghazālī's own body, and it is in this space that he both enunciated and engendered his texts. In an interesting and fascinating manner, but with the use of a single metaphor intentionally buried in the subtlety of his text, Ghazālī reached for the normativity that resides in the liminal. Thus, the need to be in between produces *dihlīz*-ian knowledge, or *dihlīz*-ian gnosis.[51] Given the fact that the *dihlīz* is such a mobile force field, one of its attractions is that it lends itself to nontotalitarian modes of being and thought.

Agonistic Dialogics

The first and enduring impression of Ghazālī is that of a person self-consciously suspended between different currents of thought and struggling to be faithful to tradition and to the demands of his own society and time. War and peace, good and bad, beauty and ugliness—these are the poles of our agonistic existence; we cannot avoid paradoxical conflicts, which pull us from both ends.[52] We, too, experience an agonistic existence, perhaps most acutely felt in the modern or postmodern age, in which individuals and entire societies are acutely experiencing the opposing pulls of transitioning from one mode of social existence to another.

As individuals and societies, we moderns are profoundly self-aware of the multiple worlds that we inhabit simultaneously. One of the questions that I implicitly pose in this book is whether the agonistic mode of existence as we experience it today has any kind of antecedents in the past. In my reading of Ghazālī, I find elements of the agonistic mode of existence to be evident in his life. Ghazālī was caught in the elaborate network of tensions of thought and a spiral of existential conditions that he embraced in all their variety like a consummate bricoleur. The strains, tensions, controversies, and disputation of a multiplicity of intellectual discourses impacted on his life, his mind, his very being. Ghazālī is the subject of heated debates in Muslim intellectual history. While some extol his brilliant expositions of faith and reason, others accuse him of imploding the edifice of reason in his sharp critique of the Muslim philosophers. It was he, his critics believe, who planted the seeds for antirationality that in turn encouraged fatalism in Muslim religious and cultural thought.

The state of being caught between antithetical positions characterized many aspects of Ghazālī's life. When he was invited by the *wazīr*, Fakhr al-Mulk, to return to teaching in Nisapūr, he at first refused to comply with the request, having vowed not to associate himself with rulers and people in power. Finally, he convinced himself that this political plea was actually a divine call, leading him to perform a larger task that required a renunciation of his earlier vows to refrain from interaction with officialdom. While his account of this event indicates that it was one of the many agonistic moments in Ghazālī's life, he nevertheless faced it with a note of optimism. He viewed the invitation as a divine sign that his role was to restore confidence at a time of crisis and to advance the public good.

But there were even more complex and agonizing moments that beset Ghazālī. As a teenager, he was admitted to boarding school largely due to the poverty of his family. That experience tortured him in his adulthood. Why did he go on to study in the first place, wondered Ghazālī? Was it to acquire precious knowledge for the sake of God or merely for the purpose of survival? Also during his youth, Ghazālī encountered thieves to whom he nearly lost his irreplaceable dissertation. Ghazālī had to ask hard questions about the divine intent behind this episode with the brigands. Finally, he was confronted with the legacy of the Muslim philosophers and again was forced to ask self-reflexive questions about the purpose of all learning and knowledge. In various ways, these episodes seem to have poisoned his tranquility and forced him to rethink a number of issues related to his being and thinking.

In more than one respect, Ghazālī's own thinking can be described as dialogical thinking. Despite the fact that he was open to Aristotelian reasoning and elements of Hellenic thought as transmitted by some of the Muslim philosophers who preceded him, he did not allow for any particular system of thought or discipline to colonize his thinking. He took neither the Hellenic sciences nor the Islamic sciences nor the Ashʿarī theological school at face value: he constantly adjudicated which parts of the different traditions were beneficial and which were harmful.[53] He explored to what extent each tradition could be a means for action that would lead to the liberation he sought. Even mystical experience—which he ultimately found to be the most desirable intellectual end—was made subject to dialogical thinking.

Dialogical thinking also informs my approach—inspired by Ghazālī—but my formulations draw on the categories of Mikhail Bakhtin, Paulo Frere, Abdulkabīr Khatībī, and Walter Mignolo. Bakhtin's insights provide the semiotic frame for understanding dialogical thinking as conceiving of all meaning to be part of a greater whole.[54] There is a constant interaction between meanings, all of which condition others in conscious and unconscious ways. This "dialogical imperative," as Bakhtin puts it, is rooted in the language-world we inhabit. Often, language users are deluded into believing that their own language is the only language of discourse. However, the overpowering force of heteroglossia and dialogism very soon punctuates such erroneous beliefs. It is the dialogic imperative that guarantees that there actually can be no monologue and that we constantly borrow ideas and inspiration from a variety of sources (like bees) toward certain emancipatory and liberatory ends.

Bakhtin argues that all discourse is heteroglot and subject to the function of a matrix of forces. Heteroglossia is that condition that ensures the primacy of context over text. It is a set of discrete criteria—social, historical, even meteorological and psychological—that ensures that a word or a sentence uttered under one set of conditions will have a different configuration of meaning if it is articulated under dissimilar conditions. Heteroglossia is at once difficult to recoup and impossible to resolve. The concept of "dialogization" is the critical insight provided by Bakhtin. For it is only when discourses and languages undergo dialogization that they effectively become de-privileged and relativized. And it is only by undergoing dialogization that our "documents of civilization" (to use Walter Benjamin's often-quoted phrase)—traditions, disciplines, discourses, scriptures, culture—can be rescued from becoming documents of barbarism.[55] For Ghazālī, intellectual decolonization meant liberation from the darker side of Hellenism, and for us it means to be liberated from the darker side of modernity.[56]

Orthodoxy and Tradition

Often, in the course of his polemical writings, Ghazālī made reference to the fact that Muslims will be split into multiple sects, of which only one will attain salvation.[57] Even though Ghazālī occasionally appeared to be skeptical of such triumphalist and exclusivist claims, one does get the sense that he believed there is a discursive path to salvation. On closer interrogation, however, the ease with which such formulaic phrases as "saved sect" or "community of consensus" at first beckon soon evaporates like mist in the rays of the sun. Intra-Muslim sectarian rivalries show that each claimant stakes a claim to the privileged "saved" position. Even adjudication among contesting viewpoints can be a challenging feat when each sect has differential standards as to what constitutes correct practices and doctrines. Aside from the major discrepancy between Shīʿa and Sunnī interpretations of Islam, there is intense intra-Sunnī rivalry between the Ḥanbalī and Ashʿarī theological traditions, each of which can become exclusionary and antithetical to the other, just as there are intra-Shīʿī rivalries.[58]

A dispute between contesting positions inevitably raises the question of how the correct position is to be adjudicated—by whom and by which standard? These concerns elicit discussion concerning orthodoxy and tradition, since the two are related. Two scholars, Seyyed Hossein Nasr and Talal Asad, deal with the notions of orthodoxy and tradition in very different ways. Nasr admits that there is no exact cultural translation for the term "tradition" in Muslim discourse; the closest approximation in his view is *dīn*, the term used to denote "religion" in Western languages.[59] In the broadest sense, tradition, Nasr points out, "is inextricably linked to revelation and religion, to the sacred, to the notion of orthodoxy, to authority, to the continuity and regularity of transmission of the truth, to the exoteric and the esoteric as well as to the spiritual life, science and arts."[60] So the Arabic term *dīn* means at once tradition and religion in its most universal sense. Nasr urges us to view religion as both the revealed principles and their later historical unfolding. Simply put, tradition for him is both metaphysics and culture.

Yet, in Nasr's view, tradition and what can be denoted as traditional are also inseparable from the sacred. Thus, when it comes to authority, tradition implies orthodoxy, or sacred authority, which is inseparable from tradition. "If there is such a thing as truth," Nasr explains, "then there is also error and norms which allow man to distinguish between them. Orthodoxy in its most universal sense is none other than the truth in itself and as related to the formal homogeneity of a particular traditional universe."[61]

Nasr goes on to lament the loss of the multidimensional character of religion, pointing out that some people castigate the mystical and esoteric dimensions of religion as unorthodox. Their atrophied conception of orthodoxy, he says, is a result of their obsessive identification of orthodoxy with simple conformity. Those who are both endowed with and engaged with the sanctified metaphysical intellect, he adds, would dismiss such a narrow version of orthodoxy as a perversion. However, Nasr is also emphatic in arguing that there is neither the possibility of tradition without orthodoxy nor the existence of orthodoxy outside of tradition. For him, both orthodoxy and tradition must be free from deviations, imitations, and aberrations of a human kind. Nasr's view, in summation, is that tradition is timeless, that it is largely metaphysical, and that it constitutes sacred knowledge. More importantly, tradition is free from the discursive traditions of rationality, and it definitely has no truck with modernity.[62]

Talal Asad posits a notion of tradition that is different. Drawing on the work of the philosopher Alisdair MacIntyre, Asad points out that tradition is essentially discourses that instruct practitioners as to the correct form and purpose of a practice.[63] Tradition, like practices, therefore, has a history, a conceptual relationship to the past, as well as a future—especially in dictating how a practice is best secured and explaining why it should be maintained, altered, or abandoned in the present in relation to other practices, institutions, and social conditions.[64] For Asad, the constitution of tradition relies on the practitioners' notion of what is *apt performance*, of how the past is related to present practices; tradition is not, he continues, the mere repetition of old forms.[65]

Having established what tradition is, Asad then frames it in such a manner that it prefigures orthodoxy, by which he means a relationship of power to regulate, uphold, require, or adjust *correct* practices and to condemn, exclude, undermine, or replace *incorrect* ones.[66] Through reasoning and argument, orthodoxy organizes modalities of discursive power and resistance, Asad argues. Even though Islamic traditions are not homogeneous, they aspire to coherence by organizing memory and desire under specific material conditions.

There is a crucial difference between the accounts of tradition and orthodoxy offered by Nasr and Asad. For the former, tradition is an a priori datum: it becomes the product of a divine archetype. For the latter, tradition is a coherent set of constructed practices with its own rules. Thus, for Asad, orthodoxy is essentially normative and a set of norm-setting practices. The latter are subject to crucial differences and are historically constructed. On the face of it, Nasr's insistence that tradition and orthodoxy be linked to truth paradoxically provides his conception of these terms a closer fit than Asad's with MacIntyre's idea of tradition as the repository of truth. Asad, as an anthropologist, does not overtly link tradition to truth claims, while Nasr asserts that orthodoxy monopolizes the truth. Indeed, Asad projects orthodoxy as the zone of coherence and discursive space for the veracity and normativity of tradition, which is always subject to the contestation of power.

Siding with Asad, we may assert that orthodoxy is at best a defense mechanism against the threatened fragmentations of incoherent pluralism. And if orthodoxy's putative aim is to protect unity by means of homogeneity, it is actually self-defeating. For, indeed, homogeneity is always elusive, since it presupposes an absolute knowledge of what is orthodox and heterodox; only in Nasr's account of tradition and orthodoxy can the orthodox be authoritatively distinguished from the heterodox.

At the practical level, no orthodoxy can admit to a heterodoxy and then run the risk of heterogeneity and self-implosion. Yet, in theory, at least in Asad's view, discursive heterogeneity is the norm.[67] Even if tradition means different things to different people, the variations in understanding tradition emerge out of reasoned debates and arguments over the form and significance of practices, which in turn establish relationships and networks of power.

One does not have to go further than the Shāfiʿī school, with which Ghazālī was affiliated, to detect such diversity of tradition. Taqī al-Dīn Ibn Ṣalāḥ (d. 643/1245), like Ghazālī a follower of the Shāfiʿī school, was nevertheless a vociferous foe of Ghazālī, claiming to oppose him on grounds of orthodoxy. Ibn Ṣalāḥ posited that correct practice can be known directly from the scriptural sources. He opposed Ghazālī because the latter believed it to be a prerequisite for the discovery of what is correct and true that one's hermeneutic be invested with logic. Similarly, the early pietist Ḥārith al-Muḥāsibī claimed to be on the path of orthodox truth, even though his contemporary, the pious traditionist (*muḥaddith*) Aḥmad ibn Ḥanbal (d. 241/855), voiced a visceral dislike for what he deemed to be Muḥāsibī's heretical views.

Iterations of Tradition

What is deemed to be orthodoxy is therefore a discursive tradition in which different forms of reasoning and the exercise of discursive power exist in a creative tension, a tension that creates resistance as well as acquiescence. In other words, orthodoxy is a contested category, variegated and diverse, and is thus not a monolithic and a reductive entity. It is perhaps best to speak about "orthodoxies" or "pluralities of discursive traditions."

The notion of orthodoxy in the Muslim tradition possibly comes closest to Michel Foucault's notion of pastoral power.[68] According to a report attributed to the Prophet Muḥammad, every individual is like a shepherd who has responsibility over his or her flock. Pastoral power in the Foucauldian sense implies a peculiar kind of knowledge between the pastor and each member of the community not unlike the shepherd's knowledge of each of the sheep in his flock, although Foucault was thinking of a pastoral setting of a different kind. Whether it is the act of the clerical pastor or of the shepherd, each act of ethical responsibility involves a type of knowledge that at first individualizes.

Pastoral constructions of power and tradition can also apply to a guild of scholars or a particular aggregation of people. In these cases, knowledge and power coalesce into the authority of a school of thought to constitute a consensus position with cumulative power, a power that is larger than the sum of its parts. Indeed, such formal power is translated into a claim of responsibility and ethics. Orthodoxy must therefore be pastoral without becoming paternal.

Early Muslim jurists were possibly most astute in their understanding of the cumulative power of authority through knowledge and responsibility. Muslim jurists identified the consensus position as the *madhhab* position, literally "the way of going out," that is, the adopted policy, rule, or procedure in law. Unfortunately, most modern dictionaries translate *madhhab* as the "orthodox rite of *fiqh*, Islamic law."[69] Despite the fact that orthodoxy is constituted through the aggregation of multiple connected authorities, heterogeneity remains a hallmark of orthodoxy. For, paradoxically, even orthodoxy can never be free of the various contradictory and antagonistic forces that shape it through acts of contestation and resistance. However, beyond orthodoxy and heterodoxy, there are discrete themes that shape all individuals within their respective communities and societies.

Ghazālī and the Poetics of Tradition

Ghazālī's life, work, and the subsequent appropriation of his ideas represent the contradictory forces and tensions of tradition in a variety of practical expressions. How can we approach someone as complex and distanced as Ghazālī without distorting his legacy? The difficulty of understanding the past begins with the present, historians remind us. We must bear in mind that the language of Ghazālī's time and place is critical to our understanding of his life. Keeping Bakhtin in mind, there is thus an important reason why it is crucial to have a dialogical process at work between the past and the present in our reading of Ghazālī, or of any other historical figure, for that matter. For even a definitive reading prefigures alternative readings to any text or history, just as orthodoxy prefigures other contesting alternatives.

At the same time, we need to recognize that the alternative possibilities we seek to explore in the past are "themselves suggested by the retrospective or deferred effects of later knowledge."[70] Crucial and intense moments of inner difference and self-contestation within "texts" present to the reader of history those moments that have an uncanny bearing on the present. The past is never simply a finished story to be narrated. It is best perceived as a process that is linked to each historian or interpreter's own time of narration. Historians cannot understand what something meant in the past unless they also recognize what kind of sense that thing, event, or occurrence makes in their own time. Both heteroglossia and dialogism are essential and indispensable conceptual tools for the historian and interpreter.

The most engaging and perhaps the most perplexing dimensions of interpretation exist at the margins. We need to interrogate instances of orthodox encrustation and settled opinion. It is in these instances where the two meanings of past and present are not simply disjoined from each other: they reach a liminal point where the dialogues between the two meanings become internal to the historian.[71] The construction of a historical culture, observes the premier modern historian of early Western antiquity, "does not begin with understanding the past but with opening oneself to the present." He continues: "It involves containing, in oneself, the confusion and dismay that ensues from the rejection of stereotypes, and from the tentative and hotly debated elaboration of new ways of understanding human affairs."[72]

Studying Ghazālī opens a window onto the Muslim discursive tradition in its multifaceted and dynamic form. It is at once pregnant with power and authority and open to creativity and hybridity. While still prone to being ideologized, a discursive tradition is also couched in a narrative form in which ideology is not the exclusive marker of identity. Examining the ideas of Ghazālī requires one (to borrow the words of Hans Frei) to be both an ethnographer and a native at once, or, as Chakrabarty would put it, to be both observer and witness at once.[73] As an ethnographer and observer, one derives meaning in a cultural-linguistic frame; as a native and witness, one searches for meaning in an intratextual hermeneutical frame. What allows an ethnographer and a native to meet in mutual respect, notes Frei, is the skill of deriving meaning in both their cultural-linguistic and intratextual interpretive frames. If the same person performs both roles, then that meaning-producing skill will provide the "bridge over which (s)he may pass from one shore to the other and undertake the return journey."[74] In that return journey, one can break away from the vexing politics of identity by embracing a third position, one that is propounded by Hannah Arendt.

Action and speech, observes Arendt, are the basic conditions of human plurality. Together, they enable humans to acquire the twofold capacity for equality and distinction.[75] "This revelatory quality of speech and action," she notes, "comes to the fore where people are *with* others and neither for nor against them—that is, in sheer human togetherness."[76] The human dilemma is also the human hope: to be bound together with others unconditionally. What binds people together is their "inter-est," that which lies not only between people but also among them. "For all its intangibility, this in-between is no less real than the world of things we visibly have in common," says Arendt. She continues: "Although everybody started his life by inserting himself into the human world through action and speech, nobody is the author or producer of his own life story. In other words, the stories, the results of action and speech, reveal an agent, but this agent is not an author or producer. Somebody began it and is its subject in the twofold sense of the word, namely its actor and sufferer, but nobody is its author."[77]

Our human togetherness beckons that spectral third position, says Arendt. When we are the subject in the twofold sense in which we have stories, agents, and heroes but can never unequivocally point out the sovereign author of any set of outcomes, it is then that we occupy the third position. Even my location as author is an in-between position, the position of a subject-agent. Similarly, Ghazālī too is a subject-agent, all of us being authored by others, events and persons, never sovereign authors in the ontological sense.

As an epochal thinker, Ghazālī evokes what Arendt describes as that "sheer human togetherness." Ghazālī crossed many boundaries and found himself in between many antinomies. While conflicting forces pushed and pulled him in opposite directions, he did not retreat from the tension that this agonism—something akin to what Gloria Anzaldúa calls mental *nepantilism*—produced in him.[78] For this "in between-ness," this engagement with more than one intellectual and cultural tradition, was precisely the source of his creativity and psychic restlessness. Reading and writing about Ghazālī is a poignant act of the imagination, a double reading of the text: every reading is at once wholly new and simultaneously unchanging, as if it were always there.

Imaginative reading and writing suggests that knowledge no longer belongs to the agent or writer but instead becomes, as Antonia S. Byatt says, "our knowledge."[79] When knowledge becomes ours, we experience our human togetherness through the act of the imagination that enables us to share a common world and language over eons and centuries. It is "the imagination," says novelist Toni Morrison, "that produces work, which bears and invites re-readings, which motions to future readings as well as contemporary ones, implies a shareable world and an endlessly flexible language." She continues: "Readers and writers both struggle to interpret and perform within a common language, shareable imaginative worlds. And although the reader in that struggle has justifiable claims, the author's presence—her or his intentions, blindness, and sight—is part of the imaginative activity."[80] What we share with our intellectual forbears, be they Augustine, Ibn Sīnā, Ghazālī, Aquinas, Rūmī, or Ibn Khaldūn, is a *common language* and the continuation of shared *imaginative universes*. And it is tradition that links us through language and practices to the different imaginative worlds that we inhabit.

Tradition and the Present

Tradition does not simply mean to receive what was handed down by a previous generation—a timid adherence and blind following roughly equivalent to the notion of adherence to authority that Muslim thinkers call *taqlīd*. Tradition is neither something that one passively inherits nor a detailed archeological map that unlocks knowledge of the past. Though we value the work of archeologists and historians, they do not embody the past and the present; they are not automatically, as members of a profession, persons of tradition. The critical element that makes an individual a person of tradition is the possession of a historical sense "not only of the pastness of the past," T. S. Eliot notes, "but of its presence."[81] The notion of tradition implies more than an awareness of the temporal and the timeless.

To be a person of tradition, one must conceive of the temporal and the timeless together; one must be acutely aware of one's place in time, of one's own contemporaneity. Instead of living in the present, a writer or thinker who engages tradition lives in the "present moment of the past" and shows an awareness, in Eliot's words, "not of what is dead, but of what is already living."[82] This is the fundamental difference between a person of tradition and a necromancer: the latter juggles the past like as if it were composed of mummies in a museum, while the former imagines the past as present and the present as past. Often, people believe tradition to be the equivalent of palingenesis, the notion that one can reproduce the hereditary features of organisms without modification. A more appropriate metaphor from biology might be that of kenogenesis, in which features derived from the immediate environment modify the hereditary development of a germ or organism. Tradition at its best functions in this manner.

Debates about tradition and modernity occupied Muslim thinkers for the better part of the twentieth century. These debates have been especially intense and soul-searing in societies where modernity was ushered in via colonization. But even modern Muslim states that were not completely subjected to European colonization, such as Iran, Turkey, and Arabia, have had to face the same questions. In the encounter with Europe, the discourses of Muslim societies came to center on categories like modernity, tradition, secularism, and nationalism. However, each category is highly differentiated, and no category can be invoked without specific attention to local context.

Of concern here is clerical traditionalism, often presented as orthodoxy—itself an elusive category covering a broad spectrum of groups and amalgamating several strands of thought. Whether we look to the *ʿulamāʾ* groups or to other groups linked to Islamic revivalism or Islamic maximalism/fundamentalism or both, we find that every group lays claim to tradition or asserts itself to represent tradition. The debate about tradition illustrates at least two characteristics of these groups. One is a desire for connectivity, or connexity, to the past that results in excessive reverence for the past along palingenetic lines: namely, anticipating the unmodified reproduction of tradition. The second is a view of tradition as being similar to biological ontogenesis, a process that maps the development of an organism from the embryonic stage to maturity. Some versions of orthodoxy and maximalism believe that by finding the origins and development of a tradition one can then claim to have access to authenticity and truth.

Some representatives of contemporary Muslim orthodoxy think of tradition as palingenesis. The result is that seminal figures and agents of tradition are given unique status in an almost mythical past. In this scheme, history is elevated to mythology, and the human beings who authored tradition are glorified without being subjected to historical scrutiny. This excessive reverence for the past in fact paralyzes dogmatic traditionalists, dwarfed as they are by the distressing self-knowledge that the achievements of the glorious past have forever exceeded those of any possible future.

A sobering voice who critiqued this reverential approach was the prodigious belles lettrist (*adīb*) and rationalist thinker ʿAmr b. Baḥr al-Jāḥiẓ (d. 255/868). Jāḥiẓ was fully aware of the double debt of the Muslim community to both the hereditary tradition and the discursive tradition. Yet, noted Jāḥiz, one's attitude toward the earliest predecessors of the tradition is like one's stance toward posterity. "For surely we inherited more edificatory admonition [*ʿibra*]," observes Jāḥiẓ, "than our predecessors ever found; just as posterity will acquire an even larger amount of edificatory admonitions than we did."[83]

Even such a concept as edificatory perspective (*iʿtibār*) is dynamic. "The notion of 'edificatory perspective' is derived from the word 'crossing' [*ʿubūr*] and the proximity of one thing to another," explains the Qur'ān exegete Fakhr al-Dīn al-Rāzī (d. 606/1209). "The word 'tear' [*ʿabra*] denotes a 'crossing/traversing,' because the tear moves from the eye to the cheek," Rāzī writes. This is also why the same root word is used in *taʿbīr*, as "the science of interpreting dreams, since the interpreter has to cross from the imaginary to the rational."[84] For this reason, a constellation of words is called *ʿibārāt*, (expressions) precisely because they, in a manner of speaking, carry meanings from the tongue of the speaker to the mind of the listener.

Keeping alive the semiotics of the notion of edificatory admonition, Jāḥiẓ propounded a moral-realist approach to history. Even if moral edification is the chief value of history, the latter requires both an interpretive and a dynamic understanding: the desire for moral edification forces us to make connections and to traverse from one site of meaning to another across time and space. The more edificatory the narrative that we accumulate, the better prepared we are to deal with the multiple lessons of history and to make the necessary crossovers and connections. Even though Jāḥiẓ viewed history to be derivative, he did not privilege historical antecedence for its own sake; he did just the opposite. It was later generations who he believed would be in a position to make more informed judgments, because they would have the advantage of hindsight.

Yet tradition is often confused and conflated with essentialist notions of "authenticity" stemming from the politics of representation and identity. Even at the risk of being contradictory, it would on the balance be fair to say that almost every representation of Islam lays claim to being the most authentic version. Who are the true representatives of tradition and the genuine standard-bearers of Islam? No one can evaluate the competing claims without interrogating the complex significations of how one defines the term "Islam." For to invoke Islam as a tradition, Eliot would remind us, it is not sufficient to signify a "pastness of the past." Such an invocation must also signify the "presence of the past." Tradition, therefore, is not a static and homogenized past laced with a romantic nostalgia. It is at its fullest when it reflects an ontological sensibility in which the temporal and timeless are seen to coexist in a complex, often mysterious, contemporaneity.

Tradition does not despise the present. As MacIntyre insightfully points out, when traditions are vital they "embody continuities of conflict." However, tradition becomes Burkean when it is viewed as being in opposition to reason. Then, adds MacIntyre, tradition "is always dying or dead."[85] Yet, too often, those who champion Islamic authenticity reify tradition to the state of either laws or metaphysics. It is coded in such formulaic phrases and repetitive practices that it is denuded of that critical element of contestation and conflict.

Mummification of Tradition

At its best, tradition produces sustainable knowledge. Alas, there are too many examples of its having the reverse effect. The standard contemporary reflex valorizes tradition as performance, reproduction, and reiteration in narrow and static frames, for these serve as the crucial ingredients in any claim to authenticity. Today, the most dismaying picture of intellectual perfidy emerges not only from the stereotypical images of Islam in the Western electronic media but also from desultory images produced in what are the bastions of Muslim traditional learning. Some of these are the renowned al-Azhar in Egypt, Dar al-ʿUlūm Deoband in India, the many *madrasas* in Pakistan and Afghanistan, the many *ḥawzīyas* in Iran and Iraq, and similar institutions around the globe. Even the slightly better-equipped modern universities in the Muslim world seem hardly to alleviate the poverty of scholarship about Islam. At best, tradition is mummified as a testimony to authenticity at the cost of creativity, while at worst traditionalism unleashes its inescapable power through the frightening violence of authoritarian discourses.

The need to rival pseudo-traditionalism, or dogmatic orthodoxy, in representing Islam and Muslims is the tenacious legacy of orientalists. Orientalism had its heyday in the nineteenth and twentieth centuries.[86] By and large, with notable exceptions, orientalist scholarship sought to further the material interests of the occident. As a rule, orientalists gave short shrift to the terms of reference and values of oriental people and of Muslims in particular while consciously devouring the orient in an imaginative geography of domination and political coercion. When it came to the question of interests, they privileged those of the occident, whether in the form of European colonial interests or of Christian missionary designs, above those of the subjects whom they studied. Condescension and thinly disguised supremacist postures marked orientalist scholarship.[87] More often than not, these experts and their legions of admirers mummified the Muslim tradition as a testimony against its adherents.[88] While not every orientalist was culpable, the orientalist study of Islamic civilization resulted in a singular outcome and judgment: Islamic civilization in its current guise produces knowledge that is unsustainable by posing an implicit demand that Muslims capitulate to Western modernity and to neo-imperial political power.

Common to both approaches—the authenticity-seeking approach of Muslim clerical orthodoxy and the expert approach of orientalists—is the effective mummification of the tradition. Dogmatic forms of Muslim orthodoxy that are obsessed with the desire for authenticity imagine tradition to be static and unshakably perfected. The effect of this conception, as reluctant as some are to admit it, is to make it questionable whether the knowledge produced within clerical traditionalist circles is sustainable knowledge and whether it harmonizes with the subjectivities of the greater number of Muslim peoples inhabiting the world today.

In their zeal to simulate authenticity, certain proponents of contemporary clerical orthodoxy turn to revanchist forms of power in the veil of orthodoxy, often accompanied by terrifying displays of power and authority. The orientalist scholars, in turn, not only appropriate Muslim tradition to psychologically disempower the subjects of that tradition but also, with sinister effect, attempt to displace tradition with alternative models of knowledge that consciously change the relations of power in a manner that benefits the modernity of the hegemonic West. Both approaches have in common a penchant for representing tradition in reductionist ways so that practices appear malformed, anachronistic, and unsustainable—but also unrecognizable to those who practice and live the tradition.

If there is anything that Ghazālī's work teaches those grappling with contemporary Muslim thought, it is how to find a better way to engage with the tradition. Ghazālī did not surrender to tradition: he imitated and invented simultaneously. Contrary to what many contemporary Muslims claim—modern educated ones as well as those who assert a traditionalist pedigree—Ghazālī shows that being faithful to tradition includes the ability to question and reinterpret it. Unfortunately contemporary Muslim thought displays two distressing tendencies: surrender to the authority of tradition or the complete jettisoning of tradition.

The French scholar of Islam Jacques Berque very pithily summarizes contemporary Islam's struggle to negotiate true progress without falling prey to an imperialist positivism. "Today, all too many militants and intellectuals," he observes, "are proponents either of an authenticity with no future or of a modernism with no roots."[89] By "proponents of authenticity," he implies the *'ulamā'* and neotraditionalist revivalist movements, and by "proponents of modernism" he clearly has in mind some secular educated Muslims who resist tradition.

In order to be faithful to tradition, one needs to do several things: to imitate, to question, and to interpret simultaneously. There is no golden formula as to what percentage of critique, questioning, and imitation places one inside tradition rather than outside of it. Every historical context determines its own requisites. To speak with tradition is to ensure that the dialogical tension is sustained and that our lived reality and subjectivity continue to inform our reading of Ghazālī. Every reading is a risk. However, that risk is reduced when our readings stake out their terrain within a range of theoretical insights derived from complex modes of reflection. Using the questions and techniques of reading I have discussed in this chapter, I hope to probe some of Ghazālī's texts in the ensuing chapters.

There are more things in heaven and earth, Horatio,
Than are dreamt of in your philosophy.
—William Shakespeare, *Hamlet*, act 1, scene 5

Properties of place, and especially of time, are the bugbears which terrify mankind from the contemplation of the magnificent.
—Edgar Allan Poe, *The Assignation*

2 Narrativity of the Self

Narrative and Poetics

Welding together rational ideas and poetic imagination was possibly one of Ghazālī's more lasting contributions to Muslim thought. In this, he distinguished himself from his peers. For not only did he acknowledge that figurative or metaphorical discourse is compatible with reason and rationality, but, more importantly, he placed metaphor at the heart of religious discourse. Sure, some of his predecessors had made similar moves. However, Ghazālī applied theory to practice, producing an intellectual legacy in which the confluence of the figurative and the rational is effortlessly narrated in a seamless web.

There is a compelling reason why figurative discourse featured so prominently in Ghazālī's thinking. His own personal search for the truth required a supplement to rational discourse—a nonrational supplement—that he found in figurative language. Ghazālī adopted narrative strategies and figurative speech in order to shield his discourse from the crudities of the intricate but transparent story of his self. He provided glimpses of certain aspects of his self in the course of his reflections on topics such as memory, writing, and the idea of exile. But understanding how his self is present in his work requires a certain way of reading, digging, and interrogating the very subtle allusions in his at times dense and intricate narratives. It is broadly true, as it has often been stated, that Ghazālī infused the ethical with the aesthetic, but the statement is oversimplified. His views did indeed have a profound, even revolutionary effect on later thought and practice. Yet it requires some close scrutiny to discover how, as well as why, he advances our understanding of figurative and poetic language in relation to both rational discourse and the self.[1]

Listening as an Event

One way of "hearing" Ghazālī is to yield to what the French philosopher Jacques Derrida calls "otobiography." "Otobiography" is derived from "otography"—a description of the ear that becomes "oto(bio)graphy" to mean narrative that gives a sense of the description of life as heard through the ear. What otobiography amounts to is a critical emphasis on listening to narratives in a way that is akin to the manner in which a reader is allied to a text in the act of reading.

The arts of listening, of "throwing one's ear" (*alqā al-samʿ*), as the Qur'ān graphically describes it, have long been central to Islamicate cultures, just as they were central to the world that Ghazālī inhabited.[2] The phrase suggests that listening is continuous and that it continues into the present. Listening, in this sense, prefigures what we today call "cowriting." It foregrounds the ear of the Other, the receiving ear. Like scores of readers, we listen, "sign," and posthumously endorse Ghazālī's texts, or those of any other writer or speaker, for that matter. This art of listening, with its multiple protocols, has deep roots in premodern cultures. One of its great merits is that it simultaneously revitalizes and expands the possibilities of understanding.

Hearing revolutionizes the possibilities of understanding when the listener not only listens but also becomes a "witness" (*shahīd*) to an "event."[3] An "event," according to the Palestinian-American thinker Edward Said, creates a mutation in history; for example, the entry of the Qur'ān into history is an event.[4] By carefully listening, the listener becomes a witness to an event. The French philosopher Alain Badiou points out that every truth has its origin in an event—an event is always part of realizing the truth and its becoming a truth—and it is a truth irrespective of whether it is a truth in nature or a truth in culture.[5] Ghazālī clearly understood certain instances and chance events in his life to have been life-transforming "events" that occurred due to divine grace.

Otobiography is crucial in reading as well as in hearing Ghazālī. It allows us to patrol and discern the membranous borderline that separates the life and body of the subject from his or her work, or corpus. In Ghazālian parlance, this intermediate state between body and corpus is the *dihlīz*, the crucial threshold, or in-between space, that one must perpetually cross and negotiate. The *dihlīz* is neither active nor passive, neither interior nor exterior.[6] Given this state of things, one can neither be content with highly esoteric readings of Ghazālī's writings nor resort to exclusively externalist and empirical readings of his life and works. Between these extremes is the *dynamis* of the *dihlīz* that needs to be questioned—the space between the "work" and the "life," or between the "corpus" and the "body," to use Derrida's terms.[7] Awareness of it forces us to reevaluate a biography in relation to a written corpus. Critical to this endeavor is the need to explore the *dihlīz*, from where new texts are engendered and interpretations are solicited, productions that are from neither the inside nor the outside but are located within the *dihlīz* itself. In relation to the self, stories and events are enunciated in the *dihlīz*.

Dihlīz-*ian Narratives*

Texts and interpretations are, in the final instance, stories about events. Muslim litterateurs had a deep appreciation of narrative (*ḥikāya*) as a literary form. Narrative is not the verbal and literal repetition of stories; the purpose of the latter is in their substance and meanings.[8] What is unique about narrative is its ability to tell the past event as if it were occurring in the present—namely, at the time of speaking. One literary scholar from Granada in Muslim Spain, Abū Jaʿfar al-Andalusī (d. 779/1378), described narrative as that moment when "you think of yourself as if you existed in that past time, or you imagine the elapsed time, as if it existed in the present."[9] The element of mutable temporality, the narrator's capacity to compress time so that he or she can speak in both the past and the present at the same time, is what so sumptuously accents the dramatic and representational capacity of narrative. In addition, noted the Indian encyclopedist Muḥammad Aʿlā al-Tahānawī (d. ca. 1191/1777), narrative has the capacity to turn events into spectacle (*mushāhada*) unconstrained by limitations.[10]

The philosopher Paul Ricoeur supplements my discussion of narrative. For Ricoeur, "emplotment," which is *muthos* in Greek, is a central ingredient of narrative.[11] *Muthos* signifies fable, a sense of an imaginary story, as well as plot, a well-constructed story. As a well-constructed story or a plot, *muthos*, French orientalist Louis Massignon concludes, resembles the concept of *ḥikāya* developed by early Arabic litterateurs.[12] Since *ḥikāya* is not a static form but is dynamic, it is able to integrate disparate and discrete elements into coherent stories. Even though it has the self-evident features of an oral form of communication, *ḥikāya* is used in both an oral and a written sense. For, often, we do not know whether a story originates from a written or an oral medium.

Ghazālī lavishly presents his most influential writings, *Resuscitation* and *Rescuer*, among others, as captivating *ḥikāyāt*. There is surely something more than gestural in his conscious decision to do so; it marks the intimate relationship of emplotment, temporality, and spectacle. Ricoeur astutely observes that the operation of emplotment is essentially to synthesize heterogeneous elements. On the one hand, it synthesizes multiple events or incidents into a complete story. On the other hand, it organizes heterogeneous fragments, such as unintended circumstances, discoveries, and chance or planned encounters—including any number of embodied interactions that range from conflict to collaboration—into some semblance of narrative coherence. Only when we gather all these elements into a plot does a totality emerge that we describe as simultaneously discordant and concordant.

The Persian scholar of Arabic rhetoric ʿAbd al-Qāhir al-Jurjānī also indirectly prefigured certain aspects of narrative in his work. He did so in some ways that are different from and in others that share similarities with modern debates on the topic. Jurjānī is credited with putting new life in rhetoric and with proposing the idea of *naẓm*, a notion of construction in rhetoric and hermeneutics. The gist of his claim is that meaning is not derived from singular words and the accumulation of clusters of meanings but rather from something more architectonic in design: we derive meaning, he suggests, from the complex *patterns* of discourse. Literary composition and discourse, Jurjānī observed, relies a great deal more than we have hitherto acknowledged on the particular patterns of construction and arrangement of words and meanings to express complex and subtle sensibilities. It would be erroneous, in his view, to suffice with merely examining the organization of words and meanings.[13]

Jurjānī's views of language and narrative seem to have faint but palpable echoes in Ghazālī's ideas. At least two points that he made are relevant to my discussion of narrative. One is that literary production is utterly dependent on the intricate figurative structures and abstract patterns that are produced in discourse thanks to the grammar of languages.[14] Thus, if one takes Jurjānī seriously, narrative is important not only as a discursive genre but also because it has the capacity to structure and shape meaning. We, of course, ignore the transformative potential of narrative at our own peril. Jurjānī alerts us to the fact that ultimately it is the combined effect of rhetorical structure and grammar that lends narrative the potency to affect our understanding and comprehension of phenomena. In this sense, and given the profound and intense debates on language and ideas that have arisen in the past half century, his insight is as refreshing today as it was innovative during his time.

The second idea of Jurjānī that is helpful is the notion of *takhyīl*, or imaginative thinking. Intended meanings conveyed by human speech, he notes, are either rational or imaginative. The difference between the two is that rational meaning can be verified as true or false, whereas imaginative thinking does not comply with this type of verification.[15] Imaginative thinking accents the subjective element. Imaginative discourse, as the literary scholar Kamal Abu Deeb points out, operates on the substance of poetic expression and not merely on the imagery of meaning. Imaginative thinking plays on the polysemy of words and allows the context to accent one pattern of meaning above another.[16]

Taken together, both the construction of narrative and imaginative thinking frame Ghazālī's discourses. They decisively shape the way he established accounts in order to produce new meanings and sensibilities. Often, his poetics tried to accomplish the impossible or attempted to stretch the limits of a paradox: he combined subjective imagination with Aristotelian representation, or poetics. Anyone familiar with Ghazālī's repertoire knows that it is a virtual gallery teeming with imagery, fragments of stories, wise dictums, exegeses of Qur'ānic passages, and reports from the Prophet. All these materials are marshaled to generate a politics of emotions in order to induce the reader or listener to action with the goal of self-transformation. Not least important is Ghazālī's recurrent and lavish use of affective images. These stir potent mixtures of ideas that result in benignly ingenuous alchemies of the imagination and discursive affect. Representational imagery, or mimesis (*muḥākāt*, which shares the same root with *ḥikāya*, or narrative) was surely Ghazālī's strongest suit.[17] He utilized it to good effect in order to externalize phenomena, to place them in view for all to gaze on and inspect.[18]

Ricoeur's insights can be constructively employed to shed some light on our understanding of Ghazālī by inflecting the role of the reader. The process of composition and the configuration of a narrative, according to Ricoeur, is "not completed in the text but in the reader and, under this condition, makes possible the reconfiguration of life by narrative." "The significance of a narrative," he continues, "stems from the intersection of the world of the text and the world of the reader."[19] So, along with Ricoeur, we need to recognize the singular fact that human beings have a built-in passion for stories, especially the stories that make up our lives. Narrative bridges the gap between stories and history, between fiction and life or art and life. Narrative understanding not only anchors our living experience but also locates us within multiple symbolic systems.

The first stage of symbolism is therefore the prenarrative quality of human experiences. Yet symbolism itself is not uniform, but differentiated. If the Ghazālian *dihlīz*, the Chicana *nepantla*, or the Derridean "borderline" are the spaces in which texts and narratives are engendered, then the interactive and reflexive Ricoeurian narrative resolves the tension between stories and life, between fiction and history, through either concordance or discordance.

Of the multiple symbols that we integrate into our lives, we most commonly identify three significant types: cosmic, oneiric, and poetic. The cosmic symbol is both a thing and a sign at the same time; in other words, it is implicitly a linguistic symbol. The oneiric symbol, unlike the cosmic one, moves to the psychic function of imagination—to dreams, fragments, and memories of our pasts. The poetic symbol, however, epitomizes both the symbolic imagination and its linguistic expression. Poetry is the welling up of meaning, and its substrate is poiesis.

Just as poiesis does not designate the finished poem but is the creative and imaginative production of the thinker or poet, poetics similarly designates those acts of imaginative production in the making. In this sense, poetics is both creation and preservation. Given that poetics constantly demands making and remaking, the element of reconfiguration within narrative, says Ricoeur, is critically important. In short, poiesis and poetics drive home the point that narrative is part of a larger notion of art.

The critical element of narrative to which Ricoeur points is that it is both revelatory and transformative.[20] That is because narrative in its universal character is that which is either true or false. Ghazālī long ago realized the transformative power of narrative as an art. Viewed from this perspective, his *Rescuer from Misguidance* is more than a partial account of his life: it is also a work of art in the sense that it is a corrective that aims at inducing some kind of transformation within its readers. In the *Rescuer*, Ghazālī comments on the work's narrative aspect. To an anonymous interlocutor at the beginning of the tract, he replies: "You have asked me . . . so let me narrate to you [*aḥkī laka*]."[21]

Ghazālī was aware of the creative power required to tell the story of his personal suffering, his myriad experiences, and his larger life story, which is mingled with sacred history—the story of his life as an emplotment or narrative (*ḥikāya*). He used the term *ḥikāya* intentionally, for he wanted to avoid the slippery and controversial term "story" (*qiṣṣa*, pl. *qiṣaṣ*). Even though the word *qiṣṣa* is used in the Qur'ān, in later Muslim history storytelling gained notoriety for fusing fact with fiction and came to be viewed as a device for embellishment. Many pietists were concerned that a preoccupation with literary effect and performance would undermine the goal of narrative, which is to promote the truth.

Theologians, including Ghazālī, were skeptical toward and often took a dim view of the confabulations promoted by specialist raconteurs and storytellers (*qāṣṣ*, pl. *quṣṣāṣ*).[22] While Ghazālī did extol some early figures like the pious Ḥasan al-Baṣrī (d. 110/728), who employed storytelling for pietistic purposes, he did not hide his dislike of the genre. Instead, he advanced the notion of *ḥikāya*, narrative telling of accounts, almost in opposition to the genre of storytelling (*qiṣṣa*) and without stating the difference between the two genres. One suspects that Ghazālī recognized that storytelling had been discredited as a genre in serious intellectual circles and pious company and that it might have proven to be a liability if he had invoked it. *Ḥikāya*, on the other hand, could approach the genre of storytelling without provoking negative reactions.

At the same time, Ghazālī deployed the paradigm of narrative as a way to provide theological conciliation to controversial ecstatic expressions (*shaṭḥ*, pl. *shaṭaḥāt*) uttered by some of the early mystics like Abū Yazīd al-Bisṭāmī (d. ca. 261/874 or 264/877–78), to whose cause he was partisan. These ecstatic expressions, Ghazālī says, should not be viewed as isolated and arbitrary utterances. Interestingly, ecstatic expressions, he notes, are part of a larger and complex narrative emanating from the depths of the advanced consciousness of the mystic. The only way one can make sense of these utterances is to relate them to the mystic's larger self-narrative. Subtly importing Jurjānī's notion of construction, he argues that it is the narrative structure that enables us to comprehend the ultimate purpose of the mystic: to speak across a variety of languages and experiences that are at once discrete and interconnected.

With this in mind, Ghazālī comments on Bisṭāmī: "It is not proper to accept what he narrates [*yaḥkī*], even if one heard it directly from him. Perhaps he was narrating it from God, the Powerful and Sublime, in a speech that he repeats to himself. For instance, when one hears him [Bisṭāmī] say, 'Indeed, I am God, there is no deity but me, so adore me,' surely it is not appropriate to understand his speech, except as a narration/as narrativity [*illā ʿalā sabīl al-ḥikāya*]!"[23] Effortlessly, he acknowledges that this kind of speech cannot be understood unless one frames it in the context of its own heterogeneity, keeping in mind the limitations of human language, the semantic overflow in mystical utterances, and the ontological state of mystics, which has changed from duality to unity. None of this makes sense without staging a prior configuration of the larger plot that mediates the mystical encounter. Without assuming that plot, Bisṭāmī's speech might amount to nonsense. From a strict juristic and theological perspective, in fact, his words are tantamount to utterances of a heretical nature. Yet once the larger plot of the utterances and their subliminal context is framed within an explanatory paradigm, the seemingly offensive elements of the utterances are diluted by their narrative pliability.

This set the stage for Ghazālī to cast his own narrative in terms of a larger frame that embraced his personal experiences, which decisively impacted his writings. There is, of course, the platitudinous sense that from the moment Ghazālī recognized the mutability of his self after his turn to mysticism he also became acutely aware of his mortality; he became more dramatically aware of his race with time. This existential change in him was precipitated by a devastating intellectual crisis that brought him face-to-face with the limits of the cognitive sciences. From that moment onward, he configured the narrative of his life almost single-mindedly in terms of temporality—in terms of his past, his present, and, with a consuming passion, his eschatological future.

In his narrative reconfiguration of the self, he did two things. First, he envisaged the self within a temporal flow of events that surrounded him as an individual in everyday existence. Second, he burdened his self with the task of giving meaning to those events. For Ghazālī, giving life (*iḥyāʾ*) to his self was a kind of auto-therapy whereby he could experience the temporal flow of events while ascribing to them nonmaterial and cosmic meanings.

Poetics of Legitimation

To understand Ghazālī's crisis, we need to hear his own account with different ears. Since a writer's biography lies in the twists of his language, we need to look at throwaway lines in his autobiography and at biographical fragments. From close readings of his writings, we get a larger picture of his identity as a subject. Imaginative readings of Ghazālī's spiritual testimony looked at alongside the various biographical and hagiographical accounts can cast an introspective light on his narrative.

The historian of religion understands better than others that mythology and myth-making play a crucial part in shaping personal life-tellings.[24] Ernst Kris, for instance, tells us that the use of "biographical formulae" transforms the mythical aspects of a subject's life into the factual.[25] Constant repetition of the same incident or event sets into motion a process whereby the image of the subject is affected. Ghazālī's biography—both his own assertions and those made by others after him—has made his image vulnerable to formulaic representations. One only has to look at the several myths in circulation that affirm his multiple roles as a theologian (*mutakallim*), philosopher (*faylasūf*), and mystic (*mutaṣawwif*) to become aware of such reproductions.

A number of myths are circulated to legitimize Ghazālī's theological works and his ṣūfī-inspired writings. Several of these are oneiric in character: it is in edifying dreams that certain pious figures have made their appearance to people in order to attest to Ghazālī's piety and spiritual achievements. Not only did Ghazālī have dreams of significance, then, but well-wishers, colleagues, and pietists have disclosed their visions of his elevated spiritual destiny. Legitimizing dreams, Leah Kinberg reminds us, are subtle ways of coding information and reinforcing the authority of a person portrayed in myths.[26] These dreams tell of Ghazālī's success in becoming an axial figure in Islamic history.

Often, dreams direct people about how to behave, think, or react to specific life experiences.[27] Oneiric communications, like all others, however, require an interpretation of their symbolic language. It is not unusual to find relational inferences drawn between dreams, poetry, and narratives of scriptural revelation. In the view of early Muslim philosophers and mystics, dreams convey information and knowledge of a higher reality. Though the intuition and information derived from dreams does not carry any authoritative value in a general sense, individuals who experience dreams find their meanings compelling. Legends abound of how certain figures were tortured by indecision over contentious matters until dreams solved their psychological dilemmas.

The founder of the influential Ashʿarī theological school, the theologian Abū al-Ḥasan al-Ashʿarī (d. 324/935–36), left the Muʿtazilī fold to develop his own following on the basis of a dream. The Prophet Muḥammad appeared to Ashʿarī in a dream, asking him why he did not come to the defense of his *Sunna*, a term that designates the edificatory statements, actions, and endorsements of the Prophet. Immediately after having this dream, Ashʿarī adopted a more literalist approach to the tradition. Then, through a succession of dreams in which he communicated with the Prophet, Ashʿarī configured his real assignment: to explain the prophetic tradition with the help of rational discourse.

Some of Ghazālī's most influential writings on ethics and theology were popularized via dreams. One Abū al-Qāsim Saʿd b. ʿAlī al-Isfarāʾīnī had a vision in which he saw that the Prophet Muḥammad approved of Ghazālī's theological text *Theses of Dogmatics* (*Qawāʿid al-ʿaqāʾid*). Very detailed sequences of similar dream representations are fully documented by annalists such as Tāj al-Dīn al-Subkī (d. 769/1368) and Abū al-Qāsim Ibn ʿAsākir (d. 571/1176).[28] In another example, an outspoken critic of Ghazālī's famous book *Resuscitation of the Sciences of Religion*, Ibn Ḥirzam al-Maghribī, dreamed that he was being whipped at the command of an offended Prophet Muḥammad for his criticisms of the book. When Ibn Ḥirzam awoke, he, to his horror, found whip marks all over his body.[29]

Poetics of Dreams

Ghazālī frequently invoked the oneiric imagination and the importance of dreams. Communications delivered via dreams were to him a valid form of knowledge, and he made several important decisions based on insights derived from oneiromancy. When he decided to end his ascetic isolation and return to teaching in 499/1106, for example, this critical decision was based on his own dreams and spiritual visions together with the visions of persons whom he had consulted.[30]

True dreams (*ruʾyā ṣādiqa*), divine communications via inspiration, and visions in a wakeful state are all different grades of revelatory inspiration. Drawing on established Muslim tradition, Ghazālī recognized dreams as but one of the forty-six aspects of prophetic inspiration, and thus as distinct from illusions and hallucinations.[31] In Ghazālī's view, there are dire consequences to faith in denying the reality of dreams as a source of knowledge out of sheer ignorance or arrogance. "Beware, if the sum total of your share of this knowledge [of dreams] leads you to deny what goes beyond your limitation," he warns, and he continues:

> For in this matter many pretentious scholars perished in their assumption that everything is comprehensible by means of rational knowledge only. For ignorance is preferable to reason if it leads to rejecting matters [that affect the integrity] of the friends of God, the Sublime. The one who denies the [validity of the science of oneiromancy] with respect to the friends of

God, also implicitly rejects the validity of prophets, and as a consequence has completely exited the pale of religion.[32]

In this passage, Ghazālī is so convinced about the self-evident nature of the symbolic realm that he issues a furious admonition that anyone who makes light of the meaning of dreams might also be unknowingly breaking with religion! Oneiric imagination, for Ghazālī, was part of a continuum of prophetic inspiration that evokes the symbolic universe, which is essential to religion. Symbols are essentially image-words that go beyond the representation of images; they privilege what an image represents and the meaning it conveys over the image itself.[33] Prophecy, with some qualification, shares the same symbolic system in which the oneiric imagination is located. An assault on one aspect of that integrated symbolic system, such as denying the validity of dreams, is deemed to be an attack on the entire system.

Dreams require presentation and re-presentation; their secrets lie buried in their interpretations. Just like the historian draws edificatory admonition (*ʿibra*) from historical data, so does the interpreter of dreams deduce edificatory meaning (*taʿbīr*, which has the same root as *ʿ-b-r*, "to cross over") from the images, symbols, and feelings experienced in dreams. One of the most thematically coherent and full stories in the Qur'ān, the chapter called "Yūsuf" (Joseph), is brimful with oneiric semiotics. The Qur'ān states that the interpretation of dreams (*ta'wīl al-aḥādīth*) is the hallmark of the prophet Joseph. Dreams are first translated from images into verbal reports (*aḥādīth*), which are then subject to interpretation. Vignettes of Joseph's saga with his envious brothers, his narrow escape from the seductive wiles of Potiphar's wife, and his conversations with fellow prisoners are included in a chapter of the Qur'ān and described as the "best of stories" (*aḥsan al-qaṣaṣ*), or, if you like, the best "re-presentations." Interestingly, in the view of most classical Qur'ān commentators, it is not so much the content of the narration as the superlative performance and style of presentation (*aḥsan al-bayān*) that is paramount in Joseph's story.[34]

The exegetes take seriously the meaning of the word "story" (*qiṣṣa*): "to follow something step by step" (*tatabbuʿ*) and "to expound something gradually and sequentially" by drawing the listener into the performance itself. In other words, listening means participating in the narrative. Another chapter in the Qur'ān is named "*Qaṣaṣ*," or "The Storytelling." This twenty-eighth chapter of the Qur'ān is filled with Israelite salvation history (*Heilsgeschichte*) detailing the encounters, suffering, and trials of Moses, the Israelites, and the pharaohs of Egypt. To grasp this story, one must adhere to the protocols of listening (and, after the Qur'ān later became primarily a written text, reading), which requires careful and attentive tracking of the subtle twists and turns in the story. To listen to a scripture like the Qur'ān and to "re-cite" it is not only an act of ordinariness, which it is, but also a search for the profound human drama that such ordinary acts embody.

Poetics of Interpretation

The interpretation of narratives and texts shares a common substrate with the interpretation of dreams: they share the use of the unconscious and the imaginal faculties. In a poignant insight, Ghazālī states: "Know indeed, that interpretation [*ta'wīl*] is analogous to the science of interpreting dreams [oneiromancy; *ta'bīr*]."[35] With this pithy but meaningful comment, Ghazālī strove to restore the classical equipoise between interpretation and the unconscious. Commenting tongue-in-cheek, he argued that if deprived of imagination to see the connection between interpretation and the unconscious, an unsuspecting exegete (*mufassir*) might get bogged down in fussing over trivia. Literalist exegetes lacking in imagination could end up with nothing but an interpretive shell (*qishr*). If they failed to grasp the complex nuances of meaning, he feared, they would be bound to miss the complex imagination that is animated by words.

Interpreting dreams is like interpreting texts, Ghazālī explained. Both require plumbing the deeper recesses of one's being. Just as the art of interpretation needs the sciences of lexicography, logic, and history, it also requires modalities to sustain the network of links with an interpreter's being and subjectivity. In short, interpretation relates to the interiority of the interpreter.

Drawing on the writing of the early pietist Ibn Sīrīn (d. 110/728), Ghazālī agreed with Ibn Sīrīn that interpretation (*ta'wīl*) involves translation from one mode of thought to another. He took several illustrations from Ibn Sīrīn's writings on dreams. For example, a person dreams that he sees himself sealing the mouths of men and the pudenda of women and seeks an explanation and interpretation for the dream. Ibn Sīrīn provides a very unexpected interpretation. The dream, he explains, means that the man in question is prematurely giving the call to the morning prayer in the month of Ramaḍān.[36] In this holy month, the morning call to prayer customarily signals the beginning of the daylight hours of fasting. Eating, drinking, and sexual intercourse cease from that moment onward for the duration of the daylight hours. So when this man prematurely makes the call, he effectively prevents people from eating and having sex at a time when they lawfully can still do so.[37] That, Ibn Sīrīn explains, is what the symbolism of sealing the mouths and the pudenda means.

Another person sees himself pouring olive oil into an olive pit in his dream. Ibn Sīrīn discloses the disturbing news to the man that he is unwittingly committing incest. How? One of his concubines is actually his biological mother! This episode requires some explanation. As a rule, Islamic law prohibits the sale of a slave who has borne her master's child. The rule prevents the occurrence of incest, which the frequent resale of female slaves can make statistically more frequent—women are purchased as concubines by people who are biologically related to them. In Ibn Sīrīn's example, it appears that the sale prohibition was violated or perhaps that the concubine was captured in a war and sold to her blood descendant. The symbolism of the dream denotes futility: the redundant act of injecting olive oil into an olive pit signals the abhorrence and futility of incest.

Ghazālī's comments on Ibn Sīrīn's interpretations are of interest to us. He hastened to point out the hazards of merely performing a workmanlike exegesis of dreams and texts. To provide literal explanations of the key words in the two dreams, like seal (*khātam*), pudenda (*furūj*), mouths (*afwāh*), and olive (*zaytūn*), would be not only highly inadequate but simply erroneous. The person who tries to decipher dreams by literally translating (*yutarjimu*) key words, as exegetes are inclined to do, is, he sardonically observes, someone who barks up the wrong alleys. Plain exegesis is very different from an interpretation that grasps (*yudriku*) the symbolic interrelations between words and their different uses. It takes a different set of skills and advanced insights to configure the links between the symbols denoted in dreams and their real-life interpretations. Only a combination of skills and knowledge allows one to decode how the sealing of mouths and pudenda signifies that someone is prematurely making the call to prayer in the month of Ramaḍān or how pouring oil into an olive pit denotes incest.[38]

Decoding or translating a dream sequence into narrative meaning requires the ability to grasp the complex semiotics at play. Ghazālī suggests that there is an irreducible connexity—a quality of connectedness—between what we "hear" in the heart by means of the regular instruments of perception available to us, on the one hand, and the complex as well as hidden recesses of the self, on the other. Being and imagination—subjectivity—are intimately linked to the words and symbols we use through the act of interpretation. Whereas many modern commentator-exegetes would wince at this cheek-byjowl consorting of denotative meaning, logic, symbolic representation, and sentiments, Ghazālī and other premodern thinkers nevertheless deemed such heterogeneity to be salutary.

This unity of meaning found in the radical heterogeneity of symbol systems is actualized via Ghazālī's commitment to a form of radical onto-theology, which will be discussed in a later chapter. Ghazālī believed that one's being is anchored in divine grace and not in an ether of bottomless rationality. This mode of thinking enabled Ghazālī to exit the linear logic of rationality and reach for other modes of knowledge. Sure, he displayed an antirational streak, but, as I will show later, he did not abandon rational discourse altogether, as some have alleged. He only framed rationality within a larger, perhaps essentializing, ontology of grace. With this ontology in hand when interpreting the unconscious in the form of dreams, Ghazālī was able to defy what Sigmund Freud later described as the "either-or" logic of rational discourse.[39] Thinkers like Ghazālī—much to the annoyance of some of his detractors—give primacy to the logic of the imaginary that is constructed as "both/and" while disavowing the limiting embrace of the "either/or" (il)logic exemplified in the English idiom, "You can't have your cake and eat it too."

Poetics of the Unconscious

Since the interpretation of symbols and images rooted in the unconscious is expressed in words, the unconscious is central to language and thus to narrative. In poetry, called *shiʿr* in Arabic, there is an emotive awareness and knowledge that profound ideas, thoughts, and words interweave in rhymed presentation. Poetry not only teaches us how words produce meaning but how words relate to the structure of the imagination in the unconscious. Richard Kearney captures this relation perfectly. "This language of the unconscious, expressed at the level of the imaginary and the symbolic, is the portal to poetry," he says.[40] As if he intuits Ghazālī's notion of the *dihlīz* as a portal, in describing the language of the unconscious, Kearney adds: "Poetry is to be understood here in the extended sense of a play of *poiesis*: a creative letting go of the drive of possession, of the calculus of means and ends. It allows the rose—in the words of the mystic Silesius—to exist *without why*." "Poetics," he continues, "is the carnival of possibilities where everything is permitted, nothing censored. It is the willingness to imagine oneself in the other person's skin, to see things as if one were, momentarily at least, another, to experience how the other half lives."[41]

A cursory overview of the links between the unconscious and poetry in the

Arabo-Islamic tradition shows that the word *mashʿar*, from the root *sh-ʿ-r*, signifies a "sacred space." And, from the same root, we derive *shiʿār*, meaning "symbol." We also derive from it *shuʿūr*, meaning "inner conscious feeling." So, if dreams are associated with prophecy and told through presentations and stories, then poetry, too, is intensely related to emotive remembering and representation. Here, remembering is not only a literary overture but is rooted in the fabric of life and practice, namely, ethics. In pursuit of framing Ghazālī's inventive making and creating—poiesis—one can hardly disagree with Brodsky that a "poem is . . . the closest possible interplay between ethics and aesthetics."[42] For if anyone has accomplished the marriage between law and ethics on the one hand and mysticism and aesthetics on the other, there is no finer exemplar than Ghazālī.

Aristotle, in the *Poetics*, tells us that poetry is also a form of "mimesis," meaning imitation or representation.[43] This insight introduces a whole new sensibility and irenic relationship between Ghazālian and Aristotelian thought. Ghazālī carefully mediated the semiotics of the Qur'ān and the Arabo-Islamic tradition when he used key terms such as storytelling (*qaṣaṣ*) and poetry (*shiʿr*) in conversation with the Aristotelian tradition. Drawing on Michael Davis's reading of Aristotle, I have come to understand that imitation and representation are ways of stylizing reality.[44] If any early Muslim thinker welcomed the concept of stylizing reality in imaginative ways, then Abū Ḥāmid al-Ghazālī was surely him. At the level of thought or reason, he points out, we understand symbols by way of simulation, or simile (*tamthīl*), and synopsis (*ijmāl*); and, at the level of human action, he continues, we cannot desist from imitation (*taʾassī*) and exemplary representation (*iqtidāʾ*).[45] His comments only reinforce what I have earlier argued, that philosophical poetics is about the interconnection of reason and action, imagination and representation. What Ghazālī and Muslim discourse more generally typify is the idea that nothing less than the conjugation of knowledge with practice (*al-ʿilm wa al-ʿamal*) leads to the completeness of being. Put differently, the synthesis is between two dimensions: being and existence.

Moral reasoning, George Lakoff and Mark Johnson point out, becomes an activity as much as it is a constructive imagination by means of what they call an "experientialist synthesis." Moral reasoning is indebted to metaphorical concepts, which assign a crucial role to the unity and fusion of reason with imagination.[46] Indeed, in this, they do not stray much from Aristotle's poetics, in which plot is the "putting together" (*sunthesis*) of deeds (*pragmata*).[47] As Michael Davis points out, for Aristotle, *poiêtikê* signifies not only the art of poetry but also making and doing by combining plots so that they hold together beautifully, even if they are made from multiple and varied parts.[48]

One can now forcefully make the case that mimesis lies behind all knowledge. For it is "only by representing something to ourselves," says Davis, "that can we single it out as an object of inquiry."[49] Not only is poetics important to the study of philosophy, but it inheres in all thinking: we cannot think about something unless we place that object in the foreground and temporarily set the other thoughts into the background for heuristic purposes. However, mimesis, or imitation, plays an even more important role: it frames reality by announcing that what is *in* the frame cannot be taken as real in an oversimplified manner.

Take as an example the Muslim requirement to emulate the model practice (*Sunna*) of the Prophet Muḥammad, what can be thought of as *imitatio Muḥammadī*, or the imitation of Christ. Every time the original act of the exemplar, the Prophet Muḥammad, is faithfully reenacted (*ittibāʿ*) by the adherent, it is clear that the original act is not repeated. To think of the imitation as "real" can be misleading. "Thus the more 'real' the imitation," Davis cautions, "the more fraudulent it becomes."[50] In other words, if one thinks when emulating the exemplar that one is repeating the exemplar's "original" act, then one has reduced one's emulation to a rational and fraudulent act. It is this rational line of reasoning that inheres in and overwhelms much of fundamentalist and maximalist thinking, irrespective of whether it is of a secular or a religious kind. Emulation requires a focused dose of the imagination in order to make it real. Thus, only an *act of the imagination* can turn the imitation of the Muḥammadan *Sunna* into an act of loyalty to and love for the Prophet Muḥammad.

Only when reason is distilled with the imagination can it make sense of emulation. Imitation is a performance that reenacts past events so that the subject becomes an integral part of the tradition and the network of truth across time and space. More importantly, imitation links the beginning of the tradition to its unfolding into the present. Uncannily, emulation parallels the function of narrative, for the purpose of narrative is the imaginative fusion of past and present temporalities.

The Self: Between (Oto)Biography and Testimony

Ghazālī thrived on two fronts: first, as a jurist-theologian who stressed the rational element of action, and second as a pious ṣūfī who placed emphasis on the imagination, combining both dimensions in his discursive thought. His dual strength as a jurist-theologian and a mystic accounts for the honorific "Proof of Islam" (*Ḥujjat al-Islām*) that has been bestowed on him. His receipt of this title was preceded by his extraordinary scholarly success and his soul-searing personal transformation.

At the personal level, Ghazālī's life history, and by implication his "self," was woven in a tapestry of engagements with multiple others. During his childhood, there was the anonymous elder of Ṭūs who supervised his early education from age eleven, that is, beginning in 462/1069. Ghazālī was decisively influenced by the scholarship and ideas of Abū al-Maʿālī al-Juwaynī, one of his later teachers. His intellectual biography was also indebted to encounters with philosophers, theologians, ṣūfīs, members belonging to heretical sects such as the Ismāʿīlīs, and to caliphs, *sulṭāns*, and *wazīrs*. One cannot ignore the influence on Ghazālī's existential formation of Niẓām al-Mulk, *wazīr* to the Saljūq *sulṭāns*, or of Ghazālī's close association with the youthful caliph, Mustaẓhir. No sooner did he reach the pinnacle of his academic accomplishments when, within four years after he attained a major professorship, restlessness and the desire to seek out the solitary path of asceticism set in. After resolving to forgo worldly endeavors and especially to avoid princes and rulers, he reversed his decision at the request of the *wazīr*, Fakhr al-Mulk. Interrupting his isolation from visible public life, he taught for some time in an official capacity at his alma mater, the Niẓāmīya in Nisapūr.

What is striking about Ghazālī's biography is the multidimensionality of his life, a multidimensionality of images, representations, emotions, and transformations that cannot artificially be compartmentalized. These elements luxuriously shaped his biography and writings. The quality of fluidity makes it difficult to stabilize his story and lends his work a certain malleability for reconfiguration through redescription. Ghazālī himself energetically engaged in acts of reconfiguration through voluminous writing. Many of his biographers also rewrite his life in manifold ways. Biographers in general, including Ghazālī's biographers, have to reimagine the past. Historical precision may be neither appropriate nor possible, as worldviews are not easily chronicled in the manner of political events. Yet this in no way detracts from the reality of worldviews for the subject.[51] In the past and the present, every effort at the painstaking reconstruction of the past is ultimately judged by its narrative outcome.

One way of examining the broad themes of a biography is to see it as poetics. Another way is to see each aspect of the subject's experience as a link in a chain of *rites de passage*. To the extent that each individual's life trajectory becomes a social drama of milestones reached, destinations attained, and wishes fulfilled, as well as their opposite, these experiences in sum constitute the pilgrimage of life. I wish to underscore three aspects that epitomize the social drama of Ghazālī's life: self, memory/writing, and exile. In the remainder of this chapter, I discuss his notion of self, while memory/writing and exile are discussed in subsequent chapters.

Of the many anecdotes that annalists record from Ghazālī's life, one particular event stands out. During his Wanderjahr, Ghazālī one day entered the Amīnīya College in the silk market (*sūq al-ḥarīr*) near the famous Umayyad Mosque in what is today the old city of Damascus. Conscious about his ascetic need to remain incognito to most of the inhabitants of the great city, he shunned all company. The anxiety that he might be recognized as the famous scholar from Baghdād weighed upon him like a catastrophe, since such acknowledgement would have prompted harmful egotistical stirrings in his soul. As a salaried scholar, Ghazālī usually welcomed fame and popular adoration. In fact, for a time in his life, many observed, such fame was all he sought.

On that day in 1095 or 1096 in the Amīnīya College in Damascus, however, he overheard one of the lecturers in a teaching circle mention his name as an authority on a particular issue, saying: "Ghazālī said . . ." On hearing the mention of his name, the chronicler Subkī tells us, Ghazālī confessed the onset of conceit. But as soon as he registered this negative impulse, he fled Damascus, fearing the effects of impious thoughts on his turbulent soul.[52] On that fateful day in Damascus, he came to detest prestige and scholarly honorifics. The world became one huge prison of self-aggrandizement and egotism for Ghazālī; it harbored vices that he learned to scorn. He realized that negative character traits prevent the soul from comprehending the truth by eroding the luminescence of the inner self.

So noticeably changed was Ghazālī as a man on that auspicious day at the Amīnīya that the transformation became evident to his friends and foes on his return to Iraq. When his new behavior was compared to his pre-ṣūfī demeanor, it became clear that the personal transformation could not have been more radical. Roughly six years prior to that fateful day in Damascus, in 484/1091, Ghazālī had arrived in Baghdād to assume the coveted post of chair of Shāfiʿī law at the Niẓāmīya College. Of all the descriptions we have of Ghazālī, the most vivid is that furnished by Abū Manṣūr Ibn al-Razzāz (d. 539/1144), himself a Shāfiʿī jurist of repute and a student of Ghazālī's. Describing the pomp and ceremony of the occasion of Ghazālī's appointment, Ibn al-

Razzāz observes: "Abū Ḥāmid entered Baghdād, and we estimated the value of his clothing and mount to be nearly 500 dirhams! When he turned ascetic, traveled, and returned to Baghdād [again], we valued his clothing to be worth a paltry fifteen kerats."[53] This account suggests how someone who experiences such dramatic shifts in life can create his or her own cast of curious admirers and resentful enemies. More than that, it indicates that such radical change is bound to invite skeptical speculation as to motivation while encouraging scrupulous historians to establish its veracity.

Personal Testimony

But images of Ghazālī's life-changing transitions, in addition to his masterpieces of writing, sustain his memory in Muslim thought. How else does one explain why, approximately nine hundred years later, Ghazālī still remains a formidable figure in Muslim thought? Ghazālī's own narrative partially accounts for his extraordinary influence: he left for posterity an explanation of his personal concerns and inner feelings in his now-famous spiritual testimony, *Rescuer from Misguidance*. As the author of a memoir, or testimony, of his spiritual experiences, Ghazālī is not unique. Many who came before and after him have written spiritual testimonies mixed with autobiography. Mystics, in particular, write for the edification of their disciples and novices.[54] Often, these memoirs are rich in content, capacious in their interpretations of events, and evocative of personal intuitions.

Roughly two centuries before Ghazālī, we find a consistent production of spiritual memoirs that the author of *Rescuer* must have had in mind as models. Unsurpassable in this genre and possibly less personal than Ghazālī's memoir is the *Counsels* (*Al-waṣāyā*) of the Baṣran-born scholar and mystic Ḥārith al-Muḥāsibī, who lived in Baghdād for most of his life. Poor Muḥāsibī ran afoul of the zealous followers of the influential and pious Aḥmad ibn Ḥanbal. Ibn Ḥanbal was a scholar who specialized in prophetic reports, and his school developed a reputation for a fideistic commitment to faith driven by a nominalist adherence to tradition. Ibn Ḥanbal had a hand in tormenting Muḥāsibī by denouncing him in lectures. His fanatical followers mercilessly persecuted Muḥāsibī, driving him to a lonely death.[55] In order to prevent posterity from judging him on the basis of the denunciations of his critics, Muḥāsibī prudently wrote about his spiritual and existential experiences, using his own voice to counter the claims of his critics.

Another partial autobiography left for posterity, less contemplative about spiritual matters, came from the pen of one of Islamdom's most well-known philosophers, Abū ʿAlī ibn Sīnā. Ibn Sīnā's intriguing account of his intellectual interests and the political challenges he faced was left incomplete at the time of his death. One of his disciples later completed it.[56] In it, the philosopher discussed a variety of issues, from his study habits and his commentary on the world surrounding his immediate milieu to the more mundane.[57]

There is a reasonable explanation as to why Muḥāsibī and Ibn Sīnā were keen to bequeath to posterity firsthand accounts of their lives. Both of them came from heterodox households. Muḥāsibī's father is alleged to have been a rebellious schismatic who was either aligned with the Shīʿa or suspected of being a proponent of free will allied with a group known as the Qadarīs. Association with either of these sects—the Rāfiḍī or the Qadarī—would have drawn disapproval from the hegemonic theological formation known generally as the Sunnī trend.[58] Ibn Sīnā's father was not only a Shiʿī but allegedly a prominent figure within the circles of the esoteric Ismāʿīlīs. This fact lends credence to the claim that Ibn Sīnā's early education took place within an eminently heterodox tradition.[59] So both Muḥāsibī and Ibn Sīnā had good reason to be apprehensive about their legacies. Affiliation with marginal groups and sects of disrepute could savagely stigmatize a person in the medieval world, as it can today. In the absence of clarification provided in their own voices, posterity might have made the wrong assumptions about these men's intellectual and doctrinal affiliations by associating them with their families.

At least some people of repute in medieval times, like their modern successors, felt it was a personal and even a religious duty to set the record straight by means of autobiography.[60] Until recently, modern Western writers have approached Muslim autobiographies in order to capture the *essentialized* self of the biographical subject, one that is easily and transparently discernible through literary interpretation.[61] With such discredited presumptions at work, the enterprise of mapping the history of the "self" in Muslim thought had limited chances of success. Others have claimed that autobiography is exclusively Western in provenance, a view now thoroughly debunked by serious scholarship. Some time ago, noted historians like Jacob Burckhardt, Charles Bushnell, and others began to acknowledge the extent to which Muslims have contributed to the genre of biographical and autobiographical writing. Bushnell, to his credit, argued that the successors to Augustine in the writing of autobiography were not Christians but Muslims. Burckhardt wrote that the "Arab had felt himself an individual at a time when other Asiatics knew themselves as only members of a race."[62]

In Muslim cultures, the frequency with which autobiographies, or spiritual memoirs, occur by the eleventh century may signal the emergence of new notions of "self" and "identity" within the cultural history of this civilization. Given that their appearance coincided with the stabilization of the major theological and juristic divisions, these documents provide some sense of the shape and form of social relations among communities and their multiple political and ideological formations. People may have begun to look for new ways of expressing social solidarity as Muslim political power in the eleventh century became unstable and unwieldy. Individuals and groups took it upon themselves to cultivate their identities independent of official dogmas and their complex surroundings with a bid to preserve their histories, honor, and reputations for future generations.

Prior to the appearance of these documents that record the identities and histories of individuals, most people were content with a form of voluntarism—with the idea that one's reputation and prestige, as well as one's good fortune to perform virtuous deeds, were ultimately in the hands of God. And if any memories were worth preserving, then Providence would ensure that others would faithfully provide accounts of those memories for posterity. However, that attitude seems to have undergone change when scholars proactively began producing several genres of historiography, hagiography, and biographical dictionaries of jurists, theologians, and pious figures that included extensive details of their accomplishments.[63]

Almost parallel to the old practice of third-party documentation, autobiography emerged in certain Muslim societies roughly in the twelfth century as a genre of writing. The timing of its emergence roughly coincided with the era that the historian Franz Rosenthal examines in his exploration of certain forms of alterity in medieval Islam.[64] Critical figures associated with the traditional Muslim law schools began to emphasize their individual authority as jurists rather than merely adhering to the consensus opinion of their regional schools.[65] It is around the same time that we begin to note a pattern by which individual scholars and figures asserted their autonomy and differentiated their viewpoints from those that society and communitarian ideologies attempted to shackle them to. Literature on Islamic mysticism, in particular, accounts for the growth in the genre of autobiographical writing in which individual identity was asserted. This literature is significant in its detailed discussions about notions of the "self," "identity," "alterity," and "subjectivity."[66]

The usual way of describing scholars in the biographical dictionaries was to state that X was "the most learned among the learned"; Y was "the most learned jurist of his time" (*afqah al-nās fī zamānihi*); Z was "more learned than so and so" or "better qualified than W"; or P was "more seductive than a fox" (*arwagh min tha'lab*). These tropes, parsed from the early literature, make comparisons on a hierarchical level, but such comparisons were not a universal feature of the literature. Elements of horizontal differentiation are also evident in the work of some early figures. The writings of the master Arabic stylist and belles lettrist Abū Ḥayyān al-Tawḥīdī and of the renowned jurist and polymath from Muslim Spain 'Alī b. Aḥmad Ibn Ḥazm (d. 456/1064) both come to mind. They are exemplary precisely because they deviate from the hierarchical differentiation that characterizes so many of the medieval works.[67]

The construction of self-portraits is indeed informative of the existence of the notion of self-presentation in Arabic literature. Many scholars bequeathed to us documents that resemble what we today would call curricula vitae. In them, they listed their family links, prestigious descent (if it deserved mention), the names of teachers with whom they had studied, the titles of the books they had written or dictated, and the most important professional posts they had occupied. Such writing may constitute an early sample of simple autobiographies, *tarjama nafsahu*, which literally means "translating/explaining one's self."[68] A plausible reason for the noticeable growth in the autobiographical genre might have been the need to accent individual agency through narratives of self-presentation. But, more than anything else, this trend confirms the growth of a notion of individualism.

Pietistic motives clearly animated some of the autobiographical writings of middle Islam. As prosperity increased, people were in a position to travel and work in far-off places, which promoted cosmopolitanism. Many mobile scholars documented their travel experiences and encounters with different teachers. Their motive for doing so was to acknowledge divine blessings bestowed on the autobiographical subject, for to do so was also to give thanks to God. The Qur'ān urges adherents to publicly give thanks: "And as for the bounty of your Lord, speak about it!"[69] Announcing the bounties the Creator bestows on one is a virtuous act; it is not meant to inspire pride but rather to induce humility, nor is it intended to demean those who are less fortunate. Some early figures, from 'Abd Allāh ibn Bulluggīn (d. ca. 1094 or after) to Jalāl al-Dīn al-Suyūṭī (d. 911/1505), were held up as role models. Suyūṭī, for instance, wrote a detailed autobiography titled *Speaking about the Bounties of Allāh*.[70]

Ghazālī and Testimony

Unlike some of his famous predecessors, Ghazālī, as far as we know, had no dishonorable family affiliations that could have stained his image. On the face of it, there was no explicit need for him to scrub his reputation by means of an autobiography. The ambiguities found in *Rescuer* provide fertile ground for speculation as to its purpose. I believe the overall thrust of it is not primarily autobiographical, nor is it a confession akin to Saint Augustine's famous text; rather, it is an expression of gratitude for the divine grace and favors bestowed on its author.[71] Ghazālī subscribed to a particular form of mysticism, as Nasrullah Pourjawadi informs us, a type in which divine grace subsumes all events and happenings.[72]

Gratitude to God for rescuing him from his paralyzing perplexity was the reason Ghazālī wrote a testimony. He felt obliged to give thanks and to identify the real "savior" in his life. The interesting subtitle of *Rescuer* discloses the testimonial character of the text. The subtitle is "*Uniting with the One Who Possesses Glory and Awe*." A closer scrutiny of this subtitle not only throws light on how Ghazālī wished to frame the *event* of his personal salvation, it also shows how such events motivated him to pursue the truth. Other versions of the subtitle read: "*That Which Unites with the Possessor of Glory and Awe*," and "*That Which Clarifies with Regard to the Possessor of Power*" (*Al-mūṣil* / *Al-muwaṣṣil* / *Al-mufṣiḥ ilā dhī al-ʿizz wa al-jalāl*).

The active participle "rescuer" (*munqidh*) is a word by means of which Ghazālī intended to suggest that his book is a complex narrative. Of course, the imagery conjures a scene in which someone in mortal danger or on the verge of drowning is rescued. However, one should not be oblivious to the fact that the notion of "rescuing" (*inqādh*) resonates with a motif in the Qur'ān that Ghazālī subtly imported into his self-narrative. It was due to God's grace that He blessed the strife-ridden Arabs of the seventh century with a Messenger who rescued the people of Makka, and later Arabia, from spiritual perdition. This is how the Qur'ān narrates that account: "And hold fast, all of you together, to the rope of Allah, and do not be divided. And remember with gratitude Allah's favor upon you; how you were enemies and He made friendship between your hearts so that you became as brothers by His grace. *And you were on the brink of an abyss of fire, when He saved you from it* [*fa anqadhakum minhā*]. Thus, Allah makes clear His revelations unto you, that haply you may be guided."[73]

In writing his personal testimony, Ghazālī drew on this aesthetic imagery from the Qur'ān by weaving the dramatic poetics of someone who has been rescued into the climactic tale. Ghazālī invoked divine grace (*niʿmat Allāh*) as the source of his guidance that, in turn, necessitated the gratitude of the recipient. The work is also a witness to his personal covenant with God, whom he believed rescued him from sure ruin. He only provided his readers with snapshots of the most significant moments that were burned onto his memory. Like a traumatized "survivor," he did not tell us the entire story of his ordeal, and therefore *Rescuer* is not so much an autobiography as it is a testimony.[74]

In several of his essay-like treatises, Ghazālī generated a combined ascetic and aesthetic paradigm that triggers a chain of equivalences between himself, God, and the divine light cast into his bosom that rescued him from misguidance. He wrote that he was profoundly indebted to God for opening the floodgates of esoteric knowledge and illumination that stilled his perplexed mind and finally brought luster to his soul.[75] He received from God, as he put it, "revelations innumerable and unfathomable in those breakthrough years of solitude."[76] It was this analogical chain and bridge with which he reached the transcendent Other, God, who authored the subject.

It was also the Other who unveiled to him the repository of that certainty that he so desperately sought, namely, the mystical path (*taṣawwuf*) that illuminates the meaning of the inner life. "I learned with certainty," Ghazālī notes, "that it is above all the mystics who walk on the road of God."[77] Even though he had been a thoroughgoing empiricist, he railed against the monstrous conflation of the analytic and the synthetic. His inner certainties compelled him to become critical of some of the disciplines and types of knowledge that he had once prized. Theological debates and discussions about logic, law, and philosophy seemed to him less fulfilling than they once had been. Indeed, he found himself drawn to the affective experiences of the self-disclosure of God that brought him such astonishing certainty. For all practical purposes, religion without experience was, in his view, a mere chimera. Preferring a sensuous religious experience, at times he singled out discursive prisms mediating religion for criticism, but he did so temperately. Only those discursive traditions that were linked to some spiritual and ethical pursuit were of value to Ghazālī.

The self, as Ricoeur reminds us, is embedded in at least two instances: first, in the temporal "flow" of events, and second in those significant moments when one attempts to make sense of complex as well as momentous personal experiences.[78] Ghazālī's now-famous and debilitating crisis was precipitated by "events" in the temporal flow of his life. And he triumphed by means of a struggle to explore the meaning of his life. In short, the self is suspended between the eventfulness of meaning or the meaningfulness of events. Events are not just chance occurrences. They are part of the unfolding life story and narrative of the subject. Events such as Ghazālī's early education on the public purse, his encounter with brigands, his exploration of the political intrigue in Baghdād, his self-imposed exile, and his personal anxiety at the Amīnīya College wittingly or unwittingly all caused him to exhibit a spectrum of feelings and emotions. He had remorse and agonizing pangs of conscience for his earlier partisanship in messy politics and his display of unbridled intellectual narcissism. Surely, the immensely heterogeneous elements in his thinking only added to the complexity of his inner struggles. But Ghazālī succeeded where others have faltered. He negotiated the antinomies of heterogeneity as well as the critical conjunctures of agonistic existence. Far from being negative, the events and struggles of his life enabled him to productively crisscross multiple boundaries.

A question to which he frequently returned was this: Can there be any meaning apart from the concreteness of existence and being? His personal crisis began when he could no longer make sense of his *experiences*, a condition of meaninglessness that led to the utter despair he eloquently recounts in the *Rescuer*. It is interesting that the most significant features of the crisis that he recalled were moments of incoherence and the haunting desire to overcome it. What troubled him most was that meaning failed him utterly. Neither the legal-moral constructs in which he had specialized nor the philosophy and theology in which he excelled could provide him with persuasive answers. In fact, as he tells us, his tongue could no longer move, a condition that drove him beyond despair to reach complete silence.

Self and Intentionality

Does Ghazālī provide any hints at self-analysis? How did he conceive of the self in terms of history and psychology? From what can be gauged, I believe that he inferred that the proper subject of the historical sciences is the moral life of communities, and that subject is what he set out to investigate in most of his writings after his turn to ṣūfism, painstakingly examining accounts of practices and how they might maximally improve the moral life of his community. It is not that he was interested in the exploits of individual kings, prophets, pious figures, and wise men, but that he viewed them as exemplars of the moral life.

The psychology of the self is rooted in intentionality. This is best illustrated by an often-reported story from Ghazālī's biographical accounts of his early education. When Ghazālī and his brother, Aḥmad, were orphaned in their teens, their education was paid for with the meager resources set aside in their father's will for the purpose. When Ghazālī's private tuition in his hometown came to a halt due to a lack of funds, he was advised to join a live-in school (*madrasa*) in Ṭūs. There, he received free boarding and tuition to complete his primary education in the interest of becoming a jurist-theologian.

By any moral calculus, it is acceptable to take refuge in a public school when pecuniary reasons force one to do so in order to survive. Later in his life, however, Ghazālī repeatedly lamented the fact that his primary education was polluted by his impure motives. This is a sentiment that may appear severe, and it has been incomprehensible to both his contemporaries and his modern readers. The jurist and historian of Islamic law ʿAbd al-Raḥim al-Isnawī (d. 772/1370) reports that Ghazālī remorsefully remarked: "We went to the *madrasa* [ostensibly] to study law [*fiqh*], [but in reality we attended it] in order to get food."[79] His regret was both palpable and consequential. No only did he recall this episode as an unholy and regrettable one, but he harbored guilty feelings that his scholarly career had tarnished beginnings. It distressed him to admit that learning could be turned from its purported noble ends into an instrument for mundane survival. "We sought knowledge not for the sake of God," he inveighs against himself and his brother, before he delightfully mitigates his condemnation by adding, "but [knowledge] refused to [surrender] except to God [*ṭalabnā al-ʿilm li ghayr Allāh fa abā an yakūna illā li Allāh*]."[80]

Ghazālī was not only tortured by the impurity of motive that he believes was inscribed in his foundational knowledge; a gaping wound also festered in his self. This entire episode, which centers on the improper acquisition of knowledge, speaks to the nakedness and transparency of his self, a self marked above all by a lack. The question he had to grapple with is this: How does one exorcise and cleanse a self that is clothed in the knowledge of expediency?

Ghazālī's guilt-ridden conscience reminds one of Abelard's memorable concern about the ethic of pure intention. "It is not the deed," says Abelard, "but the intention of the doer which makes the crime, and justice should weigh not what was done, but the spirit in which it is done."[81] If Abelard pushes the debate on intention toward the spirit of things, then Ghazālī draws our attention to how knowledge is embodied. Pure intention (*ikhlāṣ*) does not exist on its own; rather, intention is the elixir that purifies both knowledge and practice. Ghazālī exemplified in his own reflections the way that knowledge is imagined and personified in Muslim thought. Knowledge is essentially about ethics—how to live and transform the self and others. Ghazālī acknowledged that he first acquired informative discourses and reports, what we would call the facts of knowledge. But it takes something more for information and facts to morph into proper knowledge, by which one grasps a sense of reality.[82]

To bring about that change requires a psychological attitude that is fixed on intentionality. Only the catalytic elements of intentionality and purity of motive transform information into a sense of reality, so that knowledge becomes constitutive of the senses. Disciplinary practices can straighten the prior distortions of the senses and the self that block the cognition of the ends of knowledge. This is exactly what Ghazālī set out to do during the rest of his life: to reconstitute his physical senses as well as his self.

There is little doubt in my mind that Ghazālī's lifelong battle with his self—a continuous struggle to celebrate purity of motive, to maintain rectitude and moral order within his soul—was marked by self-questioning that went back to the events of his teenage years. His obsession with purity of motive and sincerity shows that he preserved his childlike impressionability. Even on his deathbed, he advised his disciples to conscientiously "cultivate sincerity of motive" (*ʿalaykum bi al-ikhlāṣ*).[83] His ethics prompted him to conclude that anything derived from talent or influence is worthless unless it serves the greater moral cause and exclusively addresses the divine. Sincerity, for Ghazālī, became the true standard, even the equivalent of true faith.

Recall the mournful soliloquy: "But [knowledge] refused to [surrender] except to God." In one sense, it is revealing. It is an expression of discontent subject to the torque of mutable feelings. In another sense, it is an index of the magnitude of the transformation that Ghazālī had undergone. Laboring to overcome the egotistical motive, turning personal defeat into victory, and transforming the mundane into the profound are all tasks of the utmost importance in the search for the alchemy of the self.

More importantly, his pithy declaration shows that he was able to visualize his past and present in terms of the sacrality of knowledge. Sacrality enters through the metaphoric domain. He attributes to knowledge a will and speaks of it as if it is a person, as if knowledge incarnates the poetics of language. He attains this via prosopopeia and personification. Prosopopeia (*lisān al-ḥāl*) is the one trope that Ghazālī frequently used, and it permeates his discourse.[84] One of the great virtues of prosopopeia as a trope is that it has the capacity to transform an idea into an anthropomorphism, as Paul de Man might say.[85] But it is not a crude anthropomorphism. Rather, it is one sustained in language and brought about by a certain verbal overdetermination that is often produced by close figural readings.

In a single move, Ghazālī regenerated meaning through an event in his life and brought to the fore the nature of knowledge. While he did allegorize knowledge, he presented it kerygmatically: knowledge is instantiated as an event. So, while the narrative shifts, telling us what happens to knowledge, it also imperceptibly turns to the subject of knowledge—the person of Ghazālī. When knowledge refuses to surrender to mundane and profane ends, it simultaneously rescues its subject, Ghazālī. In the process of describing this shift, Ghazālī demonstrates how he imagined the spirit of knowledge and how this autonomous spirit incarnated his own life.

When we explore the fragments of the life of Ghazālī, they disclose how he was often locked between positions, caught in the paradoxes and contradictions of life in a veritable threshold position, a position at the crossroads. But the possibilities of understanding Ghazālī in his complexity are sustained by certain strategies of reading. When we read Ghazālī on the borderline of the corpus and the corpse, we become aware of the range of meanings he represents. Whatever Ghazālī's corpus of writing constitutes for posterity, it is intimately related to the construction of his self. Ultimately, the internal and external battles around his self are reflected in what constitutes writing and its meaning. In other words, the need to uncover Ghazālī as the speaking subject—how he speaks within the broader context of Muslim traditions of knowledge and pedagogy—is critically important in understanding him and his oeuvre.

To come to grips with the structure of Ghazālī's narrative is to recognize that his commitment to the logocentric discourses of law, theology, and philosophy in the early part of his career prefigured their counternarratives (heterologies), the most relevant being the complex tapestry of mysticism. While every narrative does invite the counternarrative, the question that arises is not whether the counternarrative is a legitimate narrative but, more critically, whether it can supplant the hegemonic narrative as the reiteration of the original. Is the dialogical imagination in Muslim discourse premised on alterities? And can these alterities also prefigure multiple and diverse Others?[86] Or are alterities and Othering only a fiction of the dialogical encounter? If they are, will the desire to resolve it remain a cruel trick we play on ourselves?

The intelligent man knows well that nature rebels against rote learning. And whomsoever it overpowers, such a person is defeated. So when will that which is despised ever become the object of desire?
—ʿAyn al-Quḍāt al-Hamadhānī, *Shakwā al-gharīb*

3 Poetics of Memory and Writing

Perils of Writing

How did Ghazālī recover from the state of mired existence caused by his intellectual crisis? I believe that writing was his therapy; he told the story of his self by writing it and in the process "gave life" (*iḥyāʾ*) to his tormented soul. *Rescuer* is his diagnostic testimony, and *Resuscitation* contains the copious fruit of his meditations. The first text constitutes the narrative construction of the self, while the second can be considered to be an extravagant footnote. "After all," says Brodsky, "a footnote is where civilization survives."[1] When Ghazālī began to understand his own personal history as a narrative, he was challenged to reach for a deeper layer of causes (etiologies) for his condition. His self-reflection led him to explore his years as a young adult, his experiments with writing and memory, and, finally, his decision to experience exile.

An important episode in his life occurred when the young Ghazālī returned from Jurjān. There, he had studied for about two years and prepared an advanced dissertation (*taʿlīqa*) on law under the supervision of his teachers.[2] On his return journey to Ṭūs, Ghazālī and his travel party were attacked by a group of malefactors (*ʿayyārūn*) who relieved Ghazālī of his possessions, including the dissertation. He pleaded with the brigands to return his dissertation, which was the product of years of labor and his most prized possession. Ghazālī does not mention the temporary theft of his dissertation in the *Rescuer*, but it is a well-documented event, carefully recorded by the Shāfiʿī biographer Subkī and confirmed by several other chroniclers. Subkī reports Ghazālī's account of his encounter, which begins with Ghazālī's address to the head of the brigands:

> I plead with you in the name of Him who keeps you safe to only return to me my dissertation [*taʿlīqa*]. It will be of little value to you. The leader of the brigands asked me: "What is a *taʿlīqa*?" I replied: "Books in my bag. I traveled to listen and write it and to have knowledge of it." He derisively laughed at me and said: "How can you claim to have knowledge, when I have taken it and stripped you of it? You are now without any learning!" After a while, he ordered his men to return my bag. Ghazālī said: "The leader of the brigands turned into an oracle [*mustanṭaq*] whom God made to speak in order to guide me."[3]

To Ghazali's eternal relief, the leader of the brigands returned his dissertation, but the event had a profound effect on his psyche. Convinced that God had used the brigands to convey a message to him, he resolved that it was his memory that should become the prime site in which he stored knowledge, not the pages of a book.[4] During his three-year stay in Ṭūs after his return from Jurjān, he memorized his prized dissertation. The encounter with the brigands turned out to be one of many watershed moments in Ghazali's life that shaped his attitude not only toward memory but also toward what he regarded to be knowledge. This event complicated his idea of writing and its role in the constitution of knowledge. Subsequent to this event, Ghazālī came to view memory as a treasure, something that was always available and present to him, while writing was susceptible to "theft."[5]

I have identified three stages in which Ghazālī's attitude toward memory and writing developed. The first was marked by his obsession with memory. The next was one of compulsive doxological writing that served as an aide-mémoire, or, if you like, a kind of memory-writing. Finally, he entered a phase wherein he undertook what I call "heart-writing," in which writing was different from what he was accustomed to: it became part of a highly metaphysicalized self.

Writing as Theft

Some of Ghazālī's different comments and reflections on writing and memory resonate with aspects of Plato's view of writing. In the "Seventh Letter," Plato dismisses writing, saying: "Any serious student of serious realities will shrink from making truth the helpless object of men's ill-will by committing it to writing. In a word, the conclusion to be drawn is this; when one sees a written composition, whether it be on law by a legislator or on any other subject, one can be sure, if the writer is a serious man, that his book does not represent his most serious thoughts; they remain stored up in the noblest region of his personality." "If he is really serious," Plato adds, "in what he has set down in writing, 'then surely' not the gods but men 'have robbed him of his wits.'"[6]

To get a better sense of Plato's views on writing, some explanation of the myth of writing's origin is in order. In *Phaedrus*, Plato's Socrates recounts it. In the region of Naucratis in Egypt, the myth states, there dwelled a god called Theuth to whom the bird known as the Ibis was sacred. Theuth, as we will recall, was the god who invented geometry, calculation, astronomy, and, above all, writing. The king of Egypt at the time was Thamus, whom the Greeks called the Egyptian Thebes. In a bid to popularize the art of writing, Theuth visited the king in order to persuade him and all Egyptians of the wonders of writing. Writing, he believed, was a potion for memory and wisdom. The king Thebes, as Plato's voice, had an altogether different opinion about the proposal, and he replied to Theuth as follows:

> O most expert Theuth, one man can give birth to the elements of an art, but only another can judge how they can benefit or harm those who will use them. And now, since you are the father of writing, your affection for it has made you describe its effects as opposite of what they really are. In fact it will introduce forgetfulness into the soul of those who learn it: they will not practice using their memory because they will put their trust in writing, which is *external* and depends on signs that belong to others, instead of trying to *remember from the inside*, completely on their own. You have not discovered *a potion for remembering*, but for *reminding*; you provide your students with the *appearance of wisdom*, not with its reality. Your invention will enable them to hear many things without being properly taught, and they will imagine that they have come to know much while for the most part they will know nothing. And they will appear to be wise instead of really being so.[7]

Memory and the Metaphysics of Presence

Whether Ghazālī was familiar with this myth is irrelevant. What is sure is that after almost losing his written knowledge in his twenties, Ghazālī would almost certainly have agreed with Plato and made the connection between writing and "theft." Like Plato, he was not only prone to view writing as being susceptible to theft but also feared that it might precipitate the destruction of memory and rob us of wisdom. Only when learning is stored in the "noblest of regions," as Plato calls the memory, could knowledge be secure.

It was the incident with the robbers that dramatically persuaded Ghazālī to commit knowledge to a mental archive in order to remember things "from the inside," as Thebes put it. The lessons Ghazālī drew from his experience and Plato's mythical narrative share a commonality: they both privilege the spoken word over the written word. When words are spoken, speaker and listener are present to the utterance, giving the impression that the immediacy of the spoken word guarantees that we know what we mean just as we mean what we know. By contrast, the written word remains at a distance; it is liable to corruption, even theft and dispossession. Derrida identifies the feature of speech outlined above as the "metaphysics of presence." The "metaphysics of presence" is shorthand for the fiction of direct reference, a fiction that inheres in Western thought and literature as well as in Muslim literary and interpretive traditions.

Despite his critique of some of Derrida's propositions, especially Derrida's gnostic doctrines of the text, the literary critic Edward Said nevertheless broadly agrees with his French counterpart that any close reading (deconstruction) has to originate in critical receptivity.[8] Deconstruction, concedes Said, is a liberating act of reading, one that frees the prisoners of meaning, liberating the land (space) of meaning from those who colonize it.[9] The colonization of meaning takes place at the hands of all kinds of orthodoxies, starting with the elaborate dogmas attached to reading, interpretation, and how we construe meaning. The fiction of direct reference (the metaphysics of presence) is one way of colonizing meaning and, in doing so, stifling the emancipatory potential of knowledge. This happens when we valorize the spoken word over the written one and especially when we sustain the fiction of unmediated meaning in talking about writing. In fact, writing (*écriture*), says Said, aside from being a process of production and effacement, tracing and retracing, is ultimately a "process of excess, overflowing, bursting through."[10] Deconstruction, especially of writing, becomes subversive, as Plato rightly feared, because it offers the possibility of liberating meaning from the fiction of a direct reference.

Memory and Orality as Authority

The preference for memory and speech over writing has been given a lugubrious name: "phonocentrism." Phonocentrism had widespread currency in Muslim societies of the fourth/tenth and fifth/eleventh centuries and after. This preference for speech and memory continues in the Muslim cultures of the modern period and is not only restricted to traditional Muslim pedagogical practices of learning. In the heyday of Muslim phonocentrism, master scholars would permit their students to authoritatively transmit the knowledge they had committed to their "breasts." Pectoral imagery was used to symbolize that something had been committed to memory, or, in the often-used phrase, that it was known "by heart." Arabic speakers use an expression for memorizing something that literally translates as "to protect something on the surface of the heart" (*ḥafiẓa ʿan ẓahr al-qalb*), where the word "surface" is deployed metaphorically.[11]

In this ancient Islamic knowledge tradition, a written text becomes a mere certificate of authenticity that serves either as an emblem that orally transmitted material has been learned or as something that will in due time be committed to memory. The transmission of knowledge from teacher to student is governed by elaborate protocols for certification and authorization (*ijāza*).[12] The process of certification relies on a chain of authorities (*isnād*), a feature that some early Muslim writers claimed was unique to Islamicate cultures because it was a distinct feature of the followers of the Prophet Muḥammad.[13] Not only are prophetic reports (*aḥādīth*) preserved and transmitted with rigor in traditional Muslim educational practices, but all knowledge related to subjects, such as law, Qur'ān exegesis, theology, and mysticism, among others, is transmitted via meticulous chains of transmitters.

Ibn Jamāʿa (d. 733/1333), a noted Shāfiʿī judge in Mamlūk Egypt, wrote a treatise titled *The Memoir of the Listener and the Speaker in the Training of the Teacher and Student*.[14] In it, he details the required protocols for and etiquette of education in the medieval period. When a student received a certification of authorization from the teacher, it meant that the student was permitted to transmit the knowledge he had acquired to others, because his teacher had vouched for his credibility. Credibility was judged by how accurately and fluently the disciple could rehearse from memory the learning the teacher had imparted to him.[15]

As greater numbers of authorized *written* copies were gradually transmitted over time, books and reading gained importance alongside the memorization of texts.[16] Despite this move toward writing, in the premodern Muslim world the pedagogical tradition still insisted that "what a man had in his memory counted more than what he had on paper, even if he had to refresh his memory continually by reference to his notes."[17] In fact, Ibn Jamāʿa sternly warns that a student "should never depend on the books" in order to acquire knowledge, "because it is the most dangerous" of means.[18]

Ghazālī, too, believed that youths should at first memorize the catechisms of faith, a process that would eventually lead to comprehension of the doctrines and would finally result in strongly held convictions.[19] Ghazālī, Ibn Jamāʿa, and the Muslim pedagogical tradition generally preferred that the elementary stages of learning take place under the supervision of a teacher instead of exclusively from an impersonal book.[20] To be an autodidact at an early stage of one's education was not viewed as virtuous and may have been seen as the opposite.

Ibn Jamāʿa was meticulous in his emphasis on memory. He advised students to make sure that the material to be memorized was checked and corrected by an authorized teacher. Explanation of any matter was preferably to be sought from a living authority rather than an inanimate book. In other words, the role of the living authority was central to the transmission of knowledge in Muslim societies of the past. Most medieval methods of knowledge transmission sustained the fiction of the preeminent value of oral testimony and auditory forms of learning. The educational and pedagogical traditions of early Muslim societies made a fundamental ideological investment in orality.

At the same time, orality was not valorized for its benign merits. In fact, orality was both the primary means of communication and the visible performative act of a living authority. Oral communication visibly *performed* its authority. Therefore, the performance-like quality of authority was often monstrously conflated with unmediated authority and authenticity. This feature of orality eloquently demonstrates the ideological function of speech-based authority (phonocentrism): it masks the difference between signifier and signified so that the *performance* of authority is viewed to be *identical* and equal to authority itself, erasing the distinction between the two.

Yet, side-by-side with this emphasis on orality, we note that writing flourishes in Muslim societies that privilege phonocentrism. Gradually, an alternation develops between writing and speaking. It is then that we move into a gray area. For it may well be that this alternation between writing and speaking does not favor speech over writing. Another possibility arises: namely, that textual traditions that are susceptible to blending between the two modes may already be fomenting deconstruction by means of the subversive act of writing. At best, the gray area suggests that the fiction of direct reference increases and decreases depending on the extent of deconstruction at work.

Writing, Memory, and Logocentrism

In Ghazālī's case, an emphasis on memory did not inhibit him from being zealous and prolific in his writing. We know that even in the early phase of his career Ghazālī wrote several books on law. Indeed, his decision to write so early in his career in violation of the established conventions offended his teacher Juwaynī. Juwaynī viewed Ghazālī as trying to upstage him by writing a book while still an apprentice scholar. Juwaynī apparently asked him the rhetorical question "Could you not wait until I died?"

By means of his precocious and persistent engagement with writing, Ghazālī himself threw into question his stated preference for memory over writing. Even while he alternated between writing and speaking, there were differences between the kind of writing he did during his prolific early and middle career and the kind of writing he did toward the end of his career. I want to argue that at the middle stage of his career he still viewed writing as a form of memory: he used writing as a substitute for memory, a mechanical reproduction of what he knew by heart, what he had recorded in his mental archive. Writing, in other words, was only a representation: it re-presented the speech-in-memory. While this was still a form of writing, it may be described as "memory-writing," an ideological writing that generates certainty through the rhetorical and doxological closure of truth, a closure facilitated by direct reference, or the metaphysics of presence.

In the case of Ghazālī, I submit that there are some signs in his early work that indicate he was making a transition toward seeing the importance of writing. For instance, one can infer that this transition was taking place from his frequent references to *ḥikāya*, since the word has the double sense of both oral and written narrative. However, his proclivity for suggesting that writing is identical to speech did not detract from his decision to write voluminously. On the contrary, he may have been unconsciously accenting the difference between writing and speech.

One of the significant consequences of Ghazālī's undertaking to write was that in doing so he made an implicit—perhaps unconscious—admission that meaning can be deferred, stored, and possibly recuperated at a later stage. And with that admission came the possibility that any writing could mean something different than what the writer had originally intended it to mean. The very process of delaying, that is, of delaying the immediate self-presence of speech by turning it into the medium of writing, is pregnant with significance and is liberating. "Because writing itself," argues Said, "is a form of escape from every scheme designed to shut it down, hold it in, frame it, parallel it perfectly, any attempt to show writing as capable in some way or the other of being *secondary* is also an attempt to prove that writing is *not original*."[21] Writing is at the center of the struggle to free meaning from the fiction of direct reference in order to proclaim its own liberation.

At the middle stage of his career, Ghazālī juxtaposed memory/orality/speech with writing. He did so in a binary manner, just as he posited the literal against the metaphorical, nature against culture, and positive against negative. At this stage of his career, he was still committed to an exoteric interpretative paradigm and had not as yet embraced a more complex paradigm that could also account for esoteric sensibilities. Memory, speech, literalism, nature, and being positive and affirming in one's conviction—all of these Ghazālī considered to be superior terms. They were pitched against the inferiority of their opposites, namely, writing, metaphor, culture, negativity, and doubt.

The use of a superior term resulted in celebrating the *logos* (reason and speech), whereas the use of an inferior term marked a linguistic fall. In this alternation between speech and writing, absence and presence, a definite subtext persists: all analysis is strategically returned to its origins, is located in voice; by inference, writing is degraded. By privileging the oral word stored in memory over the written word, Ghazālī believed he could gain unmediated access to knowledge through phonic speech. So in transforming written texts into a voice that was locked in his memory, Ghazālī celebrated, in Edmund Husserl's words, "the solitary mental life" in which the self is present to itself.[22] Or, in the words of Paul de Man, his was a strategy that privileged "[t]he unmediated presence of the self to its own voice, as opposed to the reflective distance that separates the self from the written word."[23] My reading of Ghazālī's impulsive reaction to the incident of the temporary theft of his dissertation leads me to conclude that at that stage of his career he identified the spoken sound captured in memory as identical with meaning (thought).

However, despite its having a continuous tradition in Muslim scholarship, not even phonocentrism, with its associated preferences for the literal, the natural, and the positive, can repress the multiplicity of meaning or pretend to grasp meanings in an absolute fashion purely on the grounds of having access to their origins. Phonocentrism has produced what Derrida terms "logocentrism": an attitude or philosophy that claims that meaning emanates from speech, logic, reason, the word of God, or any other absolute origin that precedes it and, as a result, escapes the infinite play of writing. Any suggestion that a critique of logocentrism is tantamount to refuting the role of reason and logic in the process of meaning-making, as it is sometimes alleged, is an oversimplification that misses the point. What deconstruction, or a critique of logocentrism, does deny is the capacity of any single element to make meaning transparent without mediation. What deconstruction does is force us to enhance our understanding by searching for other elements that mediate meaning.

How exactly the logocentric prejudice insinuates itself into thought remains largely unexplored in Muslim critical reflections. Mohammed Arkoun has attempted to read some texts of Muslim culture against the logocentric grain, provoking controversy in the process.[24] Yet logocentrism itself takes many forms. One of these is to treat "writing" as a supplement to the oral word: in short, to argue that writing plays the role of a reminder. Another expression of logocentrism is the framing of binary oppositions, asserting that one equal term reduces the other to inequality and perpetuates ethnocentric valorization.[25] In short, the critique of logocentrism is necessary if we seek to unmask the unethical forms of reading that have domesticated themselves into ideologies of reading. Knowledge becomes a prisoner to ideology if we do not question some of the foundational presumptions about it, about transmission, and about meaning.

Ghazālī's early work is no doubt logocentric, showing proclivities toward phonocentrism that facilitate reference to an origin; they suggest that there is a pure, if not very commonly understood, source from which meaning and knowledge originates. Anyone who has lost treasured notes or whose writing has disappeared into the digital ether can have empathy for Ghazālī's panic-stricken state of mind following the temporary loss of his text. Perhaps it was that trauma, that loss, that drove him to phonocentric cultural practices.

But, with an emphasis on origins, Ghazālī could trace the source of some of his knowledge to his Shāfiʿī teachers, to the Ismāʿīlī family of jurists in Jurjān, and to Juwaynī—he could link his knowledge through chains of authorities to its sources. The impression he gave is that once he had committed learning to memory all he needed to do was to recall the words from memory, from the "inside," from time to time.

What bolsters the claim to direct reference (metaphysics of presence) is the sense sustained in the historiography of Muslim knowledge and its epistemic foundations that the chain (*isnād*) of narrators secures authenticity. There is a belief that once the chains of transmission are activated and acknowledged the authenticity of knowledge is not only re-presented but becomes a visible and specular authority. In this scenario, knowledge is traced to a site, a point, be it language or authority, beyond which we need go no further. Logocentrism and the solitariness of presence are characterized by the irrepressible desire to have a transcendental signified that engenders a closed linguistic and knowledge system.[26] Many of Ghazālī's writings on theology, law, and philosophy from all periods of his life are marked with this desire for closure, but, like all desire, it was never totally consummated.

Heteroglossia

One reason that the desire for closure remains unfulfilled is that it fails to take into account the heteroglot nature of all speech. Contemporary Muslim interpretive traditions would profit from taking this aspect of interpretation seriously. Russian thinker and linguist Mikhail M. Bakhtin has pointed out that certain base conditions have an effect on the meaning of any utterance.[27] These conditions, which influence meaning and speech at any given time and place, are of several types: social, historical, psychological, and even meteorological. When we take these conditions seriously, they give primacy to context over meaning, placing us in a position to say that all utterances are heteroglot. Put simply, this statement means that utterances and speech function within complex matrices of forces that are at once impossible to later reconstruct and, therefore, impossible to resolve.[28] Logocentric discourses fail to acknowledge that oral speech as well as writing are unmistakably heteroglot, that original meaning cannot be recovered merely by means of the repetition of a speech, by sheer re-citation. While certain sensibilities and meanings are thus beyond recovery, the words, or signifiers, of any given speech continue the signification of meaning in a process of infinite iterability and substitution, signifying new meanings under new, heteroglot conditions.

There are, in fact, continuities and discontinuities of meaning. Bakhtin convincingly explains that all languages are subject to centrifugal forces that disrupt and then reunite utterances and their meanings in a myriad of unaccountable ways. In this sense, heteroglossia has far-reaching consequences for interpretive traditions, and it remains largely unaccounted for in Muslim thought. For some authorities, the consequences of acknowledging that speech is heteroglot may be disturbing and subversive, since the acknowledgement solicits an admission that over time certain meanings are erased and new ones arise in their stead. The subversive implications are that reciting or reading the same text under a very different ensemble of conditions from the original conditions under which it was written can render very different, even radically different, meanings. Often, different interpretations of the same text are indeed radically different, but the authority structures within interpretive communities are loathe to consciously acknowledge as much.

While the adherents of logocentric approaches desire to overcome the effects of heteroglossia by emphasizing the phonocentric aspects of speech via re-citation and re-animation as well as by constructing histories of interpretation, there are limits to the extent that they can defy the conditions of heteroglossia. Assuming that one can meticulously preserve, reconstruct, and retrieve all the conditions surrounding original utterances, there still remains the challenge of creating audiences with subjectivities and conditions of heteroglossia that are identical to those that were available at the time the original speeches were produced. Thus, even oral speech is subject to heteroglossia and as a consequence is exposed to the erosion of original meaning. Interpretive communities work hard to confront and contain the corrosive effect of heteroglossia as best they can under the illusion that the moment of origin can be recovered.

Ghazālī and Heart-Writing

In the intellectual circles of the late-eleventh-century ʿAbbāsid world, writing inexorably became prominent, if Ghazālī's output is any index. And we find in his writings instances and flashes when writing is not the enemy but instead is momentarily celebrated. One can identify the discourses in which writing makes its presence felt most forcibly: they are those in which his mystical meditations are secreted into the exoteric discourses in several parts of the *Resuscitation* and at critical moments in his enormous oeuvre. One can assert with more than a modicum of confidence that Ghazālī did reach a stage when he no longer viewed writing as "theft," at least not in the way that Socrates and King Thebes saw it in Plato's recounting of the myth. Just as a close reading of Plato reveals that not all writing is bad, so, too, I would argue, can we see Ghazālī at certain moments radically change his attitude toward writing.

In summary, one can say that Ghazālī experimented with two kinds of writing. One is what I have already identified as "memory-writing," or "doxological writing"; the other is "heart-writing." Matured by time and experience, Ghazālī arrived at a point where he privileged ṣūfī metaphysics and cosmology above all other ways of seeing the world. After his immersion in ṣūfism, he experienced, in his words, "writing on the slate of the heart"—heart-writing, or what I prefer to call "dialogical writing." This form of writing was a product of the mingled intensity of his ṣūfī metaphysics and his sophisticated discursive apparatus. These conditions galvanized Ghazālī's intense mood of introspection and boosted his confidence to think more creatively about the *act* of writing in relation to his being. Gnostic and mystical elements clearly varnished the discursive repertoire that oxidized his writing and enabled him to serve it to newer audiences and communities of interpretation. Subtly, his early loyalty and privileging of speech and memory were amended so that he began to valorize writing even as he occasionally oscillated between favoring speech and writing in turn.

This oscillation, but especially the explicit accent on writing, is evident in one of his last works on legal theory, *The Quintessence* (*Al-mustasfā*). This is a work that Ghazālī completed a few years before his death. Discussing the requisite qualifications a jurist must have in order to exercise juristic discretion (*ijtihād*), he catalogues the qualifications for a master jurist (*mujtahid*). Unlike his predecessors, who provided lists of almost impossible conditions and requirements, Ghazālī lowered the bar of qualifications for *ijtihād*. Striking, though, is the fact that he did so by calling into question the importance of memory. Prior to Ghazālī, the juridical tradition required an aspirant master jurist to memorize the entire Qur'ān and commit thousands of prophetic reports (*aḥādīth*) to memory, to have scrupulous knowledge of all the rules of grammar and rhetoric, and to be a walking encyclopedia of all the recorded instances of juristic consensus.

Astonishingly, Ghazālī made a case for writing almost against memory. The concessions he made regarding qualifications favored *writing* against *memorization*, while previously memory had been privileged over writing.[29] An aspirant jurist, Ghazālī argues, need not memorize the entire Qur'ān, nor even the legal verses of the Qur'ān, nor the *ḥadīth* reports dealing with law—

nor, for that matter, need aspirant jurists store in their memories recorded instances of existing juristic consensus or the rules of grammar. All an aspirant master jurist need do, Ghazālī argues, is demonstrate a familiarity with sources and a proficiency in their interpretation. Why could an aspirant master jurist dispense with memorization? According to Ghazālī, the written source materials were sufficiently authoritative and reliable.

What caused this fundamental shift in Ghazālī's attitude toward writing and, by implication, toward knowledge? A reflexive response is that it was an effect of ṣūfism on his identity. As the influence of ṣūfī cosmology gradually entered his discourse, several parallel ontological features became more manifest in Ghazālī's work, among them the notion of writing. Gradually, he ceased to consider writing as being exclusively about establishing rhetorical and doxological truth. In his ṣūfī persona, writing became an act that also had to do with transforming the condition of the heart and the soul. Subduing the lower self by means of "self struggle" (*mujāhada*) is essential for the one seeking divine truth who hopes to experience personal enlightenment. Reasonable success in self-struggle invariably produces a change in the aesthetics of the subject that in turn becomes manifest in practical and intellectual indexes.

Ultimately, it was aesthetics that inspired Ghazālī to almost intuitively avoid "doxological or ideological dialectics" (*mujādala*), a discourse that he in the end deemed to be extremely harmful and obstructive to true enlightenment.[30] Here, I should stress that the gradual and noticeable shifts from speech to writing in Ghazālī's discursive preferences were neither incidental nor accidental to his project of reform of the self. The shift to writing in a dialogical mode signifies a transmutation in Ghazālī's self that reflected the confluence of the cosmological and discursive skeins as they threaded the ambivalence of the threshold, or portal (*dihlīz*), of his self. It is in that *dihlīz* of the self where aesthetics and ethics intermingle in the alchemy of writing.[31] Their productive tensions energized and illuminated his work by means of the addition of heady mixtures of ideas and artifacts. Ghazālī introduced these mixtures knowingly, while his critics remorselessly charged him with irresponsibly mixing multiple discourses. Unapologetically, Ghazālī carried philosophical propositions into theology and mystical insights into the arcane practices of law. He did so because he was aware of his own deconstructive move: he effortlessly moved from the semiotic in his concerns for aesthetics to the somatic, giving priority to the body of the subject, and then went on to demonstrate the pervasive interchangeability of the semiotic and the somatic.

Poetics of the Pen

Among the figurative expressions that recur frequently in Ghazālī's repertoire is the "pen" (*qalam*). He used this trope to elucidate the three phases of spiritual elevation. The highest and ideal phase in mysticism is self-disclosure, when the symbolic meanings of the angelic universe (*ʿālam al-malakūt*) are disclosed to the person on the mystical, or gnostic, path. One sign that the seeker has reached the summit of this path occurs when the mystic gives witness to the "pen." It is a pen unlike other pens that, in Ghazālī's words, writes on the "tablet of the heart" (*lawḥ al-qalb*).[32]

In *Resuscitation*, the phrase "writing on the heart" occurs several times. Since Ghazālī used the word "heart" interchangeably with the word "soul" (*rūḥ*), my neologisms "soul-writing" and "heart-writing" attempt to mirror the tropes Ghazālī used to convey the idea that the subject is open to self-transformation.[33] So the idea of writing invoked here is one that transforms the mode of existence (ontology) of the writer and exposes one to the plenitude and openness of certainty (*yaqīn*). Ghazālī did not mean certainty in the closed sense of cognitive certainty but rather an inner certainty that enables one to actively defy reason and to "walk on water."[34]

Ghazālī's sense of ontic writing thus came to constitute the opposing pendant to his understanding of the primacy of speech. As he retreated from the idea that writing is merely a continuation of speech, ontic writing began to disrupt the opposition he perceived between writing and speech. Figurative, or ontic, writing appeared to him to be a truer form of writing, a writing that inhabits speech itself. Characteristic of this form of writing is that it is a dialogue with the Other. The Other has several referents: the self-present truth, a dialogue with the self, and a writing with the divine.

Ghazālī evoked the figurative understanding of writing with greater frequency in conjunction with images such as the pen, the angel of writing, and heart-writing. In doing this, he was suggesting that knowledge is no longer grounded in a solitary self-conscious and singularly self-knowing subject. Knowledge as a sense of reality (*ḥaqīqa*) is only produced when the self engages the divine being, the transgradient Other. Only then does the self reach higher levels of intuition and become exposed to esoteric insights of knowledge. Writing in this mode is conceived of as endless and boundless.

Heart-writing is a mimesis, a re-presentation of an "event" that marks a mutation in religious history, the revelation of the Qur'ān. It recalls the dramatic event of "unveiling" experienced by the Prophet Muḥammad in his encounter with the archangel Gabriel in his first instance of revelation in the cave of Ḥirā. In that specific event of revelation, the imagery of the pen is invoked. Ghazālī's fascinating meditation on the symbolic meaning of the pen in association with heart-writing makes the parallel between his writing and this revelation all the more uncanny. Just as the pen is a central metaphor to the first Muḥammadan revelation, it also subtly moves into Ghazālī's crucial idea of heart-writing. Heart-writing elevates the author who wields the pen in search of wisdom.

Ghazālī derived his insights from the chapter of "The Blood Clot" that reads as follows:

> Recite,
> in the name of your Lord
> who created—
> who created humankind
> from a clot of blood.
> Recite!
> For your Lord is most generous,
> who taught by the pen,
> who taught humankind what it did not know.[35]

This passage and others stress the combined significance of the pen and writing. Figuratively, the pen is the means by which the inscription of knowledge is imprinted on the hearts of humans.[36] Ibn ʿAbbās, a distinguished companion of the Prophet, said: "The first thing God created was the pen. Then he took it in His right hand, and both His hands are right [hands]. Then he created the [Arabic] letter *nūn*, which is the inkpot, and then He [created] the tablet/slate and then wrote on it. Then He created the heavens and wrote what will be in the world from then on until the Hour of Judgment in terms of creation that will be created, deeds that will be done, good and bad, and all sustenance, permitted and prohibited, wet or dry."[37] In Ghazālī's cosmology, both symbols—the pen and writing—signified empowering knowledge premised on the dialogical encounters between the self and its multiple Others.[38]

Writing Heterology

There is another subversive dimension to heart-writing beyond its ability to bridge the gap between the subject and alterity. Heart-writing, or dialogical writing, in essence challenges the self-mediated certainty and pretense of memory-writing to know all the answers at the level of exterior reality. Memory-writing, like all doxological writing, is a feature of writing on law, theology, and ethics. But when writing operates dialogically, as heart-writing does in reaching the Other, then writing also decenters the diseased certainty of cognition, a cognition that constantly seeks ideological closure. It is only when ideological certainty is destabilized that writing as semiotics can effectively occur in the heart and soul—when it issues an aesthetic theory announcing openness and expansion.

Changes in Ghazālī's sensibility of writing can be attributed to his agonizing self-discovery and the altered subjectivity produced as a consequence of his encounters with the heterogeneity of the bases of knowledge, including the bases of mysticism.[39] His subjectivity was altered for the simple reason that mysticism (*taṣawwuf*) in the Muslim tradition is the science of "otherness" (alterity); in short, it is a heterology par excellence.[40] He was moved and transformed by that which resists being named, classified, and organized, by the philosophical countertradition of mysticism. In it, he discovered a special knowledge known as the science of unveiling (*ʿilm al-mukāshafa*); to put it differently, it is a poetics of imagining. The attainment of such esoteric knowledge was for him the highest achievement.

Ghazālī repeatedly referred to esoteric knowledge as subtle and not always easily grasped or appreciated by persons who lack a predisposition for it. Even when he expressed reluctance to comment on such knowledge, he inevitably was unable to restrain himself. Mysticism is the counternarrative, or heterology, in several senses. Beginning with language, the sign in the mystical universe points neither to itself nor to its agent (the signifier) in an exclusive manner but rather to another sign (the signified). And although there is gravitation toward the Sign, signifying God, the complex interrelation between signifier and signified is flexible, infinite, and inexorably edges toward the nonreferential. In Ghazālī's view, almost counterintuitively, the heterological chain does not end with the Ultimate Other, or God, where it really ought to in terms of strict theological imperatives. The reason this chain of signifiers does not end at God is because, in his view, the Ultimate Other can only be ontologically experienced; it remains beyond epistemic grasp. The chain thus culminates in the Ghazālian *unknown* God, who is unknowable, beyond either naming or classification.

Similarly, the writing subject who is engaged in heart-writing yearns for a signature on his heart that inevitably refers to a transcendent and infinite being. In the case of this kind of writing subject, the terminology of the relational system might substitute other terms for the pen, the slate, and writing on the heart, but the relational system itself will not change; the search for a graspable and intelligible object, God, remains unsatisfied. Put differently, the desire to find an origin without alterity is never fulfilled nor consummated in the esoteric realm.

However, the search for the origin, the beginning (*awwal*), is only partially realized through the act of writing itself—through dialogical writing, or heart-writing, with the pen as symbol. The closest the subject comes to an origin is to simulate an origin without alterity, the solitary pen that teaches humans what they do not know. Thus, even in relation to God, counternarrative is a permanent, unconsummated epistemic condition. Mystical cosmology, however, does widen the horizon so that there can be productive inflections with a broad range of symbols, such as oneiric and poetic ones. Ghazālī, in his ascetic and mystical mode, realized that one may only attain unmediated "presence" in order to experience the truth by expanding one's discursive apparatus so that it includes the intelligibility of symbols. But, in the end, even Ghazālī had to concede that all linguistic reference to God must by necessity be viewed as a product of metaphoric expression and figurative expansion.[41] As Roberto Calasso would say, such metaphoric expression and figurative expansion is a metaphysical contrivance, but one that delivers our offerings to their destination.[42]

One of the overarching themes in *Rescuer* is Ghazālī's struggle to make sense of phenomena and experiences that go beyond the range of our usual instruments of perception. He speaks of the several stages that one can ascend on the mystical path. In the first stage, one has revelations and visions followed by intense contemplative-cum-visionary communiqués with angels and prophets. The next and higher stage in the mystical way, he admits, is "hard to describe in the domain of language." He reminds us that anyone who "attempts to express [*yuʿabbir*] these [experiences], his words will inevitably contain that which is erroneous, with no chance of taking precautions against it [error]."[43]

To articulate such complex experiences requires one to theoretically exit from language the way we understand it, for it is only in this extralinguistic realm that "what-you-want-to-say" does *not* exist in the first place.[44] In order to express what Ghazālī calls "hard-to-describe" experiences, one is bound to fall into the imperfect lap of language. In *Resuscitation*, Ghazālī acknowledged that it is, of course, language, imperfect as it is, that mediates our experiences and gives them meaning. But once inside language, and especially inside writing—and especially heart-writing—one has, of course, entered an arena where the presence of meaning is only a promise. It is a promise that is never fulfilled, thanks to the imperfection of language. Meaning, then, is only partially transmitted; it is always associated with a certain lack.

If we could have pressed Ghazālī, he would have been likely to concede that language fails to articulate fully the presence of the ineffable interior experience—that instead it induces an endless process of deferral of meaning. Partly, this has to do with the ontological character of language, but it is perhaps more effectively due to the inevitable and corrosive effects of heteroglossia. As a result of this continuous deferral of meaning, it is an elusive task to find the appropriate vocabulary to differentiate the precise relationship between the mystic and God.

In the history of mysticism, this conundrum has been extensively discussed. Several categories and terminologies have been devised to describe in words the shapeless divine-human bond and the consequent vertiginous experiences. Ghazālī, however, showed that the descriptors we use to explain the relationship between the mystic and the divine, such as incarnation (*ḥulūl*), identification (*ittiḥād*), or attainment (*wuṣūl*), are themselves all incomplete. Language fails to convey the true reality, since the mystical states it attempts to describe are beyond description and outside the realm of ordinary speech.[45] To make his point, he took refuge in literature and poetic imagination, citing a line of poetry from Ibn al-Muʿtazz (d. 296/908) as a subtle reminder that certain experiences are beyond articulation:

> What was, was; and of the things I do not remember
> Think well; but do not ask for a report![46]

Writing as Therapy

By the time Ghazālī set out to document how one animates the sciences of religion with a spirit of ethical piety, he had a very different appreciation of writing compared to that of his earlier phases. He had come to be able to envision his "self" *in relation to* the Other (in both its ultimate and non-ultimate forms) by abandoning his juvenile dualism of opposing writing to memory/speech. By the time he wrote *Resuscitation*, he preferred to alternate between the two modes. He had come to recognize that both modes—memory/speech and writing—are manifestations of a primal writing on the heart.

The famous mystic from Balkh, Jalāl al-Dīn Rūmī (d. 672/1273), tells us that in order to end any kind of duality, we need to approach self-annihilation.

The intensity of the heat generated by the genuine but futile search for the origin in order to end alterity will finally subsume the seeker.[47] More than a century after Ghazālī's death, Rūmī served almost as a ventriloquist for Ghazālī's irenic impulses, finding the appropriate register to explain the meaning of alterity. In duality, Rūmī declares, the self affirms its own existence, as in the saying "You are Lord, and I am the servant." At the heart of our articulation are words, concepts, and the sensible. But the world of mental images, Rūmī points out, is broader than the world of concepts and of the sensible. Nevertheless, the world in which mental images are infused with their given *being* is infinitely superior and surpasses all boundaries. Animating our relationship to words, Rūmī says that the culmination of the "reality of the substance is impossible to understand through verbal expression." He continues: "The usefulness of words is to cause you to seek and to excite you, but the object of your search will not be attained through words. . . . Words are like seeing something moving at a distance: you run toward it in order to see the thing itself, not in order to see it through its movement. Human rational speech is inwardly the same. It excites you to search for the concept, although you cannot see it in actuality."[48]

Ghazālī might have come to the same conclusion that Rūmī so eloquently expressed. Yet their respective responses to this realization encapsulate the essential difference between these two towering figures of Muslim civilization. Both recognized the chasm between mind and imagination on the one hand and the limits of words on the other. Rūmī left it to his readers to find the words, if they could, to articulate their experiences. However, the theologian, the jurist, the philosopher, and, most importantly, the writer in Ghazālī compelled him to yoke the imagination and the word together. The horse of the mind had to submit to the harness of the word, for otherwise, he feared, it would lose its way.[49]

The irony about Ghazālī, and what makes him such a critical figure in Muslim civilization, is precisely that he wrote so much despite his doubts about the limits of words to express profound ideas. With more than a hint of exaggeration, one can say that Ghazālī is actually the product of a massive writing, or an enormous text. Behind the tapestry of his writings is a restless Ghazālī with pen in hand, engaging in the greatest of all thefts (writing)—engaging in the subversive, in the Platonic sense of writing.

Like all great writers, Ghazālī also exhibited a remarkable symmetry between attempts made to characterize originality and attempts made to regularize, pattern, and schematize the conditions of human experience.[50] Ghazālī had the irrepressible habit of inserting originality together with regularity, making it hard to discern his intent. The question to which we must return is whether he saw writing as the absolute origin (*arche*) or as the end (*telos*) of all thinking; did he make the written text the source and site of originary meaning, or did writing still remain memory-writing?

The answer to this question depends on the significance that we attach to the noticeable shift Ghazālī made from at first privileging memory/voice over writing/scripting to considering dialogical writing to be more valuable than memory-writing. As I said before, he alternated between the two kinds of writing. The idea of writing for Ghazālī changed: he came to see an interplay between repetition and originality. Most importantly, he discovered an intertext between the doxological and the dialogical discursivities that are produced by the two kinds of writing. This intertext, among other aspects of his writing, makes Ghazālī a fascinating figure, for in his writings there is a perpetual revision, or subtle aggiornamento, of the senses, a trait that Muḥī al-Dīn Ibn ʿArabī would later forcefully perfect and turn into his own inimitable style.

However, what is mutinous in Ghazālī's thinking is the way his views on writing also shaped his understanding of knowledge. Just as Plato's king feared when he said that writing would be subversive and change our ways of knowing, Ghazālī continuously teased the boundaries of a closed discursive tradition through his writings. It may well be that to Ghazālī the authority of writing was always subject to a primordial molestation; therefore, the discursive tradition, in his view, was both flexible and capable of engendering new texts.[51]

What Ghazālī's writing strategies accomplished is much more subtle and difficult to tell. He partially disrupted the effects of logocentrism in Muslim thought and undermined the tyranny of the fiction of direct reference.[52] Although he did not dissolve binary and dyadic formulations in the construction of knowledge, he did resist attempts to disembody knowledge into abstractions and brought to the study of philosophy and theology the concrete sensibility of a jurist. To the extent that he urged us to think and imagine knowledge as existing in relationships with alterities, a feat that he accomplished well in parts of *Resuscitation*, Ghazālī did subtly challenge logocentric currents. But insofar as one can detect in his earlier writings on law, theology, and philosophy a form of doxological writing, he unmistakably advanced aspects of logocentrism. And, given his insistence on keeping separate what he viewed as the two languages of religious discourse—poetics and an ethics of imagination versus pragmatics and an ethics of responsibility—his logocentrism remained firmly in place.

However, the heterology of mysticism that he embraced goes against the grain of logocentrism and thus might dilute its impact. For when Ghazālī insisted that ethical and moral teachings be subject to the scrutiny of the aesthetics of imagination, he was actually suggesting that anti-logocentric discourse must exercise a degree of control over logocentric discourse. But it is risky to make unqualified statements about Ghazālī, since he often occupied the *dihlīz*, the intermediate space that connects to many narratives. Since he did not, in the latter part of his life, make a rigid distinction between memory and writing, and since he did not completely abandon logocentrism, there is both ambiguity and ambivalence in his writings, allowing for the rich interplay of *logos* and *mythos* without interpretive closure.

Writing and Ambiguity

Indeed, it is this dialectic of *logos* and *mythos* that produces a richly textured narrative at the heart of Ghazālī's durable legacy. In Ricoeur's formulation, narratives are models used for the redescription of the world.[53] Consequently, they also change endlessly, since the world is endlessly capable of being redescribed, which is another way of saying that narratives tenaciously cling to their secrets. The nature of parables, and of narrative in general, the literary critic Frank Kermode reminds us, is to be "open"—open to penetration by interpretation. Kermode makes this point eloquently and deserves to be cited at length:

> The capacity of narrative to submit to the desires of this or that mind without giving up secret potential may be crudely represented as a dialogue between story and interpretation. This dialogue begins when the author puts pen to paper and it continues through every reading that is not merely submissive. In this sense we can see without too much difficulty that all narrative, in the writing and the reading, has something in common with the continuous modification of the text that takes place in a psychoanalytical process (which may tempt us to relate secrets to the condensations and displacements of dreams) or in the distortions induced in historical narrative by metahistorical considerations.[54]

It is this unique capacity of narrative to be retold and simultaneously remain original that makes it possible that something can be stored, saved, and deferred. Meaning never becomes fully apparent; it always retains some of its secrets. But we must resist the temptation to label the new traces of meaning subversive, since some of these "distortions" are themselves the product of metahistorical considerations such as heterology, while others are the product of historical conditions such as heteroglossia.

Ghazālī's corpus cannot avoid both the corrosive and the constructive effects of metahistorical and historical conditions. In fact, within his lifetime, Ghazālī himself had to deal with a number of controversies he sparked with *Resuscitation*, which will be discussed later in this book. The controversies were serious enough that Ghazālī responded with his *Book of Dictation on the Obscurities of Resuscitation* (*Kitāb al-imlā' fī ishkāliyāt "al-Iḥyā'"*), which contained clarifications in an attempt to try to placate some of his critical readers. Such readers, he complains, did not grasp the spirit that animates ideas (*arwāḥ al-maʿānī*) and failed to comprehend the complex relationship between text, meaning, and their reception. In an advisory to his critics, he pleaded for them to show greater empathy for the subtle and delicate ideas he presented in writing, especially things about which he was restrained from being more explicit. He states:

> If you examine the writing of anyone who had gained distinction in knowledge, then do not do so with condescension, like one who outwardly appears to be self-sufficient [in knowledge] but inwardly is in great need of it. And do not stop where the author's text ends. For, surely, meanings are more expansive than their literal expressions, and the bosoms [hearts] are more capacious than compiled books, for there is much knowledge in what is not articulated. So aspire to grasp all the possible meanings of his writing with the perception of your heart. Then you will know his true worth, while his purpose will also become transparent. Do not give unequivocal approval nor judge it to be wrong. Instead, let the refinement of perception preoccupy you until those thoughts in which you had reached certainty purge those that are obscure.[55]

Surely, here he came close to losing patience with his critics. But he succumbed to persuasion and urged that one look at positive aspects of an author's writing, aspects that are implied and critically understood by the reader. Great aesthetic writing ultimately resists total understanding. This is a preferable attitude toward writing, he notes, than that of being "like a fly that lands on the dirtiest spot it can find!"[56] In all of Muslim religious literature, Ghazālī's advisory to his readers most unambiguously spells out what it means to undertake a close reading. Critical receptivity in reading is an unparalleled virtue, one that a reader must seek with responsibility.

Ghazālī might have recognized that writing, like Plato's *pharmakon*, which means both remedy and poison, is both the disease (*dā'*) and the remedy (*dawā'*).[57] In a discussion unrelated to writing, he paraphrases a report attributed to the Prophet, saying: "Indeed, the one who sent the disease also sent its remedy."[58] Both disease and remedy share a common lexicography in Arabic. They depend on the same root letters: *d-w-y*. The apparent and slight phonetic difference between *dā'* and *da(w)ā'* is caused by the mutation (*qalb*) of the word, a common occurrence in Arabic.[59] Words sharing common root letters may be different in their structures and can even have opposite meanings.[60] "Disease" and "remedy" are a case in point: they are closely related etymologically, yet they project opposite meanings if they are structured differently.

Writing, too, can be subject to dual use. Unusual and opposite effects of writing materialize depending on the location and objectives of the writing subject. The advent of Ghazālī's own inner transformation and the rebirth of his soul coincided with the most creative and exhausting form of writing that he undertook. "The writing of the book, the covering of the monstrous blank page," to borrow Kermode's felicitous phrase, which is almost tailor-made for Ghazālī or Ibn ʿArabī, "is a work of mystic arrogance."[61] Whether he was propelled by the kindest mystic arrogance or by sheer desire to engage in *iḥyā'*, which means "to give new life," "to animate," "to resuscitate," "to vitalize," "to renew life" and "to revivify"—all nuances of the central word used in the project and title designated *Iḥyā' ʿulūm al-dīn*, or *Resuscitation of the Sciences of Religion*—many agree that Ghazālī filled the blank page to produce an extraordinary piece of writing.

On the pages of *Resuscitation*, more than just the sciences become animated. Ghazālī's primary desire was to see his heart come alive, and the result is a book with admirably sensitive readings of the Muslim tradition with a *carnavalesque*, even festive, eclecticism toward its revered subject: the sciences of religion.[62] Its pages are everywhere redolent of the smell of incense, pointing to the pulses of life that must throb with maximum aesthetic and ethical efficiency before the patient can be "rescued" and returned to life. If we take Ghazālī at his word, then *Resuscitation* is perhaps best viewed as the site for the possibility of truth, as the site for its awakening, not for its slumber or closure—a location for imaginative interpretation and not just rephrasing and restatement. The imperative of interpretation keeps pace with the changing force of history. Otherwise, we may—as we more often than not do—realize that the sleep of imagination, to rephrase Francisco de Goya, does indeed produce monsters.

If we take Ghazālī's writing as the remedy against the diseased writing of the jurists and theologians of his day, whom he was convinced had not only perverted but also actually smothered the discursive sciences of religion, and if we view heart-writing as a replacement for persuasive speech and rhetoric, then we can indeed say that in "writing" the *Resuscitation* Ghazālī gave life to the dialogic of writing within the self, or, more plainly, that he was *writing* his "self." Any reader of *Resuscitation* would be hard-pressed not to notice an indescribable frisson that dances off the pages of this text, culminating in Ghazālī's expanded vision, metonymically expressed in the Qur'ān as the "expansion of the bosom" or heart (*sharḥ al-ṣadr*).[63] His own liberation, Ghazālī reminds us, occurred when God inserted light (*nūr*) into his bosom, a light that became the key for the disclosure of all esoteric knowledge.[64] This expanded pectoral space liberated his self from the closed environment of a complacent certitude. To read Ghazālī as a closed and total understanding is to do the unthinkable: to kill what can only stay alive by remaining in a permanent conversation, a continuous flux.

If, during his ascetic and mystical stage, Ghazālī viewed writing as an ally, he also viewed it as dangerous, if not irresponsible, to write about everything he experienced and pondered. Not every thought, he warned, has to be stated or written. Hence, he reproached mystics and philosophers for on occasion overstating their cases. It is clear from several statements in his texts that Ghazālī, despite his mastery of the pen, was reluctant to disclose certain thoughts and ideas. He preferred to hold back, to differentiate between the forums where things could be said and those places where one should defer from saying. In the *Resuscitation*, as well as in several of his other, smaller works, he displayed this hesitation and tentativeness.

For instance, when discussing the complex idea of divine unity (*tawḥīd*), which produces a state in which the true believer is capable of witnessing God as a singular unity but evidently sees the multiplicity of divine manifestations, Ghazālī was reluctant to comment beyond stating some basic precepts. His standard refrain was that the *Resuscitation* is a book dedicated to knowing the ethics of responsibility but that it is not a forum for esoteric visionary revelations; he added that the secrets of esoteric forms of knowledge are not of those things "that are *scribbled/written* in books."[65] Gnostics, he says, had warned that "Disclosing the secrets of the divinity is a form of infidelity."[66]

Ghazālī was always concerned that disclosure of visionary revelations might lead to the impenetrable frustration of obscurity (*ghumūdh*) and complexity. He harbored a pragmatic concern about the effects of such writing on both the psyche and the religiosity of laypeople. But there were times when even he found the temptation to say certain things irresistible and failed to hold back. Here, we see another example of how Ghazālī continuously frequented the *dihlīz*, the threshold position. For he posited certain arrangements only to realize that, intellectually, one cannot observe boundaries so carefully crafted.

Beloved are men's native lands
Passions only the heart can gratify, over there.
Longing for home, men tenderly recall,
Even the seasons of the east winds, over there.
—Ibn al-Rūmī, *Dīwān Ibn al-Rūmī*

4 Liminality and Exile

Intellectuals as Strangers

The cosmopolitan Indian scholar and philologist Murtaḍā al-Zabīdī (d. 1205/1791), author of an enormous commentary on Ghazālī's *Resuscitation*, records an incident that eloquently signals Ghazālī's deep and extraordinary sense of exile. During one of Ghazālī's visits to Baghdād, Zabīdī reports, he delivered some lectures from his summa, *Resuscitation*. At some point, he spontaneously recited the two stanzas of poetry in the epigraph above. Overcome by the emotions of his own sense of exile in all its different guises, Ghazālī broke down. So intense was his sense of pathos, nostalgia, and longing that his pain also overwhelmed many members of his audience.

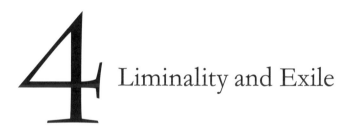

Exile is usually thought of in terms of physical separation, but the term can also mean the capacity of the self to distance itself from the trappings of the world. In distancing oneself from such creaturely dependencies, one may have to forego the pleasures of home, family, and one's intimate knowledge of the breezes of the seasons and instead suffer the pain of distance and alienation. One notion of exile Ghazālī articulated is the idea of consciously placing on hold or banishing into exile our sentiments, namely, our desires and passions. He had a simple rationale: absence and renunciation only enhance the desire for an object denied. When the lover reunites with the beloved, be it an earthly beloved or a sublime one, then the reunion takes place with heightened intensity and enjoyment.

Self-exile, or self-banishment, was truly a characteristic feature of Ghazālī's life. Self-exile means voluntarily taking a position that is not always the beaten track. But "exile" can also be thought of in another sense: it can mean taking a position that brings one into the center of several tensions that lead to a certain amount of estrangement, described as the position of a *gharīb*—in the best sense of the word, a "stranger." Despite his commitment to the mainstream, Ghazālī often found himself at the center of conflicting viewpoints that positioned him to experience what it is to be both an insider and an outsider at the same time.

He was a jurist, but a jurist with a difference; a mystic, but one who fastidiously adhered to the juristic requirements of normative practice. Theology came to him almost intuitively, as did philosophy; yet no one can reduce his identity to being exclusively a theologian or a philosopher. He inhabited the in-between space, or passage (*dihlīz*), between disciplines. In doing so, he did not always meet the criteria to be counted among the philosophers and was often scowled at by more crotchety theologians. Monasticism is not a creedal statement that he adopted, but he did elect isolation and a hermetic life for long spells.

All Ghazālī's minor self-exiles are framed by one rather spectacular and dramatic self-exile, one that occurred after a four-year spell of staggering intellectual production in Baghdād. Around 488/1095, Ghazālī chose exile and departed Baghdād, "the city of peace," ostensibly for pilgrimage but actually for undisclosed destinations. His single purpose was to discover true virtue and rid himself of his inner doubts and moral indifference.

The moralist and poet-philosopher Abū al-ʿAlā' al-Maʿarrī might have said that solitude and inner contentment provides the greatest peace, not the protective walls of a medieval metropolitan city.[1] Ghazālī realized, in the words of Maʿarrī, that "separation from men is a convalescence from their malady, inasmuch as association with them is a disease which infects [both] conscience and religion."[2] Escaping from his professorship and college life was perhaps the most explicit statement—or ritual act—that Ghazālī made to announce the beginning of his passage toward forming another identity. Of course, as a scholar of repute and standing, it was unusual for him to radically separate from society. However, as a mystic, it was not an abnormal activity to undertake penitential ordeals in search of self-purification. Among the most well-known mystical figures who clocked Wanderjahre were Manṣūr al-Ḥallāj and Abū Yazīd al-Bisṭāmī.

Anxiety and the (Im)Possibility of Decision

When Ghazālī faced the paralyzing crisis of his life, prevaricating as to whether he should leave Baghdād, it was also a critical juncture in the development of his self. His first dilemma was whether to end his term as a professor, a role for which he had acquired great renown. He agonized as to how others would view his decision to abandon this position. After all, the dissemination of knowledge as a teacher was one of the highest ethical duties that a Muslim scholar could perform. So before leaving Baghdād, he tried to reduce the excessive amount of stimuli accumulating in his mind and tugging at his ego, to diminish what Freud would call the "pleasure principle," the stimuli in a cognizant self.[3]

Another dilemma Ghazālī faced was his incurable desire to retreat into the world of asceticism and to live in isolation. This would mean abandoning all glory, fame, and engagement with society in search of the truth. He set his sights on the everlasting and eternal future that is promised for the truly devout in the eschatological realm and is known as the hereafter. When the ego, or self, is educated and disciplined with reason in order to understand that the temporary denial of pleasure can result in something more long lasting and permanent, then the self is governed by what Freud calls the "reality principle." While the reality principle is also intent on obtaining pleasure, it is a way of instructing the ego to accept the fact that the pleasure in question can be either postponed or diminished.

Ghazālī believed that it was important to discipline his self to understand that true pleasure is associated with the world to come (*ākhira*) and not with the material world. The *ākhira*, the eschatological future, was for Ghazālī the *real* world, a domain of ultimate truth (*ḥaqīqa*). Having made his decision, Ghazālī chose to live in isolation, to adopt the life of an ascetic as far as possible from the penetrating eyes of the material world. Yet, as he later reflected, the decision to leave Baghdād was not made by his own volition; it was made for him by a higher power.

Acting on his decreed choice, Ghazālī responded to the reality principle, the impulse to postpone true pleasure to the afterworld. Whether the pleasure in the afterworld is corporeal or figurative remains a subject of debate; Ghazālī seemed to favor a corporeal afterlife, since he affirmed the progressive and forward development of the ego. He also realized that yielding to an "other-worldly" reality principle can provide dividends in this material world. It opened him up to new experiences of esoteric realities by enabling him to understand his self through the multiple refractions of the imagination, with its symbolic, oneiric, and poetic aspects. In search of the ultimate reality or sense of reality (*ḥaqīqa*) as the desideratum of mysticism, Ghazālī embraced the life of constant meditation, seclusion, repetitive remembrance (*dhikr*) of the divine, and self-purification. In so doing, he reached out to the future with hope (*rajā'*).

Ghazālī realized that the objects of his desire and ultimate pleasure required that he subject himself to the Other, namely, God, by submitting to the discipline of the ṣūfī path. He acknowledged that although he had acquired all the theoretical knowledge about mysticism, he lacked the experiential dimension. His failure to experience the esoteric realities meant that he was unable to successfully encounter the divine. At this stage, as well as at other moments in his intense engagement with ṣūfism, Ghazālī experienced both subjection and alienation. Subjection and alienation are two perspectives of mystical experience. On the one hand, his engagement with ṣūfism placed him in an intense relationship as a "subject" of the divine Other. On the other hand, in terms of the criteria held by his adversaries, especially among the jurist-theologians such as Ibn al-Jawzī, he had strayed from the divine Other, at least according to their moral and ethical portrayal of the divine will through law. If one compares this view to Ghazālī's own theological pronouncements, there is little doubt that his discourses show signs of vacillation and subjectivity, reflecting the undulating pendulum in his psychology and being, but consistent with his overarching commitment to experience.

The location of Ghazālī, his in between-ness, his occupation of the intersection of many paths—the *dihlīz*—was also his strength: it permitted him to function within several discursive traditions. It did not prevent him from writing on legal theory or from producing allegorical writings like *The Niche of Lights* and *The Alchemy of Happiness* (*Kīmyā' al-saʿāda*). Some of the narratives found in the *Resuscitation* and the *Niche* have kept scholars debating endlessly about the nature and turn in Ghazālī's intellectual project. For others, his forays into Neoplatonic thought were puzzling. Many wonder whether it might not have been judicious on his part to keep silent about highly esoteric matters. Nevertheless, in all this, Ghazālī maintained a delicate balance between intellectual sobriety and mystical esoterism.

One can possibly attribute Ghazālī's sobriety to the fact that he was thoroughly grounded in the study of theology, dogma, and law, a formative orientation that prevented him from fully surrendering to whatever intoxicating thoughts he may have contemplated. Almost childlike, he left behind the sober world of dogma and law in pursuit of the reality principle, entering into the symbolic order of language, a journey that inflamed his ambition to attain spiritual distinction. If the journey into the symbolic universe replenished his fatigued soul, then this spiritual energy reciprocally stimulated his imagination and mind. However, in order to articulate the world of symbols, he still required language to mediate his thoughts. Since language itself is imposed from outside, it had an alienating effect on him. Unfortunately, the prison-house of language is inescapable, and submission to its code a prerequisite. Once one's identity is molded in the limitations of language, then the terrain of identity has to be constantly replowed in order to accommodate new foliage. It is therefore not surprising to see Ghazālī subtly and constantly reformulate issues: he twisted and turned the register of language in order to excavate meanings that could express his experiences. And so Ghazālī's dilemma continued as a religious subject, for the tensions of this world versus the other world, the dynamic between the imperatives of the pleasure principle versus those of the reality principle, endlessly played out in the antinomies of his identity.

There is a dialogical relationship between what Ghazālī deemed a world of pleasure and finitude on the one hand and a world of ultimate reality on the other. The world of pleasure requires continuous supplementing by the real—enrichment by means of the counterfactual imagination. The real not only supplements the finite world of pleasures but at times also contradicts it. This tension between pleasure and the real, or between realities and ideals, played out through the process of construction and reconstruction of Ghazālī's thoughts in the various stages of his life. Reconstruction, while necessary, is also fraught with dangers that must be carefully considered and adequately legitimated.

In much of Ghazālī's writings, especially those that deal with ethics and mysticism, one sees a reconstructionist at work. For he was explicit in stating that his project was about resuscitating the discursive corpse of religion. So, as he furiously engaged the status quo during different stages of his life, he simultaneously furnished a critique of the existing conditions, insofar as the purposes of the ultimate contradict the world of pleasures. Therefore, reconstruction is not only based on validating the status quo; it is also designed to critique existing conditions.

Pilgrimage and Liminality

Perhaps Ghazālī took a leaf from the life of Abraham (Ibrāhīm), the prophet, whom he frequently invoked. Abraham also went into temporary exile, though he went to a deserted part of Arabia with his son Ishmael (Ismāʿīl) and his slave wife, Hagar (Hājar), where, according to tradition, he was instructed to abandon his offspring and spouse for some time. Abraham was compelled to do this by God in order to break his love for his progeny. Ghazālī, similarly, sought exile in order to break his love for his self, which was manifested in vainglory and scholarly hubris. In the Islamic tradition, it is Abraham who is the exemplar of pilgrimage to Makka. One of the ritual goals of pilgrimage is to place the subject in a temporary state of liminality, away from the everyday rhythms and normality of life, in order to experience an abnormal state during which rehabilitation and healing take place. And so the irony should not be lost on us that, just as Abraham bequeathed the ritual of liminality to Islam, Ghazālī took liminality seriously and left Baghdād under the pretext of fulfilling the ritual of pilgrimage to Makka but then chose to extend his liminal journey for a longer period and into other cities of religious and spiritual significance.

Anthropologists have observed that in the major religious traditions pilgrimage is the functional equivalent of a ritual of passage as well as part of a set of rituals of affliction.[4] In preliterate small-scale societies, but also in cultures where pilgrimage systems are strongly developed, people often undertake a penitential journey to some shrine or sacred space in order to cure illness; to find relief for the difficulties of their bodies, minds, and souls by miraculous power; or even simply to cultivate better morale.[5] Ghazālī's own experience could not have been very different from those of other people engaged with such established pilgrimage patterns. His was an unusually dramatic and celebrated pilgrimage, however, and it was fraught with social consequences.

Instead of undertaking the obligatory pilgrimage (*ḥajj*) to Makka, Ghazālī spent much of his time in solitary meditation in and around Damascus and Jerusalem, both sites of nonobligatory pilgrimage in Islam. In order to leave Baghdād, he realized that he needed a convincing pretext, and so, he recounts: "I announced that I had resolved to leave for Makka, all the while planning secretly to travel to Syria. . . . Then I entered Damascus and resided there for nearly two years. My only occupation was spiritual exercise and combat, with a view to devoting myself to the purification of my soul and the cultivation of virtues. . . . Then I traveled from Damascus to Jerusalem, where I would go daily into the Dome of the Rock and shut myself in. Then I was inwardly moved by an urge to perform the duty of pilgrimage. . . . So I traveled to the Ḥijāz [Arabian Peninsula]."[6] Locales of the great spiritual traditions of the Jewish prophets and saintly figures equally revered by Islam became the sacred geography for Ghazālī's mystical quest.

It is possible to think of Ghazālī's exodus from Baghdād as an "event"—an act that transformed him and the equally transformative legacy he left behind. To view it as such is also to observe his capacity to transgress, to break out of boundaries, and to embrace innovative ideas and practices. If one views the entire period of Ghazālī's spiritual isolation as one long, drawn-out liminal period, then he underwent an almost formulaic transition, which included all the rituals of making the passage from one state of being to another.

In my view, his rite of passage neatly coincides with the three-part sequence experienced by the ritual subject that anthropologist Victor Turner has identified, namely, separation, transition, and incorporation. In fact, the social and personal drama of Ghazālī is almost tailor-made to fit the *rites de passage* theories associated with an individual's life crisis. Demarcating sacred time from secular time and sacred space from secular space, the first phase of Ghazālī's ritual transformation was clearly his separation from routinized life in a big city. Separation changed the quality of his time as he began a life of renunciation that required extensive self-reflection and meditation. It was this qualitative change in *time* that was effective in transforming Ghazālī's social status from scholar to ascetic (*zāhid*).

In an inquiry into language, symbol, and experience, the political philosopher Eric Voegelin notes that we humans have discrete relationships with the cosmos.[7] There are at least two types of human relations to the cosmos. At one level, the relationship to the cosmos is expressed in the language of mythical tale, while at a second level it derives from a heightened perception and experience of existential tension. It is particularly at such moments of perception that cosmic temporality is polarized into *time* and the *timeless*. This experience of time, in turn, is expressed and coded into the language of noetic and spiritual life.

We can see that Ghazālī experienced something similar to this if we follow the way he structured his narrative account of the self and the manner in which time framed his enhanced consciousness. Not only did he detach himself from familiar surroundings, family ties, and other mundane things, but he also shared with us in his testimony that the period of exile was the most fecund of all times for exposing him to unprecedented spiritual experiences; the latter brought home to him a profound awareness of the timeless aspects of his life and beyond, especially of issues related salvation in the afterlife.

Between the stages of separation and incorporation, Turner tells us, is the most crucial of all stages: the liminal, or intermediate, phase. The ritual subject passes through a period of ambiguity and social limbo that does not have any specific time. During this stage, the subject possesses few of the attributes of the preceding or subsequent profane cultural states except for the continuous noetic intuitions and the wonders of the spiritual life.

The period between 488/1095 and his return to Ṭūs in 493/1099–1100 or shortly thereafter can be described as Ghazālī's extended liminal phase. It was during this phase that, in all likelihood, he began writing the bulk of his opus, *Resuscitation of the Sciences of Religion*. Some scholars view this as an unconventional writing but at the same time appreciate it as a prized piece of religious literature with inexhaustible possibilities as a model for the narrative of religion. The work clearly coincides with Ghazālī's increased awareness of what may be called his gratifyingly complex *mundus imaginalis*, the imaginary universe that is strongly connected to a sense of the timeless.

Not only did allegorical realities of divine revelation unfold to him through intuitions with great clarity, as he stated, but the work also represents the fulcrum of his spiritual and imaginative productions. *Resuscitation* is a writing by an author who envisioned himself to be part of a sequence of epic performances and dramatic episodes, one who was transformed into a stronger personality and who assumed that he was destined for important responsibilities as the "renewer" (*mujaddid*) of the faith at the beginning of the sixth Islamic century. At one level, Ghazālī was a man of the sixth/eleventh century. From another perspective, his increased noetic intuitions did not simply heighten his sense of his individuality but also enabled him to enter a zone of timelessness. The tension between time and the timeless, ethics and cosmology, became so acute that it at times expressed itself in paradoxes, in the appearance of antinomianism and transgression.

Some of Ghazālī's utterances and writings reflect what the Scandinavian thinker Søren Kierkegaard more than seven hundred years later encapsulated in his famous phrase "the teleological suspension of the ethical."[8] This comparison may surprise some, but in terms of their respective quests the two scholars were not so different. The European thinker's exemplary struggles with faith caused him to agonizingly reflect whether "faith is precisely this paradox, that the individual is higher than the universal."[9] Ghazālī too suffered for a long time and struggled with a similar set of questions: Where and how does the person of faith fit in relation to the community of faith and the rest of the world? Is the individual quest for the truth a higher obligation than the truth claimed by the community and society? And what happens when these two sets of interests clash? Which of the two prevails?

Liminality of Ethics

Some of Ghazālī's actions during his personal crisis elicited strong criticism from religious authorities and scholars. He stood accused of not only suspending or ignoring some of the rules of religion but, ironically, of enthusiastically undertaking new spiritual experiments in total disregard for the well-defined boundaries of the law. In other words, there are signs that Ghazālī may have cultivated a hermeneutic of transgression when his concerns for the cosmological and metaphysical domain predominated or came into conflict with the imperatives of ethics.

No less an authority than the sometimes involuntarily zealous Ḥanbalī moralist and chronicler ʿAbd al-Raḥmān Ibn al-Jawzī focused on these uncomfortable aspects of Ghazālī's views and practices. Ibn al-Jawzī sharply criticized Ghazālī for antinomianism and charged him with "abandoning the standard of law" (*taraka fīhī qanūn al-fiqh*) in several instances.[10] Ibn al-Jawzī was a persistent critic. In his undisguised thunderbolts, he audaciously insinuated that Ghazālī had taken leave of his senses. Commenting on Ghazālī's view that there is no legal prohibition on listening to music (*samāʿ*) for purposes of spiritual elevation, Ibn al-Jawzī not only disagreed with Ghazālī, as many others did, but was brusque with him: "Abū Ḥāmid al-Ṭūsī supports [those who approve of music] with such arguments [as if] he has rejected the status of common sense."[11]

But Ibn al-Jawzī's indignation turned into shrill protest when he considered Ghazālī's remedy for certain spiritual diseases of the heart. In his advocacy of certain techniques whereby ṣūfī novices might remedy flaws in their characters, Ghazālī flirted with some real controversy. He proposed exceptional spiritual remedies for those who suffered from an overdose of arrogance bred by narcissism, the haughtiness of self-prestige, and egotism (*jāh*). In the *Resuscitation*, Ghazālī described the practices adopted by a ṣūfī group known as the "Blamers," or Malāmatīs, whose members went to extraordinary lengths to perpetually blame themselves for their shortcomings, even embracing punishing ordeals in order to perfect their sincerity (*ikhlāṣ*).[12] "[They] nominally embrace sins in order to despise themselves in the eyes of people," Ghazālī notes, "but in fact they try to rid themselves of the scourge of egotism [*jāh*]."[13]

There was a theatrical aspect to the practices of this group. When their actions finally elicited the condemnation of people frustrated by their antics, it was exactly the response they expected. They perversely reveled in the words of repudiation uttered against them and believed that such humiliation would contribute to the breakdown of their egos. The goal of the Malāmatī ṣūfīs was to forget their past solidarities with humans and they only desired to experience the omnipotent representation of the divine.

Some of the Blamers, Ghazālī informs us, intentionally drank nonalcoholic beverages that looked like wine so that onlookers would condemn them as fallen and sinful individuals due to Islam's taboo against intoxicating beverages.[14] Referring to this unusual practice, Ghazālī candidly points out that "from the point of view of the law [*fiqh*], of course, there is disagreement as to its permissibility," but he then almost apologetically adds that "the mystics treat their souls with means that a jurist would not sanction [*lā yuftī bi hi al-faqīh*], no matter how much healing to their souls they [the ṣūfīs] saw [in such practices]."[15]

If Ghazālī had unambiguously distanced himself from the Blamers, then the response of his critics might have been different. But in his own comments on these practices, he walked a tightrope. On the one hand, he dispassionately identified the legal and ethical limits beyond which certain practices cannot be tolerated. At the same time, he offered an empathetic clarification to state how different the rationales of the jurists were from those of Blamer ṣūfīs for pursuing such practices. But if anything turned his Ḥanbalī critic Ibn al-Jawzī apoplectic, it was Ghazālī's unspoken endorsement of the idiosyncratic practices of an ascetic whom Murtaḍā al-Zabīdī identifies as Abū Jaʿfar Ibn al-Kuraytī al-Baghdādī, one of the masters of the famous mystic Abū al-Qāsim b. Muḥammad al-Junayd (d. 298/910).[16]

It is alleged that Ibn al-Kuraytī's piety brought him so much acclaim and fame among the multitude that he was repeatedly mobbed by admirers.[17] Such excessive adulation and publicity harmed him spiritually, since the status (*jāh*) he enjoyed in the eyes of people inflated his ego and sense of self-importance.[18] In a bid to defeat the hostile enmity of Satan in his soul, Ibn al-Kuraytī devised a strategy. He orchestrated a plan to commit certain reprehensible and forbidden acts in order to invite public odium and in the process suffer the humiliation of being apprehended; all this, he believed, would aid his pursuit of pious ends. Setting aside the relationship between torture and mysticism, which is too complex to be discussed here, it is clear that the desire on the part of Ibn al-Kuraytī to undergo this penitential ordeal was unstoppable. So he entered a public bath incognito and purposefully put on clothes belonging to other patrons, an act that would unmistakably be perceived as theft. He then slowly and purposefully walked out of the bathhouse wearing the illegally acquired clothes in order that he might be detected and apprehended by the patrons. When the alarmed patrons of the bathhouse discovered that their clothes were missing, they apprehended the anonymous "thief." As outraged owners of property are inclined to do, they assaulted, humiliated, and stigmatized Ibn al-Kuraytī as a rogue and scoundrel (*ṭarrār*), blissfully unaware of his identity as a pious man.[19] In his view, however, the exercise had achieved its goal. He delighted in the display of divine omnipotence on his body as his ego was systematically eroded by the self-inflicted torture.

Ghazālī offered careful commentary on this orchestrated practice of inviting humiliation, introducing several caveats. While he lauded the purpose behind the practice of self-odium as a unique way of disciplining the self, he expressed doubts about its legal validity. People in leadership positions who serve as role models for others, he observes, are not permitted to engage even in acts that simply appear to be sinful practices.[20] Therefore, he explicitly states that laypersons in search of punitive ordeals should only choose permissible practices, as it is forbidden to transgress the law. Despite his cautionary advice, any impartial reader of this passage is left with the impression that Ghazālī approvingly cited the vignette about Ibn al-Kuraytī, and by doing so he invited controversy.

The celebration of humiliation is a tropism; it offers a self-inflicted response to negative spiritual stimuli. The idea is to put the subject (the mystic) through an ordeal involving subversion in order that he or she will desire the good as a remedy. This line of thinking is not without precedent. Even the stern but brilliant Andalusian jurist Ibn Ḥazm, notorious for his intolerance of people who have weak spots in their mental fences, endorsed a moderate form of subversive thinking in ethics. He cited a report attributed to the companion Abū al-Dardā' that states: "Unwind the spirits with a modicum of distraction [*bāṭil*, literally "falsehood"] so that they may aid you in the search for truth [*ḥaqq*]."[21] Here, one is reminded of the work of two nineteenth-century Frenchmen, the poet Charles Baudelaire and the novelist Gustave Flaubert.

Both forcefully remind us in their respective literary work that the aesthetic expression of evil also implies the keenest appetite for the good, the highest possible moral goal.[22] One may wonder if Ghazālī also imagined that by stimulating something evil one actually invites the desire to do what is morally good.

By now, Ibn al-Jawzī's response should be predictable. He was scandalized by the mere suggestion that ṣūfī novices could contemplate such offensive practices as he suspected Ghazālī of condoning. That Ghazālī entertained such themes in his book only underscored Ibn al-Jawzī's conviction that Ghazālī had at times flirted with an intolerable level of antinomianism. Ghazālī's apparent declaration of his loyalties on this matter was, for Ibn al-Jawzī, a clear sign that Ghazālī had been "excluded from the circle of law [*fiqh*]" by a higher power.[23] In his righteous indignation, Ibn al-Jawzī viewed such exclusion as a good omen; the implicit endorsement of Ibn al-Kuraytī's actions discredited Ghazālī, and Ibn al-Jawzī was confident that a negative reputation would protect the practice of law from Ghazālī's perverse suggestions.

Taking clothes from the public baths, Ibn al-Jawzī continues, is nothing short of theft. And, according to at least two founders of the traditional law schools—the leading third-/ninth-century jurist Muḥammad Ibn Idrīs al-Shāfiʿī (d. 204/820) and his contemporary Aḥmad Ibn Ḥanbal—such an offender is liable to amputation for such a crime, irrespective of his intent. Describing Ghazālī's apparent sympathy for Ibn al-Kuraytī's actions and his other views as "utterly detestable" (*fī ghāya al-qubḥ*), Ibn al-Jawzī relentlessly cataloged what he believed to be Ghazālī's other misdemeanors in several of his writings.[24] Not even Ghazālī's later clarifications helped to mitigate his case in the court of Ibn al-Jawzī and other critics.

Now it may well be that Ghazālī's fatigue with the profane life of an academic jurist, coupled with his belief that law fails to deliver the truth, prompted him to seek these fleeting adventures with antinomianism during his drawn-out and transitory liminal phase. Through a variety of experiences and an exacting pilgrimage of the self, he gradually transformed himself into a ṣūfī with a new mission, redefining his own position in society. During his transitional stage, Ghazālī came to view things that he once saw as clear-cut in a different light—more tentative and opaque, as his comments on the Blamer ṣūfīs illustrate. It has been observed that during liminal phases ritual subjects tend to invert their previous social status in search of a new one. Could Ghazālī have sought a new social status during his liminal phase? It is a fair question, since there was an unmistakable desire on his part to abandon his role as a scholar-jurist. We know, for instance, that there was a period when he refused to be called a jurist (*faqīh*), during which he castigated jurists and came close to labeling law (*fiqh*) as practiced in his day a vulgarity. In fact, he described law as "a mere science of this world."[25]

There may, after all, have been a point to Ghazālī's attempted subversion of the law. There was something both subversive and playful in his explanation of the controversial events, which he implicitly endorsed by including them in his corpus. His narrative strategy decentered and isolated some powerful multivocal symbols and characters. For instance, he implicitly or explicitly distinguished between the good person and the bad person, the ṣūfī and the jurist, intentionality and its absence. By both decentering and creating axiological binaries, Ghazālī generated a set of relations between things. Thus, he distinguished between a fact or a statement in the corpus of the law and a speech act as it relates to the body of the mystic, as in the example of Ibn al-Kuraytī; he was then in a position to relate the two dimensions in a nuanced tension, a move that frustrated the intensely logocentric interpreters, among them Ibn al-Jawzī and Ibn Taymīya.

Ghazālī demonstrates that in making a moral judgment it is not only important to know the facts but also to know *how* the facts are made and what motivations enliven them. Then, the moral action alone is not the sole warrant for a judgment, but something else is, namely, intention and purpose. Once an element that sublimates the moral discourse, such as intention or purpose, enters into the equation, it takes off the hard edges of absolute moral judgment in which one must choose between good and bad, right and wrong. Moral judgment becomes humanized. Then the question can legitimately be raised: Is the person who ostensibly steals clothes from the public baths in order to humiliate himself really a thief in the true sense of the word? Has he really broken the law? Stealing clothes is surely a crime, but does Ghazālī's coding of this narrative not urge us to ask *why* he is stealing?

Permission or prohibition in the eyes of the revealed law, *sharīʿa*, is usually presented as a fairly clear-cut matter. But Ghazālī smuggles in the question of intent and purpose: *Why* does a person commit a particular act, and *who* sits in judgment over such acts? Was Ghazālī subtly decentering the status of the law? Was he trying to liberate Muslim discourse from a suffocating juridical ethos that only produced a law with a stifling hand? And in doing so, does he not force us to ponder this issue more critically?

Writing Heterology

The story about stealing clothes in the bathhouse resonates with the dilemmas and paradoxes experienced by the prophet Abraham, who was commanded to sacrifice his son. Each story in its respective way points to that paradox of faith, namely, an inwardness of faith that is incommensurate with its outwardness—an exterior of faith not identical with its interior. Strikingly, two languages are operative, corresponding to the two aspects of the paradox: the language of the law (*fiqh/sharīʿa*), or the discourse of outward conduct, which represents the logocentric axis; and the language of esoterism, that of reality-seeking or sense of reality (*ḥaqīqa*) of the inner self, which represents an anti-logocentric axis, or the heterological polarity of faith.

Even as Ghazālī became fully aware of the incommensurability of the two narratives, he attempted to bridge the distance between them. On several occasions, he permitted the individual to attain the higher end, even if it meant that the universal rule of the law would be broken (or seemingly broken). Ideally, in Ghazālī's view, qualities of inner certainty and faith determine the relation of the individual to the law and ethics. This perspective is contrary to the views held not only by Ibn al-Jawzī but also by modern philosophers like Immanuel Kant. For the Ḥanbalī moralist and the German moral philosopher alike, it is law and ethics that determine the content and nature of faith. Ghazālī, to the contrary, requires the dialogical encounter of the letter and the spirit. It is an encounter where the borders and intersections are never easily identifiable or verifiable but always present, always in need of being experienced anew.

Subtly, Ghazālī posed the question as follows: Are the loathsome, boneheaded jurists, who only understand the law as written dicta, going to judge the acts of those whose superior spiritual aims and morality are beyond their ken? Should one not in these instances defer to those virtuous jurists who have developed a sensibility to fathom the purposes of the law? The virtuous would be in a better position to understand that the need to remedy the malignancy of the soul takes priority over the prohibition against simulating the consumption of alcoholic beverages. When one stumbles into such streaks of relativity in Ghazālī's texts, it leaves one breathless to note with what vehemence he simultaneously appealed to the principle that the exoteric rules of the *sharīʿa* must be properly applied before one plumbs its depths to grasp the esoteric meanings. Whether Ghazālī's apparent desire to join irreconcilable ends was a mere platitude or an enviable conviction is hard to tell, but it is safe to say that this oscillation between the relative and the absolute lent an extraordinarily creative and deep edge to Ghazālī's writings.

Admittedly, there is something unusual about these subversive streaks in his writings. The multiple and mingled discourses, as demonstrated in the example discussed above, create unusual conditions in his normative narrative. They shake our complacency about what we accept as normal, producing novelty by defamiliarizing the familiar. The major beneficiary of this iconoclastic edge in Ghazālī has been the heterological element in his work, namely, the element of ṣūfism. As the proverbial "savage in the kitchen," ṣūfism partially neutralized and destabilized the logocentric character of the prevailing juridical discourse.[26] No wonder that most of his defenders on the allegation of antinomianism, like Zabīdī, also happened to be strong partisans of mysticism and were less disturbed than others when Ghazālī allowed novices on the ṣūfī path to choose between the lesser of two legally prohibited practices. Ghazālī and his protagonists, for their part, argued that if the goal of such subversive acts is to fulfill a higher purpose also endorsed by the law, such as attaining morality and piety, then there is some tolerance for the temporary engagement in antinomian practices.[27] Subtly, this narrative suggests that one can derive wisdom and guidance even from something that is not permissible in law and ethics.

In fact, it is worth poring over Zabīdī's eloquent defense of the subversive and playful sequence of events in Ghazālī's writings. "Indeed, it is required that an ascetic [*faqīr*] medicate his heart with some prohibited substances in order to repel a calculatedly more prohibited thing," reflects Zabīdī. "So, if by analogy [it is permissible] to treat bodies with the antidotes of their diseases," he continues, "then how can one compare the perishing of the body with the destruction of the hearts?"[28] Clearly, Zabīdī uses the a fortiori argument, namely, if the health of the body permits the use of prohibited substances, why then cannot the same be done to medicate the most important spiritual organ in the body, the heart? Both in Zabīdī's narrative and in Ghazālī's snapshot narration of the incident of Ibn al-Kuraytī, we see how effective the role of narrative is in framing law and ethics, how effortlessly we can receive a complex idea and communicate it within a larger framework. Legalistic practitioners like Ibn al-Jawzī were confounded by the use of the aesthetic sensibility in the normative realm of law and ethics and deemed it to be intolerably subversive, while Ghazālī and others had no such qualms.

Ghazālī's critics who took issue with the deleterious effects of ṣūfism on his normative allegiance to the *sharīʿa* insightfully acknowledged the counternarrative (heterology) he was mounting against the dominant narrative. Ibn al-Jawzī's language requires closer scrutiny. He charges that Ghazālī and other ṣūfīs "invented" or "fabricated" (*ibtakarū*) a normative discourse (*sharīʿa*) and called it "mysticism" (*taṣawwuf*).[29] So whenever he turned to Ghazālī, he repeatedly lamented the fact that the scholar from Ṭūs had abandoned the rules of law. Unable to withhold his cynicism, Ibn al-Jawzī says: "What surprises me more than the robber taking clothes from the bathhouse is this jurist, whose knowledge and rationality were clearly robbed by *taṣawwuf*!"[30] Even a friendly observer, ʿAbd al-Ghāfir al-Fārisī (d. 529/1134), the official preacher of Nisapūr, expressed reservations about Ghazālī's *Alchemy of Happiness*, which bristles with mystical exegesis of selections from the Qur'ān.[31] Fārisī argues that Ghazālī's heavy borrowing from the sciences of the Greeks fueled suspicions about his theological views, harming his credibility and reputation. In keeping with a sentiment of the early patristic community, Fārisī adds that many known things ought to be kept hidden and not told in public.[32] If anything, Ghazālī would have agreed with him—he, too, staunchly advocated that esoteric knowledge not be publicized—yet Fārisī found Ghazālī's discretion to be lacking.

Revisiting Abraham

The symbolic and scriptural leitmotif at work in Ghazālī's narrative uncannily bears resemblances to the story of the prophet Abraham, as a cursory reading of *Rescuer* will show, just as there are similarities in how liminality played out in their respective pilgrimages. Abraham, in his bid to discover God, according to the Qur'ān, began by pondering the heavenly bodies. At first, he saw the sun and the moon, momentarily mistaking these natural phenomena as deities, but he quickly realized his folly: ephemeral bodies are not ultimate beings.[33] Ghazālī committed a similar error. He, too, at first thought that rational discursivity via law and theology were ends in themselves that could lead to the discovery of ultimate truth. But as he grappled with the cognitive sciences, he recognized their limitations to show him the path to true happiness and felicity. Just as Abraham showed contrition for mistaking the cosmic bodies for the truth, the seductive glamour of doxological knowledge wore thin for Ghazālī.

In fact, he admitted that he learned the art of dialectic from Abraham's debates with Nimrod. Abraham tells the tyrant king, "My Sustainer is the giver of life and death," to which the king replies, "I am the giver of life and death."[34] Realizing that the dialectic is not suited to the opportunity, Abraham resorts to a more appropriate polemical technique and says, "'[Okay,] God causes the sun to rise from the East, so [why don't] you cause it to rise from the West?' And dumbfounded was the infidel!"[35] From this episode, Ghazālī extrapolated a nugget of wisdom that he believed served Abraham well and from which he profited. Abraham discontinued his first line of debate and adopted a more potent polemical line of argument for a good reason; his goal was "not to annihilate [*ifnā'hu*] him [Nimrod], but to resuscitate him [*iḥyā'hu*]," a goal that required a change in polemical strategy.[36] And it was from Abraham, Ghazālī says, that he learned the categorical syllogism *analytica priora*, which also implicitly surfaces in the Qur'ān: Whoever can make the sun rise is God (first principle) / But my God can make the sun rise (second principle) / Therefore, my God is God—and not you, Nimrod (conclusion).

Ghazālī intentionally imitated Abraham. There is a clear intertextual narrative at work here. The subtleties of Abraham's discourse only become apparent, says Ghazālī, if one can have access to the spiritual illumination derived from the world of prophecy.[37] He found in Abraham the paradigmatic figure who is constantly on trial and struggles with his emotions and inner self in order to gain proximity to God. Unsurprisingly, the paradigmatic figure of primitive monotheism (*ḥanīfīya*) became the hero of the preeminent medieval Muslim figure.

When Ghazālī reached a state of mental desperation and anxiety, he recognized that his convictions were under threat. It then dawned upon him that he would have to sacrifice his love for the cognitive sciences in order to attain a more solid conviction, which he found in divine grace and love. Once again, Abraham was the paradigmatic model; the latter was prepared to make the ultimate sacrifice, ready even to offer his son if such was the need in order to show obedience to God. In the end, he became a sincere lover and friend of God. Abraham thus made the transition from the pleasure principle to the reality principle: he was ready to abandon certain sources of immediate pleasure and satisfaction and to put up with some extraordinary earthly discomforts and ordeals. In so doing, Abraham renounced this world, at least for a period of time, to become the true friend (*khalīl*) of God. In Ghazālī's own renunciation of prestige for the life of asceticism and his transition from the pleasure principle to the reality principle, he followed Abraham for a higher purpose: to seek friendship with God.

Convinced that no one in Iraq would understand how he could abandon a prestigious teaching position for an ostensibly compelling religious motive,

Ghazālī contrived a white lie: "I announced my intention to go to Makka, meanwhile knowing full well that I planned to head for Syria." He explains: "I took this precaution so that the caliph and my colleagues would not detect my plan to go to Syria. So I gracefully executed my exit from Baghdād with the intention to never return again."[38] Abraham told the king of Egypt, pointing to his wife, Sarah, that she was his sister, fearing the king might kill him in order to claim her if she were his wife. Like Abraham, Ghazālī was prepared to sacrifice the pleasures of family, children, and career for a higher purpose: to find the ultimate truth.

It is perhaps here that the paradox that Kierkegaard so starkly posed with respect to Abraham haunts us and also has implications for Ghazālī. Kierkegaard interprets Abraham's response to the divine imperative to mean that there are occasions in life when the imperative to act on a particular and extraordinary command, or to act as an individual, is higher than the need to always consider the universal imperative and the greater good. The most traumatic ethical moment is precisely the one in which one has to abandon a universal ethical imperative in response to what may appear to be a supra-ethical imperative, in order to respond to the divine call itself. Abraham faced the impossible dilemma of flouting the universal prohibition against murder, speaking white lies, and neglecting his responsibility, all in order to reach a personal truth, a truth that only benefited him as an individual.

Was this not the challenge that confronted Ghazālī and countless others caught in agonistic dilemmas? Why did Ghazālī voluntarily resign from an important and responsible role in public life as a scholar, from which he could influence and improve the destinies of many individuals and direct the well-being of public life? He resigned in order to develop his self, to strive for his own personal salvation, and to gain proximity to God. Ghazālī describes his illness as "God locking my tongue." By divine intervention, he suggests, he was prevented from teaching. It was at once a divine sign and a trial of sorts.[39] This was Ghazālī's supreme test, similar to the occasion when, in the words of the Qur'ān, "his Lord tried Abraham by a number of commands."[40] If Abraham had heard the command to kill his son in order to please his Lord, then Ghazālī, following his paradigmatic hero, was also ready to slay his idols of self-pride and arrogance in obedience to God.

To be sure, the dilemmas of Ghazālī and Abraham were of a different magnitude, but they do resemble each other in their ethical dimensions. Ghazālī's dilemmas raise the same contested questions as Abraham's about the imperatives of ethics and the law on the one hand against the imperatives of inner faith or certainty (*yaqīn*) and the question of being on the other. His quest for assurance and certainty was remarkably similar to Abraham's. For, in his soliloquy, Abraham says that he longs for the "contentment of my heart."[41] Both figures also contravened the law; as we saw, there was an instance when Ghazālī's critics said he did not strictly advocate the law against theft when a mystic had violated it. Abraham viewed the prohibition against murder as fungible when confronted with a divine call to break it. We saw how Ghazālī's defenders thought he navigated the paradox of breaking the law for a higher purpose. What might appear as breaking the law is actually the only pragmatic way to eliminate one evil with another.

Aporia and Creativity

One's judgment of Ghazālī depends on a variety of factors, including a consideration of temporality, place, and aesthetic sensibility (*dhawq*). Viewed through the lenses of a nonliteralist contemporary hermeneutic that is also imbued with a sense of mysticism, his transitional phases and idiosyncratic views offer us opportunities to explore new possibilities of the imagination. Some of these opportunities are inspired by Ghazālī's personal experiences and the contexts that he explored, which his eighteenth-century commentator Zabīdī fully justified, and which also turn out to have been seedbeds of creativity.

In modern terms, some of Ghazālī's views would be termed "subversive," since he went against the grain of established legal practices.[42] Yet, when examined from the perspective of the mystical path in which paradox, aporia, and narrative play are welcome tropes, Ghazālī clearly offers new models, fresh paradigms, and hopeful symbols for religious creativity. Of course, he was not the first to invent these, since he built on an existing tradition of ṣūfī narrative and practice. Yet, given his stature and reception by later generations, he does play a major role in validating these subversive moments within a juridical and normative idiom. Over the centuries, as Ghazālī's thought gradually gained acceptance in traditionalist circles, the subversive narrative was recycled into the religious and cultural imaginations in different proportions, both reinvigorating and regenerating the social imagination.

In his own lifetime, but even more in the memory of later generations, Ghazālī's personal transformation into a pious mystic not only became legend but was gradually incorporated as a pious model into the community of traditionalist thinking. Ghazālī is generally considered to be among the pious, *sharīʿa*-observing figures of the Muslim intellectual tradition, even though there would be some who would demur at this. His contemporary, Fārisī, played a critical role in providing for posterity a picture of his transformation: "I visited him several times. I watched him, remembering how he used to conduct himself in bygone days with maliciousness, looking down upon people with contempt, making light of their [views] in arrogance and haughtiness, boasting his extensive natural gifts of thought, eloquence, and mind, and only seeking glory and status. Now he was just the opposite of all that. He was cleansed of that detritus. At first, I thought all this was contrived and deliberately cultivated in order to show off what he had become. But after a long observation and examination of the man, my doubts were proven wrong. The man had really recovered from his earlier delusion."[43]

Fārisī gives us a picture of the rites of passage that our subject had undergone. He presents Ghazālī in the proverbial "before" and "after" account. In his view, Ghazālī completed his life pilgrimage by arriving at the destination of mysticism (*taṣawwuf*). In embracing mysticism, Ghazālī's old form acquired new content. His prestige as a scholar par excellence, combined with his accomplishment as a mystic, gave him authority and power. The influence of the "new" Ghazālī did in the long term lay the groundwork for the making of a new intellectual structure and intellectual community. It will indeed be a worthwhile exercise to explore how additional new readings of Ghazālī might stimulate the possibilities for a revisionist orthodoxy or a critical traditionalism in Muslim thought.

Abū al-Aswad said: "Sovereigns are rulers over people, but it is the learned who rule over the sovereigns." . . . ʿAlī said: "Esteem is tethered to failure and modesty to privation. Wisdom is the lost property of the believer. He should seek it, even if the idolaters possess it."
—Ibn Qutayba al-Dīnawarī, *ʿAyūn al-akhbār*

5 Grammar of the Self

Grammar of Religion

The philosopher Ludwig Wittgenstein noted that languages of faith are grounded and embodied in epistemic practices, namely, in the *way* we construct and imagine what is knowledge and in *how* we know.[1] Yet the evidence that we proffer for our beliefs is actually only formulated in the latter instance. In other words, established beliefs are preceded by the events and experiences that inform them. Needless to say, numerous ways of thinking and a range of practices precede beliefs that finally crystallize into a dogma, or article of faith.

People embrace the same doctrines or beliefs in somewhat different ways because we each have different pictures of such claims. Wittgenstein calls such pictures a "grammar," or the "grammatical effect" of beliefs. "Grammar" here simply means a network of ideas or meanings.[2] Conflicts between competing discourses within a religion are often not disputes over a common language as much as they are clashes between entirely different "grammars," or networks of ideas. Put differently, we could also say that people apprehend different pictures of what it is they believe or hold to be sacred in the context of their lived experiences.

One of Ghazālī's most challenging tasks was to find the most appropriate and acceptable grammar to talk about religion in the public space. In his world, as in ours, there were contesting grammars of religion. Muslim thinkers were divided then, as they are now, as to whether any extrascriptural and noncanonical materials could be used in order to expand on religious discourse. For some, tradition resembles palingenesis; such people subscribe to the view that a religious tradition must, like a biological organism, identically reproduce without modification. Defenders of this view are those who are generically identified as the "partisans of the prophetic tradition" (*ahl al-ḥadīth*), among whom the Ḥanbalīs are the most notable. For believers in this trend, the plain meaning of scriptural and prophetic authority serves as a sufficient warrant for action and thus ends all further interpretive possibilities. Opposed to this group are the dialectical theologians (*mutakallimūn*), who espouse more complex hermeneutical theories. For believers in this latter trend, the interpretation of the text also includes a serious consideration of the question of context, time, and history.

Fully aware of these theological minefields, Ghazālī moved cautiously but determinedly in order to construct a grammar in which he combined dialectical theology, philosophical rhetoric, and logical propositions without dropping from his view the ethical objectives this grammar had to fulfill. In pursuing this goal, he had to mediate several discourses and their accompanying metaphysics. This was a task fraught with risks that he had to carefully navigate, and even negotiate. If he appears contradictory in some of his positions, then it is understandable. For he did indeed work within a maelstrom, forced to negotiate multiple antithetical positions. And if he appears tentative and undecided from time to time, it suggests that he did not entirely subscribe to a totalitarian epistemology, but one that was partly open to cautious reconstruction. How open he was to epistemological reconstruction is difficult to quantify.

One thing is certain. Ghazālī must have anticipated that his venture into the uncharted waters of intellectual exploration would both affect the construction of his own religious identity and influence the way he imagined religion. In fact, his critics, especially Ibn Taymīya, later forcefully made this very point, asserting that Ghazālī's intellectual forays into philosophy polluted his religious imagination. Ibn Taymīya actually argued that on several issues Ghazālī committed epistemic treason. Not only did he do the unthinkable by buying into the epistemology of the philosophers, but he did worse, in Ibn Taymīya's view: he failed to jettison philosophical modes of thinking.

After listening to Ghazālī's critics, one is often left with the impression that they admired his intellectual abilities and talents as much as they regretted some of his utterances. Many admired his command of multiple sciences, his razor-sharp insights and boundless creativity, as much as others were envious of these qualities. Some commented that he had combined the good with the bad, an almost irreparable blemish on one's personal and scholarly record.[3] The key concern was that he had entertained too many conflicting ideas and worldviews in prizing creativity over consistency. In the view of some of his contemporaries and later scholars, this kind of intellectual ferment did not lead to stability, but only prompted more questions and inquiries. As discussed in the last chapter, others viewed his creativity as part of a veiled antinomian streak. His critics believed that knowledge could readily be classified into the categories of either beneficial or harmful, since everything is either black or white. Ghazālī believed that in the ordering of human experiences there are intermediate stages and shades of gray.

But Ghazālī's own apologia on occasion is marked by indecision. There are times when he adopts an aggressive impatience toward slavish minions of narrow intellectual trends, flaunting his familiarity with the skills of logic, theology, and philosophy to prove his opponents wrong. Yet, in other instances, he comes across as very traditional and on the rare occasion not indistinguishable from a Ḥanbalī dogmatist. If some of his contemporaries did not appreciate the tentativeness of his views, it is clear that his very openness provided the productive side of his legacy. It is precisely his openness that has enabled legions of scholars to continue the conversation with Ghazālī and his legacy over centuries. It is the multiplicity (heterogeneity) of his sources of knowledge as well as the multiple notions of time (heterotemporality) inherent in his narrative that give his writings an unprecedented richness. In Ghazālī's own view, of course, the different moods and formulations reflected in his prolific oeuvre of writings were entirely natural and acceptable. Each statement, he argues, is determined by the context and the audience one addresses.

Following the teachings of religion, Ghazālī firmly believed in speaking to audiences according to their level of understanding. In fact, he chastised speakers who confused audiences by employing a language or narrative that was not appropriate to the addressees. And speakers who publicized incredulous material only caused their audiences to become despondent and confused.[4] He was fond of quoting a report from the Prophet that states: "Talk to people in a familiar idiom and omit what they may disapprove. Do you want them to refute God and His Prophet?"[5] This advice aims to optimize communication between speakers, who are societal guides, and their audiences. It is certainly not paternalistic advice designed to mollycoddle audiences and avoid meaningful exchange. For Ghazālī, there was a fine balance between educating one's audience and alienating them with ideas that they were unable to bear. He maintained that one must not forfeit any opportunity to share wisdom with people in a constructive manner.

And yet Ghazālī himself struggled to find the right message and tone for his intended target audiences. Ibn Ṭufayl, the philosopher from Muslim Spain, leveled the serious charge that Ghazālī was a crowd-pleaser, implying that he was expedient. "His [Ghazālī's] books . . . well, it depends who he addresses among the populace," complains Ibn Ṭufayl. "For he prohibits in one instance and permits in another; anathematizing certain practices and then deems the same permissible in other instances."[6] Clearly, Ibn Ṭufayl did not appreciate Ghazālī's narrative strategies, preferring the philosopher's disembodied intellectual clarity and transcendent truth above all other types of discourse.

Fragments of Truth and Method

There are instances when Ghazālī untied the Gordian knot of Muslim theology. Knowledge of the truth, in his radical view, is contingent upon the conditions for knowing the truth. For example, according to standard Muslim theology, anyone who hears and recognizes that Muḥammad is a prophet but then fails to act on such knowledge is culpable for not choosing the truth when it revealed itself. Most theologians make the case that if a person never hears of Muḥammad's prophecy, then, by the requirements of justice, there is no ground to obligate such a person to the warrant of Islam. However, Ghazālī went one step further, arguing that even if a person does hear about Muḥammad, the conditions under which the person knows of him are also important. Christians and people of other denominations are excused from the obligation to believe in Muḥammad's prophecy, according to Ghazālī, if the Prophet of Islam is so publicly demonized in their societies as to obstruct people's judgment about him and prevent them from recognizing his prophecy in good conscience.[7] In other words, Ghazālī admitted that sociological and psychological factors shape knowledge and its reception. He affirmed a rather important principle that ideas and beliefs, even the truth, are organically constructed within social and political environments.

A humanistic impulse complicates the historicist underpinning of the previous insight, as Ghazālī also spiritedly argued that the truth is independent of the knowing subject. In fact, he maintained, the true integrity of a person is measured by the veracity of the truth that person professes and not the other way around. A truth is wrongly judged, he believed, if measured exclusively by the standing, identity, or politics of its author. He, like Rāghib al-Iṣfahānī before him, drew inspiration from an aphorism attributed to the fourth Sunnī caliph, or first Shīʿī *imām*, ʿAlī bin Abī Ṭālib (d. 40/661), who said: "Do not apprehend the truth via the men [that hold it]; know the truth, and then you will recognize its possessor."[8] Opposed to Protagoras and Nietzsche, for whom "man was the measure of all things," Ghazālī, together with many thinkers, held that the truth is the measure of all humans. While Ghazālī acknowledged that the truth is mediated by the environment through which it is refracted, he argued that it remains a robust standard that can vouch for its possessor.

What is the objective measurement of the truth? In this respect, Ghazālī was an empiricist and acclaimed the sciences—both the empirical and the rational sciences. One can avoid or drastically minimize error in the discovery of the truth, he argues, if one adopts the methodology of logic. Immunity from error is proportionate to the validity and theoretical efficacy of the method employed. What is required is a process of abstraction that is indifferent to the worldview of the investigator. It does not matter, says Ghazālī, whether the author and practitioner of a science or a craft is a believer or "the most sinful and gross liar," since the empirical outcome is independent of his negative qualities.[9]

Skeptics may suspect that Ghazālī is here making a crass separation between facts and values. However, he draws our attention to the dominant element of objectivity in the discovery of a truth and the need to be vigilant for the seepage of subjective elements that are separable from the process itself. Subjective impulses, he concedes, do impact on the *recognition* of the truth. Furthermore, it is precisely the objectivity of truths that facilitates the transfer of knowledge between civilizations, since people can evaluate the merits of a value or practice in terms of the objectivity they share with others across cultural and particularistic differences. The logic of Ghazālī's position advances the cross-cultural exchange of knowledge, and cosmopolitan Muslim culture profited from this approach over the centuries. Concerns about contamination or error creeping from foreign sources of knowledge into Muslim intellectual life, as some puritan figures feared it would, did not give Ghazālī any pause. He was confident that the safeguards of logic would alert him to rational errors.

Imagining Knowledge without Its Sources

Since the truth can be verified independently of its author, transmitter, or bearer of facts, Ghazālī railed against Muslim scholars who disqualified knowledge on the basis of its origins or the inadequate moral and religious credentials of the persons claiming it. During his day, the adversaries of foreign knowledge tried to discredit the transfer of knowledge to Islamicate societies by attacking those who originated knowledge or transmitted it on the grounds that their identities as Christians, Jews, or their status as persons of minority sects negatively implicated their knowledge claims.

In a polemical exchange, Ghazālī asks the rhetorical question: Does it make sense to abandon certain proofs, sources, data, and methods merely because one's opponents employ identical methods? If it did, he retorts, then this act would lead to a certain absurdity. An adversary could effectively empty one's arsenal of arguments by appropriating every view and rendering it untouchable simply because it had been appropriated. Ghazālī sarcastically asks if one would push this absurdity as far as refraining from believing certain verses of the Qur'ān and prophetic reports just because a controversial group called the Brethren of Purity (Ikhwān al-Ṣafā) cited these materials in its writings for subversive ends.

In his view, both philosophy's unthinking foes and those opposed to the adoption of "foreign knowledge" among Muslims held an absurd position. Intelligent people, he argued, should not allow their objectivity to be blurred by the psychological fallout of an argument or phenomenon. Even a discredited and polluted source ought not to deter someone in search of the truth from recognizing knowledge.

Those susceptible to emotive impressions due to a lack of education could be forgiven for making hasty and simplistic conclusions about the identity of knowledge. But it was unpardonable if educated persons and intellectuals did the same. "An educated person," observes Ghazālī, "does not loathe honey just because he finds it in the surgeon's cupping glass [a container for blood]."[10] The idea of honey being placed in a container customarily used as a surgical glass for blood is aesthetically repugnant, but it is not substantively repugnant. Intelligent people are in a position to distinguish between the aesthetic aversion created by the association of honey with a surgical glass and the substantive value of honey.

In Ghazālī's view, the repugnance is created by a psychological state of mind. While a surgical glass is an unconventional form of dinnerware, it would make little sense to toss out the useful honey, especially if the surgical glass were sterile. Ghazālī's point was that a discriminating observer will make a distinction based on fact and not on emotions. He exemplified the difference between those who instinctively think in an utterly reductionist fashion and others who avoid simplistic conclusions. Ghazālī employed the example of the honey in the surgical glass in order to rebut his detractors who chided him for his appreciation of the value of philosophy and sciences inherited from non-Muslim cultures of ancient times. His opponents not only declared such knowledge to be distasteful, but they deemed it unequivocally subversive and dangerous.

Ghazālī's opponents used what the nineteenth-century German philosopher G. W. F. Hegel called "abstract" thinking, which Hegel suggested is a trait of the uneducated. Even earlier, Michel de Montaigne also objected to abstract thinking.[11] Hegel spoke about it in the context of spectators witnessing a handsome and strong murderer being led to the gallows. For the ordinary folk, the man is nothing but a common criminal. They can find no extenuating circumstances for his deed. Any mitigating facts about the murderer's dysfunctional childhood, which may have contributed to his career in criminality, are ignored by the group of spectators. So overcome are members of the audience by the single fact of murder that they see no redeeming qualities in the murderer, nor do they appreciate his attractive physical features. "This is abstract thinking," observes Hegel, "to see nothing in the murderer except the abstract fact that he is a murderer, and to annul all other human essence in him with this simple quality."[12]

Ghazālī was opposed to reductionist and abstract thinking. An insensitive and unthinking observer may annul all the other properties of the murderer and reduce his identity to a single, albeit heinous, criminal deed. Similarly, someone who does not reflect deeply may view the surgical glass to be essentially a container for blood and nothing else. In both examples, a simple and single essential quality precludes the consideration of other, positive qualities. Differences among people in terms of material background, social status, and education can have a significant impact on their knowledge and actions. If the educated or upper classes were to see anything good in the murderer, the lower classes would accuse them of a corruption in morals, to use Hegel's example. Similarly, if the lower classes approved of something, it would be dismissed by the upper classes as the preference of the hoi polloi that deserved to be ignored merely because people of a different educational background and class status recommended it. In other words, knowledge and practices that are inspired by reductionist thinking based on prejudice about status, gender, or identity are antithetical to complexity and the dialogic nature of knowing.

Like his critics, Ghazālī himself announced prohibitions. In this sense, he was a product of his time, even though he was ahead of his time in other matters. To be fair, the prohibitions he issued were not comprehensive bans. For instance, he had an elitist streak that made him believe that only certain kinds of educational materials were suitable for consumption by the masses. Therefore, he believed that sophisticated and risky investigations in matters of theology, philosophy, and metaphysics, for instance, had to be restricted to qualified and serious scholars and kept at a safe distance from the masses. It is therefore ironic that Ghazālī later criticized the philosophers for adhering to elitist notions of religion.

But one also has to keep in mind that Ghazālī's world, that of the end of the sixth Islamic century (the eleventh century of the common era), was hierarchical and vertically structured in both its social and intellectual norms. He had no hesitation about discouraging laypersons and amateur scholars from reading the books of philosophers. Amateur scholars with inadequate training, he feared—especially the unwary among them—might indiscriminately become infatuated with the ideas of the philosophers. The question is whether Ghazālī's overall arguments on the methods of knowing can still be of value under changed circumstances, now that we eschew strict class, hierarchy, and status formations.

Ghazālī may have been speaking from personal experience, for we know that he had no teacher in philosophical studies. Like a good autodidact, he acquired books of philosophy and absorbed their contents during his tenure as a professor in Baghdād. When he spoke of his drift into skepticism in that ʿAbbāsid capital city, he may very well have been relating his encounter with philosophy. We have good reason to believe that the philosophical materials he read unhinged him intellectually and brought him to the brink of chronic doubt and reflexive uncertainty, from which he had a narrow escape. He recognized the depths to which philosophy can drag even an educated man's faith, leading to mental turmoil. Perhaps, from his own experience, he had reason to believe that neither laypersons nor mediocre scholars should dabble in philosophy.

The Role of Intellectuals

One of Ghazālī's almost paranoid obsessions was with the idea that scholars should not give laypersons the impression that religion is based on expediency or ideological concerns. Even if religious thought does represent ideological positions, his rare populist dimension compelled him to express concern for the faith and beliefs of those who were at the mercy of the doings of the elite, namely, the laity. Therefore, he went to great lengths to explain what scholars should and should not do. Only serious intellectuals should engage with philosophy and deal with the subject in a responsible manner, he felt. As role models, intellectuals had to think of how their intellectual and personal conduct would affect the public, since he feared that the conduct of some intellectuals might have a negative impact.[13]

He worried that laypersons and amateurs would try to imitate the intellectuals, thereby causing mischief and damaging the faith of others. Ghazālī had in mind the kind of choices that scholars might make in legal and theological matters that bordered on the permissive. Even though choice is at the core of scholarship and differences are legitimate, his fears led him to caution scholars against giving the impression that there is no consistency in religious practices. He wanted to keep religious authority under strict surveillance and balked at making it seem as though intellectual authority is plastic and malleable.

Even a snake charmer, Ghazālī explained by way of example, has to avoid touching a snake in the presence of his young son. For without the requisite skills, the son's imitation of the father could be catastrophic. While he cherished intellectual inquiry, the thrust of his complaint was against dilettantism. In fact, he blamed serious scholars who publicly flaunted their skills in risky intellectual ventures for giving the dilettantes the courage to undertake similar actions.[14] Ghazālī's firm caveat against amateurism and his promotion of hierarchical authority may ruffle our modern sensibilities. But he appears to have been directing his diatribes against harmful and fraudulent scholarship, a bane of which no age can categorically claim to have acquitted itself.

Ghazālī, I think, was making a larger point. Producing innovative scholarship, nurturing creativity, and harmonizing and internalizing ideas from a variety of sources are obviously legitimate enterprises. People equipped to execute such responsibility must shoulder it. However, I suspect that his point was to ensure that risk taking in the moral and ethical spheres did not undermine the public confidence in the intellectual edifice that governs society.

Ghazālī believed there is a responsible way and an irresponsible way of undertaking cutting-edge scholarship. Ironically, he has been accused of doing the very things against which he cautioned. Scholars like Abū Bakr al-Ṭurṭūshī (d. 520/1126) and Abū ʿAbd Allāh al-Māzarī (d. 536/1141) charged that Ghazālī was not only dabbling in theology but had been duped by the lure of philosophy. They both said that Ghazālī might have been better off if he had stuck to the safe shore and only studied the law.

Intellectuals, in Ghazālī's view, shoulder a significant burden in order to secure society's well-being. They require skills of discretion similar to those of a money changer or goldsmith who can distinguish between a genuine gold coin and a counterfeit one even if both are kept in the same purse. And just as the proximity of genuine and counterfeit coins does not affect the quality of the metals, so too the proximity of truth to falsehood does not magically turn the truth into a falsehood or a falsehood into the truth.[15] For Ghazālī, responsibility was commensurate with capacity.

The credentials of the individual scholar are vital to the intellectual enterprise, but there are other factors that also play an important role. In the sectarian world of Ghazālī's time, affiliation itself created boundaries and limitations. Scholars belonging to the Sunnī sect would often not only be skeptical of the views of Muʿtazilī or Shīʿī scholars but would also argue that these scholars' sectarian affiliations alone created a permanent ideological prejudice that nullified their testimony and contributions to knowledge.[16] Knowledge, or at least certain kinds of knowledge, relates intimately to the identity of the scholar. More than the merit of an idea or concept, it is the credibility and identity of the producer of knowledge that is often in question.

Ideas and Their Identity

Going against the dominant trend, Ghazālī held that an idea is not marked by its provenance or the identity of its author. He believed that any idea can be measured and evaluated on its merits and knowledge value. He lamented the rejection of any idea on the ground that its author was a philosopher or a person of a different religion. Even the arguments of philosophers with whom one has major disagreements, Ghazālī argued, should be countenanced. Furiously denouncing certain theologians, he called them "a group who have only the faintest of intellect claims that since those [beneficial ethical] discourses occur in the books of philosophers adulterated with their [the philosophers'] own falsities, reference to them should be avoided."[17] Since such people believed that philosophers held false views, they maintained that philosophers' arguments should be rejected without giving them any thought. "Their reason for such thinking is due to the fact that they heard of these notions from the philosophers for the first time," Ghazālī explains in disagreement, "and thus their weak intellects conclude that such views are false, since to them the author of ideas [philosopher] is deemed a liar."[18]

His vehemence was directed at those self-declared puritan scholars of religion who find an idea repulsive purely on the grounds of its origin and the identity of its author. Explaining his approach, Ghazālī declared that one must disaggregate an argument and evaluate each element of it for its merits. According to this standard, even a monotheistic Christian committed to his doctrines follows the truth, albeit only in part, if he does not acknowledge the Prophet Muḥammad as a prophet. As I pointed out earlier, Muslim doctrine expects humanity to recognize the prophecy of Muḥammad. Thus, when a Christian living in the post-Muḥammadan period rejects him as a prophet, such a person is, in Ghazālī's view, an "unbeliever"—but, surprisingly, he is an unbeliever only to the extent that he rejects Muḥammad.[19] The deficiency in his Christian doctrine does not invalidate the remaining monotheistic belief that he affirms. "If he is an infidel, [he is so] only in terms of his denial [of Muḥammad's prophecy]," observes Ghazālī. "Thus, there is no need to contradict him in assertions unrelated to his denial, especially when these [other] assertions are true in themselves."[20]

Elsewhere, Ghazālī notes that there are different levels of monotheism. "When Christians refer to God as the third of the three," he writes sagely, "they do not mean that God is [numerically] three."[21] They are affirming, says Ghazālī, that "indeed, God is one in his essence [*dhāt*] and three with respect to his attributes [*ṣifāt*]. And this is the wording of their statement: 'One in substance [*jawhar*] and three by way of hypostasis [*uqnūmīya*].' By 'hypostasis,' they mean 'attributes.'"[22]

Clearly, Ghazālī's views are radical by both historical standards and the standards of the mood of contemporary Muslim theological debate. He provides insightful and conciliatory grounds to bridge the different religious traditions. To draw the conclusion from the discussion above that Ghazālī was an apologist for Christian trinitarian doctrine, as some are likely to do, is to mistake his real purpose in this illustration. Yet his ideas can serve as a model and provide grounds for an emancipatory pluralism. His purpose was to foster a broad-gauged epistemology, one that is susceptible to plurality. A truth is not invalidated by the status of the one holding it, he argues, since this would be reductive, throwing the baby out with the bathwater. It is vulgar to declare a monotheistic Christian to be an unbeliever, he argues, for to do so from a Muslim perspective is to be both totalitarian and lacking in nuance. Only a part of this hypothetical Christian's beliefs clash with Muslim doctrines regarding the status of believers who adhere to non-Islamic creeds, after all, namely, that part related to the Prophet Muḥammad's prophecy.

Knowledge and the Other

Ghazālī appears to have distanced himself from viewing knowledge as embodied in the identity of its holder. In many instances, he tended to stand aloof from that narrow trend within his intellectual milieu. Dogmatists and puritans have criticized him for being too liberal in his use of material from politically incorrect sources. Among the fiercest detractors was Ibn Taymīya, the eighth-/fourteenth-century polymath. Ibn Taymīya eloquently illustrated the difference between himself and Ghazālī, which is symptomatic of the larger debate about knowledge and identity.

Ibn Taymīya criticized Ghazālī for citing a line of poetry composed by a Christian poet, Akhṭal, in a crucial argument about the nature of language.[23] "Akhṭal" was the sobriquet of the renowned Arab poet Ghiyāth b. Ghawth b. al-Ṣalṭ (d. 927/710). The polemic turns on Ghazālī's defense of the view that the book of God, the Qur'ān, constitutes "a speech that is self-sufficient in the essence of God, the Sublime." "Furthermore," Ghazālī argues, "it [speech] is an eternal attribute among His attributes [*Huwa al-kalām al-qā'im bi dhāt Allāh ta'ālā, wa huwa ṣifa min ṣifātihi*]."[24] The word "speech" (*kalām*), according to Ghazālī, is a homonym. The signified of the term "speech" sometimes refers to only the verbal utterance; on other occasions, it refers to the intentions and meanings behind an utterance. Ghazālī cites a line of poetry by Akhṭal as proof for his claim that the Qur'ān is a "speech" and that it signifies meanings and intentions that are interior, located in the psyche of the speaker or listener. The poetry on which Ghazālī relies reads:

> Speech lies in the heart
> And surely the tongue has been made a signifier for what is in the heart.

Without mentioning any name, Ibn Taymīya refutes Ghazālī's argument with his characteristic thunderbolts but, interestingly, ends up defending the idea that knowledge is inseparable from identity. Ibn Taymīya rebuts the claim that the divine speech, the Qur'ān, is primarily an inner speech (*kalām al-nafsī*), as many Ashʿarī theologians have maintained. Ibn Taymīya then elaborates and provides a fuller context for the lines quoted by Ghazālī from Akhṭal's poetry. He wanted to show that once the reader has a fuller idea of the meaning intended in the remainder of the poem, it becomes clear how wrong Ghazālī was to use it for his proof citation (*istishhād*). For, if one reads the cited line with the preceding line, one gains a different idea of the intended sense of the poet:

Let not the effect of his utterance impress you
  Until it is authentically linked to the speech
Speech lies in the heart
  And surely the tongue has been made a signifier for what is in the
    heart.[25]

Ibn Taymīya's point is to show that Ghazālī got it wrong. In the fuller version of the poem, an enunciative utterance is also called "speech" (*kalām*). So Ghazālī scored no major points in citing Akhṭal, Ibn Taymīya points out. In fact, Ghazālī selectively cited the poem to prove that the word "speech" may signify inner speech, but in the previous line "speech" means "utterance," which belies his point. What Ibn Taymīya omitted to mention is that the word "speech" (*kalām*), used in different senses in two successive lines, can signify two very different meanings, and that the play of the poem is precisely on the ambiguity and polyvocality of this word.

Tantalizing as the debate about divine speech as inner speech may be, what deserves our attention is the substance of Ibn Taymīya's ad hominem attack. His main objections were threefold. First, he found it incredulous that a poet's verse could qualify as evidence in issues of linguistic argumentation. Second, since Akhṭal was not a classical poet but was from among the postclassical poets (*muwalladūn*), he questioned how Akhṭal's words could be viewed as authoritative. Third, and in Ibn Taymīya's view most important, he found it utterly unacceptable that the view of a "Christian trinitarian infidel" (*naṣrānī kāfir muthallith*) named Akhṭal was cited as the deciding linguistic evidence for an argument related to the Qur'ān in Muslim theology.[26]

Points one and two of Ibn Taymīya's polemic are odd and disturbing. For, in linguistic issues, poetry does qualify as evidence even in the clarification of ambiguities related to the Qur'ān. His objection as to which generation of poets qualifies as authoritative is also moot. But Ibn Taymīya's main objection —his objection to Akhṭal's identity as a Christian—is a more candid one and is representative of the fault line between him and Ghazālī and their respective views on knowledge. He believed that identity and knowledge could not be separated. Thus, identity politics played a crucial role in the interpretation and transmission of knowledge for Ibn Taymīya. Once Akhṭal was discredited as an evidentiary source on the ground of his religious identity, Ibn Taymīya could begin to make the case that if his ideas and philosophy were secreted into Muslim knowledge they would subvert the pristine purity of tradition.

Akhṭal's view on language, he implied, was not doctrinally neutral. The Christian poet's predilection for linguistic ambiguity presaged shades of trinitarian figurative interpretation, doctrines that are antithetical to Muslim belief. Therefore, in his view, importing Akhṭal's linguistic ambiguity—whether an utterance can be deemed as "true" or "real" speech, or as "interior" or "exterior"—was not innocent, but rather a form of ideological contamination. Ibn Taymīya remarks that Akhṭal's semiotics was inseparable from his ideological commitments as a Christian. For Christianity's key doctrine is based on the fundamental ambiguity regarding whether Jesus was human or divine or both at the same time, and that ambiguity also has a linguistic component.

Ibn Taymīya clarified his position: "And the Christians have erred in the denotation [*musammā*] of speech [*kalām*], so they made the messiah [Jesus] self-sufficient in himself, who is then identical to the word of God."[27] To state that divine speech is not the literal word of God, but a strange kind of "inner" component of speech, as many Muslim theologians claim, is in Ibn Taymīya's view an absurdity that does not meet the standard of rational scrutiny.[28] Only prophetic dicta can dispense with the required standard of rational and conceptual validity.[29]

Ibn Taymīya was remorseless in pointing out that Ghazālī not only followed the Christian premises of arguments that were harmful to uniquely Muslim ways of thinking but was also indiscriminate in his use of spurious and suspect sources.[30] For this reason, Ibn Taymīya wryly observed, Ghazālī and those who held similar views repeated the errors that non-Muslims committed: they employed abstract rational arguments that could not be actualized. In his witheringly patrician style, Ibn Taymīya, who resisted cosmopolitanism, wrote: "What is repulsive about these persons [Ghazālī and others] is that in matters that affect the foundations of their religion, and in knowing the essence of speech—the speech of God as well as the speech of the entire humanity—they employ arguments of a Christian poet, whose name is Akhṭal."[31]

Ghazālī, along with other theologians, Ibn Taymīya pointed out, resembled a Christian in his conception of language and speech.[32] By stressing the ambiguity and incomprehensibility of the ineffable and eternal divine speech of revelation, these Muslims were more like Christians who in turn talked of "hypostases," "trinity," and "unification," all formulations that, to his mind, did not survive rational scrutiny.[33]

Apart from his microanalysis of the debate, Ibn Taymīya's interest lay in prosecuting an intra-Muslim polemic—with puritanical zeal—about the inadvisability of taking knowledge from the Other. Ghazālī, too, was aware of this risk but nevertheless embraced a critical cosmopolitanism and therefore proceeded with caution. But his caution gave him no immunity from scathing criticism. The underlying dread that animated Ibn Taymīya's views was that borrowing ideas across confessional frontiers would graft alien and repulsive ideas onto the recipient tradition. Little attention was given to the fact that Islam was itself the hegemonic culture in Ghazālī's world and thus that the likelihood of it becoming subservient to foreign ideas was rather remote. Ibn Taymīya did not show the slightest awareness that religious traditions continuously borrow ideas from each other. Within a single culture, there can be different translations and interpretations of concepts, and people who face similar issues in different times and places may arrive at similar solutions. In fact, Isaiah Berlin has a sage comment that is appropriate here: "Similarity is not identity; one must see both the wood and the trees, although only God can do this perfectly."[34]

Theology and Ambivalence

Ghazālī provided several clues to suggest that he hovered between antithetical positions, shuttling between the extremities of his mental *dihlīẓ* when it came to theology and philosophy. On the one hand, he felt compelled to refute the philosophers with their own arguments, while on the other he was acutely aware of how fastidious the intellectual milieu around him was about the use of the grammar of philosophy and theology. Already, the use of dialectical theology (*ʿilm al-kalām*) in defense of religious dogma had created unending controversies and tensions. Strict scripturalist tendencies, represented by the amorphous partisans of *ḥadīth*, who claimed to adhere to the authentic tradition, were opposed to the dialectical theologians (*mutakallimūn*), who espoused a more complex hermeneutic framework.

Ghazālī, together with his teacher Juwaynī, was often the target of criticism by scholars from the opposing school for succumbing to the charms of dialectical theology. There is no scriptural warrant or authority from the patristic community, his critics argued, to validate resort to dialectical theology. While Ghazālī acknowledged the absence of dialectical theology in the first Muslim community, he maintained that there was a necessity for it during his time in order to defend the tenets of faith, given the rise of heretical tendencies that required proper refutation.[35] Dialectical theology is, in this view, like surveillance equipment that polices the boundaries of religion and prevents harmful intrusions. Its purpose is to keep the public space free from subversive discourses that may harm the convictions of the common folk. Therefore, he tolerated public debates in order to rebut and refute heretical views.

In an unusual comment in *Resuscitation* that reflects his vacillation on dialectical theology, Ghazālī criticized theologians who saw their role to be that of polemicists and debaters. Such theologians, he argues, should not mistake their labors as the equivalent of "devotional acts that lead to [salvation in] the hereafter, nor are they engaged in caring for the heart and its betterment." Theologians of this type, he states indignantly, are "not at all among the persons who could claim to be learned in religion!"[36]

Among those figures who preceded him with whom Ghazālī might have found some common cause in the pursuit of theology were humanists like Abū Sulaymān al-Manṭiqī (d. ca. 392/1001) and his student Abū Ḥayyān al-Tawḥīdī. Ghazālī would surely have concurred with them in their assessment of the deficient methods of the theologians. Manṭiqī said:

> The method of the dialectical theologians [*mutkallimūn*] is based on comparing single words or things. It is based either on rational proof or, without it, relying on disputes and whatever occurs to sense perception or to the mind [at that moment]. Or [it relies] on a combination of impulses ranging from sense perception and illusion to imagination that coalesce in the mind. All this is related to a distortion and an impulsive need to silence an opponent with whatever means appropriate. To issue a statement lacking in comprehensiveness as well as reference, together with blunders, is incompatible with the status of knowledge. Often poor behavior and, yes, little devotion, questionable bona fides, the corruption of conscience, and a total rejection of piety accompany this.[37]

In short, Manṭiqī saw no value in *kalām* and actually dismissed it as a useless pursuit. Philosophy, in turn, suggested Manṭiqī, was much more specific and disciplined in its intellectual endeavors, free from subjective claims and a rigorous empiricism.[38] Ghazālī agreed with Manṭiqī to the extent that *kalām*, as practiced by some of his predecessors and contemporaries, surely lacked intellectual rigor, but he would have disagreed with him about the unqualified merits of philosophy.

Kalām, as its name suggests, was nothing more than disputatious and unsystematic polemical debates. Ghazālī nevertheless defended the value and role of this science as the queen of all sciences and as a universal discipline. For, in his view, all "the sciences of religion" (*al-ʿulūm al-dīnīya*) rely on dialectical theology for their foundations and justification; it is thus "the superior science" (*al-ʿilm al-aʿlā*).[39] The deficiencies of theology, Ghazālī argues, can be remedied by supplementing it with logic.

Indirectly, the logical supplement brings to theology some philosophical rigor, a feature that Manṭiqī found indispensable. Although Ghazālī was reticent to give all the credit to the philosophers for producing logic—for they claimed it to be a universal language—he nonetheless admired the coherence and intellectual satisfaction that logic brings to the sciences of religion. He went so far to say that logic is a "preamble [*muqaddima*] to all the sciences; and whoever does not grasp it, then as a matter of principle there can be no reliance on their claim to have acquired science [*ʿilm*]."[40]

The question is whether Ghazālī would have agreed with Manṭiqī and Tawḥīdī that there is a complete disjuncture between philosophy and religious truth. According to Tawḥīdī, the humanist Manṭiqī proclaimed "philosophy as truth, but it has no claim on religion; and religion, while it is truth, has no connection with philosophy at all."[41] Tawḥīdī imputed to philosophy a prophylactic character, whereas religion in his view was medicinal. "Religion is the medication of those who are ill," he asserts, "while philosophy is the medicine of the healthy." "Prophets administer medicine to the sick," he continues, "in order to restrict [the impact of disease], so that in the end [the patient] recovers from the disease. Philosophers, [on the other hand], wish to immunize their followers, ensuring that their health remains at an optimum [at all times] so that they are never afflicted by disease."[42]

Ghazālī may have been troubled by such triumphalist rhetoric on the part of the philosophers, and the above formulation was challenged by the scholars of religion. But, if pressed, even Ghazālī would have conceded that, while religion and philosophy perform different functions in society, there may indeed be some mutual reinforcement of principle. His personal experiences taught him that philosophy could not heal diseased souls, but it did help him clarify things discursively. Only the intense practice of religion and the experience it provided could give satisfactory relief to him in the end.

The Qur'ān, in Ghazālī's view, sufficed as a discourse to ensure doctrinal rectitude in public discourse. "The likeness of arguments from the Qur'ān," he says, "is like that of nourishment, from which every person can benefit; whereas arguments of the dialectical theologians are similar to medication, in that they only profit some individuals, and rather cause harm to most people." He continues: "In fact, the similarity of the Qur'ānic arguments is like that of water; they benefit a suckling infant as well as a strong person. All the other arguments are like regular foods: they are beneficial to the health of those who are fit in some instances, but they can also be the cause of their illness on other occasions. Infants, it is clear, cannot profit from these [foods, that is, theological arguments] at all."[43]

It remains contested whether Ghazālī would have credited philosophy with providing immunity from disease, as Manṭiqī proposed. Ghazālī criticized philosophy on several points. But his real motive in criticizing the philosophers was to puncture their arrogance, their belief that their ideas were beyond the dictates and authority of religion. Such intellectual conceit, he felt, was symptomatic of a disease of the soul that far outweighs the merits of logic and reason. It is as if Ghazālī was asking: Could such a spiritually harmful philosophy be of any benefit?

Several decades before Ghazālī was born, the leading scholar of Muslim Spain, Ibn Ḥazm, made a bold statement with respect to philosophy and theology. He asserted that the goals of philosophy and revelation were identical. "Philosophy in reality, in terms of its meaning and benefit, as well as the desired goal for its acquisition," Ibn Ḥazm said, "is nothing other than reforming the self. So in this world, virtues and good conduct can lead to success in the hereafter and good management in the domestic and public spheres. This is identical and in no way different from the goal of the revelation [*sharīʿa*]. There is no dispute in this matter between scholars of philosophy and scholars of *sharīʿa*."[44] Ibn Ḥazm's view of how religion and philosophy both promote virtues that lead to human flourishing was one that Ghazālī endorsed wholeheartedly.[45]

Critique of Theologians

Ghazālī was exasperated by the behavior of fellow Ashʿarī theologians whom he believed were misguided by their zeal into attacking philosophy for the wrong reasons, and with impoverished intellectual assets to boot. He vigorously pursued this critique in a book titled *Decisive Criterion for Distinguishing*

Islam from Masked Infidelity (*Fayṣal al-tafriqa bayna al-Islām wa al-zandaqa*), and the critique is littered throughout many of his other writings.[46] This was in part Ghazālī's response to criticisms directed at him by chauvinistic and narrow-minded Ashʿarite theologians who were offended by his independence vis-à-vis some of the school's doctrines. Once *Resuscitation* gained circulation, the attacks against him increased and became more visceral.[47] He possibly had the attacks from these kinds of theologians in mind when he remarked that a rational foe is better than an ignorant friend.[48]

Driven by outrage at the actions of some zealous Ashʿarīs who could easily be coaxed into issuing decrees of anathema and excommunication against anyone who slightly digressed from the Ashʿarī interpretation of dogma, Ghazālī decided to define the boundary between belief and heresy.[49] It is assumed that much of his venom was directed at some uncritical North African Ashʿarī scholars. Among them was Māzarī, who was bitingly critical of Juwaynī and Ghazālī for their independent positions on several issues. It is well known that Māzarī identified Ghazālī to be among those thinkers who did not fully endorse all the doctrines of the Ashʿarī school.[50]

In Baghdād, too, tolerance for adversaries or even friendly criticism of Ashʿarism was unpopular. When Ghazālī was in his early twenties, a prominent Muʿtazilī scholar and propagandist best known as Abū ʿAlī ibn al-Walīd died in Baghdād in the year 478/1084.[51] Abū ʿAlī was a student of the famous Baṣran Muʿtazilī theologian and jurist Abū al-Ḥusayn al-Baṣrī (d. 436/1044).[52] For his allegiance to Muʿtazilī views, Ibn al-Jawzī informs us, the man was subject to extraordinary victimization by the Sunnīs. Intolerance threatened Abū ʿAlī to the extent that he did not risk making a public appearance and remained closeted at home for nearly fifty years![53] Prior to that, in 465/1073, the famous Ḥanbalī scholar Abū al-Wafā' Ibn ʿAqīl (d. 513/1119) had also been subject to an inquisition for being sympathetic to the "doctrines of the heretical innovators, Muʿtazilis and others" and for frequenting impious intellectual circles.[54]

Ghazālī was scathing in his remarks about some theologians who, despite their moral depravity and intellectual fraudulence, continued to pontificate on matters of anathema and heresy in a self-righteous manner. He denied them the privilege of becoming the defenders of God, Islam, and the truth. With a combination of caustic language that almost amounted to denigration and disdain, he stated that those theologians whose hearts were polluted and impervious to prophetic wisdom disqualified themselves from serving the cause of defending religion. "How can the secrets of the [angelic] kingdom enlighten people whose deity is their desires?" he thunders. In a passage of savage irony that reveals a great deal as to how he viewed his colleagues and the social and political context, he asks how the learned theologians could provide guidance "when their rulers [*salāṭīn*, sing. *sulṭān*] [were] their object of worship; their direction of worship [*qibla*] their dirhams and dīnārs [the currency of the time]; frivolity their law; glory and lust their intention; and serving the rich their act of worship; when evil whisperings [substituted for] the remembrance of God [*dhikr*]; when politicians [were] their treasure; and legal fictions [were] the sum total of their ideas to the extent that decency demanded [that they adhere to laws]?" Such frightening levels of moral depravity begged the question, in his view, as to how such theologians could "differentiate between the darkness of heresy and the light of faith."[55]

Responding to the chauvinism of the heresy-mongering theologians, Ghazālī showed that he suffered fools badly. "Whoever thinks that heresy [*kufr*] is defined by opposing the Ashʿarī, Muʿtazilī, Ḥanbalī, or any other school of thought, then know that such a person is not stupid! He is a prisoner of authority [*taqlīd*]," Ghazālī scolds. "Actually, he is the blindest among the blind," he continues. "Do not waste time in trying to rehabilitate him, let alone trying to silence him by comparing his claims with those of his opponent."[56] Such people, in his view, were effectively a lost cause; they were beyond persuasion and also perhaps beyond redemption.

And by which authority, he asks sardonically, does this group of theologians have a monopoly on the truth?[57] Would such bigots have the courage to condemn a towering intellectual like Abū Bakr al-Bāqillānī (d. 403/1013), who disagreed with the founder of Ashʿarism, Abū al-Ḥasan al-Ashʿarī, on the question of the divine quality (*ṣifa*) of duration (*baqāʾ*)? Bāqillānī, as we know, did not view duration as an *additional* quality of the godhead, a position contrary to the one held by the Ashʿarīs, who argued it had an existence outside the divine essence.[58] Ghazālī also lashed out against the standard Ashʿarī view on this topic: "So whoever said," he states provocatively, "that 'duration is a quality additional to the Everlasting' is actually far off the mark."[59]

By contradicting Ashʿarī and supporting the view of Bāqillānī, Ghazālī was himself engaging in some rough polemics, but he felt emboldened to create a space for theological toleration. If one applied the zealot standard for adjudicating anathema, then merely disagreeing with Ashʿarī on an important issue like duration would negatively implicate both Bāqillānī and Ghazālī and place them outside the strict fold of Ashʿarism, which in turn could have all kinds of implications for their adherence to Islam by standards of orthodoxy.

Some Ashʿarī apologists, Ghazālī tells us, tried to downplay the differences between Bāqillānī and Ashʿarī, arguing that both men agreed that the quality of "duration," irrespective of whether it was part of or separate from the divine essence, has the characteristic of perpetual existence (*dawām al-wujūd*). This contorted interpretation seemingly reconciles the positions held by the two men in order to protect Bāqillānī from having imprecations of anathema directed at him. But Ghazālī was unconvinced by the apologia and declared that the bigoted Ashʿarīs had failed to be consistent. Nothing could be more fundamental, he asserted, than the disagreement between Ashʿarī and Bāqillānī on the nature of the attributes of God, and thus the attempted reconciliation was futile.

Pushing the point further, Ghazālī then asked: If the Ashʿarīs could find a way to compromise with Bāqillānī, then what prevented them from doing the same with the Muʿtazilīs on a doctrinal matter that was logically analogous? The difference between the Muʿtazilīs and the Ashʿarīs centered on the notion of God's attribute of knowledge (*ʿilm*). The Muʿtazilīs believed that God "knows" through his essence, whereas the Ashʿarīs claimed that God "knows" through an additional attribute of knowledge, one that stands apart from his essence.

The differences in the intra-Ashʿarī dispute between the two individuals, Bāqillānī and Ashʿarī, and the debate between two rival theological schools, Ashʿarī and Muʿtazilī, are of the same magnitude. Just as the Muʿtazilīs argued that God "knows" through his essence, Bāqillānī, whose doctrinal pedigree was Ashʿarī, also argued that God's "duration" (*baqāʾ*) occurs as a result of certain qualities inherent to his essence. In both instances, the Ashʿarīs required additional attributes to make God's "duration" and "knowing" possible. If the differences between the two schools were on the same scale as the differences between two individuals who disagreed within the same school, then why, asks Ghazālī polemically, "the differential treatment toward the Muʿtazilīs"? Why foster hostility toward the Muʿtazilīs but reconciliation with Bāqillānī when in fact the latter committed the same theological offense of which the Muʿtazilīs stood accused? One explanation may be that the Ashʿarīs in Ghazālī's time had realized that it would be self-defeating to anathematize Bāqillānī. So, pragmatically if not expediently, they reconciled with him. Bāqillānī was the foremost theologian of the eleventh century affiliated to the Ashʿarī school. Not only would the Ashʿarīs damage the reputation of their school if they drew their theological daggers against him, they would also renounce a stellar figure in their intellectual tradition.

Ghazālī actually had a more personal motive for taunting the Ashʿarīs of his day by exposing their doctrinal inconsistencies vis-à-vis Bāqillānī and the Muʿtazilīs. There was an element of intellectual challenge and daring on his part in publicly going on the offensive with his Ashʿarī counterparts. He was encouraged because on the issue of the divine attribute of "duration" he shared Bāqillānī's view and not that of Ashʿarī. Thus, his discussion of the issue amounted to flinging down a gauntlet and making a frontal challenge to the heresy-mongers, who may have momentarily contemplated anathematizing and then excommunicating him for deviating from the correct doctrine.

Ghazālī took courage in knowing that the Ashʿarīs had not anathematized Bāqillānī or others who dissented from the school's position, like the prolific jurist-theologian al-Ḥusayn b. ʿAlī al-Karābīsī (d. 248/862)[60] and the *qāḍī* and leading theologian of his time Ibrāhīm b. ʿAbd Allāh al-Zabīdī, better known as al-Qalānisī (d. ca. 359/970).[61] Ghazālī reckoned that if the Ashʿariīs did give vent to their folly it would be self-defeating.[62]

In a bid to expose the charlatanism of certain Ashʿarī theologians, Ghazālī provided his reader with a set of prosecutorial questions. While these questions were part of a polemical exchange, they were designed to serve as leading questions to be put to any persons whom he considered to be fake theologians. The idea was not so much to test their abilities as to disclose their incompetence during informal cross-examination. Beyond that, his purpose was also to show that the adherents of the Ashʿarī school committed the very same intellectual errors and contradictions that they accused their Muʿtazilī opponents of committing.[63]

If you asked an Ashʿarī why he anathematized the Muʿtazilīs, Ghazālī mused, he would give a standard reply along the following lines. In their understanding of God, the Ashʿarī would say, the Muʿtazilīs believe that a single divine essence generates the function of knowledge, power, and life. This is wrong, the Ashʿarī would say, because in reality and by definition, these are different attributes. Logically, it is impossible to describe a unity or represent a plurality of essences if these are only represented or signified by a single entity. Ghazālī then proceeded to find an analogous Ashʿarī argument; he asked why the same logic did not apply to the Ashʿarī explanation of divine speech. The same contradiction that the Ashʿarīs identified in the Muʿtazilī reasoning as absurd, he pointed out, was evident in their own reasoning on divine speech!

It is known, for instance, that the Ashʿarīs maintained that the attribute of divine speech (*kalām*) is also associated with the divine essence and is thus an attribute of essence. Having established this, the Ashʿarīs also maintained that, while God's speech is one, it becomes manifest in the form of multiplicity through manifestations that we identify as divine revelations in the Torah, the Psalms of David, the Bible, and the Qur'ān. Furthermore, we know that these scriptures consist of informative historical narratives (*khabar*, pl. *akhbār*) that are liable to verification or falsification, but that they also contain performative predications, such as commands and prohibitions, that are not liable to being tested for truth or falsity. In other words, each of these revelations contains multiple essences. Ghazālī prompted his fictional interlocutor to put the following question to the theologian under cross-examination: How is it then possible that in a single scripture two types of speech—performative and informative utterances—can coexist? In his view, the Ashʿarī view allowed for the coexistence of two contraries in a single instant—a blatant contradiction in terms!

If the charlatan Ashʿarī theologian was unable to respond to this query or fumbled in his response, it would be clear that he had a layman's qualifications—that he was a mere journeyman (*muqallid*) who lacked the skills of an original and serious investigative thinker (*ahl-naẓar*).[64] Such a theologian should remain quiet, Ghazālī advised, if he wished not to be banned from engaging in public debates or leading investigations into heresy charges. Concerned that such characters only caused harm in the public realm, Ghazālī was dismissive of their efforts, which he compared to those of an ironmonger who tried to shape cold iron on an anvil.

Ghazālī was, of course, referring to boneheaded lay theologians. Such individuals may have been slightly more educated than laypeople, but their real expertise was in intimidating others with threats of anathema. It appears that some may have been sniping at him and that he was returning fire. When retaliating, Ghazālī himself was not reticent about playing the heresy card. After pointing out that demagogue theologians were not original but blindly followed some revered authority, Ghazālī went on to suggest that in this way heresy-mongers themselves might have been guilty of heresy. "Perhaps if you are fair," he taunts his opponents, "you will realize that the one who believes that a single speculative thinker has the exclusive monopoly over the truth, such a person is closer to unbelief and contradiction. It is unbelief, because he elevates such a mortal to the status of a prophet. A prophet alone is infallible. For faith [doctrinally] is established by compliance with [the teachings of a prophet], and opposing him [his prophetic teachings] is a warrant for unbelief."[65]

Ghazālī, then, accused charlatan inquisitors of contradiction. He made an unambiguous and compelling point: self-righteous and unqualified heresy-mongers and inquisitors pretended to have original insight but lacked the qualifications to acquire it. Therefore, they could, ironically, commit acts of unbelief themselves in following the errors rigged in the views of the authorities they claimed to obey.

Ghazālī's goal in mounting these polemics was to point out that imputing charges of heresy is such a serious business that most theologians are just not qualified for it. Just as he believed that laypeople should not get entangled with complex theological doctrines, so too did he believe that run-of-the-mill or journeyman theologians should refrain from such tasks, since their involvement only exacerbated social harm. Such serious tasks required original thinkers and persons qualified enough to be recognized as master theologians and juridical authorities (*imāms*). Interestingly, in his view, the chief offense of unqualified theologians was rooted in their unthinking imitation of authority. Their actions bred a cult of personal authority and sacralized the authority of ordinary mortals to the elevated status of prophetic authority. Ghazālī's larger point, in my view, was that often the very sword dogmatic and unthinking heresy-mongers brandish becomes the instrument on which they can be impaled.

During much of these polemical exercises, Ghazālī played devil's advocate. One would err to think that he did not have his own disagreements with the Muʿtazilīs. When he playfully cast them in a positive light during the course of his polemical exchanges to score points on his Ashʿarī adversaries, it did not amount to an endorsement. Interestingly, it is precisely because polemical gestures are playful and fluid that it becomes startlingly obvious that theological doctrines are themselves flexible, if not plastic. For in the playfulness of polemics, the constructed nature of theological discourse becomes transparent. Ghazālī was petrified at the prospect of such polemics being displayed publicly in debates, and he thus strongly opposed such exhibitions. He was acutely aware that they had the potential to make many people skeptical and to undermine their beliefs and religious commitments.

What is remarkable about Ghazālī's theological discourses is the considerable amount of self-reflexivity that he demonstrated. Actually, his theological writings represent some of his most insightful dimensions; they were the coalescing point for all his skills, talent, and passion. Ghazālī himself had no intention of abandoning theology or wishing it away. To the contrary, he tried to use it as productively as possible in order to define the borders between unbelief and faith while at the same time raising the bar as to what qualified as heresy. He realized that his greatest challenge was to create a plurality of views within a faith tradition and that, to that end, theology was a valuable instrument to legitimate diversity. It is obvious that Ghazālī had such a fine mind that if he had wished to make a theoretical argument for the recognition of all the contending theological schools in Muslim theology he may have been the one person who could have made the case for it.

At the same time, he was also acutely aware that a superfluous and rootless pluralism would be worthless; knowledge has to be rooted in the specifics of practice. While he viewed knowledge to be universal, unaffected by creed or identity, true knowledge, he believed, is not obtained by the use of reason. True knowledge requires an inexpressible cosmic orientation as a sense of reality (*ḥaqīqa*), the knowledge of *how* to live. Only an imaginative self-identification with some central principle such as a belief in God and divine inspiration, he felt, can produce true knowledge.[66] True knowledge is the reason why theology becomes such an indispensable grammar for certain classes of people who require conviction through empirical observation. The great masses of people, Ghazālī often asserted, know and identify with the truth better than the learned. This is probably the main reason why he was so skeptical of the publicized antics of the learned, for their discourses had the potential to cloud that natural affiliation that ordinary people have with their beliefs.

Ghazālī was personally ambivalent about theology. At some stages of his life, it served him well, especially as he recovered from his personal crisis. He was also aware of its potential to mediate public discourse and make the environment more tolerant, allowing for a plurality of views to flourish within certain limits. At the same time, he was conscious of the fact that theology is a double-edged sword, one that can be indiscriminately wielded both politically and privately. He knew how he had used theology in the service of the politics of the Saljūqs—the very *salāṭīn* he accused other theologians of slavishly serving—when he ideologically combated their Ismāʿīlī adversaries on their behalf. Perhaps there was even a hint of remorse in some of his jeremiads for his role in all this, but it may be a contested point. At the private level, individuals can pursue fratricidal vendettas against each other in vexatious heresy-mongering, producing social chaos and disruption in endless and futile pursuits that stray from the tenets of faith. The landscape of Muslim religious history is littered with the corpses of such sectarian disputes fuelled by theological partisanship, as is the landscape of the present. Personally, Ghazālī found very little use for doxological theology and drifted toward a Neoplatonic theosophy, much to the chagrin of the more rigorous theologians who criticized him for making what seemed to them an unfortunate turn. He, in turn, appears to have been content in his rediscovery of faith and self, a faith, as he acknowledged, that was not grounded in reason inasmuch as it was inspired by the divine afflatus.

Therefore, there is no salvation except in independence of thought.

"Forget all you've heard and clutch what you see
At sunrise what use is Saturn to thee?"

If writing these words yields no other outcome save to make you doubt your inherited beliefs, compelling you to inquire, then it was worth it—leave alone profiting you. Doubt transports [you] to the truth. Who does not doubt fails to inquire. Who does not inquire fails to gain insight. Without insight, you remain blind and perplexed. So we seek God's protection from such an outcome.
—Abū Ḥāmid al-Ghazālī, *Mīzān al-ʿamal* (*Balance of Deeds*)

6 Metaphysics of Belief

Faith in a Nutshell

Ghazālī remained primarily committed to two constituencies in his explicitly theological writings: intellectuals and ordinary people. He reveled in plumbing the complicated arguments of doxological theology mingled with philosophical insights, which he used with great effect in public discourse against political and ideological opponents such as the Muʿtazilīs, the Ismāʿīlīs, and others. At the same time, he was eager to protect the simplicity of faith found among ordinary people from the disruptive influences of theological polemics. A public domain overloaded with theological polemics, he feared, would lead to confusion and, worse, would spoil the naive and simple faith of ordinary people. Since he had been deprived of such unspoiled faith—simple faith unblemished by the exaggeration of intellect that destroys the harmony of any faith—Ghazālī genuinely wished it for others and explicitly expressed this wish in some of his writings.

In *Resuscitation*, it appears forcefully in a discussion in which monotheism (*tawḥīd*), yoked to the idea of absolute reliance (*tawakkul*) on God, is elaborately treated. Ghazālī demonstrated his argument by using as an analogy the walnut. The four graded stages of belief in the oneness of God (*tawḥīd*) are analogous to the four parts of a walnut: the outer shell, the peel, the nut, and the oil extract.[1] A mere verbal confession of the article of faith is the first and primary stage. It is equivalent to the walnut shell. Like the shell protects the nut, elementary faith protects the individual from harmful and injurious elements of unbelief. It is, simply, a protective fiber, very little else. It discloses nothing about the quality of the faith, just as the shell tells the connoisseur very little about the quality of the nut inside it. Even a heedless believer, or a hypocrite for that matter, can make a declaration of faith, but it will remain superficial; so, from the perspective of the other, more developed stages of belief, this elementary stage appears to be almost equal to "hypocrisy." Submitting to Islam on this nominal level has the benefit of admitting an individual into the community of believers. Its greatest advantage, of course, is political. Even a nominal Muslim enjoys immunity from the aggression of conquering Muslim armies. In the premodern Muslim political system, a non-Muslim's allegiance to the Islamic empire was demonstrated by paying special taxes in exchange for the status of a protected subject (*dhimmī*).[2]

When a person commits to faith with the heart, understands its meaning, and consciously takes certain measures to avoid making a superficial confession, then this person conforms to Ghazālī's second stage of belief. Faith at this level protects the individual from harm, just as the peel surrounding the nut protects the nutritious substance from deterioration and decay. In Ghazālī's words, a person at this stage of faith has "a firm knot on the heart" (*ʿuqda ʿalā al-qalb*). Provided, of course, that sin does not erode faith, at a minimum such an individual can expect protection from the torment of hell in the afterlife. But salvation is not automatic. A number of factors constantly threaten the knots of faith, he points out. Heretical beliefs (*bidʿa*)—in other words, beliefs unsubstantiated by canonical authority—Ghazālī warned, can be extremely corrosive to one's faith.

Just as the protective peel insulates the nut from rotting, so does dialectical theology (*kalām*) protect the individual's faith from harm. Here, despite his occasional scorn for theologians, Ghazālī approved the role of the decent theologian, whose purpose is to repel the heretics who undermine the knot of faith in the hearts of the majority of people. Interestingly, he qualified his description of the theologian as one who is a "confessional monotheist" (*muwaḥḥid*). Ghazālī appears to have been saying that such a theologian's discourse is designed solely to defend the monotheistic beliefs etched on the hearts of ordinary folk and to protect their faith and commitment from dilution. At the level of conviction, Ghazālī explains, the dialectical theologian and the layperson might be similar. However, the two differ in one crucial respect: the theologian is able to circumvent the snares of the heretics thanks to his superior intellectual talents, whereas the layperson, who lacks such skills, is vulnerable.

The third stage of commitment to faith produces yet another kind of monotheist. Here, the believer witnesses the truth "as it is" in its manifest reality. In terms of the integrity of faith, such a believer is akin to the kernel of the nut. Unlike a person whose faith is only "skin deep"—the one covered by the peel of faith—the believer who grasps the kernel of faith understands that only a single cause animates all reality. Truth at the deepest level thus becomes singular, even though externally truth may appear to be multiple.

The person who not only attests to a singular reality but also witnesses the existence of a singular being as the essence of all reality has reached the pinnacle of faith. Such a person embodies the essence of faith, just as the oil of the nut embodies the essence of the walnut. "He [a believer] does not witness the totality," explains Ghazālī, "from the perspective of multiplicity, but views it from the perspective of a singularity or indivisible unity."

Thus, the four stages of monotheistic confession correspond to four existential and embodied formations of religiosity: hypocrisy (*nifāq*) is the lowest rung of faith, followed by doctrinal rectitude (*iʿtiqād*), then faith as trusting in God in an ultimate sense (*tawakkul*), and culminating in contemplative vision (*mushāhada*) at the apex. Despite his concern for the beliefs of the ordinary folk, Ghazālī's language of faith may only have been accessible to people when he used analogies to explain it. Once he began to explain the complex gradations of faith as he commented on the faith-as-a-walnut analogy, his language gravitated toward a sophisticated, elite discourse.

As a creed, says Ghazālī, monotheism must ultimately lead the religious subject to attain religiosity by means of the contemplative vision, when the totality of reality as a multiplicity of parts is both apprehended and witnessed as a single reality. Reaching this goal, he admitted, is an extraordinary challenge. But Ghazālī quickly elaborated that what he meant by "contemplative vision" was the monotheism of the intellect (*tawḥīd al-ʿaql*), the desideratum of the seeker after truth. He conceded that in witnessing God a person cannot totally be immune from the distractions of the multiplicity of the Other, or non-God, from time to time. It requires a tremendous amount of spiritual labor to grasp and experience the contemplative vision, the highest level of perfection in monotheism.

Explaining how the multiplicity of self-evident substances, contingents, and bodies can be reduced to a unity of essences is something that Ghazālī was reluctant to indulge in. His stock answer was that these matters fall within the realm of revelatory knowledge (*ʿilm al-mukāshafa*), a subject beyond the goals of the *Resuscitation*, which is devoted to ethics. Disclosing sensitive esoteric knowledge in writing is a most risky and imprudent undertaking, he notes. What he was prepared to say, though, was that seeing reality in terms of multiplicity and seeing it in terms of unity are not mutually exclusive perspectives; instead, they are perspectives viewed from the same frame.

To show how the various perspectives on reality are interlocking components of a single manifold, he used the analogy of the relation of the limbs to the unity of the body. For instance, a human being who is deeply introspective and knowledgeable about human anatomy might look at the various body parts and imagine the body to be several disjointed units, placing the emphasis on the unique capacity of each limb. Another observer might see the variety of limbs to be the uniqueness of an integrated and unitary being. Most people view humans as a composite of multiple organs and limbs, not a collection of disjointed limbs. Similarly, says Ghazālī, everything in existence, from the Creator to the created, is the product of multiple and diverse perspectives (*iʿtibārāt*) and contemplative visions (*mushāhadāt*). From one perspective, an object might be viewed as unitary, while seen from another perspective it looks multiple.

Addressing skeptics who might question his explanation, Ghazālī cautioned that common sense requires that we not deny anything simply because we have not yet attained it or do not yet understand it.[3] He was fond of quoting the first caliph, Abū Bakr, who said, "Acknowledging an inability to comprehend something is itself a form of comprehension."[4] It is precisely when one concedes one's inability to comprehend something as profound as the divine unity in all of creation that one is compelled to accept faith by means of verification.[5] (Others attain to faith by intuitive means and do not require rational verification.) The ideal of comprehending the singularity of all being in the multiplicity of creation, while not part of one's essential reality, is sufficiently compelling for one to acquiesce to the truth by way of faith.

For instance, one may not be a prophet, Ghazālī notes, but that does not preclude one from believing in prophecy and becoming a stakeholder in the concept. In doing so, one does not become a prophet, since it is not necessary to be a prophet to experience the effects of prophecy.[6] Faith at its optimum unveils complex realities to the believer in the form of contemplative visions, experiences that might occur only momentarily, like transient shafts of lightning. It is very rare that visions become a permanent condition and feature of a religious life.

Ghazālī narrated with some relish the exchange between Ibrāhīm Khawāṣṣ (d. 903/291), an early mystic, and the famous mystic and martyr Manṣūr al-Ḥallāj. The story epitomizes the different existential stages of religiosity. As an ascetic, Khawāṣṣ regularly undertook penances by living in the desert. On an occasion, Ḥallāj asked him, "What condition are you in?" To which Khawāṣṣ replied, "I undertake journeys so that I can correct my state of absolute trust in God [*tawakkul*]." Ḥallāj retorted, "You have ruined your life in order to inhabit your inner dwelling; where is the assimilation into divine unity [*fanā' fī al-tawḥīd*]?"[7] Commenting on this exchange, Ghazālī observes that Khawāṣṣ was engaged in the third level of divine unity, whereas Ḥallāj was urging him to ascend to the highest level of expressing the unity of God in contemplative visions.

Reaching perfection of faith and apprehending the absolute unity of God unveils the unseen realities, according to Ghazālī. Contemplative vision is a superior vision to biological sight. In the former, all the realities are observed through the heart and mind, whereas the latter depends on the organic instrument. As one draws closer to the most advanced stage of faith, one transcends the perception of the divine, just as an idolater beholds his idol as a means to reach for a higher and more personal encounter with the Real. In Ghazālī's view, there are two serious conditions that secrete an element of polytheism into a monotheist's faith and impede the individual from attaining an exclusive encounter with the divine: when a religious subject places his ultimate reliance on the discretion of human beings, and when a religious subject depends on the efficacy of inanimate objects.[8]

For example, it is entirely contrary to the spirit of trust in God (*tawakkul*) and belief in the singularity of the divine being (*tawḥīd*) to say that the ultimate cause of the growth of crops is rain, just as it is offensive to suggest that the movement of ships is due to the winds on the sea. In fact, to make claims that ultimate causes can be located in natural phenomena is tantamount to associationism (*shirk*), an anathema to pristine monotheism. For such a claim reveals an ignorance of the reality of all causes. Moreover, human beings are not capable of providing sustenance, nor is it in their discretion to give life or to withhold it. To attribute the ultimate cause of things to human beings while remaining oblivious to God's hand in such matters is contrary to monotheism.[9]

Let's presume, says Ghazālī, that a monarch writes an order of reprieve that at the last minute commutes the execution of a person on death row. Imagine how offensive it would be to the king if the person whose life was saved announced that it was the pen and the paper on which the order of reprieve was written that saved his life, unless he meant it figuratively. In saying the pen saved his life, the reprieved criminal would deliberately deprive the king of his efficacy, nothing short of lèse-majesté. If the denial of such effective causation is offensive in an earthly setting, then it stands to reason, Ghazālī implies, that it gives offense in the divine court when the role of the ultimate cause of causes is not acknowledged.

Even when Ghazālī tried his best to explain faith for laypersons with the use of the most elegant of analogies and the plainest of language, he was handicapped by his own intellectual makeup; his scholarly labors inevitably took him into the philosophical and metaphysical thicket, at a distance from lay audiences. Was it a caprice that made him yearn to be the defender of the popular cause? Certainly, his lifelong passion was for mastering the elite sciences and discourses, especially the philosophical discourses, where he oscillated between Aristotelian and Neoplatonic narratives. Any cursory survey of Ghazālī's writings confirms that he was committed to metaphysics without showing any qualms about using the language of philosophy to explain religion—nor did he hesitate to use very explicitly Islamic formulations in order to frame philosophical debates.

This lends some credence to the criticism, often vicious, that his contemporaries, such as Ṭurṭūshī, directed at him; they said his writings were "woven with the views of philosophers and the constructions of the Brethren of Purity [Ikhwān al-Ṣafā]."[10] The latter were avant-garde intellectuals in Islam's early centuries who were viewed with deep suspicion by traditional pietists. Ghazālī's critics held them in contempt for believing that prophecy is a talent that can be acquired and for regarding miracles as trickery, among other things.[11] While Ghazālī did not explicitly subscribe to any of the controversial group's views, there are indeed strong resemblances between his philosophical hermeneutics and those of the Brethren of Purity. A hallmark of their interpretations that also corresponds to certain mystical traits is the idea that all reality is constituted by a dualism, having exterior and interior (exoteric versus esoteric), hidden and apparent, visible and invisible dimensions.[12]

What the Brethren of Purity really aspired after was to provide a hermeneutic in which religion and philosophy could ideally be reconciled as mutually reinforcing each other—or at least not viewed as antithetical to each other. It is on this matter that Ghazālī left his most important signature on early Muslim philosophical discussions. Whatever sympathies he may have had for the agenda of the Brethren of Purity remain moot. If he had them, they remained subordinate to what he thought were the essential elements of Islam as a creed. His forays into philosophy and his critique of the views of certain philosophers earned him notoriety in philosophical circles, where his views were received with a passion that equaled that of his critics who were theologians.

The Trouble with Philosophy

A popular anecdote often invoked to portray Ghazālī's infatuation with philosophy is a report attributed to Ibn al-ʿArabi al-Mālikī (d. 543/1148), once a student of Ghazālī's. "Our master Abū Ḥāmid al-Ghazālī," declares Ibn al-ʿArabī, "swallowed philosophy and then tried an emetic but failed to expurgate it."[13] The imagery is revealing in its attempt to both infantilize Ghazālī and portray him as a victim of his own intellectual appetite. In some ways, it would be an apt description if it were not for the malice and the intended backhanded insult, for Ghazālī did indeed have both an intellectual curiosity about philosophy and an ongoing struggle with it. However, this statement has been employed with great effect by his critics, who have used the fact that he borrowed from foreign sources of knowledge to discredit aspects of his intellectual legacy and impugn his credibility.

It is Ghazālī's complicated engagement with philosophy that is of interest to us. During the second half of his four-year stay in Baghdād as professor, Ghazālī embraced philosophy, either as a kind of therapy or as a weapon to further his ideological agenda. It was not the last time that philosophy would be viewed as a therapy, for Wittgenstein later observed that "the philosopher treats a question like a disease."[14] Ghazālī had several questions—or diseases, if you like—for which he sought a remedy in philosophy with a passion for logic. Philosophy, in his view, was not a single discipline, or science (*ʿilm*). He saw it as a rubric for four related disciplines, namely, mathematics and geometry, logic, metaphysics, and physics.[15]

Among the compelling grammars of philosophy, Ghazālī at first found solace in logic and deployed it to advance his theological propositions. Mastering the repertoire of logic, as well as of metaphysics and physics, clearly furnished his narrative with additional clarity, subtlety, and sophistication. However, it also provided him with new possibilities to share and exchange ideas with audiences beyond his limited fraternity of jurists and theologians. This is also what makes his scholarly labors so distinct—that he managed to innovate a very early interdisciplinary approach, mixing metaphors and paradigms in order to illuminate ideas and problems. Despite the fact that he was ruthlessly criticized for "mixing" types of knowledge, he succeeded in reaching audiences familiar with philosophical discourse, literature, and mysticism in his own culture and beyond.

Ghazālī's major trouble with philosophy was twofold. First, he was disturbed by the attitude of the philosophers and the impact of philosophical discussions and theology in the public domain. Second, and related to the first point in a slightly different manner, he took issue with the ideological nexus that was formed between philosophy and the political opposition to the Saljūqs that was spearheaded by the Ismāʿīlīs.

His encounter with philosophy, especially the work of Abū Naṣr al-Fārābī (d. 339/950) and Abū ʿAlī Ibn Sīnā, brought him face-to-face with a new epistemic grammar that both enchanted and dismayed him. He was enchanted by philosophy since it aided him in making more persuasive theological arguments. What he found odious was the hubris that familiarity with philosophy bred within elite scholarly circles. The condescending attitude of some philosophers toward religion and its practitioners especially concerned him. Since he did not view the philosophers as taking religion seriously, he feared that if such attitudes became widespread they could damage the general public's confidence in religion and undermine the ethical and moral system that it underpinned. What may have further provoked Ghazālī's righteous indignation was the absolutism that he discovered to be common to Ismāʿīlī and philosophical thought. Ghazālī was not opposed to rationality; he cherished it. What particularly horrified him was the rationalist absolutism that he found in both groups, which in turn was succeeded by the more serious and, in his view, more dangerous problem of antinomianism.

The Muslim philosophers, Ghazālī maintained, were infatuated with "high-sounding names such as Socrates, Hippocrates, Plato, and Aristotle" and boasted of the excellence of their science as a tool for unraveling and understanding reality. Enamored by this intellectual legacy, the philosophers, Ghazālī observed, "den[ied] revealed laws and religious confessions and reject[ed] the teachings of religion and religious communities, believing them to be man-made laws and embellished tricks."[16]

But he was unable shake off his love-hate relationship with philosophy and the Muslim philosophers. He esteemed philosophy's use as a means of persuasion and argumentation, and he internalized a good deal of it. As a believer in revelatory truth, the theologian in him precluded him from accepting philosophy as an end in itself. For all the reasons just mentioned, he not only challenged the aura of invincibility of the philosophers' arguments but also consciously labored to undermine and displace that aura. With this attitude, he went to great lengths to show that philosophy itself is subject to critical interrogation and that philosophers hold views that are flawed by other standards of truth, such as those of theology.

What may have inflamed his ire was the common trait of antinomianism that he detected in the discourses of the philosophers and the Ismāʿīlīs, whom he claimed also "render[ed] invalid the revealed norms."[17] He spoke disparagingly of the Ismāʿīlī belief in an absolute authority that alone can provide authoritative and morally correct knowledge to the community. In his political-cum-theological treatise *The Obscenities of the Esoterists* (*Faḍāʾiḥ al-bāṭinīya*), he systematically refuted the Ismāʿīlī claims. But Ismāʿīlism, in his view, was not only a political challenge to the ʿAbbāsid-Saljūq establishment. It posed an intellectual and theological challenge first and foremost, since it also drew on certain philosophical strains of Neoplatonism. His goal in writing *Incoherence of the Philosophers* (*Tahāfut al-falāsifa*) was not confined to the task of identifying the theological lapses in the thinking of the philosophers. It also attempted to expose the predisposition of philosophical thought to absolutist and authoritarian appropriation, an element he feared that the Ismāʿīlīs might gainfully exploit, which they purposefully did.

It is this ideological convergence of two influential ideological trends—Ismāʿīlism and philosophy—that formed the subtext for his philosophical and theological writings. Frequently, he refuted an Ismāʿīlī claim only to allude to the sinister resemblances it had to the ideas of the philosophers. The common thread shared by his adversaries was the overweening emphasis on the part of the philosophers on discursive rationality and the Ismāʿīlī tendency to dismiss any reliance on human capacity and mortal intellect, seeking instead refuge in infallible authority.[18] It would, therefore, not be incorrect to view the *Incoherence*, in part, as the philosophical pendant to his political theology documented in *Obscenities of the Esoterists*. The latter is a bruising critique of Ismāʾīlī doctrines, as well as of some ideas of the philosophers.

I believe Ghazālī was perhaps more offended by the reasoning and justification that the philosophers provided in support of their views than by their substantive ideas themselves. He was outraged by their ratiocination that religious discourse is an expedient to pacify the intellectual mediocrity of the subaltern classes while the elites are entitled to derive a different and higher truth from revelation. This might have been the provocation that led him to make overtures to protect the religion of the masses from corruption by scholars.

There may be at least two further reasons why he found the philosophers' approach to religion offensive. First, he, too, may have personally believed that the elites could appreciate the more subtle and deeper meaning of revelation and religion. Yet he also recognized that if he conceded the coexistence of two parallel religious discourses, one for the masses and almost another religion for the elite, it would give a completely utilitarian and instrumental character to religion. This would not only undermine the confidence of the populace in religion per se but also make of religion a useful fiction. Second—flowing from the first, and perhaps more important—one suspects that Ghazālī feared that the philosophers' interpretation of religion would in the long term pillory the ethical imperatives of religion, which might have a domino effect by making people skeptical about all other doctrines, from the authenticity and authority of prophecy—namely, the person of the Prophet Muḥammad—to the Qur'ān. Philosophy unchecked and unrestrained, he thought, might wound Islam as a religious tradition.

The point I want to make is that as a philosophically minded intellectual Ghazālī may have believed that there is a genuine place for an elite interpretation of religion, since people are naturally inclined to perceive things differently. But Ghazālī the realist theologian viewed the social cost of permitting such an attitude to flourish to be too high; such a view could imperil the core and essence of his religious tradition itself. Would Ghazālī's attitude have been any different if the philosophers had not been so brazen as to articulate their view of religion in crude terms of "expediency"? While this remains a speculative question, I do believe that if the philosophers had been less partisan and high-minded about solving all the difficult questions about religion, from prophecy and values to theodicy, Ghazālī may have responded differently. At least, he would not have perceived them to be so threatening and may not have pursued them so doggedly. The cardinal flaw in the philosophers' approach was their hubris, in his view, which made them overstate their case.

Philosophy wanted to be the master narrative, even though the philosophers made overtures toward partnership with religion. Religion, in turn, saw itself as the master narrative. And, in the case of Islam, there was an additional political contest. As Islam was the new master narrative in regions that had only recently obeyed other gods and followed different faiths, it would have been political suicide to concede that Allah needed a helping hand from Zeus. So while some religious scholars accepted the bona fides of philosophy, placing it in a subordinate position to the dogma of religion, Ghazālī was skeptical, despite his admiration for aspects of the discipline. He preferred some ambiguity. Philosophical ideas, like mystical formulations, Ghazālī repeatedly stated, are so complex and multidimensional that it is often preferable to leave some secrets unspoken and implicit. When such complex ideas are publicized, he argued, they invariably cause great harm, since they are often the cause for miscommunication and dangerous misunderstanding.

At the personal level, however, philosophy prompted Ghazālī to ask the larger ontological questions. Despite its merits, the study of logic had limitations in its ability to help him overcome some of his more complex epistemological and ontological doubts. As he indirectly indicated in his spiritual testimony, he was driven to ask: Who am I? How do I know myself? Where am I on the chain of being? What is the purpose of my existence? Why am I? What is my particularity?

At some stage in the prime of his life, Ghazālī remarks, the thirst to get a grip of the sense and true reality of things became so overpowering that he often imagined that certain things were involuntarily and providentially happening to him. It was at this stage of his life, he confesses, that, like a snake's skin, the fetters of compliance to tradition and adherence to inherited beliefs just peeled off.[19] He does not tell us for how long this state of mind continued. He does admit, though, that his intense reflections on the question of knowing things a priori only precipitated more questions. It led him to ask: Why are the children of Jews, Christians, and Muslims raised in their specific religious traditions and not in others? Who determines their choices? He was aware that the teachings of the Prophet Muḥammad state that everyone is born in a natural state and with a built-in disposition for the truth (*fiṭra*). Tradition teaches that people are shaped in their beliefs by the socialization provided by their parents in childhood. This only prompted Ghazālī to probe further, for the average comprehensibility only provokes further incomprehensibility.

He recognized how critical it is to grasp the content, or substance, of *fiṭra*, the innate disposition within humans. At first, an unnerving vacancy surrounded the question of *fiṭra*, which then led Ghazālī to conclude that *fiṭra* must be something of the original condition equivalent to true being, where reality is perceived in all its luminescence. In its natural state, being has an a priori predisposition for knowledge as well as for comprehending the unity of God (*tawḥīd*), Ghazālī concluded.[20] His conclusions about this innate predisposition of *being* only led him to explore the value of intuitive and ontological knowledge. Intuitive knowledge, or aesthetic sensibility (*dhawq*), literally means "to taste." Muslim mystics explain *dhawq* as a cognitive condition that follows spiritual ecstasy, when the subject experiences the first steps in witnessing "true reality."[21] In other words, *dhawq* is the metaphor for ontological knowledge and experiential wisdom. Vico defines the Latin word *sapere* to mean "tasting," a term that metaphorically becomes the word for "wisdom" (*sapientia*, or "tastefulness") because wisdom puts things to their natural uses rather than to artificial ones.[22] It is this aesthetic sensibility that allows us to configure how knowledge is made as poetic wisdom, *sapientia poetica*. Knowledge derived from mystical and self-reflective experiences, like all true art, is a more reliable form of knowing than culturally constructed epistemologies.

Ghazālī thus distinguished between a priori knowing (ontic knowing) on the one hand and discursive knowing on the other. Discursive knowledge, like philosophy, theology, and ethics, delivers one to the threshold (*dihlīz*) of this pure ontology. But it is from the ontological realm that being derives its transcendent and ineffable character. If knowledge and knowing cannot account for this vital ontological dimension of being, then knowledge itself, in Ghazālī's view, is deficient.

The way he narrated his experience deserves some attention. Once he recovered from his searing emotional crisis, which was partly occasioned by his skepticism of all knowledge, he at last recognized that discursive knowledge is a necessary component in the quest for certainty but that it is not the only component.[23] From that point onward, Ghazālī construed discursive knowledge very differently. Discursive knowledge from then on had unshakeable foundations in rationality. After his recovery from his knowledge crisis, Ghazālī observes, he regained his confidence in the self-evident data of reason (*al-ḍarūriyāt al-ʿaqlīya*) as a reliable source for certainty.[24] A characteristic of discursive knowledge, says Ghazālī, is its irreversible certainty to withstand the most inexplicable trickery and attempts to falsify it. For example, it is accepted that ten is greater than the number three. But what if someone asks you to invert this elementary certainty of arithmetic and believe that three is greater than ten on the ground that the challenger can miraculously transmute a rock into gold or a stick into a snake? Ghazālī's response was an unambiguous "No." "I will not doubt my knowledge because of this feat," says Ghazālī. "The only effect it will have on me," he continues, "is that it will make me wonder [*taʿajjub*] as to how he could accomplish such a [feat]; but as to doubt about what I know? Never!"[25]

Discursive knowledge was thus, for Ghazālī, equal to verisimilitude. He was grounded in essentialist discursive rationality, in causation and empirical certainty. Reason is a single scientific discipline, Ghazālī maintained, citing an unnamed poet, whereas insanity has varieties.[26] His trust in reason is what gave him an unshakeable certainty and confidence. Parenthetically, we have to mention that he was not closed to the idea of wondering and was open to *imagining* beyond discursive knowing, an imagination that would not affect the empirical data. However, his confidence in reason and rational data stemmed from a new experience. His attachment to reason, Ghazālī explicitly states, was "not based on a constructed proof [*naẓm dalīl*] or systematic argument [*tartīb kalām*]." "Rather," he reveals, "it is by means of a light [*nūr*] that God had cast in the bosom. And that light is the key to most knowledge. Therefore, anyone who thinks that the unveiling of truth depends on carefully formulated proofs has indeed placed the abundant mercy of God under restraint."[27] One cannot ignore here the way he depicts the role of innate nature (*fiṭra*) as a receptacle in the heart for the light associated with divine mercy and grace. This form of ontic knowing, knowing from being, is what Ghazālī and the Muslim tradition generally metonymically refer to as the "expansion of the bosom" (*sharḥ al-ṣadr*), a code for the essential vitalization of the self.

In an effortless move, Ghazālī grounded reason in a transcendent ontology. So, while the protocols of reason and discursive logic remain intact, rational discursivity can be viewed as continuing into a pure ontological realm. At least, the ontological horizon is in theory both opened and naturalized in conjunction with reason; epistemology and ontology can coexist side by side as neighbors without creating an impermeable divide between them, as certain strands of post-Enlightenment thought have construed the relationship between the two aspects. The protocols and disciplines governing both would, of course, be different, but the main point is to demonstrate that continuity is possible from one mode of knowledge to another. It is the ontological moorings to which reason is anchored that provided Ghazālī with the kind of unshakeable epistemic certainty and inner confidence that René Descartes might have longed for but was reluctant to embrace.

Given the fluidity between epistemology and ontology in the Ghazālian scheme of things, often his explanatory statements of causation require careful attention in order to discern in which register and in what key he spoke.[28]

It is, therefore, not surprising that his references to ontological propositions frequently get confused with epistemological propositions and vice versa. Ghazālī's ontology was unapologetically theistic; in fact, it was an ontology centered on divine grace. His epistemology thus had metaphysical backing and was unmistakably mingled with theistic presuppositions. To put it slightly differently, one can say that Ghazālī gave priority to the ontological chicken, whereas Ibn Rushd later gave priority to the epistemological egg. And another, younger contemporary of Ibn Rushd, namely, Muḥī al-Dīn Ibn ʿArabī, viewed the entire universe as just one big ontological chicken. Or one could say, to be sure, that Ibn ʿArabī combined the chicken and the egg—but as ordinary mortals we see a great deal more of the chicken than of the egg.

A Clash of Epistemologies

Ghazālī's major disagreement with his philosopher and Ismāʿīlī adversaries was on the question of epistemology. As a consequence of Ghazālī's commitment to revealed authority, both his metaphysics and his epistemology were flooded with theistic foundationalism. So even when his epistemology consisted of certain self-evident rational propositions, they were tinged by an a priori theological fidelity to revelation. He took issue with the philosophers when their views on a whole number of issues did not conform to some of the foundations that he deemed to be incontrovertible and necessary elements of his theory of knowledge. Similarly, he was skeptical of Ismāʿīlī epistemic claims that resulted in ontological transgression, especially of their belief in the authority of charismatic leaders who possess absolute knowledge. Manṭiqī spelled out the essential differences between religion and philosophy, differences that Ghazālī doggedly wished to retain despite his predilection for philosophy. The repertoire of religion, says Manṭiqī, consists of key words and concepts like revelation, seeking the satisfaction of the divine, acting on divine commands, being guided by the light of reason, invoking God without compunction, seeking the plain meaning of revelation and the true meaning of the tradition, and upholding the consensus of the community as an ideal.[29] The repertoire of the philosophers, on the other hand, consists of key words and concepts like investigation and pride in intellectual labor; using expressions such as "I examined," "I abhorred," "I approved," and "I walk in the light provided by the Creator of creation"; invoking names like Plato and Socrates and others; talking about nature, natural causation, primordial matter, form, and essence; and employing terminology that no Muslim, Jew,

Christian, Magian, or Manichean would dare invoke, says Manṭiqī with ill-disguised sarcasm.

Philosophers hold that doctrines are true only if they meet the criteria of rational arguments. Belief in God and the truth of revelation are certainly not among the elementary propositions. A proposition regarding God stands in need of rational justification, a philosopher would argue. Thus, a philosopher seeks evidence for the existence of God. If it is difficult to prove, philosophers work on certain assumptions to demonstrate the reality of a realm of existence beyond the physical—the metaphysical—and build a narrative around such a probability. Some Muslim theologians borrowed heavily from the metaphysical narratives of the Muslim philosophers. While there were commonalities between the two epistemological systems, there were also significant differences that resulted in disagreement.

Ghazālī accused the philosophers of sleight of hand. He found that they were inconsistent. They claimed fidelity to the empirical tradition but did not perform to its requirements; it was an empiricism to which he also swore loyalty. The philosophers, Ghazālī says, "use[d] the appearance of their mathematical and logical sciences as evidentiary proof for the truth of their metaphysical sciences, using [this] as a gradual enticement for the weak in mind."[30] But in practice there was no such comparable metaphysical proof. Perfection, a feature of the mathematical sciences, was absent in the metaphysical sciences, which explains why the philosophers disagreed among themselves. Were metaphysics an exact science like mathematics, Ghazālī argues, then it would not be susceptible to error.[31]

When interpreting religious and revealed discourse, Ghazālī was, of course, neither a literalist nor a commonsense scripturalist. He often lost patience with those who asserted that the language of religious discourse *exclusively* relied on the warrant of scriptural authority (*naṣṣ*), namely, the Qur'ān and the *Sunna*. Aware of the damage that a blunt-edged scripturalist approach inflicted on the image of religion, Ghazālī habitually increased the discursive and rationalist torque of his arguments. He became impatient with religious scholars who relied on theistic arguments without striving to provide any rational explanation for their views. It is because Ghazālī effectively used two discourses, religious and philosophical, to explain his arguments that his writings demonstrate such an extraordinary depth and sophistication.

Scholars who wished to defend religious arguments, Ghazālī argued, had to be equipped with the best and most advanced intellectual tools; if not, they did religion a disservice and parodied the discourse of religion despite their best intentions.[32] Consider his response to some theologians who tried to refute the scientific arguments provided by philosophers as to why lunar and solar eclipses occur. Muslim philosophers were as well-versed in astronomy, science, botany, and medicine as they were in the sciences of religion. They, of course, had a scientific explanation as to how and why a lunar or solar eclipse occurs. They believed that lunar eclipses occur when the earth interposes between the moon and the sun and the latter's light is obscured from the moon. A solar eclipse occurs, they explained, when the lunar orb interposes between the observer and the sun.[33] These matters now seem self-evident to us, as they did to Ghazālī. He was convinced that geometric and arithmetic calculations as well as empirical demonstrations cumulatively made the philosophers' explanation of these natural phenomena incontrovertible and convincing.[34]

Yet some theologians of his day rejected such explanations on dogmatic grounds, and their poor arguments seem to have elicited his pique. In the face of empirical evidence, he comments, some theologians foolishly contested the scientific explanation as to why an eclipse occurs because in their view the heavenly bodies submit to a direct divine revelation, or an instruction from God. The evidence that these theologians adduced, Ghazālī explains, was a fragment of a prophetic report (*ḥadīth*) of dubious provenance that says, "But, if God reveals himself to a thing, it submits itself to Him."[35]

First, Ghazālī undermined their evidence by arguing that it was a disputed fragment of a prophetic report—that it was in fact scandalously false evidence. Second, and perhaps more interesting, he argued that even if this report were sound, it would still lend itself to interpretation (*ta'wīl*). The fragment of the report, Ghazālī explains, means that things submit to God in a figurative and effective sense rather than in a literal and empirical sense. Understanding scientific matters by means of literal interpretation amounts to "rejecting matters that are conclusively true," Ghazālī states unequivocally.[36]

Hermeneutics, he concluded, can resolve the apparent conflict between empirical evidence and scriptural mandates. Interpretive conflict took place because a too-narrow hermeneutic was brought into play. Instead, he preferred to use a larger interpretive aperture in which the canonical texts were interpreted in conjunction with scientific data and common sense in a complex intertextual approach. Armed with this paradigmatic approach, he confidently refuted the views of those scholars who felt compelled by their religious commitments to reject self-evident scientific data.

In a rebarbative tone, Ghazālī charged that such persons actually "harm religion and weaken it." "For these matters," he continues, "rest on demonstrations, geometrical and arithmetical, that leave no room for doubt." He explains: "Thus, when one who studies these demonstrations and ascertains their proofs, deriving thereby information about the time of the two eclipses [and] their extent and duration, is told that this is contrary to religion, [such an individual] will not doubt science, but [will come to doubt] religion. The harm inflicted on religion by those who defend it in an improper manner is greater than [the harm caused by] those who attack it in a proper way." Frustrated by the violation of common sense demonstrated by some implacable theologians, Ghazālī reminds us of the wise dictum that "a rational foe is better than an ignorant friend."[37] With bruising sarcasm, he said elsewhere: "To shun an ignoramus is to make an offering to God!"[38]

In a more buoyant mood, Ghazālī cast his epistemological concerns in the form of demonstrative or syllogistic arguments. These, he explains, are the best means to achieve certainty and security from error in logical propositions. He was not prepared to exchange fact for fiction, firmly believing that the imperatives of logic must seem to have the intransigence of a tornado even in the face of a magician's tricks. In this, he was indebted to the Aristotelian tradition. He used hegemonic tools to create counter-hegemonic narratives. So enamored was he with Aristotelian syllogism that he translated it into an Islamic idiom and found its scriptural equivalents in the Qur'ān, claiming to be the pioneer in this respect. Careful not to concede every logical proposition to the Greeks, he informs us that many categories of demonstrative arguments date back to ancient times. But in order to make the categories more palatable to the intellectual sensibilities of his audiences, he deemed it necessary to update and renovate the terminology of logic.[39] Not only did he believe that arguments presented in a discourse familiar to his audiences would have more persuasive value, but he also implied that logical and rational thinking is inherent to all cultures, including those cultures that are inspired by the teachings of the Qur'ān.[40]

Causation: Natural or Habit?

Inspired by the Qur'ān's notion of God's unsurpassable sovereignty, and coupled to an ontology of divine grace, Ghazālī felt confident in presenting the doctrine of the habitual order of occurrences (*istimrār al-ʿāda*, or *iṭṭirād al-ʿāda*).[41] This doctrine has received a great deal more attention than Ghazālī might have anticipated, evoking a variety of protestations from his adversaries. It has often been used to discredit him as a thinker and as proof of his antirationalism and antiempiricism. It is clear that Ghazālī made this argument in a polemical context against his philosopher adversaries. Against the commonplace notion of material causation, Ghazālī argued that the causes and effects we attribute to things are not what he called *necessary* causes and effects. It is important to follow his qualifiers. It might appear to us that things occur *with* causes and effects, but they do not occur *because of* them.[42]

Denying effective material causation obviously placed Ghazālī at odds with the general understanding of natural causation. Theologians before him had used other formulations to articulate a similar point to his, the best known among these being the doctrine of acquisition of the Ashʿarī school. But Ghazālī took the opportunity to clarify what he meant in order to align and harmonize his theology with the notion of rationality in a seamless narrative. Let's take the example of the burning of cotton when it comes into contact with fire. Ghazālī says that we understand cotton to burn because we are accustomed to seeing it burn on a regular basis. Our observation is therefore one of habit rather than one computed after consideration of the number of causes that make fire burn cotton. We assume that it is the fire that causes combustion and burns the cotton to ashes. But the experiment in itself does not rule out the possibility that there might be another cause, or several causes, for the combustion and the subsequent incineration of the cotton to ashes.

Similarly, through the act of copulation, sperm reaches the womb, but the male sperm producer cannot be viewed as the agent who produced the child or even any of the capacities inherited by the child. Ghazālī viewed what we generally describe as causes to be in reality "instrumental" causes. In other words, certain instrumental causes such as fire and cotton are utilized to produce combustion. We witness procreation after a successful sexual encounter results in a pregnant female. The visible actions, Ghazālī insisted, should not be confused with the efficient causes. "Existence 'with' a thing," he observes, "does not prove it exists 'because of' it." Both he and the philosophers, Ghazālī says, agree that things exist due to something coming from the "direction of the first"—meaning the first cause, or God—either directly or indirectly.[43]

Where Ghazālī parted company with the philosophers was in the explanatory narrative that he provided about the nature of existence and how it is sustained. This differs substantially from those of his philosopher counterparts and of modern empirical scientists. Ghazālī believed that the philosophers had no convincing argument to demonstrate that what they called the principles of existence caused fire to burn or copulation to result in pregnancy.

The reason we expect a match to light is that it happened the last time we tried to light it. If there was something Ghazālī remained skeptical about, then it was permanent and universally necessary causes. For these principles or causes, he believed, can appear and disappear: the best thing we can do is say that they occur regularly. It is this radical aspect of his thinking that inscribed a nontotalizing dimension in Ghazālī's metaphysics.

He agreed, though, that when contact between various bodies does occur a number of properties that philosophers designate as accidents (*aʿrāḍ*) and events (*ḥawādith*) inherent in the substances or bodies are activated. The existence of these properties in their respective forms, Ghazālī continues, "emanates from the one who bestows forms [*wāhib al-ṣuwar*] to things, who is one of the angels."[44] In other words, whether it is due to angels or some other cause, the existence of the substance or body is sustained by the will of God. For instance, when the eye recognizes a color, what really happens is that certain receptacles that Ghazālī calls "readiers" and "preparers"—like the sun, the healthy pupil of the eye, and the colored object viewed—all accept the forms of the accidents and events that have occurred. However, in his view, there is nothing essential in these receptacles that means they *ought* to take on the shapes that they do or the colors that appear in them the way they do. In fact, Ghazālī would say, the only reason they occur in the way they do is because of a divine deliberation and choice: in short, divine voluntarism. The philosopher, on the other hand, says Ghazālī, believes that temporal events stem from certain principles inherent in the nature of things. Therefore, it is necessary that things proceed in a manner that is dictated by the nature of things. According to these ingrained natures, a shiny body will receive the light of the sun and reflect it, while mud will only absorb the light.

Obviously, Ghazālī held on to this doctrine of habitual occurrence in order to prove that the habits or patterns he described could on occasion be suspended. The suspension could then explain and justify the occurrence of prophetic miracles. He had in mind miracles like Abraham's survival in Nimrod's fire and the virgin birth and miraculous conception of Jesus. Even though Ghazālī could not provide a thorough explanation as to how these miracles occurred, he attributed his inability to explain them to the limits of human knowledge, to the fact that we cannot know everything fully. He did, however, provide a ratiocination to suggest that whatever inexplicably happens must have a cause beyond the apparent cause.[45] In other words, the lack of a complete explanation suggests that there is a penumbra of uncertainty in human existence that resists a totalizing narrative.

Reason is something that Ghazālī did not abandon, even though he denied naturalistic causation. And many of his critics confused his skepticism about natural causation with a denial of rationality. He would certainly have conceded the limitations of reason to know things in their totality, but to deny rationality would to his mind be to debauch the imagination. In fact, Ghazālī admitted that there are certain operational patterns of nature at work. However, he insisted that we can call these patterns principles only provided that we do not view them as autonomous principles but rather as part of a domino effect that ultimately connects to divine choice and voluntarism. What Ghazālī wished to stress was that God is actively in charge in both human actions and of the function of nature and cosmos: God *does* micromanage the universe, if you like. The philosophers preferred a Deist God, one who winds up the clock and leaves it to the determinants of its own instrumentation. (And, of course, Ghazālī's position would prompt many moralists to have questions about divine justice due to recurring floods, deaths, war, dispossession, and disease. Eric Ormsby's book on divine justice is a helpful guide to this topic.)[46]

Anticipating that his adversaries would burlesque his reasoning, Ghazālī mounted a preemptive intellectual strike. Paraphrasing the objections of his opponents, he heard them ask: You expect us to believe that if one leaves a book at home, by the time one returns in the evening the book will have turned into a handsome servant, ready to do household chores? By indulging in the caricature of his own reasoning, Ghazālī acted as ventriloquist for his philosopher adversaries, who asked him: So it is eminently possible that a clutch of stones and a bag of dust could turn into gold nuggets and fragrant musk? He had two kinds of answers to these questions—a typical put-down and a serious answer.

Continuing to indulge in his penchant for mockery and humor, Ghazālī says: "I do not know what is at the house at present. All I know is that I have left a book in the house, which is perhaps now a horse that has defiled the library with its urine and its dung. All I know is that the jar of water I left at home might have turned into an apple tree. For God is capable of everything. It is not necessary for the horse to be created from reproductive material [sperm] nor a tree from a seed! In fact, it is not necessary for either of the two to be created from anything." Addressing his readers with a full dose of sarcasm, he adds: "Well, perhaps God did create things that did not exist previously!"[47]

The serious reply that Ghazālī gave to his skeptical interlocutors turned on an epistemology with metaphysical backing or, to use a domestic analogy, an epistemology with a theistic doorstop. All fantasies are possible, he replies, if one believes that a known thing can coexist with its negation. "These absurdities only follow," says Ghazālī, "if the established existence of the *possible* does not permit the creation of knowledge for a human where [the same possible thing] can become nonexistent."[48] In other words, the problem centers on how the *possible* is imagined. If the imagination only permits the existence of one iteration or one incarnation of two identically possible things, then surely the absurd fantasies imagined by Ghazalī's philosopher in the entertaining passage cannot be possible. For the possible existence of one will make the existence of the other impossible. To put it differently, Ghazālī points out that if your system of knowledge and reasoning allows you to believe that the same person can be a man and a horse at the same time, then these fantasies are possible. If the possibility of the one negates the possibility of the other, however, the problem is solved, and your absurd fantasies are voided in reality.

In order to expose the flaws of his interlocutors, Ghazālī polemically led them into an ambush to concede epistemological nihilism. Implicitly, he said that the fantasies of his fictional philosopher—even if they were made by way of polemics—amounted to suggesting that one can actually claim to have *knowledge* of something absurd without having to rationally justify its grounds and its existence. For that is what he believed underpinned the irrational proposition that books can turn into horses. Only a nihilist can believe in nothing. For a nihilist, either the grounds for knowing never existed or it is not possible to discover them. Therefore, a nihilist can believe anything, for a nihilist can claim that one does not have the grounds for knowing in the first place.

Turning the tables on his opponents, Ghazālī suggested that if they could momentarily join him in this fantastical mode of thinking then they might conclude that they were prepared to believe in the abstract existence of something without ascertaining whether such a proposition was feasible in epistemic terms. In other words, he drew them into thinking about knowledge in imaginative terms, not empirical terms. Ghazālī clearly anticipated all the possible responses his doctrine of habitual order might receive and thus prepared his rebuttals. Superficially and at first blush, the impulse is to say that if he did not believe in natural causation and if he believed in miracles that suspend the naturalistic order of causation then surely he was arguing that anything ridiculous and fantastical is possible. Instead of surrendering to such unreason, however, as some extreme forms of postmodernism are inclined to do, Ghazālī took refuge in reason and knowledge. In fact, he cautioned his opponents by saying that in their polemical zeal they had carelessly abandoned epistemic integrity by imagining horses reading books in a library. For even in a hypothetical argument, Ghazālī notes, one cannot abandon reason. It was his adversaries, he pointed out, who were openly flirting with nihilism.

In defending himself, Ghazālī denied any charge that could tie him to nihilism. He conceded that he shifted the grounds for causation to another realm, for he denied philosophical or natural necessity. He posited divine self-sufficiency and sovereignty as the ultimate cause, which is to say that he believed nothing is impossible for the divine. Because he adopted this theistic stance, it compelled him to polemically concede the imaginal *possibility* that anything could happen by divine self-sufficiency. But imagining the possibility of something and realizing it are two different things. A far-fetched fantasy is ruled out of bounds by reason and is only possible by the act of divine will, which is not bounded by reason. So while he did not abandon reason, he did push reason into a conversation with the poetic imagination.

Ghazālī's reason was grounded in a form of ontological antiessentialism. His ontology was premised on the infinite grace and capacity of the divine. This ontology kept any theoretical *possibility* unbounded. But he did concede that there is a world of a difference between being open to the possibility of something happening and it actually happening. There are possibilities, Ghazālī concedes, "that may or may not occur."[49] Furthermore, he differed from the philosophers in believing that the *possibility* of something existing cannot be equated to the *necessity* of something existing: the former is premised on a will, while the latter bears the markings of an autonomous and involuntary natural causation. Because he was a believer, will was nonnegotiable for Ghazālī, for his will was utterly dependent on the will of God.

His alleged skepticism with respect to natural causation, Ghazālī conceded, was limited. This limitation stemmed from an admission on his part that in the macro scale the possibilities of knowledge that God has created for us are bounded. Therefore, it is knowledge (epistemology) as a human enterprise that prevents the realization of the fantasies that his fictional interlocutors suggest are possible within his schema. He reiterated his golden rule that something is only actually possible by repeated occurrence, by continuous habit. It must occur "one time after another," he says, which then "fixes unshakably in our minds the belief in [its] occurrence according to past habit."[50] Therefore, only when all the libraries of the world turn into overcrowded equine stables and this repeatedly and observably occurs can we say that knowledge allows for the absurd to be realized as a habitual occurrence. But if it happens that a book turns into a horse only once, then all we can say is that the occurrence is contrary to knowledge and reason. But, of course, one would be intrigued and would be led to wonder how it happened. Wonder, he hints, may titillate our imagination to explore the mysteries in the realm of the unfathomable.

If Ghazālī exhibited epistemic skepticism, then, paradoxically, it was a skepticism inserted into his thinking by his theistic foundationalism. Unlike a nihilist, who denies there is any way of knowing, Ghazālī acknowledged that there are limits to knowing, that there are different ways of knowing. Implicitly, his ontology inhered to a transcendental signifier that acts as the glass ceiling to knowledge. And even though humans cannot really know what that ceiling is in practical terms, the theoretical limits should induce humility and surrender to an all-knowing Creator.

The limits of knowledge itself stem from a self-reflexive reason. Not only does reason recognize its own limits, but at the precipice, or *dihlīz*, of its limits reason opens up onto an ontological shore. This limitless ontological shore imagines all possibilities that are possible, but its articulation is restricted by the limitations that inhere in language and reason. Surely, in language and reason, a thing and its opposite cannot exist in the same epistemic reality. The only realm where the coexistence of a thing and its opposite is possible is that of imagination; an ontological fantasy, or just a plain fantasy, is not constrained by epistemology. Epistemology is the *knowing* face of ontology. The unknown face of ontology is that realm where a *taste* for things and intuitions flourishes and where subjects have experiences in a unique state where essences are annihilated and pure being subsists.[51]

Ghazālian epistemology has at its base a premise of the possibility of not knowing, the ethical and egotistical readiness to embrace humility and say "I do not know."[52] Ghazālī cited an insightful report: "Knowledge is threefold: an articulate book, an abiding tradition, and the ability to say 'I do not know.'"[53] Everything comes with its alterities: knowing and not knowing, growth and sclerosis. It is self-awareness of this alterity, this human limit, that inspires an ethical humility and curbs vainglory. Ignorance can be turned into a virtue if it is properly received. Genuinely confounded at the periphery of knowing, the subject evinces ignorance only to be endowed with a new sense of profundity called "wonder" (*taʿajjub*).[54] Ghazālī describes being at this outer periphery of knowing as accompanied by an ineffable feeling that is contrary to all the habits of knowing.

By engaging in wonderment, the knowing subject, of course, recognizes the occurrence of certain phenomena; but, simultaneously, in the act of wonderment itself, the subject also confesses that she has no rational grounds to know and believe what is observed. Surely, one can only believe in inexplicable happenings and events with a leap of faith, not with knowledge. For all the studied vagueness of his position, there is a reason why Ghazālī made this turn to wonder. All his life, he sought the holy grail of certainty, and he found it in foundationalist epistemology. So while Ghazālī was antiessentialist in elements of his ontology, he could not concede to an epistemic antiessentialism.[55] What kept his thinking pellucid was his commitment to epistemic coherence. Thus, he did not undermine his epistemic system, but rather allowed the mind to pass from the discernment of order and rationality to the wonderment of the miraculous and inexplicable.

When Ghazālī held forth on the habitual order of occurrences—on the absence of natural necessity and causation—then he was speaking from an ontological vantage point; it tinged his epistemology with the color of his ontology. At the epistemological level, he was an essentialist, albeit one who espoused a foundationalist epistemology without succumbing to a totalizing order of reason. For he recognized that without an essential knowledge there can be neither ethical values nor theological judgment.

He applied this line of epistemic thinking in his criticism of some of the views of the Muslim philosophers. With it, he defended the doctrine of *creatio ex nihilo*, the idea that God knows particulars as well as universals and that bodily resurrection is what religion teaches. These were the products of his epistemology that clashed with outcomes of philosophical thinking. Therefore, the two forms of thinking, theology and philosophy, each produced very different and sometimes overlapping cosmological, ethical, and moral viewpoints.

Ghazālī's epistemology reflected a panoramic view of his self. What is remarkable indeed is his ability as a bricoleur to suture and negotiate these multiple textures of thought into a seamless epistemology and ontology. With extraordinary intellectual dexterity, he grounded his epistemology in a theistic ontology of grace. From this vantage point, knowledge does not turn on an ungrounded cogito but on an unfathomable, unknowable, and nonrepresentable divine being whose sovereignty extends to both history and science.

For this reason, Ghazālī labored hard to ensure that human endeavor did not erase that divine presence, whether in abstract or empirical forms of reasoning. At the same time, he retained human agency and refused to accommodate epistemological determinism or nihilism. While he refused to acknowledge natural causation, he did admit that nature has a predilection for dispositions, but he argued that these are not ultimate, reserving ultimate causation to a theistic will. In other words, he had an alternative narrative for causality, one that was not oblivious to the theistic dimension.[56]

His own self-reflexivity also made him realize that knowledge is ultimately interpretative, given the central role of one's being and subjectivity in the enterprise of creating knowledge. This opened him to more conciliatory forms of knowing, culminating in his hermeneutic of reconciliation while retaining a threshold of consensual meaning as the yardstick for inclusion in or exclusion from the confessional community. His conflict with the Muslim philosophers did not occur because he rejected reason, as some of his unfair critics allege. Rather, his disagreement with the philosophers was over the way they configured reason. For the philosophers, reason almost became autonomous, whereas Ghazālī wished to tether reason to subjective imagination, furnishing it with the self-reflexivity to question its own limits and explore all possibilities in the face of the Other.

A foundationalist epistemology with metaphysical backing allows the imagination to flourish optimally, unencumbered by linear limitations. There was indeed in Ghazālī's thinking a transcendental signifier that relativizes all others. That transcendence is a form of freedom from the restraints imposed by an instrumentalized rationality. An instrumentalized rationality that is oblivious of transcendence and unrestrained by moral authority flirts with idolatry.

Skillfully woven into the gossamer skein of the implications of Ghazālī's complex ideas about the habitual order of things was his implicit but radical proposition of a nontotalizing order of reality. It is this nontotalizing order that makes it possible for multiple notions of time (heterotemporality) and multiple forms of reasoning (heterology) to coexist contrapuntally within a single, complex narrative without being encumbered by the linear and exclusionary logic of rationality. Of course, a thing and its opposite cannot coexist at the same time on the same epistemic register, as Ghazālī pointed out. However, things can coexist with a modicum of harmony at different ontological levels in relation to the thinking self—some aspects of which are representable and others of which are nonrepresentable. But it requires a particular agility of the mind and a particular style of self-reflexivity to hold such a complex apparatus intact—characteristics that modern secular reasoning regrettably regards as antithetical to rationality.

Spoke the Voice: "Your tale is indeed full of sorrow;
Your tears tremble at the brim and are ready to flow.
Your cry of lament the sky has rung;
What cunning your impassioned heart has lent your tongue!
So eloquent did you word your plaint, you made it sound like praise.
To talk on equal terms with Us, man to celestial heights did rise."
—Muhammad Iqbal, *Shikwā wa jawāb-i-shikwā* (*Complaint and Answer*)

7 Dilemmas of Anathema and Heresy

Names of Heresy

Despite his differences with both the philosophers and some theologians, Ghazālī had an abiding interest in pursuing a version of epistemological diversity as well as exploring the grounds for intra-Muslim reconciliation and tolerance. He gave considerable attention to the process of anathematizing (*takfīr*), which puts into question a believer's affiliation to the community of Muslims. Even though there are no institutional modes of punishing heresy in Islam, political authorities often decided to enforce the penalties for heresy via juridical organs. Given the role of the state in these matters of religion, there was often considerable political freight involved in prosecutions of heresy. Successful inquisitorial prosecutions required the interests of religious orthodoxy and the institutions of state power to coalesce. Needless to say, heresy-mongering masked in a variety of legal forms continues to have a lively existence in contemporary Muslim societies and is exercised by the institutions of the modern state; at the level of civil society, this discourse is pursued by religious institutions and forms of vigilantism.

Translating terms related to heresy from Muslim theology into the English language creates several problems; chief among them is that translation has to negotiate the Christian theological sensibilities encoded in English terms. Therefore, a certain amount of interpretation and adaptation becomes necessary when translating terms from Muslim languages into European languages. One of the terms that features prominently in Muslim heresiology is the notion of *bidʿa*. Literally, the term means "innovation," but a literal translation makes very little sense; in fact, it conveys the false idea that invention is a religious offense in Islam. *Bidʿa* means deviation from sanctioned beliefs and religious practices, especially those of a moral and ethical nature, in a way that undermines established conventions, customs, and tradition. Alternate practices that supplement or realize ends similar to or better than tradition do not constitute *bidʿa* unless they cause grievous harm to the body politic. Perhaps *bidʿa* is closest to the idea of "heresy," a word that comes from the Greek word meaning "choice" (*hairesis*). In this sense, revulsion against *bidʿa* is really a mechanism to prevent individuals from exercising moral and doctrinal choices without restraint to the extent that those choices damage the approved, normative ethos of tradition—*Sunna*.

Literally, the term *kufr* means "to reject" or "to hide." Theologically, it means to repudiate the truth after knowing it; in other words, it describes the conscious act of declaring that one is an unbeliever by verbally rejecting the doctrines or, according to some authorities, by the willful omission of obligatory practices. Unbelief by omission is a controversial doctrine. I will use the following terms to correspond with the following Arabic equivalents: "unbelief" for *kufr*; "infidel" for *kāfir*; "to declare something as anathema" or "to anathematize someone" for *takfīr*; and "heresy" for *bidʿa*. A fourth term employed by Ghazālī is *zandaqa*. This word was used to brand heterodox elements during the late Umayyad period as well as by the successor ʿAbbāsid authorities, but it is less frequently used in modern times.[1] Often, a person suspected of harboring Manichean or dualistic beliefs, together with his Islamic association, would be charged with being a subversive (*zindīq*, pl. *zanādiqa*). The accusation referred to a form of doctrinal subversion, or "masked infidelity," as Sherman Jackson has elegantly rendered it. Prominent figures, including the talented ʿAbd Allāh b. al-Muqaffā (d. ca. 139/756), a foremost member of the ʿAbbāsid bureaucratic intelligentsia, and the eloquent Bashshār b. al-Burd (d. 167–68/784–85), one of Islamdom's most outstanding poets, as well as a few philosophers and mystics, met their deaths following charges of doctrinal subversion when their religious activities were deemed to be masks for their infidelity.[2]

Degrees of Subversion and Heresy

Ghazālī admitted that subversion comes in different forms. Not all evaluations are clear-cut, and as such they produce uncertain interpretations that are not prone to unequivocal judgments. He cautioned against making hasty judgments against fellow Muslims and warned of the enormous "risk involved in anathematizing, whereas there is no risk in maintaining silence."[3] Every judgment involving anathema depends on an understanding and investigation (*naẓar*) of the phenomenon, an investigation which is a product of independent intellectual exertion (*ijtihād*).[4]

Ghazālī differentiated between two levels of subversion. The first is absolute subversion (*zandaqa muṭlaqa*): embracing Islam with the treacherous intent to undermine the foundational beliefs of the faith. Examples of absolute subversion include claiming that the Creator does not exist and saying and believing that there is no afterlife.[5] Restricted subversion (*zandaqa muqayyada*), on the other hand, involves a serious lapse in the interpretation of a fundamental doctrine of the faith. One might, for instance, acknowledge the existence of a Creator but refuse to subscribe to doctrines that insist one can have bodily and sensory experiences in the afterlife. Or a person might subscribe to doctrines that deny that the Creator has detailed knowledge of human and natural events.[6] Such individuals do, of course, in principle assent to the authority of the Prophet, but they are viewed as sectarians because they do not follow the established doctrines. This view sheds light on what is meant by "sectarianism": breaking with the established, if not hegemonic, discursive tradition. While restricted subversion is still a grave charge, it is the product of human fallibility and not of malicious motive. Hence, this kind of subversion has mitigating features insofar as it is reversible by retracting and correcting the subversive opinion or interpretation.

One can view those charged with restricted subversion as partial outcasts. They continue to belong to the confessional community of the Prophet Muḥammad, but they are pushed to its margins. Ironically, they fulfill the prophecy that predicts that the confessional community (*umma*) of Muslims will divide into more than seventy sects. Ghazālī implicitly suggested that such partial heretics ought to be included in the confessional community. In part, this was because he took his own caution seriously and showed restraint in anathematizing. As long as one has grounds to doubt and to show hesitation, he argued, it is preferred that one refrain from anathematizing and keep people inside the tent of the confessional community.

Indeed, the process of pronouncing anathema, according to Ghazālī, is not only a rational and abstract act; it is also one that carries profound legal and material consequences. A person who was anathematized was liable to the full punitive effect of the law. His property was legally expropriated, and he almost certainly faced the death penalty if he did not retract.[7] Theologically, such persons were also condemned to eternal damnation in hellfire. "Those who rush to anathematize," warns Ghazālī, "can be known by their extravagant predisposition toward ignorance."[8] Even in instances where he thought anathema and heresy applied, he was tentative, always trying to mitigate the charge by giving the accused the benefit of the doubt. Stating that scholars hold different opinions on a matter was always a mitigating defense.

Diagnosing Anathema and Heresy

Ghazālī set two criteria for anathematizing someone: unbelief can only be imputed if someone has first violated certain fundamental doctrines of faith or, second, if a person holds heretical beliefs that induce public harm. Strictly speaking, declares Ghazālī, it is only in matters of foundational beliefs that one can impute unbelief. He introduced a unique benchmark: a distorted belief amounts to unbelief (*kufr*) only when it is tantamount to "refuting" (*takdhīb*) the authority and incontrovertible teachings of the Prophet.[9] The choice of the term *takdhīb* is intentional: the antithesis of *takdhīb* is the term *taṣdīq*, meaning "to assent by verification," or by means of the grammar of assent, to the teachings of the Messenger. When an act of verification amounts to its inverse, then by any objective standard it is a false acquiescence and constitutes a grammar of dissent. It takes extraordinary ingenuity to detour one's assent into its opposite, and it is even more difficult to prove that someone has done so while harboring malicious intent.

The grammar of assent (*taṣdīq*) in Islam is threefold. Every believer must verify in principle (1) a belief in God, (2) a belief in the Prophet Muḥammad, and (3) a belief in the Last Day. Rejecting any one of the three elements is grounds for exclusion from the community. The tripartite doctrine is extremely limited. The authority for each part is incontrovertibly established to stem from the Prophet. To reject what is indisputable dicta from the

Prophet, says Ghazālī, is to deserve to be anathematized. Ghazālī exempted from anathema any flawed or unconventional juridical views and dissenting views on doctrine beyond the three essentials of the grammar of assent; lesser forms of dissent may be solemn, but they do not warrant anathema, he argued.[10]

Even though Ghazālī raised the bar for proving anathema, any verdict of anathema was left entirely dependent on interpretation. Therefore, it stands to reason that the most important and critical question remained: How does one determine that a particular statement constitutes an offense against the essential dogma? To test any reality, Oscar Wilde reminds us, we must see it on the tightrope.[11] Since prosecuting people for their complex beliefs often involves contentious processes of interpretation, any heresy-monger would have to find a watertight interpretation in order to determine the offense in question. To find a sound interpretation, he would have to accomplish the unenviable if not impossible feat of turning dogmas into acrobats and then judging their performances. Heresy prosecutions, after all, require painstaking investigations and impartial arbiters. Each sect anathematizes its rival by claiming that the other sect dissents from the essential grammar of assent, an act tantamount to refuting the authority of the Prophet.[12]

To let us know that he was aware of the legacy of vexatious heresy-mongering in Muslim history, Ghazālī used several examples in his astringent meditation on anathema and heresy. A Ḥanbalī might denounce an Ashʿarī for rejecting the authority of the Prophet because the Ashʿarīs deny that God can be associated with direction and space: the Ashʿarīs do not give a literal interpretation to God's ascension to the throne as the Ḥanbalīs do; rather, the Ashʿarīs view the language of this Qur'ānic passage to be figurative. Yet, for the Ḥanbalīs, the Ashʿarī interpretation is in stark contradiction to the plain meaning of incontrovertible prophetic reports. The Ashʿarīs, in turn, accuse the Ḥanbalīs of anthropomorphism for their literal reading of canonical statements and for saying that God ascends his throne the way that humans sit on chairs. Ironically, now it is the Ashʿarīs who charge the Ḥanbalīs with rejecting the plain meaning of the Qur'ān's description of God's uniqueness, the statement that "Nothing resembles Him."[13]

Similarly, the Ashʿarīs denounce their nemeses the Muʿtazilīs for denying that humans will be able to apprehend God on the Day of Judgment. They also charge that the Muʿtazilīs deny God's attributes of knowledge and power—both attributes that they believe exist independent of the divine essence. In denying these *doxa*, the Muʿtazilīs denude God of his essential characteristics, the Ashʿarīs allege. In their rebuttal, the Muʿtazilīs denounce the Ashʿarīs for inventing and fabricating divine attributes. In fact, they charge, the Ashʿarīs espouse beliefs that were unknown to the members of the founding community of Islam. The Ashʿarīs, in turn, counter by arguing that the unsanctioned ideas and practices (*bidʿa*) that they have adopted are necessary in order to explain the nature of the godhead in a language that is accessible to human beings, stating that they now have to make the beliefs of Islam understandable to cultures outside the founding context of Arabia.

The Muʿtazilīs, in a counterpolemic, allege that the argument advanced by the Ashʿarīs is implicitly a backhanded and retrospective way of imputing heresy to the early community of believers. The Muʿtazilīs add that since the early community of pious Muslims did not subscribe to any of the theological formulations devised by the Ashʿarīs the latter are saying that the early Muslims did not have sound beliefs! More outrageous still, they continue, is the Ashʿarī embrace of the doctrine of the independent attributes of God. To claim that God has attributes that are as eternal as is his divine essence, as the Ashʿarī doctrine states, compromises the pristine monotheism of Islam.[14]

Such futile sectarian polemics certainly irked Ghazālī. The rhetoric in intra-Muslim theological disputes became so overheated that the intensity blurred the difference between legitimate disagreement in faith and dissent. In the absence of a universal benchmark for measuring assent to Islam, what constitutes masked infidelity remains a problem. Ghazālī, for his part, proposed a hermeneutical approach to seeking a resolution to this conundrum. Careful rules of interpretation, if dispassionately applied, he believed, could substantially reduce the intra-Muslim discord about doctrinal matters while simultaneously establishing reasonable boundaries for the tolerable diversity of belief. His definition of the grammar of assent included elaborate criteria for determining whether an interpretation affirms and verifies the teachings of the Prophet or whether it does the opposite.

The grammar of assent is thus essentially an epistemic construct; it is a claim based on knowledge that is naturalized as true and self-evident. For the very act of verification implies that the believer acquiesces to a body of knowledge—data that cannot be verified in history. Often, belief involves claims about the unseen world and the afterlife that are beyond an empirical grasp. And when one submits to such knowledge claims, one is also verifying the existence of an original informant, namely, the person of the Prophet Muḥammad, who is the source of these doctrines.

It is striking how Muslim creedal doctrine—and Ghazālī's formulation thereof—is utterly reliant on discursivity. But it is equally true that the shift to knowledge, a phenomenon that remains understudied, only took place when prophecy ended with the death of the Prophet Muḥammad. After his death, there was a noticeable change in the structure as well as the form of the Muslim grammar of assent. During the lifetime of the Prophet, believers were in personal contact with him; attesting to his person also meant affirming his human and prophetic identity at once. Muḥammad was the source of his followers' beliefs and teachings. When the possibility of this personal affirmation ceased with his death, from then onward the Prophet was *mediated* to his followers. They began to access him through multiple media: via the tradition of the community (consensual practices), the charismatic authority of the learned, or, most importantly for theologians, via apodictic knowledge. And in modern times, the Prophet, the community, and every conceivable artifact of historical Islam are affirmed via the Qur'ān by some in ways that differ markedly from the earliest affirmations of the Prophet's authority. But this is a topic that cannot be treated in detail here.

In short, from personal verification of prophetic authority, a switch occurred so that verification became discursively mediated. Knowledge is a substitute for the charismatic authority of the Prophet in the post-prophetic community. Knowledge is therefore coequal to prophecy; to put it differently, knowledge simulates prophetic authority since it is the only trace left of the Prophet. Muslim modernists and revivalists understand this knowledge to be virtually limited to the Qur'ān. Mediated knowledge, however conceived, has become the basis of the normative practices of the community. It should by now be clear why the fulcrum of Islam resides in knowledge and discursiveness. The relationship between learning and prophecy is described in a famous prophetic report: "The learned are heirs to the prophets."

Ghazālī's insightful formulation of a hermeneutic that mediates between knowledge and belief, faith and unbelief, and truth and falsehood in a doctrinal context was unprecedented. If one follows his schema, then there are at least five ways whereby one can assent to the Prophet Muḥammad's existence or presence (*wujūd*) and thereby verify prophetic knowledge. In any doctrinal matter of substance, an interpreter would be immune from charges of heresy and unbelief if that individual's interpretation conformed to one of the five levels of interpretation that Ghazālī configured. The categories of affirmation of the Prophet's presence or existence are (1) essential existence, (2) sensory existence, (3) conceptual existence, (4) cognitive existence, and (5) analogical existence. This hermeneutic of reconciliation is at its core an epistemological paradigm with emancipatory designs to induce tolerance and foment a plurality of beliefs within the Muslim faith tradition.

Hermeneutic of Reconciliation

ESSENTIAL EXISTENCE

Essential existence is the most basic and self-evident form of affirmation. The sky, earth, animals, and vegetation are self-evident and do not require interpretation. Similarly, reports from the Prophet that tell us of a cosmological order involving a divine throne, a cosmic chair, and the seven heavens all have an ontic existence; affirming these as they are narrated is an essentialist way of assenting to prophetic authority. Believers affirm these cosmological symbols in terms of their plain meanings. Since these symbols exist independently and are part of an absolute reality, they are not interpreted, irrespective of whether our sensory and imaginary apparatus apprehend them, says Ghazālī.

SENSORY EXISTENCE

Sensory existence occurs when the senses conspire to grasp reality, as in everyday experience. Of the two examples Ghazālī provided, one illustration will suffice. The Prophet said, "On the Day of Judgment, death shall be presented in the form of an elegant ram that will be slaughtered [at a place] between heaven and hell." This statement means that from the moment the ram is slaughtered the reality of death will be annihilated. An interpreter, says Ghazālī, might view death either as an accident (an attribute or an idea) or a non-accident (a substance). Theoretically, it is impossible for an accident to be transformed into a body. Those who will witness the ramlike embodiment of death on the day of resurrection, Ghazālī points out, will be convinced that they have beheld death in its "true" form. Why is it possible to affirm such statements in a sensory manner? Well, if we remember that there will be only a singular reality in the afterlife, it becomes clear that the ram will be the form and reality of death in the afterlife. Affirming an incredulous statement, such as this prophetic report about death looking like a ram, by means of background knowledge of the kind that Ghazālī provides constitutes the second legitimate form of assent.

CONCEPTUAL EXISTENCE

When something only has an imaginary existence, then it stands to reason that it can only be affirmed conceptually. So the Prophet Muḥammad once said: "It is as if I am seeing Jonah, the son of Amittai [Yūnus bin Mattā], wearing two woolen wraps with short fibers, announcing his readiness to serve [God] [*yulabbī*]. To which the mountains reply and God the Sublime says to him: 'Here I am [*labbayk*], O Jonah.'" It is evident that this prophetic report involves a simile (*tamthīl*), because Jonah preceded the Prophet Muḥammad in time. Therefore, the report is not a statement enunciated in chronological time.

Another way to get at this statement, says Ghazālī, is to view it as a dream sequence wherein one apprehends images. The phrase in the report employs the simulating mode "as if" in order to indicate beyond doubt that the goal of the statement is to "instruct" (*tafhīm*) the audience of listeners; it is not designed to describe a reality. Imaginary representations use metaphor and simile as synecdoche (a connection) for ocular observations. They have a lasting and powerful effect on the listener or reader, so much so that even if one uses evidentiary proof to disprove them it is hard to dislodge the impressions they leave, according to Ghazālī. Interpreting prophetic reports as imaginary representations is another legitimate form of assent to dogma; it does not constitute refuting the authority of the Prophet if his words are interpreted in this manner.

COGNITIVE EXISTENCE

Cognitive existence is the abstract apprehension of reality without associating prophetic words with either an image or the senses. The word "hand," for instance, can signify power, or the word "pen" can signify knowledge. In a report, the Prophet said, "God the Sublime fermented the clay of Adam with His hand for forty mornings." Those who deny that God could have a physical and sensory organ such as a hand rightly understand that this means that God has "an immaterial and abstract hand" (*yadan rūḥānīya ʿaqlīya*), says Ghazālī. The expression portrays a meaning of "hand" without necessarily signifying its image.

Another report states, "God first created the intellect [*ʿaql*], saying to it: 'With you I give, and with you I prevent.'" The meaning of "intellect" here cannot be the contingent meaning of the word we are accustomed to, as some theologians have understood it; a contingent cannot be among the first created things. *ʿAql*, or intellect, in this context signifies the essence of an angel that can perceive things with its substance and essence without any need for instruction. Sometimes the term "pen" (*qalam*) is employed to convey a similar meaning, as in the prophetic report, "God, the Sublime, first created the pen." "Pen" here means the angelic intellect as well as the means whereby knowledge is conveyed to the hearts of prophets, to saints, and to angels by means of revelation and intuition. A single referent like "angel" can also have several signifiers depending on its relational construction. So an angel can be called *ʿaql* with reference to its essence or it can be called *malak*, an angel as we normally imagine it. An angel can also be signified by the word *qalam* when the referent is knowledge of a revelatory and inspirational kind. Therefore, the angel Gabriel is called "the spirit" (*rūḥ*) with reference to his essence; he is designated "the trustworthy" (*amīn*) as the keeper of secrets; and he is referred to as both "the strong" (*dhū mirra*) in terms of his power and "mighty in power" (*shadīd al-quwā*) with reference to the perfection of his might. Gabriel is also called "influential" (*makīn*) with respect to his proximity and status to God and "the obeyed one" (*muṭāʿ*) with reference to his direction of the other angels. Thus, "pen" and "hand" can have abstract meanings without signifying their sensory and imaginary meanings, and it is perfectly legitimate in terms of doctrine to understand them in this way.

ANALOGICAL EXISTENCE

Something has an analogical existence in Ghazālī's schema when it does not fit any of the four categories discussed above: essential, sensory, conceptual, or cognitive. If knowledge from the Prophet does not fit in any of the four registers, then it is legitimate to affirm it by interpreting it as analogous to or resembling something else. When two things resemble each other due to a common quality or attribute that they share, we have a case of analogical existence. For example, in many reports, God is described as having desire, happiness, patience, and anger, all qualities found in humans. Anger, says Ghazālī, is a physiological description; the subject experiences an increase in blood pressure in order to give vent to feelings. Since such physical symptoms cannot be ascribed to God in an essential (or ontological), sensory, conceptual, or cognitive sense, then one needs to find an approximate attribute that resembles anger by analogy. So we say that anger is an analogy for taking revenge. God's anger can only be ascribed analogically, meaning that God is exercising his wrath, or taking revenge. Ghazālī's examples under the category of analogical affirmation open the door wide for figurative interpretation in its multiple forms, which is possibly what he intended to do with this generic rubric.

Mediating Reconciliation

One assents to the teachings of the Prophet if one's interpretations fall into one of these five hermeneutical registers. All sects, according to Ghazālī, need to use a form of interpretation (*ta'wīl*). Interpretation begins with affirmation at the existential register. If that proves not to apply, then one of the other registers is applied. As long as any statement from the Prophet affirms any one of the five registers of interpretation, a person cannot be charged with heresy. Even Aḥmad Ibn Ḥanbal, one of the staunchest opponents of figurative interpretation, had to concede, says Ghazālī, that at least three reports require a nonliteral explanation. So Ghazālī declares confidently, "Anyone who has a viewpoint that corresponds to the viewpoint of the owner of revelation [the Prophet] in one of these registers, know that he is among those who have verified and assented in faith."

Interpretative disagreement among scholars is legitimate. Scholars will disagree among each other, especially if they do not have consensus on a method and a criterion (*mīzān*) for the resolution of intellectual conflicts. In Ghazālī's view, such disagreement can be overcome by deferring to logic; he elucidated this view in his books *Touchstone of Speculation* (*Miḥakk al-naẓar*) and *The Weighscale of Balance* (*Al-qisṭās al-mustaqīm*). But even if logic were made a yardstick, he admits, scholars would still disagree, since each has a different standard for determining what are acceptable criteria and each subscribes to varying fundamental premises. Evidence, says Ghazālī, sometimes requires empirical knowledge (*tajrībīya*) to establish it. On other occasions, reports of consecutive testimony (*tawātur*) suffice as proof. Yet in regard to both empirical and narrative forms of evidence, people disagree as to what constitutes sound criteria.

However, in the principal doctrinal matters (*uṣul al-ʿaqā'id*), Ghazālī required adherence to the apparent meaning of reports. He only permitted reaching for a figurative interpretation when there was a compelling argument that justified abandoning the plain meaning of a doctrine. If someone denies bodily resurrection or physical punishment in the hereafter without a compelling argument for doing so, Ghazālī argues, it is justified to anathematize (*takfīr*) and excommunicate such a person for holding erroneous beliefs. He reasoned that such deviant beliefs caused harm to the very institution of religion. "It becomes necessary," he says, "to anathematize all those associated with this thought; and this applies to the viewpoint of most of the philosophers."

One notices that Ghazālī's animosity toward the Muslim philosophers only increased when they provided justification for their viewpoints. The philosophers, from their perspective, argued that to believe in bodily resurrection is appropriate for laypersons. Subalterns are not inclined to apprehend the idea of an afterlife in an abstract and cognitive sense. But the intelligentsia, the philosophers pointed out, cannot interpret descriptions of the hereafter in corporeal terms. Hence, the philosophers did not subscribe to corporeal resurrection.

These are the arguments that Ghazālī deemed harmful and deserving of being anathematized. How do these views constitute an attack on religion, as Ghazālī claimed they do? Creating two standards of interpretation—one intended for the elite and another for the plebeians—strikes at the credibility of the Prophet, implying that he advocated doublespeak. And such a blow at credibility might have a domino effect, impugning the entire structure of the faith. For if fundamental doctrines of the faith are subject to such variant interpretations, then they will create an infinite variety of ways of assenting to prophetic authority and will make affiliation to the community superfluous. The philosophers did not indulge in unsanctioned choices (*bidʿa*), but their extreme choices negated the very grammar of assent, which had truth telling and verification (*taṣdīq*) at its core.

The reason why Ghazālī viewed such interpretations to be outrageous is that they implied that religious discourse is subject to "expediency" (*maṣlaḥa*) and "deception" (*talbīs*). He explained why he deemed the philosophers' position to be so grotesque—to be, in fact, a hanging offense. Their position, says Ghazālī,

> is tantamount to the categorical refutation [*takdhīb*] of the Messenger, on whom be peace. This falls outside the scope of the levels of interpretation that we mentioned earlier. Evidence from the Qur'ān and prophetic reports providing clarification about bodily resurrection, the knowledge of God, the Sublime, [and] about whatever happens to people is not subject to interpretation [*ta'wīl*]. In fact, they [the philosophers] concede that their view is not an interpretation. Instead, they contend: "Since it is in the best interests of common people to believe in bodily resurrection, for their intellects cannot grasp an abstract afterlife; and, further, since it is to their benefit to believe that God the Sublime knows all that happens to them and is constantly guarding over them in order to generate a desire and awe in their hearts, it was permissible for the Messenger, on whom be peace, to make it comprehensible to them through literal language. One does not become a liar if one's intent is to reform someone. So he [the Prophet] states

it in such a manner that is in a style that reforms them, even though the reality is not as he states it."

Ghazālī's response should by now be predictable. Such an argument, he thunders, "is categorically invalid." For it is tantamount to refuting the teachings of the Prophet, and in his view that was "the ultimate form of subversion [*zandaqa*]." On the scale of offensiveness, the views of the philosophers, he felt, fell between the Muʿtazilīs and outright heresy [*kufr*]. Furiously protesting the discourtesy of the philosophers, Ghazālī notes that for all their ills even the Muʿtazilīs are better, since they never tolerate attributing lies to the Prophet.

Ghazālī astutely observes that core doctrines, as speech acts of a tradition, are rendered incoherent and transformed into something else if they are instrumentalized or subjected to rational intentions. What the Muslim philosophers did, one can say, was engage in an early iteration of a form of proto-secularization of religious doctrine. Perhaps they thought that the pursuit of ideas had a built-in "heretical imperative," to use a phase made famous by Peter Berger. Ghazālī reclaimed the epistemic sanctification of doctrines linked to the authority of the Prophet; this was his obsessive concern. His intellectual brilliance made him realize that if the position of the philosophers were to succeed it would strike at the heart of Islam's epistemic sanctuary. After all, prophetic truth in Islam is tenuously tethered to the epistemic umbilical cord that leads to Muḥammad.

He also adopted a very tough stance against some ṣūfīs, even though it would be fair to point out that his rhetoric in this regard was moderated. Some ṣūfīs claimed, Ghazālī explains, that their spiritual elevation exempted them from some of the obligations in Islam and that they could thus abandon daily ritual prayers, drink wine, commit sins, and illegally consume public funds. "There is no doubt," declares Ghazālī, "of the obligation to execute such a person, even though there may be some reservation about him being eternally condemned to remain in hell." By their public advocacy of antinomian and permissive practices, these ṣūfīs disseminated harmful ideas in the public space; they transgressed proper social norms, and hence their actions required their excommunication.

Despite his rhetorical fury, Ghazālī was careful to draw subtle distinctions between various kinds of antinomian ṣūfīs. Someone who merely advocated permissiveness without providing justification for such advocacy was less offensive to the public good than someone who also provided arguments and propaganda in support of it. Ghazālī's reasoning followed the rule of suppressing the causes of maximum harm. The unbelief of a passive advocate was self-evident, and the chances of such a person causing societal damage by attracting a following were small. By comparison, an active and articulate defender of antinomianism who justified his beliefs as a bona fide religious discourse was assessed to be a greater threat. Such a person, in Ghazālī's view, posed a grave public danger and deserved excommunication because, in his words, "he destroy[ed] religion by means of religion [*yuhaddim al-sharʿ bi al-sharʿ*]."

If Ghazālī tirelessly and repeatedly warned that finding in favor of unbelief is always a task fraught with danger, it is equally true that when he did actually decide to prosecute he was absolutely unyielding. He took an extremely tough stance against the antinomian ṣūfīs. Thus, he was unambiguous in his view that certain ṣūfīs and other subversives (*zanādiqa*), such as the leadership of the Ismāʿīlīs, deserved the death penalty. "Executing such [persons] is preferable to killing a hundred infidels [*kuffār*]," Ghazālī proclaimed with Olympian fervor, "since these [subversives] cause greater harm to religion." One is, of course, baffled by the harsh stance he took against high-ranking Ismāʿīlī leaders and toward the philosophers. In the case of the Ismāʿīlīs, especially their leaders, he argued, their masked infidelity could not be accepted even if they recanted. The essence of Ismāʿīlī doctrine, he believed, was perpetual dissimulation and deceit. Hence, no subsequent statement could be accepted once a person had graduated into the high-ranking leadership of this sect.

Did Ghazālī lose his balance in judgment on some of these issues? Did he slip into subjectivism and become actuated more by the imperatives of the political than by the ethical and the humane elements in his theology? Ghazālī himself would not have denied that an element of subjectivity is evident in all acts of reasoning; especially when it came to moral decision making, he was acutely aware of this dilemma. Up to a point, he nevertheless pursued a coherent, rational line of reasoning. Part of the problem was that on occasion Ghazālī did not clarify his presumptions as he moved from one context to another. His reader has to supplement his texts with informed intuition. Given his own caution about wrongfully anathematizing people and his preference for erring in favor of not anathematizing, his lack of equivocation in the case of the Ismāʿīlīs and, in part, of the philosophers is surprising, as it went against his own caution. The matter is especially grave, since excommunication brought the irreversible death penalty.

My view is that Ghazālī shifted positions: a careful theoretician who wished to create tolerance and interpretative diversity within Islam, he was at the same time haunted by his political concerns. Just when he took the turn in theorizing diversity, he saw the apostates, his political foes, from the corner of his eye, triggering his impulse to think like a jurist. When he thought like a jurist and a political animal, social harm and the impact of subversive beliefs on the broader society were foremost on his mind. Thus, he deferred to protecting the social good of the aggrieved community. But it is obvious that in protecting the community he excessively valorized the notion of good as an absolute, placing it beyond all the refinements of theological discourse. And when he did make the abrupt turnabout, it was a transition from theological vigilance to temporal expediency made due to concern for the social good. He readily conceded that people might disagree with him about some of his extreme views, since he admitted that the matter of anathematizing involved a great deal of discretion (*ijtihād*).

It was the courageous and brilliant Indian thinker of the early twentieth century, Shiblī Nuʿmānī, who most recently challenged Ghazālī about his uneven application of the hermeneutic of reconciliation.[15] Ghazālī left a conundrum unresolved in his hermeneutic, Nuʿmānī states, because of a problem of definition and an inconsistent application of his own principles. In matters of fundamental doctrine, Ghazālī insisted that one could not abandon the apparent meaning of a text unless compelled by an apodictic or categorical proof (*burhān qāṭʿī*).[16] Nuʿmānī points out that, according to Ghazālī's own standard, if a commonsense reading produces a meaning that is rationally impossible (*muḥāll ʿaqlī*), then one ought to abandon the commonsense interpretation in favor of another register of interpretation.[17] But since there is no consensus as to what constitutes a rational impossibility, there has been persistent inconsistency in the proper application of this rule—an inconsistency, he alleges, that Ghazālī also failed to avoid.

For instance, Nuʿmānī points out, Ghazālī considered it a rational impossibility that God could be spatially determined. Thus, Nuʿmānī questions why Ghazālī tolerated a Ḥanbalī viewpoint that attributed a spatial substrate to God. Similarly, he continues, Ashʿarī theologians deemed the proposition of death turning into an embodied ram to be an impossibility. However, many *ḥadīth* scholars have argued that such an event is eminently possible. If we keep Ghazālī's treatment of these groups in mind, says Nuʿmānī, then we must note that Ghazālī did not anathematize the Ḥanbalīs on the basis of fundamental doctrine either. In fact, Ghazālī gave sympathetic consideration to the Ḥanbalī epistemology. Then, according to Ḥanbalī discursive standards,

Ghazālī judged their claims about anthropomorphic views to be permissible and did not deem their beliefs objectionable.

"Clearly, this is a sign of Imām [Ghazālī's] generosity," notes Nuʿmānī, who then mischievously asks: "Why did he not extend this generosity to the Muslim philosophers?"[18] Like the Ḥanbalīs, the Muslim philosophers espoused a principle: that it is rationally impossible to replicate that which is nonexistent. It was on this basis that the philosophers refused to subscribe to bodily resurrection. They believed that what had become disinterred and ceased to exist could not be replicated. Therefore, they rejected the claim that earthly bodies will be resurrected. It is because they abnegated bodily resurrection, we will recall, that Ghazālī charged that the views of the philosophers deserved to be anathematized.

Nuʿmānī believed we should ask why Ghazālī would attribute unbelief to this view of the philosophers, especially if such a paradigm was consistent with their standards of knowledge. For we know that in the case of the Ḥanbalīs Ghazālī took into consideration their own subjective standards of what they did not deem to be an impossibility; in so doing, Ghazālī actually endorsed anthropomorphism, Nuʿmānī alleges. However, when it came to the philosophers, Nuʿmānī points out, Ghazālī applied the full objective standard and did not give them the benefit of the doubt.

There are similar lapses in argument unrelated to fundamental doctrines that nevertheless have a significant impact on the way he set up his paradigm. Ghazālī offered a controversial interpretation of a prophetic report that states, "Angels do not enter a house in which there is a dog."[19] The charge that Ghazālī's critics have directed at him is that he abandoned the plain meaning of this report and resorted to a figurative interpretation without a valid and compelling justification for such a detour—that he ignored his own rule of interpretation.[20] The key word in the report, "house," Ghazālī explained, signifies the human "heart" and not a brick-and-mortar building that a plain reading suggests. The word "dog," in his view, signifies carnality and not the four-legged canine we know. So Ghazālī argued that angels do not enter a heart that is home to corrosive moral traits such as anger, carnal desire, envy, arrogance, and vainglory. The negative human qualities are personified as barking dogs. After executing a brilliant exegetical pirouette, Ghazālī rhetorically asked: How could angels ever enter a heart that is filled with such animalistic characteristics?[21]

If he got applause for his figurative interpretation of this text from the mystics and literary connoisseurs, he also scandalized a section of the scholarly community. For most scholars, the report Ghazālī interpreted means that canines are prohibited from living inside the home of a faithful Muslim. In the face of rough criticism, his ripostes were equally profound, marshalling a range of materials to support his claim.[22] He admitted to interiorizing the meaning of the report but rebuffed suggestions that he had negated the literal meaning: "I do not say that the word 'house' means heart and 'dog' means anger and other despicable traits," he explains, "But I do say it alerts you to it." He continues, "There is a big difference between declaring the literal as the figurative difference and being alerted to the figurative by the mention of the literal and to also endorse the literal."[23] This kind of interpretation is approved by the virtuous scholars, he states in his own defense.

He had observed that it is perfectly acceptable to the canons of the Arabic language to interpret statements blooming with anthropomorphic imagery as having metaphorical meanings.[24] Now while this helped Ghazālī in the interpretation of the dog story, it worked against him in his disavowal of the philosophers' figurative interpretations. His claim that doctrines related to eschatology—such as the meaning of paradise and hell, body and spirit—have acquired such translucent clarity and endorsement within the Muslim tradition that they are beyond any metaphorical interpretation is unconvincing and inconsistent with his own interpretative paradigm. It is, further, difficult to see how Ghazālī could have even partially redeemed himself on strictly theoretical grounds from the charges that Nuʿmānī made about his leniency toward the Ḥanbalīs and his severity toward the philosophers. His defense would have had to involve an element of the politics of interpretation and human frailty.

By reinvigorating the standards of theological interpretation, Ghazālī offered his contemporaries—and us—an important starting point for pursuing the noble end of doctrinal pluralism in Islam. The age-old conflicts over interpretation in law and theology have left a checkered and unflattering legacy of heresy-mongering and anathematizing in their wake. Ghazālī's intervention was an important one. At the same time, his political context and commitments handicapped him from pursuing a fully fledged ecumenism in Islam, since his paradigm did not shift any of the major sectarian divisions. At most, it modestly moderated the intra-Sunnī polemics.

The narrow theoretical frame for ecumenism that he adopted allowed him to add his very influential voice to some of the less sanguine aspects of Muslim political theology. He mustered a severe political theology against the Ismāʿīlīs and the Muslim philosophers while not even offering a fig leaf to the Muʿtazilīs. One has to wonder, though, why after all his invectives against the philosophers he retained a category of "restricted subversion." It is as if he had second thoughts and thereby offered a backdoor redemption to whoever needed it. His conflicted wish to protect the ʿAbbāsid state and, perhaps more important, his impassioned desire to shelter the community from harm got the better of him in political theology. Despite his extraordinary brilliance, in his writings on political theology his polemical talents overshadowed the vatic largeness so evident in the bulk of his oeuvre. In this respect, Ghazālī left the theological landscape rather untouched in its substance; cynics might say he left it worse for the wear.

If there is one area of his copious writings and reflections where Ghazālī's thinking was not shaped by the liminal space of the *dihlīz*, then it is his theological and political writings. It is as if he could not shake off the absolutism of his time. It is indeed a pity that Ghazālī's best intentions in theology did not lead to the flowering of intellectual diversity. While his five-level interpretive framework aimed at lessening heresy-mongering and social upheaval, it is not exactly a theological Rosetta stone, and it had a negligible impact on Sunnī Islam. However, it is a potential starting point for fostering a more extensive hermeneutic of reconciliation if it can be supplemented with a critical engagement of the tradition.

> Whatever else it might be, the divine is certainly the thing that imposes with maximum intensity the sensation of being alive. This is the immediate: but pure intensity, as a continuous experience, is "impossible," overwhelming. To preserve its sovereignty, the immediate must come across to us through the law. If life itself is the supreme unlivable, the law, which allows both mortals and immortals to "distinguish between different worlds" is what transmits life's nature to us. . . . Chaos generates the law, but only the law will allow us to gain access to chaos. The unapproachable immediate is chaos—and "chaos is the sacred itself."
>
> —Roberto Calasso, *Literature and the Gods*

8 Hermeneutics of the Self and Subjectivity

Resuscitating Ethics

Even a cursory glance at Ghazālī's *Resuscitation* reveals one crucial project—perhaps his most fascinating project—at the heart of his work, namely, ethics. This text, more than his other texts, vibrates with cognitions that are ultimately not submissive to their author. Combining the traditional genre of ethics (*ʿilm al-akhlāq*) and the science of positive law (*ʿilm al-fiqh*), he explained them by playing them out in recognizable forms. Yet Ghazālī not only revitalized Muslim religious thought by establishing *adab* (pl. *ādāb*) at the heart of law (*fiqh*), he also felt compelled to reincubate ethics in the cauldron of tradition.

Adab is a word that does not translate as easily into its approximations of "civility" and "etiquette" as is often thought to be the case. *Adab* is something more: it is that pedagogy that results in the cultivation of a virtue and motivates all human practices. It is both the education itself and the practical formation of norms for right and exemplary conduct; and, more, it is the internalization of norms in order to ingrain into the psyche a certain virtue (*faḍīla*).

When virtue becomes an indelible part of what Muslim philosophers and ethicists call one's inner disposition, or habitus (*malaka*) of the soul/self, only then can one claim to have acquired *adab*, or ethical norms.[1] Not only is *adab* that learning acquired for the sake of right living, but it is a knowledge that goes beyond knowing. Muslim ethicists describe *adab* firstly as a disposition toward knowledge. It is, then, primarily the attitude and disposition that enables one to experience the effects of knowledge and be transformed by its animation in the self. Ghazālī described the goal of *adab* as the disciplining of the spirit (*nafs*) so that the spirit may direct the body to perform deeds of merit almost instinctively.

As I have pointed out in previous chapters, Ghazālī's main quest was ultimately about identifying the right ethical conduct in order to attain salvation. In his view, this desire for ethical rectitude was the central challenge of his time, and in order to meet it self-knowledge was indispensable, even inescapable. Of course, it was particularly his turn to mysticism (*taṣawwuf*) that leavened his insights and prodded him to earnestly reflect on the reformulation of law and ethics.

He began by recuperating those seminal surface and deep meanings of law that were prevalent during the period of the Muḥammadan proclamation (*risāla*) and of Islam's kerygmatic orientation. If the early legal writings of Ghazālī were the pedestrian output of a graphomaniacal young scholar, then the *Resuscitation* was an outpouring of contemplative heart-writing, a sensitive rereading of the juridical tradition that did not abandon the idea of law. Some excellent work has documented the substance of Ghazālī's ethical virtues and their relationship to the soul.[2] What is of interest to me is to explore how Ghazālī related metaphysics to subjectivity and then to follow his exposition of ethics as a discursive tradition. I specifically wish to track the interaction between law and the caring of the self in the practices of both individuals and the community.

The Treason of the Scholars

The Ghazālī we encounter on the pages of *Resuscitation*, it is fair to say, is a radically different person compared to the one we come across in his other writings. The work opens with moral and prophetic indignation conveyed through unflattering observations about the practice of law (*fiqh*) and stinging rebukes of the jurists (*fuqahā'*) and their profession. One cannot dismiss Ghazālī's criticism of the jurist-theologians (*ʿulamā'*) as mere senescent prejudice. His critiques not only reveal a major shift in his understanding of the law but serve as a preamble to his discussion of how he thought about the function of law in relation to individuals and society. With this turn, he abandoned his own previous indulgence in legal hair splitting and interschool polemics. Implicitly, Ghazālī alerts us in the *Resuscitation* to the prevailing political practices of his time. To ignore his jeremiads is to overlook elements of social history that may help us understand his era.

Ghazālī was uncharacteristically blunt in his criticisms in the *Resuscitation*. The jurist-theologians of his day, he argued, had not only failed to fathom the essence of the teachings of religion, they had also turned their backs on their responsibility as heirs of the prophetic tradition. Ghazālī used the jurist-theologians as an index of the level of degradation his society had reached: the very people who were charged with keeping alive the conscience of society had reached a nadir of praxis because they treated religion as an expedient. More disconcerting to him was that the all-important ethical aspect of religion, which culminates in law (*fiqh*), was being instrumentalized for questionable purposes. He did not hide his sulfurous contempt for the jurist-theologians as a group. In a fierce polemic against them, he declared that Satan had misled most of them and that many had been seduced by tyranny: "The *ʿulamāʾ* make people believe that knowledge is nothing but three things: [they obey] ordinances issued by a judicial authority (*fatwā ḥukūma*),[3] on which judges rely to resolve disputes, especially when mobs are incited;[4] [they] dupe people into believing that polemics is the only worthwhile knowledge, used for boastful flouting in order to brusquely silence others; [and they] beguile laypersons with rhetorical flourishes that pretend to be knowledge. Besides these three things, they see nothing of value. This is surely a hedonistic snare and a trap for sin."[5]

But not all scholars were like those just described, Ghazālī explained. Many could be classed into a sliding scale of three groups.[6] To the highest rank belonged those who received the honorific of "proof" or "testimony" (*ḥujja*). Such scholars were not only knowledgeable but were also living testimony of a pious and ascetic life spent in reverence for the divine. In the second rung were those called "protector" (*ḥijāj* or *ḥajāj*), who eloquently defended the discursive tradition. In the third rung were the "defeated" or "overcome by argument" (*maḥjūj*).[7] It was only these scholars who demonstrated no reverence for God. To the contrary, scholars in this rung were only interested in hubris and material gain. The greatest accomplishment of a scholar of this ilk, Ghazālī wrote with colorful contempt, was to be "puffed up by his visits to his prince and meetings with his *sulṭān* and by the deferential graces the judge, the prime minister, and the chamberlain all show him." Decent scholars, he lamented, were no longer to be found, because the "corruption in the judiciary and the absence of people of piety and rectitude" had precipitated a great malaise.[8] Ghazālī not only gave us a glimpse of how he felt about his peers but also of how he felt about those who governed his world—about officialdom and the bureaucracy.

It is the duty of scholars and intellectuals, Ghazālī remarked, to be the conscience of society and to become the standard-bearers of truth and justice. Instead, the jurist-theologians of his day peddled pointless polemics and harmful propaganda, forfeiting their duty as the producers of knowledge. Perversity had the better part of them, he charged; they freely sold their souls to the devil, allowing immoral practices to be viewed as virtue and vice versa.[9] Such a blanket condemnation of moral perversity coupled with charges of intellectual treason is an extraordinarily strong charge to have come from the pen of Ghazālī. Often, he was forthright, but he was also usually careful and balanced. Perhaps these statements reflect the high moral ideals that he set for himself. As an alternative to all the corruption to which he was a witness, he proposed a narrative of religious practices that would result in ethical outcomes.

Unless those who follow religion are endowed with certain predispositions, Ghazālī argued, the teachings of the Arabian Prophet would just not inspire people to piety and moral rectitude. Happiness (*saʿāda*) as an end would be elusive if the teachings and practices did not transform the psyche, or spirit (*nafs*), of adherents. Ghazālī thus embarked on an elaborate project of describing how one can attain a virtuous self that will be compatible with the teachings of religion. Some of this program is spelled out in capsule form in the *Balance of Deeds* (*Mīzān al-ʿamal*), but it is pursued in intricate detail throughout *Resuscitation*.

Ghazālī structured a dialogic between virtue (*faḍīla*) and law (*fiqh*) that created an ethics. But what really binds the law to the self, he suggested, is the cement of *adab*. For Ghazālī, ethics was not only based on an intelligible relationship between virtue and law but was also the embodiment of virtues through practices. Of course, he recognized that there is a gap between the imperatives of the law and the attainment of virtue. To bridge that gap, he argued that ascetic practices (ascesis) as well as mystical meditative practices could transform the indifferent practice of the law into a vibrant practice that would lead to a virtuous self.

Ethics of the Self

Of all the methods he experimented with, Ghazālī found the method of the mystics to be the most attractive and conducive for his purposes. Thus, his ethics was, in a sense, traditional jurisprudence mediated by mysticism. What I think Ghazālī found persuasive about mysticism was the kind of imagination it cultivates within an individual. He was fascinated by the way mystical practices school the self and conscience in order to produce a virtuous state of mind and virtuous predispositions. Once the pedagogy of the self is accomplished, then certain skills and practices spontaneously become part of one's habit, which is reflected in the dignity of one's spirit or self.[10]

The study of the self has gained a great deal of prominence in contemporary philosophy and anthropology as well as in religious, cultural, and literary studies. French anthropologist Marcel Mauss stressed the need to explore the cultural variations of the idea of the individual in great civilizations. Our knowledge of how the self is culturally conceived in Islamicate societies and how it has served as a historical index of personal and social transformation is still at its infancy.[11] Studies in ṣūfism and Muslim philosophy have yet to reach such a critical mass that they enable us to talk about the subject of the self in synthetic and general terms. However, we can say with great confidence that Ghazālī, like Augustine centuries before him, was fully aware that the self is an entity that can be transformed. He was living proof of his own transformation.

What is characteristic of Ghazālī's ethics is that he not only presented an abstract theory that maps the self, defines the role of reason, and explains the soaring potential of the soul and the faculties, he also provided elaborate diagnoses of problems and prescriptions for transformation. This specificity and comprehensiveness is what differentiates his ethics in quality from similar discussions by Muslim humanist philosophers such as Maʿarrī and Ibn Miskawayh, both of whom also wrote on ethics. Not only did Ghazālī write with more passion, but he was also a man with a mission. Thus, he did not hesitate to employ persuasive arguments to make the individual see the need for personal change. But he also saw the individual self not as an isolated entity but instead as related to a broader cosmic reality. Attempting to sever it from this larger scheme would be, he thought, a self-defeating enterprise.

Human beings and the universe around them, according to Ghazālī, resemble a script (*taṣnīf*) and a composition (*ta'līf*). His description is delicate: "The universe, and whatever mystery it hides, is God's script and His composition, His original creation and invention. And the spirit is a part of the many components of the universe. And every unit of its multiple parts teems with mystery."[12] It is as if Ghazālī had in mind a score, an orchestra, and a conductor. He did not revel in the fragmented nature of the universe, as some postmodernists do; rather, like a musician, Ghazālī sought harmony and symmetry between the various units of the universe. Just as the composite is unique, so too does each component independently reflect the mysteries of the divine. Exploring the marvelous operations of human biology, Ghazālī drew our attention to understanding the intimate relationship between creation and the Creator.[13]

A careful study of a score of music, a writing, or poetry not only allows one to marvel at the genius of the artist, it does something more: it creates a sense of intimacy that enhances one's admiration for, reverence of, and confidence in the creator of the work. Similarly, there is a remarkable difference, Ghazālī tells us, between a mere factual accounting of the universe and a more calculated examination of creation, one that starts with the human self and enables the subject to stand in awe of the Creator.

Anthropology of Adab

To talk about Muslim ethics is to talk seriously not only of the subject but also of the Creator and a discursive tradition of normativity. To secularize ethics is to denature it. What I call Ghazālī's "ethics" is an amalgam of what was previously discussed under the rubric of law (*fiqh*) and was extensively treated in the pedagogical tradition as the science of proper conduct (*ʿilm al-akhlāq*), which ṣūfī treatises developed more synthetically. Ethics is thus the narrative that combines the theory of right conduct with its applications.

Writing around 1909, the Anatolian scholar Uways Wafā al-Arzanjānī, better known as Khānzāda, defined ethics, writing: "The entire path to true reality is about right conduct [*Ṭarīq al-ḥaqq kulluhā ādāb*]."[14] The ethics of conduct is central to Muslim salvation practices. Ghazālī considered ethics to have an impact on both a macro level, corresponding to society, and a micro level, corresponding to the individual. Even though his best labors were dedicated to the ethics of the individual, he was not unmindful of the relationship of ethics to society as a whole, contrary to the charges of his modern critics. I would argue that, for Ghazālī, there was a dialogical relationship between macro and micro politics, namely, between the governance of the polis and the governance of the body. In *Balance of Deeds* and wherever Ghazālī discussed the ethics of the self, he utilized the same organicist metaphor that he used in discussing politics. The organicist metaphor is one in which governance of the worldly realm is discussed in terms of the body of the sovereign. On occasion, he used other images, such as the topographical imagery of a king's city. Metaphors and images are abundant in Ghazālī's repertoire where he discusses complex issues, since he realized that the images with which his readers were familiar were more effective at conveying his ideas than abstract words.[15]

"The relationship of the human spirit to his body," says Ghazālī, "is like [the presence] of a ruler in his city or kingdom."[16] The monarch represents the spirit, while the ministers represent the organs and limbs of the body. Just as each minister must fulfill his responsibilities in order for proper and just government to exist, similarly, each bodily limb and faculty must comply with its assigned task to prevent degradation in an individual's behavior and character.[17] Another metaphor of the body-soul relationship drew on the topography of a medieval city. In this imagery, Ghazālī identified the locus of pragmatic rationality to be in the middle of the brain, which he compared to the central location of the residence of the king in his capital.[18] All the remaining faculties, equivalent in Ghazālī's scheme to the various ministries, are marked in terms of their importance by their proximity to the king's residence. Just as the sovereignty of an earthly monarch requires the optimum functioning of all organs of government to secure justice and order, similarly, all the bodily organs must be disciplined—must curb the lusts and passions emanating from the lower self—so that the monarch of the body, namely, the spirit, may reign supreme and turn the person into a true vicegerent (*khalīfa*) of God on earth. In a third variant of this metaphor, Ghazālī describes the body to be analogous to a city (*madīna*) and the perceptive faculty, namely, the intellect (*ʿaql*), to be its contemplative sovereign. Here, all the king's physical and abstract sensory capacities of perception, including the sovereign intellect, serve as his aides and army, while the limbs become his subjects.[19] The enemies of the city are lusts and anger. Therefore, the city—the human body with the help of the intellect—should be turned into a fortress (*ribāṭ*), while the soul should be trained to become a warrior-ascetic (*murābiṭ*).[20]

Two issues deserve comment here. The first is that information—both the "facts" of knowledge and "true" knowledge, namely, the knowledge of how to live—is as imperative for the governance of the body-natural as it is for the body-politic. Especially with respect to the body and the self, self-knowledge is indispensable. The second is that the earthly kingdom, or polis (*mulk*), mimics the realm of the sovereign king (*mālik*) of the universe; in other words, the ethical imaginary is anthropomorphic. Though the earthly monarch lacks the perfection of the absolute sovereign, he nevertheless strives for perfection. His lack of perfection is compensated for in the politics of presence; both the earthly ruler and the intellect deploy instruments of surveillance in panopticon fashion, the former over the polis and the latter over the body. Here, the dialogical continuum between individual and society is sustained, just as Ghazālī fosters a continuity between the secular order of politics and the ultimate order of religion. His ethical paradigm is thus configured on three interlinking aspects: the disciplining of the soul (*tahdhīb al-nafs*), the governance of the body (*siyāsa al-badan*), and the administration of justice (*riʿāya al-ʿadl*) in society.[21]

If governance of the body-politic and the body-natural are construed as the two sides of the ethical coin, then sovereignty and autonomy, or responsibility, are the two necessary outcomes, respectively. A ruler's sovereignty increases with effective governance, just as the responsibility of the individual subject increases when bodily desires and appetites are placed under the governance of reason. "For if a human being is unable to govern and control his own self," Ghazālī asks, "how will he be able to govern others?"[22] In other words, the mimetic self must uphold the highest sovereign status as an edificatory ideal in order to become a "subject" of the divine king. To become a subject of God, the self must become subject to itself in a necessary and voluntary act of self-surrender. Liberation, in Ghazālī's scheme, consists in subduing one's animal nature and turning instinctive drives into ideas, thoughts, and imagination. It is when the corporeal body is allegorized that the possibility of realizing one's higher theomorphic nature also increases. Our theomorphic nature goes back to the genesis narrative of Adam; all humans are delegated representatives of the absolute sovereign (*khalīfat Allāh*).

For it is ultimately the upbringing and moral formation of the individual members of the community that will result in predictable conduct conforming to the desired moral order, under which optimum human flourishing and happiness can occur. That moral order is enshrined in the revealed law (*sharīʿa*), which only becomes manifest and known through the positive law. Even though the law is grounded in a discursive tradition, it is a means to attaining higher cognitive intuitions and spiritual knowledge. The law, in effect, becomes a technology for the care of the self. Not only the body but also the psychological apparatus, in Ghazālī's view, becomes a site for engagement with the law. Ghazālī was clear in arguing that the purpose of the law is self-formation, which may occasion some hardship until the body acclimatizes itself to willing conformity. One must immediately sound the caveat that law, in his view, had a role beyond enforcing obligations and sanctions. The law also interacted with both the body and the spirit.

Corporeal or Allegory?

The body-spirit relationship cannot be reduced, in Ghazālī's view, to a neat and convenient Platonic dualism, where the soul, or spirit, is the self and the body only its dwelling place. Ghazālī's position was perhaps closer to that of early rabbinic Judaism, where the encounter of body and soul is a dialogical one.[23] Opposed to this viewpoint is that of the Platonists, who first arrived at a hermeneutical resolution of body and spirit and then translated it into an anthropology in which the soul is the self and the body something less. Although Ghazālī did not draw a direct line between hermeneutics and anthropology, there is certainly a Platonic strand or, if you like, a body-soul tension in his conceptualization. Indeed, if the body-spirit relationship is framed along the lines of a dialogue between a benign monarch and his subjects, then the body-soul relationship can also be imagined to be a dialogical one. Just as a king without a kingdom ceases to be a monarch in any meaningful way, so does a spirit without a body (and vice versa) fall short of our understanding of what both body and spirit are.

This tension between the literal and the figurative, the corporeal and the allegorical, creates a semantic space that offers wide latitude for interpretive maneuver, ambiguity, and productive imagination. Arising from within this space is an anthropocentric imagery, one that resists the Platonic drive to go beyond material language and to discover an immaterial spirit.

However, Ghazālī was not entirely consistent on the matter of literal and figurative, corporeal and allegorical. On occasions, he insisted that one can provide both an allegorical interpretation and a literal one simultaneously. The allegorical, he argued, constitutes one "face" (*wajh*) of interpretation among many equivalent aspects or, literally, "faces of interpretation" (*wujūh al-ta'wīl*).[24] When he was more precise, Ghazālī was adamant that the corporeal sense was the primary one and the allegorical sense secondary. But both can coexist in creative tension, he believed, without contradiction. Ghazālī made this rhetorical move more than once, especially when charged with taking liberties with the literal meanings of the Qur'ān or prophetic reports. A case in point is provided by the novel allegorical interpretation he offered of the prophetic report prohibiting dogs from Muslim homes, which is discussed in the previous chapter. He averred that the allegorical was but one of several meanings of the report. The literal meaning was equally valid, he argued, but was not negated when one also considered the report's allegorical sense.[25]

Ghazālī's style was to exploit the semantic space between literal and figurative senses. He made productive use of interpretive subtleties in order to produce new and fresh meanings. While his literalist critics have taken him to task for such interpretive liberties, few have noticed that Ghazālī's theory of language foregrounded this flexibility. He almost routinely made a binary distinction between an utterance and its meaning. For him, meaning existed as a disembodied substance prior to its incarnation in language. Given this position, he often tended to slip into dualism, and when pushed he would privilege spirit over body, meaning over utterance, perhaps neglecting to uphold the well-established literal meanings. But his ability to defend his views with a very complex intellectual apparatus and hermeneutic was his recipe for success.

Theonomy, Heteronomy, and Autonomy

In theistic traditions, it is accepted that our nature is a God-given nature. Thus, there is also an expectation that human lives should be lived according to a God-given set of norms and values. What is most contentious is the question whether the interpretation and application of these values corresponds to that human nature, which in itself is based on discursive knowledge. Theonomy, literally meaning "God's law," raises this question. Christian and Muslim ethicists have for centuries debated how God's will is to be determined from their respective scriptures. In Christendom, the debate has centered on the status of the laws stipulated in the Hebrew Bible following the advent of the New Testament. It continues to occupy thinkers in that tradition.

For Muslim thinkers in the past and present, whether a Muslim ought to live by God's law has never been seriously debated: theonomy is a theological given. The idea of revealed norms (*sharīʿa Allāh*)—the idea of "God's ruling" or "God's ethical judgment" (*ḥukm Allāh*)—despite its ambiguity, has been an a priori concept within the tradition, hardly contested by even the most extremist sectarian groups. However, there has been considerable debate about the authority of knowledge developed in ethics, especially knowledge that stems from a revealed source. Do the interpretations derived from the authoritative sources constitute categorical truths or mere probable truths? For, indeed, it is difficult for a textual and hermeneutical tradition to escape the hazards of interpretive relativism. Therefore, the question of authority and of who is permitted to engage in the production of knowledge regulating discursive practices is a central concern in Muslim ethics. This is also possibly one of the most important questions that occupy contemporary Muslims. One of the reasons ethics and law in the Muslim tradition is such a serious matter is that it is related to questions of being, to an ontology of transcendent and divine proportions.

Since the formative classical period, Muslim theologians have tied legal values to theological doctrines in order to provide them with an ontological grounding. Often, the debates about hermeneutics and epistemology that dominate discussions of law and legal theory mask the ontological dimensions of the problem. But it is the force of ontology that lends integrity to the discursive system and, moreover, animates the power and authority of the tradition. Against this background, one can begin to see why interpretive transgressions in the law often generate such extraordinary violence—what can be thought of as ontological violence. When transgressive ethical reasoning clashes with authority, it also violates theological doctrine, often resulting in theological anathematizing (*takfīr*) and stigma. An example may be useful. A later native of Ghazālī's home province of Khurāsān, Saʿd al-Dīn al-Taftāzānī (d. 793/1390), said that even the mere "wish" to see certain prohibited practices, such as adultery and homicide, become permissible deserved anathematizing. Such an illegitimate desire, he reasoned, is tantamount to the denial of apodictic truths that are in conformity with wisdom and established in all religions.[26] Here, we clearly see how epistemology becomes coupled to larger cosmological and ontological premises.

Ghazālī himself agonized about questions of law, as is evident in his parody of the jurists of his day for their crass legalism and formalism. In his view, the law could have no meaningful effect unless the psyche and self-understanding of the ethical subject were disciplined in order to synchronize with the demands of God's law. Ghazālī was at his best when he detailed the ideal conditions necessary for the disciplining of the soul so that it might comply with the demands of the law. For the law to have an effect on the conduct of the ethical subject, something had to occur *before* the law: the cultivation of the self through the disciplinary practices of *adab* education (*ta'dīb*) and moral cultivation (*ta'addub*).

Just as the Greeks sought perfection of the soul in philosophy by means of *paideia*, so Muslims sought perfection of the soul through the teaching of *adab*, or norms of conduct. The historian of late antiquity Peter Brown correctly identifies two crucial differences between *adab* and *paideia*.[27] First, *paideia* in late antiquity had no religious code and imposed no religious sanction. It was essentially a secular system of grooming. Second, *adab* became part of a public discourse in Muslim societies at various levels, whereas there was no equivalent of a general Christian *adab* except in the monasteries of the late antique world. The *adab* that Ghazālī proposed was for a world outside monasteries; it was directed at a more general public.

However, both *adab* and *paideia* function as means of education. Knowledge in both cases is not about storing information in the memory. Rather, knowledge is a conviction that "evokes a desire for action."[28] Ghazālī, like his predecessors, did not make a point of showing that knowledge must be performed; implicit in the idea of knowledge, for him, was the understanding that it is performed and practiced. Just as for the Greeks "educating oneself and taking care of oneself [were] interconnected activities,"[29] in the Muslim tradition the interconnectedness of knowledge (*ʿilm*) and practice (*ʿamal*) culminated in the discipline of exemplary conduct (*adab*).

Even though the disciplinary practice of *adab* prepares the ground for the proper inner conditions of the soul to be governed by *fiqh*, there is a dialogical relationship between the cultivation of the self through knowledge and living according to the law. Sometimes, one gets the sense that Ghazālī believed that the practices of *fiqh* were meant to reinforce the dispositions cultivated by *adab*. Ghazālī did, of course, suggest that by observing the rules of exemplary conduct one could more fruitfully profit from the law. Therefore, he spent a considerable amount of time in trying to explain the ethical content and purposes of practices instead of explaining the legal minutiae related to them, as the jurists were in the habit of doing. On other occasions, one gets the sense from Ghazālī that *adab* is really the glue that binds *fiqh* to the self or, to use a different expression, that he sought to grow *fiqh* in the fertile ground of *adab*.

Ghazālī excelled in perfecting the dialogical relationship between the outer (*ẓāhir*) and inner (*bāṭin*) dimensions of the human self. It goes without saying that he sought to create a degree of compatibility between the two dimensions. His goal was to perfect the inner self so that it would consequently regulate the external dimensions. Ghazālī was unambiguous about the importance of such regulation; he observed that the "exemplary conduct of the exterior [*ādāb al-ẓawāhir*] is an emblem of the exemplary conduct of the interior [*ādāb al-bawāṭin*]." He continued: "Movement of the limbs is the fruit of thoughts, actions are the product of character [*akhlāq*], and right conduct is the dissemination of knowledge. Know that the purest concealed core of the heart [*sarā'ir al-qulūb*] is the orchard of deeds and their wellsprings.[30] The interior luminescence illuminates the exterior by giving it ornamentation and luster. Right conduct transforms loathsome and sinful deeds into virtues. If a person has no humility in his heart, do not expect to find it in his limbs. And whose heart is not a niche for divine lights, the beauty of prophetic example will not radiate [through] his exterior."[31] In this passage, Ghazālī explicitly refers to the dialogic tension of the self between the inner and outer, between law (*fiqh*) and conscience (*sarā'ir*), between actions and intentions, and between body and spirit. A special kind of discernment is required to master the synchrony of the inner and outer dimensions of the self. The Arabic word for discernment and refined knowing is *fiqh*, which is more often translated as "law" or "positive law." Ghazālī offered some insightful readings on *fiqh*, which will be elaborated later. In his hands, *fiqh* became part of critical practices that regulate human actions and elaborately care for the inner self. It is this dimension of *fiqh* that he believed was neglected in the scholarship and practice of Islam in his time.

Ghazālian Subjectivity: From Individual to Subject

Debates about the formation of the self and the understanding of subjectivity in Islamicate societies require more study. One of the main concerns has been to avoid projecting onto the past notions that are unique to our times. If we turn to Christendom, we find that there is an extensive debate among scholars of late antiquity about whether the individual was a discovery of the twelfth century. Caroline Bynum has pointed out that what the twelfth century did achieve was a rediscovery of "the self, the inner mystery, the inner man and inner landscape," with an equal emphasis on the prosperity of the community.[32] What has preoccupied thinkers is the question of whether the idea of the individual is identical to the modern notion of the subject. Clearly, the modern concept of the subject is differently constituted from its premodern antecedents. Without denying the existence of the concept of the subject in earlier times, it is this difference that is important to grasp.

In Islamdom, the idea of the individual predates its emergence in Christendom. Even though some intellectual historians are critical of Jacob Burckhardt for his exaggerated focus on the individual in Renaissance society in the service of a history of great persons, his remarks about Arabo-Islamic societies were accurate. He held that Arab society arrived at the notion of an individual at a much earlier period than other Asiatic societies, whose people saw themselves as members of races.[33] Shlomo Goitein, Franz Rosenthal, and Amin Banani, among others, have pointed out that dating back to the pre-Islamic period the notion of an individual was already valorized in Arabian society. Marshall Hodgson takes the argument several steps further. He draws our attention to the fact that at the most elementary level the very term *Islām* "refers to the inner spiritual posture of an *individual* person of goodwill."[34] Since Arabic cultural thought provided the first impulses for emergent Muslim thought, it is not surprising to find that the idea of individuality seeped into nascent Islamicate cultures. The theme recurs frequently in literature, art, and philosophical treatises. But it was perhaps most effectively elaborated in the development of theology, Islamic mysticism, and law, while the Qur'ān and prophetic traditions explicitly excoriate ideas of group and ethnic salvation and lay stress on individual accountability.

There is hardly any doubt that by the twelfth century the idea of the individual was well entrenched in Ghazālī's Persianate world. In fact, the idea of the individual qua individual runs like a golden thread through almost all of Ghazālī's work. He articulated the notion of individuality by using different signifiers and composite constructions of ideas. Terms like *shakhṣ*, denoting a "person as an individual,"[35] or words such as *wāḥid*, which indicates "one person," as in the colloquial "*one* can think of," are littered throughout his prose.[36] Ghazālī unapologetically stated that an individual is "by virtue of his soul, not his body, since the parts of the body keep on changing from childhood to adulthood."[37] The idea of individuality is also inscribed in the capacity concept, called *taklīf* in Muslim ethics. It is the idea that one is morally accountable when one reaches puberty and becomes an addressee of the normative discourse of revelation. Without the notion of an individual self, which in turn generated the idea of individual responsibility, Muslim law and ethics in themselves would be unintelligible.

Subjectivity: Beyond Autonomous Individuality

It can be argued, however, that an individual is always a "subject"—from the Latin *subjectum*, a word that literally means "that which is thrown under." Or, if one assumes that all ideas are always discursively constructed through language and ideology, then there is still, no doubt, a subject, but it is "subject" as a product of imaginary misrecognition of the ego, in the extreme position adopted by the French Marxist scholar Louis Althusser. Subjectivity and self-centered humanism are the products and outgrowths of the imaginary, according to Althusser. "Individuals are always-already subjects," Althusser writes, meaning that we are always the products of ideology. The subject is the one who is discursively called upon to participate in a cultural substrate, which is what is meant by "subjectivity": it is at any given point very specific and demystified. In other words, subjectivity is always an individual substance like the soul, self, or person.

Subjectivity is not something that exists ab initio. "Subjectivity," explains Fred Dallmayr, denotes an underlying foundation or pre-given substance in which human experiences are rooted.[38] That rootedness suggests that subjectivity is constituted by a discursive formation. A discursive formation signifies ways of systematically organizing human experience of the social world in language and thereby constituting knowledge. As Michel Zink points out, "subjectivity is dependent on antecedent texts and prior 'truth'; the subject is 'subject to' preceding values with which it identifies, and is thus generalized."[39] This idea of subjectivity being dependent on prior truths, preceding values, or a pre-given substance means that subjectivity is intimately tied to an understanding of tradition, a topic discussed in the first chapter of this book. Tradition, says Hannah Arendt, is both the thread that guides us to excavate the vast realms of the past and at the same time the chain that fetters each successive generation to a predetermined aspect of the past.[40] In this sense, subjectivity is very closely related to the idea of tradition, a dimension that provides depth to human existence in profound ways.[41] Often, this sensibility is couched in ambivalent psychological terms that inflect notions of the autonomy of the self. Does this mean that individuals are defined not by their social relations but by an inner sense of self-presence, a sense of their own subjectivity? And would a discursive formation not be an appropriate means to mediate their subjectivity? For Ghazālī, the answer to both questions is "Yes."

Mapping Subjectivity

A recurring theme in Ghazālī's work is his strong desire to develop an inward subjectivity. This inner world of subjectivity repeatedly comes into confrontation with an external world that alienates the inner from both itself and its divine source. All Ghazālī's arguments in the *Resuscitation* focus on the world of subjectivity, for it was the fundamental economy of the early Muslim idea of selfhood.

His idea of subjectivity was related to the dialogue between the self and others (divine and human). In his post-ṣūfī writings, Ghazālī consistently went to great lengths to demonstrate that ritual practices have as their primary goal serving both God and humans. This servitude starts with proper intention and protecting the mind and soul (*nafs*) from peril. Humans only put themselves at risk when they succumb to their base instincts and live the life of vice. In the end, it is human vices that pollute the soul. Therefore, Ghazālī gave an extraordinary amount of attention to the diagnostics of the soul and its rehabilitation. What we moderns call subjectivity is approximate to what early Muslims discussed in various theories about the soul. The soul, of course, embodies but is also part of something larger that we call the "self," a point that will be discussed later. For Ghazālī's intellectual forebears and contemporaries, the soul was the seat of subjectivity, the essence of selfhood. However, in any exploration of the soul in Muslim literature, one is also bound to discuss it as part of a network of relations with entities described as the spirit (*rūḥ*), the heart (*qalb*), and the intellect (*ʿaql*).

Ghazālī's doctrine of intention (*nīya*) formed the critical nexus between the soul and the heart. Even if the body fails, the soul can still be healthy with the purity of its intention. Intention is the "condition and attribute of the heart, which comprises two elements: knowledge and practice."[42] Knowing what is required and then acting on the knowledge acquired with sincerity and truthfulness are the crucial elements in the cultivation of the self. Even if one is unable to practically fulfill a virtuous task, the self grows in excellence by the mere intention and desire to do good. Ghazālī had a very clear sense of the self and of subjectivity mediated by the soul. The soul is the subject of multiple desires, the seat of true freedom, and the essence of the individual person.

In order to frame subjectivity, Ghazālī and many of his predecessors resorted to the language of pectoral psychology. The chest, or pectoral region of the body, referred to as *ṣadr* (bosom), is a critical space denoting spiritual enlightenment in the Muslim tradition. All guidance is due to the enlightenment received in the bosom, or, as the Qur'ān puts it, it is due to the "opening of the bosom" (*sharḥ al-ṣadr*).[43] Of course, it is not so much the pectoral biology as it is what is housed in the pectoral region, namely, the heart, that is important in this image. Pectoral psychology views the heart as the psychosomatic center of the human being, and this view was common to the traditions of late antiquity in Judaism, Christendom, and Islamdom. All viewed the heart as the traditional seat of emotion.[44] Possibly due to the influence of Galen on Muslim cultures, some thinkers like Ibn Sīnā thought differently and began to view the brain as the seat of cognition and perception, conflating the brain and the heart in their respective functions. Ghazālī, too, acknowledged the brain as an organ of sensory perception, yet he related it more intimately to the specular aspect, what we would call "the mind" or "reason." For the perception of knowledge and the inner reality of things, the intellect (*ʿaql*) is the critical faculty. However, Ghazālī pointed out that the intellect is actually more intimately related to the heart than to the brain.[45]

Polyvocality is characteristic of each entity in Ghazālī's pectoral psychology—the soul, spirit, intellect, and heart. Due to the plurality of meanings, a remarkable blurring of distinctions between them occurred. His discussion of the heart and the soul highlights some of the elements relevant to my discussion of subjectivity. He was somewhat dismissive of the biological heart, writing that all animals have one and that it is a subject best left to medical doctors. Of significance to him was the distinct part of the biological heart, the hollowed cavity with dark blood, which is the locus of the spirit (*rūḥ*). However, what captivated Ghazālī was an abstract entity that has the most tenuous relations to the biological heart, an entity he identified as a "divine, spiritual subtlety" (*laṭīfa rabbānīya rūḥānīya*). Properly speaking, the "heart" (*qalb*) for him meant only this. To grasp that subtlety, Ghazālī states categorically, is to understand "the true reality of a human being." Privileging the more subtle psychosomatic definition of the heart was something that Ghazālī did with a purpose. For it is in the heart that three vital capacities of a human being coalesce. They are also the quintessential characteristics, Ghazālī believed, of a human being: "the ability to perceive, the capacity to know, and the capability to experience things [*al-mudrik, al-ʿālim, al-ʿārif min al-insān*]."[46] According to Ghazālī, it is the heart that can integrate these complex competencies so that humans are at once perceiving, knowing, and experiential subjects. It is these capacities that constitute the true reality and essence of a human being.

Using the categories of Muslim theology, Ghazālī proceeded to draw our attention to why the heart is integral to the discourse of law and morality. Muslim legal and moral theory as propounded by the Ashʿarī school, as we know, starts with the presumption that human beings are morally accountable (*mukallaf*). For this reason, they must take seriously the revelatory address (*khiṭāb al-sharʿ*) directed at them. There is general agreement among Muslim jurists that the normative address of revelation assigns one of five values to all human acts: obligatory (*wājib* or *farḍ*), recommended (*mandūb* or *mustaḥabb*), indifferent (*mubāḥ*), disapproved of (*makrūh*), and forbidden (*ḥarām*).[47] Failing to perform an obligation or contravening what is forbidden has consequences, which are also spelled out in the divine address. That normative discourse, Ghazālī reminds us, is directed at no other entity than the heart. For, in his own words, it is ultimately the heart that is "addressed, punished, reproached, and held accountable."[48] In addition, the heart is the seat of sensation, which is intricately related to imagination, memory, and knowledge, and which is integral to the soul and the spirit; often, the term "heart" as the location of the soul is metonymically inflected to mean "the soul." The human heart, Ghazālī clarifies, is a perfect "eye" that is sometimes called the "rational faculty," the "spirit," and the "soul."[49]

Similarly, the soul, too, is polyvocal. One set of meanings of the soul denotes its various states of elevation or degradation: it indexes the presence or absence of virtues in the soul.[50] What is of interest to us is that Ghazālī—in almost identical terms to his description of the heart—describes the soul as "the subtle entity which is the true reality of a human being and is the self/identity [*nafs*] and essence [*dhāt*] of a human being."[51]

The uncanny resemblance should come as no surprise. Despite the distinct function of each separate entity—heart, soul, spirit, and intellect—all form part of a psychosomatic network, or an intriguing intertext with the heart at its center. For even the definition of the term spirit (*rūḥ*), for example, corresponds substantively with the meaning that Ghazālī proffered for heart (*qalb*) and reason (*ʿaql*). In sum, the heart not only plays the role of majordomo of this psychosomatic network, it is also the delta, if you like, into which various tributaries from the intellect, the spirit, and the soul flow.

Early Arabic poetry offers a more nuanced interpretation of the word "soul" (*nafs*) in the sense of the "self" or "person." The semiotics of this sense is retained in the field of meanings for the word. In fact, Ghazālī unmistakably used the term *nafs* to mean "self" and "identity."[52] Without this gloss on the word *nafs*, Ghazālī's own definition of the concept makes little sense. The soul, he explains, is a subtle entity that constitutes "the human self/identity and essence."[53] For to say the soul is that subtle entity which constitutes the human "soul" and essence would be a tautology; therefore, the word *nafs* in Ghazālī's definiens must accent the sense of self or identity in order to avoid obscurity.[54] The point by now should be clear: Ghazālī imported the sense of self, person, and identity into the meaning of the soul.

To shed more light on the concept of self, we turn to Ghazālī's eighteenth-century commentator Zabīdī. In a useful gloss on the topic, Zabīdī points out that every time we make reference to *anā* in Arabic or "I" in English we are making reference to the self.[55] Scholars over the ages have disagreed, Zabīdī explains. Some say the self is the visible sensory body, only to further argue over whether the self is the body itself or merely the idea of corporeality. Favoring the viewpoint of the metaphysicians and some mystics, Zabīdī then describes the self as a "spiritual substance" (*jawhar rūḥānī*). He cites the thirteenth-century Khurasānian exegete and polymath Fakhr al-Dīn al-Rāzī as saying that the self can never merely be the sensory skeletal frame, because it constantly mutates and deteriorates. Aligning himself with Rāzī, Zabīdī then proposes that it is "imperative that the self be dissimilar [*mughāyir*, an alterity] to this skeleton."[56]

The foregoing discussion suggests that Muslim thinkers, including Ghazālī, were cognizant of notions of selfhood and identity. This further reinforces my claim that subjectivity is implicit in the psychosomatic network of meanings centered on the heart in its relations with the spirit, intellect, and soul/self. It is, therefore, no coincidence that the modern Arabic equivalent for the notion of subjectivity (*dhātīya*) is derived from the classical Arabic formulation of essence (*dhāt*).

One must therefore wonder why Ghazālī, in concluding his discussion of the multiple meanings of each of these interrelated entities of self/soul, spirit, heart, and reason, proceeded to say that these four terms cumulatively signify a fifth sense, or signified, which he described as "the knowing and perceptive subtlety of a human being."[57] The ideas of knowing and perceiving were common functions of the heart, spirit, and intellect, but not of the soul. So what does the representation of a fifth sensibility mean here? In my reading, Ghazālī was indeed articulating a particular and discrete understanding of subjectivity, drawing on the multiple dimensions of pectoral psychology. As a spiritual substance consistent with the views of Ghazālī, Rāzī, and Zabīdī, the heart-soul dialogic is actually the self, which is the true reality of the human being. The Ghazālian self is a gnoseological notion of the self having to do with a philosophy of cognition. With the fifth essential meaning, Ghazālī was cryptically denoting an underlying foundation, or pre-given substance of the self, in which human experiences are rooted and with which the Muslim subject identifies. Indeed, the self is loosely woven to the extent that it is premised on a psychosomatic network. Within this network, the self is exposed to a temporal flux, where it has the capacity to transform itself for better or for worse depending on the kinds of choices the individual makes. So, while the subject is rooted in a cosmology, it is thus not an impermeable self but rather one that can deal with multiplicity and temporality.[58]

In *Niche of Lights* (*Mishkāt al-anwār*), Ghazālī deploys a set of metaphors in order to describe the constitution of the self.[59] Here, the "Verse of the Light" (Qur'ān 24:35) provides him with his main inspiration, forming the centerpiece for the metaphorical imagery that describes "the five luminous human spirits [*al-arwāḥ al-basharīya al-nūrānīya*]."[60]

> God is the light of the heavens and the earth.
> The simile of God's light is like a *niche* in which is a *lamp*,
> the lamp in a globe of *glass*,
> the globe of glass as if it were a shining star,
> lit from a blessed olive *tree*
> neither of the East nor of the West,
> its light-giving *oil* nearly luminous
> even if fire did not touch it.
> Light upon light!![61]

Each of the similes, or tropes, in this verse—niche, lamp, glass, tree, oil—is represented by what he calls a "spirit" (*rūḥ*) that has an assigned function. I would call this the tropological description of the spirit, or the spiritual-ontological paradigm. The niche is the simile for the sensory spirit, the glass for the imaginal spirit, the lamp for the rational spirit, the tree for the discursive spirit, and the oil for the prophetic spirit. Each spirit is dependent on its predecessor and grows in an ascending order. Starting with the most visible of all, it is the sensory spirit that progresses to the imaginal spirit. The latter, in turn, prepares the way for the rational spirit. The discursive spirit grows in complexity like a tree, and as a tree it is also capable of reproducing itself through its seeds. At the apex is the holy prophetic spirit that can partake of different kinds of knowledge due to its absolute purity and inner luminescence.

If one examines the three paradigms that Ghazālī offered in terms of epistemology, ontology, and the self, one gets the sense that he sought symmetry between these dimensions. Notice the parallels between the existential paradigm of hermeneutics (epistemology), the spiritual-tropological paradigm (ontology), and the pectoral paradigm of the self: they all unmistakably represent five dimensions, or meanings, of an integrated phenomenon. Each paradigm is almost identical with the others in the quintet structure, with slight differences in terminology. In fact, it would be fair to say that there is a homology—a correspondence in origin and development—between the three paradigms as Ghazālī described them.[62] In the existential hermeneutical paradigm, he pointed out that in order for an interpretation to be valid it must correspond to any one of five interpretive registers of meaning, namely, the essential, sensory, imaginal, rational, and analogical. It is no coincidence that each element of the quintet of registers corresponds almost identically to an element in the spiritual-tropological paradigm of the self. If we pair the models, it amplifies the homology:

essential existence—prophetic spirit (oil)
sensory existence—sensory spirit (niche)
imaginal existence—imaginal spirit (glass)
rational existence—rational spirit (lamp)
analogical existence—discursive spirit (tree)

Given the degree of compatibility between these two models, and given Ghazālī's configuration of the self, the coherence becomes even more remarkable. Here, Ghazālī pushed for epistemic and ontological modular coherence that then coalesces in the self, which combines the ontological and epistemological dimensions. In other words, Ghazālī almost instinctively understood that knowledge and knowledge-making procedures have an intimate connection with the formation of the self. Knowledge and subjectivity are intimately linked without creating either radical alterity or identity.[63] In fact, Ghazālī placed the onus and responsibility of finding the appropriate conjuncture between epistemic and ontic concerns on the self. Thus, Ghazālī's ethical project strongly veered toward the formation of a responsible ethical subject, one who embraces an ethics of responsibility.

Constructing the Ethical Subject

To comprehend the ethical subject is to grasp how the integrated soul/self becomes the addressee of divine discourse. Furthermore, to recognize the ethical subject is to understand how the soul/self is held accountable and liable for sanctions if it fails to uphold the given norms.[64] But the self also fluctuates in relation to the conditions that it encounters within the subject. These conditions can transform the self into a variegated spectrum of states: into a blaming or lamenting self, a self that enjoins vice, or a contented self.[65] In each of these states, the self is capable of performing certain functions that are transparent: that is, the acts performed by the subject reflect the state of the self. Thus, the self is an ethical subject related to actions rather than to pure intentions, even though intention is a crucial preliminary to action. Put differently, the self is a locus of responsibilities and a space for transformation. It is indeed this complex, mutable, and mediated self that Ghazālī wished to make the focus of the law, rather than making an exterior self the exclusive focus of the law, as some positivist jurists have attempted to do.[66] Hence, the law (*fiqh*) has to converse and engage with the soul/self (*nafs*) in ceaseless activity, to engage in producing words and actions within which the ethical subject is couched. In other words, Ghazālī believed that the body and psyche ought to be subjected to repeated disciplinary practices until virtues become naturalized within the self.

Ghazālī's ethics was rooted in an epistemic structure, or discursive formation, par excellence. Ethics, for Ghazālī, were based on "knowledge of transactions," or *ʿilm al-muʿāmala*, the latter word derived from the Arabic verb *ʿ-m-l*, which signifies "to act" or "to practice." Another form derived from this root is *muʿāmala*, which means "interactive action" or "to act in relation to others." *Muʿāmala* is interactive and reaches its fulcrum in the subject's ethical relations and acts with others. "Each one of you," Ghazālī wrote, citing a famous prophetic report, "is a shepherd, and each of you is responsible for his flock."[67] Translated into a contemporary idiom, this statement might read: "Each one of you is an ethical subject; therefore, each of you is obligated to an ethics of responsibility." Transactions in Muslim jurisprudence are viewed as being part of *ḥuqūq al-ʿibād*, meaning "fulfilling one's duties and responsibility toward fellow human beings," which in today's rights-centered discourses is often translated as "fulfilling the rights of human beings." But the underlying point to the discourse of *muʿāmala*, which Ghazālī repeatedly insisted was at the heart of *Resuscitation*, is precisely the intersubjectivity of ethics, the idea of having meaningful relations of responsibility toward others. Ghazālī's ethics thus did not ignore its transitive dimension. In this paradigm, ethics is not conceived without the Other being fully integrated in the discursive process. Thus, the ethical act is not an exclusive transaction with the self but is conditioned in relation to the Other. This Other is encountered at two levels: at the level of an intersubjectivity with other human beings in history and at the level of a transcendental intersubjectivity in relationship to God, often expressed as *ḥuqūq Allāh*, the duty toward God.

Ghazālian intersubjectivity thus could not loosen the existential axis from the transcendental axis. Intersubjectivity, in his view, was essentially about proper and normative modes of conduct between the ethical subject on the one hand and both the divine and fellow human beings on the other hand. This view represents the two polarities of intersubjectivity, which correspond to the ethical and ontological configurations of the self. The divine element is always present and never suspended. At the ethical level, the self or subject is defined by practices in the present but is always mediated, either by the divine Other through revelation or by the past in terms of the historical traditions. Historical memory, as well as the state of being subject to prior and past truths, is etched onto ethical practices. All the elements that provide social cohesion and reinforce communal sensibilities are part of the subject, whether they are the idea of the monotheistic community (*umma*) that surrenders to God, the notion of human consensus on norms (*ijmāʿ*), or Ibn Khaldūn's concept of social cohesion (*ʿasabīya*). Intersubjectivity is thus a hybrid notion in which a subject in the present attempts to construct an ethical claim in conversation with the past, the divine, and the present. In other words, it requires one to be fully cognizant of the past and the way that tradition and past memory also both shape the present. It is thus inconceivable to imagine a Ghazālian ethics and subjectivity that is radically severed from tradition.

For Ghazālī, ethics was heteronomous. "Heteronomy" means "other" and "law." The ethical imperative, for Ghazālī, was not derived from the will of the autonomous agent, as Immanuel Kant would have it.[68] Rather, the will of the agent is a response to the divine address and an invitation to give willing assent (*taṣdīq*) to revelation.[69] Thus, it is the Other that provides the human will with the law, instead of human reason being the provider of the universal law. A heteronomous agent derives principles of action from outside himself or herself. Such agents allow themselves to be influenced by the will of others —in this case by God's will—by giving primary consideration to the goal or consequences of their choices. Thus, in the heteronomy of the will, morality and ethics are external to reason. A heteronomous ethics is derived from religious beliefs; it depends on social, cultural, and theological resources. Ethics, piety, and ritual, for Ghazālī, were in the end designed to construct a largely heteronomous self, not an autonomous one. However, it does not follow that a heteronomous self is lacking in individuality. Individuality is not the opposite of heteronomy. Rather, individuality is the locus of agency and ultimately responsibility.

So, in the light of a Kantian critique of heteronomy, how do we make sense of Ghazālī's ethics? The critical difference between Ghazālī and Kant is that the latter privileges rationality and intelligence as the exclusive sources for moral principles, whereas for the former the sensible world is also a ground for ethical guidance. For Ghazālī, both the rational and the sensible worlds could be—and in fact had to be—employed in moral philosophy. So Kant could conveniently dismiss heteronomy as the "source of all spurious principles of morality" in order to privilege autonomy and to justify all human actions in terms of the supreme principle of a rational morality. For those who take heteronomy seriously, however, the principle of happiness is the ground for actions.

Ghazālī and Kant each gave a different weight to responsibility and duty. Ghazālī saw happiness as a telos and a heteronomous ethics of responsibility as the means to reach that end. For Kant, in turn, a rational order was the telos and an autonomous ethics of duty was the means to achieve such an end. For Ghazālī, what overrode the response to the call of reason was the responsibility to respond to the imperative of the Other.

The French philosopher Emmanuel Levinas helps us to make the point that responsibility is also subjectivity, a subjectivity that was commanded at the outset, by which I understand him to mean the primordial command to humans. In contrast to an ethics of duty, an ethics of responsibility favors heteronomy, and "heteronomy," Levinas adds, "is somehow stronger than autonomy."[70]

That Other evokes a reference to another order, another modality of order rooted in the transcendent. Hence, when there is an aberration—as in the case of Ghazālī's subtle toleration of the controversial deed of Ibn al-Kuraytī stealing clothes from the bathhouse in order to be humiliated—there is a signal pointing to another world and its unique metaphysical order. When Ghazālī tried to defend this obviously transgressive act, or when his defenders grappled with the controversial act of stealing in search of pious ends, they all desired to grasp the fundamental codes and to rediscover a principle of order. "Heteronomy," as de Certeau invites us to think about it, "is at the same time the stimulus and what is inadmissible. It is a wound in rationalism."[71]

Autonomy

For Ghazālī and Muslim ethicists in general, heteronomous subjectivity meant being an *ʿabd*, a servant, to God. The word *ʿabd* in its verb form signifies "to serve," "to be a slave," "to be a devotee," and "to adore," to sample but a few of its meanings. It is not viewed as a blemish to be a servant of God; quite to the contrary, it is an honor to be subservient and to take control of the ego. For the purpose of the Creation, according to the Qur'ān, was for humans to serve and adore God.[72] On the face of it, this Qur'ānic view may appear to be different from Levinas's view of subjectivity. However, on closer scrutiny, Levinas's insight could also supplement and deepen one's reading of the Qur'ānic view. When Levinas argues that a heteronomous subjectivity is neither bondage nor slavery, he is asking us to look beyond the rhetoric and to recognize who the addressee is, rather than asking who is the one commanded as a slave.[73] In fact, the addressee is a human being; it is an affirmation of the human through the command. So, when A gives B a command, then it is only at the level of form that B is no longer autonomous and is bereft of subjectivity. If one thinks in terms of what content has been passed on between A and B, says Levinas, then the subject B has received an order from A; in other words, it means that the subject has received powers from A. Thus, subjectivity is a form of empowerment and not really servitude or slavery. For subjectivity is meaningless if one is not subject to a command, to a heteronomous voice, and in a position to respond willingly to that command. Someone who is subject to a heteronomous voice has a more informed sense of being a subject than does a subjectivity that narcissistically avows a gnostic self—a subjectivity in which the self is the subject to the self. Far from being enslaved, a heteronomous subject is empowered in terms of the Levinasian view.

For Ghazālī, responding to a divine command was the act of autonomy within heteronomy: the autonomous exercise of the will to say yes or no, to take responsibility and face the consequences of one's decisions, was for him the ultimate act of autonomy. Giving a shepherd a command to take care of a flock, to use the expression Ghazālī employed, makes him responsible, and in exercising that responsibility—despite the fact that he was commanded to exercise it—the shepherd receives powers and becomes autonomous.

Ghazālī's notion of autonomy within heteronomy was consistent with his idea of the individual. His writings projected a heterogeneous understanding of the individual—namely, one who is subordinate to a socioreligious hierarchy—instead of imagining the individual exclusively in terms of political and economic autonomy. One gets the sense that the individual in the Ghazālian scheme of things is not merely defined; the individual is also normatively required to experience life in terms of social relations. If there is any space in this understanding for an autonomous ego, then it is at the very private level of personal piety and personal religious experiences. Beyond that, Ghazālī imagined the individual as a transcendent subject, one who is held accountable beyond the confines of time and space. However, the focus of ethical and spiritual fulfillment could not be found within hermetically sealed conditions, but only in social relations with other human beings.

Yet even a heteronomous ethics requires a locus and substrate for its performance. For if there is no ethical subject, then there is also no heteronomy. Thus, in the self-knowledge of the subject, there is also an attempt to reach out to the heteronomous, divine Other. Ghazālī drew on Qur'ānic resources in order to make this link. "There are numerous signs [of the divine] in the earth for people of sound understanding," says the Qurʿān, "as well as in your own selves. Will you not then reflect?"[74] The perfection of the soul takes place when it internalizes and imprints the divine signs in such a manner that the sign and soul become indistinguishable. Perfection, Ghazālī reminds us, occurs when the soul/self "is engraved with the essence of the divine commands and is united with it, as if it [soul/self] is it [the divine commands]."[75] So the soul/self is, indeed, the locus for the incarnation of the divine commands in terms of immersion and total obedience to the divine. This is attainable after extensive purification through self-mortification, which then manifests itself in happiness.

While it may appear that Ghazālī advocated complete immersion in the divine Other, there is a certain indeterminacy about his understanding of autonomy. While the essence of ethics is heteronomous, there remains a liminal space within his ethical paradigm for a notion of autonomy. Of course, Ghazālī did not use the term "autonomy," but, in my reading, he nevertheless described a liminal, indeterminate autonomy. It was not an autonomy of reason, but rather one of aesthetics. Whatever the ethical command is to which the subject yields, the source and measure of the experience lies within the subject. It is the subject who experiences it, and the experience is unique to the subject. Ghazālī orchestrated a number of concepts and ideas to construct the aesthetic dimension of the self. Specifically, he used metaphorical terms. His imagery was that of spiritual geography, which he mobilized from Qur'ānic narratives. Most of it related to the search of the prophet Moses for divine intimacy. The key terms are mountain (*ṭūr*), riverbed (*wādī*), and burning brand (*qabas*).[76] He also deployed other Qur'ānic imagery in order to signify a spiritual subjectivity with key phrases such as "blessed riverbed" (*wādī al-aymani*, 28:30), "bank of the blessed riverbed" (*shāṭi al-wādī al-aymani*, 28:30), "light-giving lamp" (*sirāj munīr*, 33:46), "spirit of our command" (*rūḥ min amrinā*, 42:52), "live coal" (*jidhwa*, 20:10), and "flame" (*shihāb*, 27:7). Moses's encounter with the divine presence took place near the "blessed river," where he went in search of combustible items to provide warmth (*iṣṭilāʾ*) for his companions. Instead, he found divine warmth in a sanctified riverbed.

For Ghazālī, these metaphors represented the aesthetic sensibility that one experiences as a subject: it is the aesthetic dimension of any kind of subjectivity, irrespective of whether that subjectivity is in search of the divine or is the subject of artistic, ethical, or musical discourse. This aesthetic sensibility is designated as *dhawq*, or intuitive cognition, literally meaning "taste." As a judgment of taste, our aesthetic sensibility is related to the most intimate human feelings, pleasures, and sensations, which are intuitively experienced. But as an aesthetic judgment, it can also be shared with others and explained to others by means of language, regardless of the inadequacy of language to carry such meaning and communicate it. And it is not only a self-indulgent aesthetic pleasure. One can also forge interpersonal agreement on aesthetic meanings, even if such agreement is always incomplete. Thus, human beings can agree on aesthetic questions without exhausting their meanings. In that sense, taste (*dhawq*) signifies the autonomy of the moral and ethical judgment that is exercised by the subject. Only someone who has himself sat in front of a fire can warm himself and experience heat, says Ghazālī. One who has heard about the warm hearth cannot experience the heat. Similarly, only one who hears music being played can enjoy its rhythms; it is not enough to read the score.

Aesthetic sensibility is, Ghazālī clarified, "discovery through experience" (*wijdān*).[77] This experience, too, colors one's understanding; hence, there is a free play between imagination and understanding. The purpose of aesthetics, says Ghazālī, is to illuminate understanding with a deep imagination. What sets intuitive knowledge, or gnosis (*ʿirfān*), apart from discursive knowledge is that the former is flush with imagination, while the latter has much less of it. One is exposed to the aesthetic imagination through the nondiscursive experience and intuitions that mysticism acknowledges.[78]

In coming to terms with how to understand and interpret the self, one is reminded of Fyodor Dostoyevsky's character Marmeladov in *Crime and Punishment*. Marmeladov encapsulates in his character the dilemmas of autonomy, subjectivity, and the wounded rationalism found at the core of a heteronomous ethics. Heteronomy reaches its apogee when Marmeladov, like Ḥallāj or perhaps even Ibn al-Kuraytī, cries out: "Crucify, oh judge, crucify me, but pity your victim! Then I will come to you to be crucified, for I thirst for affliction and weeping, not for merriment."[79] Marmeladov in his soliloquy is confident that the Lord will forgive every human being, even those with the most beastly characters. Aghast at the idea that the Lord will give blanket amnesty to sinners, the learned and wise men object, proclaiming: "Lord, why dost Thou receive these?" The reply given to the wise men goes to the heart of the human dilemma. The human dilemma is precisely the ability to experience a devastating paradox. Only a heteronomous ethics can effectively shed some light on this paradox. Surprisingly, Ghazālī in the case of Kuraytī and Dostoevsky in the case of Marmeladov both resolved the ethical transgression of their characters within a framework of heteronomy. Ghazālī would not have disagreed with Dostoevsky's reply, as stated in the voice of the Lord: "I receive them, oh ye wise men," says the Lord. "I receive them, oh ye learned ones, inasmuch as not one of these has deemed himself worthy."[80] This is a shattering response, filled with irony and paradox, tropes that a heteronomous ethics, with its logic of practice, is best equipped to handle through narrative. For the core values, if we may call them that, in a heteronomous ethics are deferred to a time outside serial time when the ego is obliterated and only the narrative remains. Dostoyevsky writes: "And He will stretch out his arms to us, and we shall fall at His feet and weep, and we shall understand all things. Then we shall understand, . . . and all shall understand."[81]

The Tradition teaches men how to cross the desert, and how their children should marry. The Tradition says that an oasis is neutral territory, because both sides have oases, and so both are vulnerable. . . . But the Tradition also says that we should believe the messages of the desert. Everything we know was taught to us by the desert.
—Paulo Coelho, *The Alchemist*

9 Technologies of the Self and Self-Knowledge

Alchemy of the Law

How did Ghazālī sustain the self, balancing between discursive knowledge and experience? In other words, what technologies did he propose in order to give a unique shape to the self, and what was the nature of his ethical power and authority? Early pietists—and later jurists, theologians, and scholars in general—were preoccupied with the cultivation of the self through elaborate sequences of practices, specialized disciplines, literature, and institutions. Ghazāī's contribution to *adab* and *fiqh*, cumulatively referred to as ethics, was his ability to draw on the established vocabulary and give it a fresh interpretive gloss. In terms of method, one of the first things he did was examine how certain terms had undergone a corruption or change over time, denoted as "catachresis." One such term is the word *fiqh*, meaning "understanding," "discernment," or "intelligibility."[1] Over time, the term *fiqh* increasingly came to be used in the very narrow sense of "positive law." The renowned philosopher Abū Naṣr al-Fārābī, for instance, described *fiqh*, or the art of jurisprudence, in analogical terms. Jurisprudence, in his view, meant to transfer to acts for which there are no given ethical values those values that are known and given on the ground that the two acts—the act with a known value and the act with an unknown value—share certain essential properties.[2]

While Ghazālī was aware of this formal definition of law, which was common among jurists and philosophers alike, he was not interested in it or others like it. In fact, the positivistic definition of the discipline of law, he pointed out, was contrary to the usage and meaning of the term *fiqh* among the first community of Muslims. During the prophetic and immediate post-prophetic era of Islam, Ghazālī argued, *fiqh* meant the "knowledge of the path to the afterlife and cognition of the subtle perils afflicting the soul, as well as those actions that corrupt good deeds; the capacity to grasp the insignificance of the world and the burning curiosity to experience the pleasures of the afterlife with a heart overwhelmed by reverential awe [for the divine]."[3]

"Discernment" (*fiqh*) and the ability to "discern" (*tafaqquh*) were highly valorized in Ghazālī's lexicon. The word *fiqh* has been used to denote the rules of positive law because positive law is the outcome of the process of discernment. Yet Ghazālī was disillusioned with the jurists (*fuqahā*ʾ) for their inability to discern what he deemed to be the true meaning of things, namely, the transformation that the practices prescribed by the law should bring about in the legal and moral subject. In the *Balance of Deeds*, he postulated another meaning for *fiqh*. The real purpose of the discursive sciences is to find a reliable manner by way of personal intellectual effort (*ijtihād*) to discern the state of the soul/self (*nafs*).[4] And Ghazālī became increasingly emphatic that the primary concern of the law should be not so much establishing rules as demonstrating a concern for the state of the soul, or self.

Ghazālī's notion of *fiqh* as discernment of the self resonated well with certain antecedents in the pietist-juristic tradition. The founder of the Ḥanafī school, Nuʿmān b. Thābit (d. 150/767), better known as Abū Ḥanīfa, defined *fiqh* as "the cognition of the soul/self as to its rights and its duties."[5] To state it in slightly different terms, *fiqh*, then, is the self-cognition of one's duties and responsibilities. The latter conception of *fiqh* has a deeply entrenched genealogy in the tradition that has been displaced especially by more positivistic interpretations that emerged in the nineteenth and twentieth centuries. Among the scholars of the formative period, the sense of *fiqh* described by Ghazālī was well established. Hence, the highly reputed eighteenth-century Indian encyclopedist Muḥammad Aʿlā al-Tahānawī demonstrates how the early scholars recovered the substance of Abū Ḥanīfa's description of the self-cognition of rights and duties. He applies Abū Ḥanīfa's meaning to both his own definition of conventional positive law (*fiqh*) and his definition of the science of proper conduct (*ʿilm al-sulūk*).[6] Clearly, there is a great deal of fluidity between the disciplines of ethics (*ʿilm al-akhlāq* and *ʿilm al-taṣawwuf*) and the science of positive law. Ghazālī, building on this tradition, tried to suggest that the disciplines of law and ethics are two strands of a double helix, and that ideally one should look at the complementary genetic material in each and not view each as separate, which one does to the detriment of both law and ethics.

In fact, Ibn Khaldūn perceptively points out that Ghazālī combined two genealogies, or narratives, of what came to be known later as "the science of transaction."[7] One genealogy corresponds with what Ibn Khaldūn called the mysticism (*taṣawwuf*) of the first generation of Muslims, which was epitomized by the mystic Ḥārith al-Muḥāsibī. It combines the purification of the heart with the observation of the law. Thus, human actions produce the appropriate pious effect on both the inner and the outer self, culminating in the seeker becoming an expert at "inner discernment" (*fiqh al-bāṭin*). The other tradition was pioneered by Abū al-Qāsim al-Qushayrī and Abū Ḥafṣ al-Suhrawardī (d. 632/1234), and its goal is to bring the seeker "supreme happiness" (*al-saʿāda al-kubrā*) by means of spiritual enlightenment. In pursuing this method, the seeker develops a unique integrity (*istiqāma*)[8] within the self, which enables the seeker to avoid sin and remain obedient. After a prolonged engagement in this state of piety, the chances increase that the divine mysteries will be unveiled to the seeker. Ibn Khaldūn argues that Ghazālī, in his *Resuscitation*, distilled the core elements of each genealogy and then combined both into his own presentation of the science of transaction.

By recuperating these earlier iterations of the essential meaning of *fiqh* at the core of the "science of transaction," and especially by emphasizing self-reformation, Ghazālī developed an ethical theory that stressed self-knowledge, or self-intelligibility, which in the end would result in self-production, or auto-poiesis. The Prophet Muḥammad, he argued, due to his status as Prophet, was intuitively endowed to be a "discerner of the soul/self" (*faqīh al-nafs*)—in short, one who possessed self-knowledge. Given the perfection of his soul, the Prophet did not need to engage in the discursive process of intellectual effort (*ijtihād*). However, Ghazālī hastened to add that anyone other than a prophet who wishes to attain such a level of self-intelligibility by exclusively relying on the help of ascetic practices is actually being overambitious. Ascetic practices are necessary, but these must, as a matter of necessity, be coupled with discursive knowledge based on investigation and inquiry.[9] Of course, it is more than apparent that Ghazālī worked hard at moderating his tone in order not to sound as if he was saying that the ṣūfī path was the exclusive path by which one can attain happiness, even though in his own view it was the ideal one.

To counter any scurrilous charge of monasticism and isolationism, he repeatedly warned that his personal bias favoring knowledge of the afterlife need not be interpreted as causing him to feel contempt for other disciplines that are essential to the discursive tradition.[10] To gain mastery in any discipline requires arduous training, he added. At first, any disciplining of the self causes difficulty and requires constraint. But, with practice, the disposition becomes natural. This applies equally to training for long-distance running and to practicing in the art of calligraphy. To become a discerner of the spirit —or to acquire "self-intelligibility," as I prefer to describe it—is to be subject to an elaborate process of self-reflection. This means one must learn about the various conditions that afflict the soul and then, on the basis of that knowledge, become a master at offering advice in ethical matters. The training process and experiences involved are similar to those required in order to become a conventional jurist. Similarly, intuitive knowledge requires regular practice until one develops a habit of understanding the phenomena of the spirit in such a manner that it becomes a spontaneous part of one's identity.[11] Those who seek to improve the condition of their souls will not reach perfection in a one-night vigil, Ghazālī cautions.[12] Self-development is a gradual process of growth, and one should guard against complacency and against regular minor infractions that may deter progress. True happiness comes when one's faculties are so attuned to the divine patterns that obedience to God becomes a pleasure and committing a sin is instinctively experienced as reprehensible.[13]

Another way to construe this is to say that through the concept of the discernment of the self (*fiqh al-nafs*) Ghazālī was making a push toward a deontological foundation for law.[14] By interiorizing his renovated understanding of the law, Ghazālī moved against the grain of universalizing an exterior law that was often viewed as lacking in sensitivity to social conscience. Linking the literal rule of law to an understanding of the self, which in turn connects law to the divine, is a move that is consistent with the proclamation, "Whosoever knows the self has indeed known their Sustainer [*Man ʿarafa nafsahu fa qad ʿarafa rabbahu*]." And, indeed, the one who understands the self also comprehends the knowledge that paves the way to felicity in the hereafter. This is an audacious and radical thought, even in a sense perilous. For by this radical move, Ghazālī took the law out of the narrative of justice and enunciated it, even inscribed it, in mystical authority, as in the Abrahamic call, "I am here Lord, at your service [*Labbayk, allahumma labbayk*]." By connecting the law to the self, one that is dyed in the "color of the Divine" (*ṣibghat Allāh*),[15] Ghazālī placed the interiorized alterity of the law above reason and universality. The self-comprehending and self-understanding subject bypasses the universalizing narrative of reason and justice and takes refuge in the aesthetics of a beautified life: "And who could better decorate a life than God, if only we truly adore Him."[16] Thus, one could say that when Ghazālī described the essence of law to be located in the self he was making a reference to the irreducible singularity of each ethical situation. It is this unique and singular ethical context that is inscribed on the self, a self that must of necessity also engage in a dialogical relationship with the universal and with the exteriority of the discursive law.

Therefore, Ghazālī was unambiguous about the role of *fiqh* as positive law, a body of knowledge to which he as a jurist had made significant contributions; he did not reject it outright. He knew that the law was routinely prescribed by jurists in the external process of self-intelligibility and the acquisition of righteousness.[17] Since he was aware that his views could be misinterpreted as a rejection of the norms of conventional positive law, he quickly supplemented his comments on the self-intelligibility of the subject. The norms as deduced by the jurists, he noted, were indispensable. Here, Ghazālī prefigured what later Western moral philosophers like Thomas Hobbes and others would confirm: that the human being, to paraphrase Reinhart Koselleck, is embedded in an eternal and immutable legality.[18] What made Ghazālī different from some of his peers, and where a Ghazālian understanding of law and ethics was radically different from Derridean notions of the mystical foundations of the law, was that he established a dialogical channel between external law and internal law for the comprehending ethical self, or conscience.[19] He devised a hybrid concept, conjoining two ideas: he combined intelligibility and understanding with the self—that is, *fiqh* plus *nafs*—in order to produce self-intelligibility (*fiqh al-nafs*).[20] Ghazālī, in fact, employed a whole range of terms in his writings to highlight the efficacy of the interiorization of ethics.[21]

Addressing the black-letter jurists, whom he criticized for saying that *fiqh* only obliges the will in its external action, he forcefully made the counterpoint that *fiqh* also obliges the inner posture (*bāṭin*) and compels the moral subject to submit to an ontological call. Self-intelligibility, thus, is the combination of knowledge and morality; fact and value are not separate. The facts and the values are determined by deep self-reflection as well as comprehensive reflection on the world. Therefore, the inner and outer posture of the ethical subject—conscience and law—ought to remain in constant conversation with each other; otherwise, they will part ways, much to the detriment of ethics. If the will has to submit with pure and exclusive intentionality to the command of the law, then such a will ought to be grounded in the transcendent ontological space of the self. It is at this point that the dialogical relationship between conscience (ontology/fact) and law (epistemology/knowledge) is most acute. While we know that the law comes from outside the self, we simultaneously recognize that the locus of the law is both the body and the self. In other words, engagement with the law cannot just dispense with an exterior formality of acquiescence: it requires an embodied subjectivity. Ethics in the Ghazālian key, one might say, means a bid to sustain the dialogical as well as the performative aspects of the law. This occurs through the symphonic relationship of the external action performed by the limbs to the inner posture of the conscience. For what Ghazālī effectively did was combine ethos with poiesis. In fact, this combination is not as outlandish as it may sound at first blush. The contemporary Doha-based and Egyptian-born Muslim scholar and jurist Shaykh Yūsuf al-Qaraḍāwī put the same proposition slightly differently. In a booklet on Ghazālī published some years ago, he urged future researchers to probe how Ghazālī infused ethics into mysticism and how he managed to inject spirituality into ethics.[22] That question goes exactly to the heart of the matter, which is to investigate how mystical poetics, or art, leavens the study of the law and ethics (ethos).

It is, of course, possible that a universal law (*ḥukm*) could be in tension with the subjective and ahistorical authority of the law. Could this then create a situation where the universality of justice is in contradiction with the ethical intuitions of subjectivity? Put differently, can conscience intervene in the performance of the outer law, especially in the light of changed and altered subjectivities? Can the ethical content of the law be realigned with the righteousness of the law through a dialogic of conscience? From the Ghazālian perspective, this is in theory possible, but the theory has thus far remained untested and unexplored. In the same way that the human is embedded in legality, in the Ghazālian scheme legality in turn is embedded in the purest dimension of the self and conscience. The dialogic of action and conscience may be intense, but it is indispensable; without an intense dialogic, a historical textual tradition of ethics will face insurmountable challenges.

This prompts another question. Can an ethical subject be freed from the cultural particularity of the originary moment (the enunciating moment) of an ethical tradition and its subjectivity? How the ethical subject can transcend the particularity of the historical moment of the enunciation of her ethics while still retaining a historical subjectivity is a major question in contemporary Muslim ethics. The dialogical imagination offers the possibility that one may negotiate subjectivity in temporality. For one may have to consider the effects of heteroglossia on language and from there explore the possibilities of a new ethics in relation to changing social contexts. Temporality is part of subjectivity. Thus, if an insurmountable contradiction, or aporia, arises in which the demands of conscience are irreconcilable with the external law, it will only be a temporary conflict; ideally, the dialogical process will, over time, attempt reconciliation, synchronization, and restoration.

Irrespective of whether one seeks esoteric knowledge through inspiration and revelatory means or by way of discursive reasoning, it is imperative that one's faculties be disciplined by the routines of disciplinary practices. Reeducating the desires, in short, is a critical part of ethical formation.[23] Both reason and knowledge are critical to self-transformation in order to achieve the true discernment of the self, Ghazālī argues. Practically, Ghazālī points out, we need three types of knowledge in order to advance on the path of self-knowledge.[24] The first is psychology, knowledge that provides an understanding of the self and the possible ways in which self-discipline can be exercised. The second is skills related to domestic management. Here, knowledge relevant to raising children and taking care of dependents, such as wives, husbands, children, family members, and, in his day, slaves, comes into play. The third is knowledge of politics and the skills to manage the polis, where jurisprudence and civil administration are critical requirements. Harmony in the three spheres—personal, family, and political—he believed, creates the optimum conditions for the realization of true happiness. Knowledge is central to all three spheres, and in order for this knowledge to flourish three faculties have to be trained and disciplined. Ghazālī's three faculties (*quwwa*, pl. *quwwāt*) are the faculty of contemplation or reason (*tafakkur*, or *fikrīya ʿaqlīya*), the faculty of desire, or appetite (*shahwa*), and the faculty of anger (*ghaḍab*).[25] These three faculties partially correspond to Plato's three elements of the soul, namely, intellect, desire, and emotion.

The refinement of the contemplative faculty results in wisdom (*ḥikma*), says Ghazālī, as promised in the Qur'ān: "He gives wisdom to whom he pleases; and the one to whom wisdom has been given, has received much good."[26] One endowed with a refined contemplative faculty can easily make a judgment between truth and falsehood in doctrinal matters. Such a person can distinguish between truth and untruth in speech and can discriminate between acts that are aesthetically pleasing and those that are abominable. The contemplative faculty is intimately connected to epistemological, ethical, and aesthetic sensibilities. By refining the appetite, moreover, one acquires the virtue of abstinence (*ʿiffa*) in order to avoid indecent acts. And in refining the faculty of anger, finally, one attains temperance (*ḥilm*), the ability to show restraint and thus acquire courage (*shujāʿa*). As long as the latter two faculties—desire and anger—are governed by contemplative reason, a certain amount of harmony, equilibrium, and justice (*ʿadāla*) is achieved between the various faculties.

Ghazālī believed that once the faculties are educated they not only perform harmoniously but also reach, in his view, the highest ethical standard, which is the fulcrum of prophetic teachings. At that point, perfection in faith is synonymous with excellence in character. Ghazālī cites a report of the Prophet Muḥammad in support of his claim. "The most perfect of you in faith," the Prophet said, "is the one who attains excellence in character and is most kind to his kin." In Ghazālī's words, one only attains equilibrium (*ʿadāla*) and harmony when one's actions coincide with "the aggregate of most noble virtues of the revealed norms [*jummāʿ makārim al-sharīʿa*]."[27] It is with the perfection of the three primary faculties that the self acquires "sovereignty" over the body.

The idea of justice and equilibrium (*ʿadāla*) features prominently in Ghazālī's thought, where it is almost akin to the tripartite Platonic schema in the *Republic*. It has not only a material and corporeal manifestation but also a cosmic resonance. In order to understand the place of equilibrium in Muslim ethical thought, it is helpful to refer to Rāghib al-Iṣfahānī. Whenever the word "equilibrium" (*ʿadāla*) is used, Iṣfahānī tells us, it is always relational, either to humans or to God.[28] In relation to humans, it is a disposition (*hayʾa*) that *in potentia* means to demand some amount of equivalence and *in actu* means to apportion according to an amount of leveling and equality. When equilibrium is used with reference to God, it does not again signify a disposition, but rather signifies how God's actions become manifest with an unsurpassable sensibility of "harmony" (*intiẓām*). Humans who strive to acquire a sense of justice perfect virtue and realize the disposition to accomplish such an act. Sometimes, all virtues are called justice, and occasionally justice is called the most beautiful virtue.[29] Iṣfahānī captures this meaning in his exegesis of the Qurʾānic verses "He revealed the Book with the truth and provided the measure [*mīzān*]" and "He elevated the firmament and placed [therein] the measure [*mīzān*]."[30] Iṣfahānī renders the Arabic word *mīzān*, literally meaning "scale," "balance," or "measure," as metonymically meaning "justice," "harmony," and "equilibrium." He glosses his interpretation with a prophetic report that states, "The heaven and earth is framed on justice [*ʿadl*]."[31] The harmony of the cosmos, for Ghazālī and generations of Muslim scholars, rested on the realization of justice. Justice thus not only has a value in terms of personal ethics and the training of the faculties, which is a primary goal, but also inhabits all realms, from the private to the public to the cosmic. Realigning personal justice with public and cosmic justice makes the realization of justice the main goal of the *sharīʿa*, the revealed norm of God.[32]

The noted fourteenth-century Ḥanbalī jurist Ibn Qayyim al-Jawzīya (d. 751/1350) eloquently defined *sharīʿa* with justice as its centerpiece:

> The foundation of the *sharīʿa* is wisdom and the safeguarding of people's interests in this world and the next. In its entirety, it is justice, mercy, and wisdom. Every rule that transcends justice to tyranny, mercy to its opposite, the good to evil, and wisdom to triviality does not belong to the *sharīʿa*, although it might have been introduced into it by implication. The *sharīʿa* is God's justice and mercy amongst His people. Life, nutrition, medicine, light, recuperation, and virtue are made possible by it. Every good that exists is derived from it, and every deficiency in being results from its loss and dissipation. . . . For the *sharīʿa*, which God entrusted His prophet to transmit, is the pillar of the world and the key to success and happiness in this world and the next.[33]

What Ibn Qayyim does is render the *sharīʿa* into abstract principles. This is akin to creating a Muslim version of a moral law, except that the moral law in this case is not natural law but revealed law. The revealed moral law is neither an oracle nor a legislature, but rather a discursive tradition intimately tied to actions of the body and conditions of the soul and self. Therefore, education is important, as is discipline, in inculcating a harmony between body and soul. Indeed, this education challenged Ghazālī, insofar as he relied exclusively on experiences derived from subjective ṣūfī practices. For when pressed as to whether he was advocating a new ethical project based on mysticism (*taṣawwuf*), he momentarily equivocated about its place in his ethical scheme.[34] In a rhetorical interlude with a fictional interlocutor who asks if one can independently determine whether what the ṣūfīs say is true or false, Ghazālī retorts: "This book is not about providing demonstrable proofs about truth and falsehood in these matters, but it is about counsel [*waṣāyā*] to alert the heedless ones."[35]

The pedagogical project Ghazālī had in mind involved an extensive cultivation of the appropriate faculties and sentiments in order to give rise to the proper virtues. Knowledge (*ʿilm*) and the intellect (*ʿaql*) are critical components in the realm of education. "Knowledge," says Ghazālī, "is the worship of the soul, and in the lexicon of revelation [*sharʿ*] it is called the worship of the heart."[36] On the other hand, this education cannot take place in isolation from society, despite Ghazālī's desire to create opportunities for novices to isolate themselves from worldly engagements for some time in order to contemplate and acquire enlightenment, which in his words occurs when the secrets of the kingdom of the heavens and the earth are disclosed. But society is the ideal habitat for humans, since we are essentially social animals who can only survive as collectivities.[37] Notwithstanding his criticism of the juridical practices in his day, Ghazālī felt that the rule of law was absolutely essential to advance equity (*ʿadl*) and principle (*qānūn*) in social practices; without these, chaos would reign.[38] Ghazālī the jurist, in the end, still believed that law had a role in worldly concerns and that it possibly offered the best elaboration of the principle of justice, a concept he did not neglect in his late ṣūfī phase.

Ghazālī's own life crises forced him to understand the civil war between conscience and action—the obligation to uphold the law while at the same time making sure that the law is just and fair. He understood the dialogic between conscience and deed. Few grasped the notion of exile (*hijra*) the way he did; he then went on to substitute physical exile by exiling the conscience to a state of good. But if there was one arena in which Ghazālī struggled for most of life, then it was with knowledge, its certainties and contingencies, even after his mystical turn. In his engagement with ethics, he could not import the entire narrative of mysticism without alienating his audiences.

Grounds for Ethics: Epistemology and Praxis

Ghazālī succinctly traced the place of knowledge and action in Muslim thought. Knowledge, he pointed out, only has a reality in an embodied form. In fact, knowledge has a "virtual" quality of producing aesthetic delight. He explained:

> The pleasure an intellectual [*ʿālim*, literally "learned person"] gains from his knowledge does not go unnoticed. He gains even more pleasure when he makes discoveries in the resolution of complex matters, especially when these relate to the kingdom of the heavens and earth and matters divine. This is an enjoyment that cannot be understood unless one has experienced the bliss of unveiling the mysteries. . . . This is an unending pleasure, because there is neither limit to knowledge nor any competition in this re-

gard. For the true student, knowledge expands no matter how many may seek it. Affection, for an intellectual, grows in proportion to the growth of his conversation partners. It is especially delightful when knowledge is sought for its own sake and not for worldly gain and leadership.[39]

Ghazālī points out that the sanctity of knowledge brings "perpetual honor" to its bearers. The learned, he says, are the envy of both the powerful and the wealthy. Because people of power and privilege realize that they are dispensable while the learned are indispensable, they envy the learned.[40] Knowledge not only creates self-awareness but also has the salient quality of making the individual reflective and independent in thought; it immunizes against futile conventions and motivates one to seek perfection and introspection.

Ghazālī uses an analogy from medicine to illustrate his point. A patient who strictly follows the physician's instructions regarding medication and diet will no doubt experience a certain form of healing. But a patient who not only follows the physician's advice but in addition tries to understand the cause of the disease by way of personal research and investigation will enjoy a different kind of healing. Additional information about the nature of the disease not only provides the patient with a better understanding of the illness but also enlightens as to its cure. The difference between the two patients, says Ghazālī, is that the second person transcends conventions of imitation and authority in order to gain insight.[41]

Knowledge and insight are essential requirements for self-understanding. Knowledge enlightens and motivates; it is a virtue in and of itself, and therefore it has a sanctity. But since knowledge is not an uncontested phenomenon, it is not the exclusive grounds for moral conduct. In moral philosophy, says Ghazālī, we make decisions as to what is good or detestable on one of two grounds. In some cases, we decide something is good or bad on the basis of a commitment to normatively revealed discourse (*sharīʿa*). As he put it, we show "obedience to the ultimate order by acquiescing to normative discourses [*al-tadayyun bi al-sharāʾiʿ*]."[42] At other times, we choose what is morally good or bad on the basis of subjective motives (*aghrāḍ*); in other words, our decisions are based on inclinations fuelled by personal preferences.[43]

Ordinarily, we use the words "good" and "bad" in a very loose manner. In so doing, Ghazālī reminds us, we are inattentive to the subjective nature of our ethical decisions. Contrary to the rationalist Muʿtazilī theologians, who argued that things and acts are intrinsically and inherently good or bad, Ghazālī, in line with the Ashʿarī theologians, maintained a different opinion. From

Ghazālī's perspective, good and detestable are not qualities that are attached to the essence of things, but rather are qualities that are discursively mediated by theology. He conceded that goodness and detestability can be rationally comprehended, but he nevertheless maintained that good and bad are both "relational predicates" (*awṣāf iḍāfīya*). This means that they are not essential properties but rather contingent attributes that adhere to things, substances, and human acts.

Opposed to the view of Ghazālī and the Ashʿarīs is the Muʿtazilī claim that moral judgments inhere in the essence of things, substances, and acts—that they are "essential predicates" (*awṣāf dhātīya*).[44] Illustrating his view, Ghazālī argued that we are often oblivious to our prejudices when declaring something to be detestable. When we say something is "detestable in itself," we ignore the fact that the real reason we say so is a psychological one. The object we dislike is contrary to our inclinations, and thus we deem it detestable. Or we say that something is "absolutely detestable," ignoring others who may find the very same thing attractive. In fact, Ghazālī insisted, we declare things to be good when they correspond to our subjective inclinations and deem them bad when they conflict with our inclinations.[45]

In order to demonstrate that even consensus cannot impose moral values, he pointed out that the very fact that human beings differ in their judgments as to what is good or bad is in itself sufficient proof that good and bad are not essential qualities. Likewise, norms provided by a divine legislator are also subjective and do not necessarily cohere with any rational norm. For this reason, a revealed normative code advances what is deemed good or detestable irrespective of whether the acts in themselves cause us benefit or harm.

Indeed, as a rule, we understand almost intuitively that speaking a lie is a detestable deed. However, imagine, says Ghazālī, that a pious and morally upright person, or a prophet for that matter, seeks your assistance because agents of a despotic king or frenzied, loutish killers are pursuing him. In order to protect the person in question, you offer him safety and refuge in your home. When the enemies come and knock at your door in search of the fugitive, do you speak a lie and say he is not in your home? Would it be deemed a detestable act if you spoke a lie to the persons pursuing him with murderous or harmful intent? Would you be regarded as a dishonest person if you deflected them with a ruse? Ghazālī's response to these last two questions was an unequivocal "No." Detestability is not intrinsically related to lying, for telling a lie in the circumstance described above saves the life of an innocent person.

Saving a life is certainly not a detestable act; in fact, it is obligatory to rescue a person in such mortal danger.

The Muʿtazilīs, Ghazālī rhetorically pointed out, who deemed killing to be inherently detestable, also permitted capital punishment as a just recompense for murder and allowed the killing of animals for food. Surely, argues Ghazālī, an essential attribute does not change according to circumstances.[46] Killing should under all circumstances be a "single reality or essence," and hence consistently detestable, if detestability is an essential attribute of any act. Something as detestable as killing is justified for purposes ranging from capital punishment to killing for food, just as speaking a lie is justified in order to save someone's life, says Ghazālī. In order to justify such actions, we must conceive of good and detestability as nonessential qualities, or relational predicates, that are relative to circumstances and conditions: we kill for certain motives and ends. We admit that on occasion our own subjective consciousness creates within us an illusory belief that something is bad. For instance, on seeing a speckled rope, one might mistakenly believe it to be a snake and recoil in fear. Similarly, one would be repelled at the idea of drinking water from a water fountain that resembled a urinal. The only valid reason why we perform good deeds and refrain from committing bad ones is to comply to authority, whose sanctions deter us.

We also deem something to be good or detestable, Ghazālī points out, on the grounds of a subjective assessment of our own best interests (*maṣāliḥ*). Here, it is possible to see that the command theory of moral philosophy, or subjectivist ethical philosophy, made sense to Ghazālī. He found several flaws in the Muʿtazilīs' objectivist theory of morality. In the grand scheme of moral philosophy, Ghazālī's account was clearly aligned to a notion of divine voluntarism. It may also be the only narrative among existing explanations that is convincing to many adherents of religion. For if one follows the Muʿtazilīs and their objectivist moral philosophy that good and bad inhere in acts, then several vexing questions remain unanswered. We know, for instance, that the offspring of Adam and Eve engaged in what we today call incestuous relationships in order to procreate. Camel meat was prohibited for the ancient Israelites but not for the Ishmaelites, the progenitors of today's Arabs. Rationalist explanations cannot provide convincing answers as to why Muslims and orthodox Jews should not eat pork, especially when such meat can be cultivated in extremely hygienic conditions free from disease. Earlier ratiocinations stated that pig meat was infected with disease, a view that no longer has any scientific credence.[47] Nor can reason explain why Muslims are required to abstain from alcoholic beverages if good and detestability are not attached to the essence of wine. In fact, Ghazālī offered what resemble cultural ratiocinations to explain why people adhere to dietary rules. They serve, he says, as markers of distinction between different religious communities. In the absence of rationalism as a convincing ground for moral reasoning, ethics as the command of the sovereign makes eminent sense.

In his view, the dispute about good and detestable boils down to epistemology. At the heart of the disagreement between the Muʿtazilīs and the Ashʿarīs was their disagreement about what constitutes knowledge. Given the inescapable element of human subjectivity, ethical matters, too, cannot escape this dilemma. Those inclined toward rationality like the Muʿtazilīs try hard to argue that knowledge in and of itself is objectively verifiable. The Muʿtazilīs conceded that people might disagree about the sources of knowledge, but it was unthinkable to them that people could disagree about what constituted knowledge itself.[48]

Ghazālī explained that the reason for disagreement was the lack of consensus about this very issue. For if there were to be an objective and self-evident standard for establishing knowledge, there obviously would be no disagreement in the first place.[49] Ghazālī then argued that if killing and causing pain to animals were an inherently detestable act then both he and his Muʿtazilī opponents would instinctively have agreed to its detestability. They did not agree because they disagreed about what constituted the elusive facts of knowledge. While both sides recognized that animals experience pain, they nevertheless agreed to eat animal meat on different grounds of reason, or as a result of different kinds of reasoning. That difference in reasoning was itself an indication of disagreement about what constitutes knowledge.

A very important point that Ghazālī stresses is that knowledge construction, or epistemology, is intrinsically and intuitively related to certain values. These values cannot be verified empirically. Instead, they are subjectively, if not surreptitiously, inserted into the knowledge equation, a fact that the Muʿtazilīs failed to grasp. So while the Muʿtazilīs might have cringed at the suffering of animals, they rationalized their meat-eating habits on the ground that God would reward the animals in the hereafter for the pain caused them in serving as a source of animal protein for humans. Ghazālī disagreed with this reasoning. He had no qualms about the pain caused to animals, believing it to be a commendable thing in that God was at liberty to cause animals pain. Unlike the Muʿtazilīs, Ghazālī was not sure whether causing animals pain at the time of slaughtering was either a crime or a deed worthy of reward.[50]

Thus, in order to escape the epistemological quandary and endless contestation, the Ashʿarīs opted for an antiessentialist ground for establishing goodness and detestability, namely, the idea that values are provided by divine revelation and prophetic authority and that we are thus compelled to abide by these imperatives. Both good and bad are subjective values, since they are not grounded in any universal, absolute theory of objectivity. Reason can to some extent provide us with secondary reasons in order to make us understand why something is good or detestable and thus make the realities more palatable, but there are instances when reason cannot fully explain the rationales behind certain commands.

If good and bad are not empirically verifiable, then why do human beings live virtuous and ethical lives and conduct themselves accordingly? To this question, Ghazālī has an unequivocal answer: in order to attain happiness. In theory, if one wishes to attain happiness, one will have to make certain choices and take responsibility for those choices. Surprisingly, he refrained from saying that one is virtuous because God's law commands one to be virtuous. Instead, he chose the rational language of ethical formation, arguing that happiness is the end of a virtuous life. Happiness was, indeed, the centerpiece of Ghazālī's ethical thought, and he spent much of his life trying to configure the best way to achieve it. But happiness is not a goal that one attains by accident; nor was he interested in material happiness, but rather transcendent happiness. It is the ultimate goal of religious life to attain felicity and salvation in the afterlife. While happiness is primarily an ultimate question, it also has a dual role in that it ensures that one is happy in this earthly life.

The Arabo-Islamic concept of happiness (*saʿāda*) is similar to eudaemonia, the state of having a good indwelling spirit described by some Greek thinkers. But happiness, for Ghazālī, was not a state, but a striving or a seeking. One strives to achieve happiness, but it is never fulfilled. One attains a sense of happiness by taking certain steps to create a balance between the three faculties of anger, appetite, and knowledge. In this sense, Ghazālī's notion of happiness was closer to Aristotle's understanding of the same concept than to the idea of eudaemonia: both believed that happiness is not only a state of mind but also an activity in accordance with virtue. However, the state of mind that the one who seeks happiness enjoys is not insignificant. Happiness is not so much a bodily pleasure as it is the effort expended to reach perfection. To experience the paradisiacal tranquility in one's heart is part of the earthly experience. Nevertheless, happiness is also the desired end of ethical practices. One can attain it by fully grasping the ethical imperatives behind the normative or revealed prescriptions (*sharīʿa*) of religion. By combining practices with knowledge, one can achieve happiness. "There is no path to happiness," says Ghazālī, "except by means of knowledge and practice."[51]

If properly assimilated, there is no reason why the untrained or neglected self of a person cannot be transformed into a superior and fully illuminated entity. For Ghazālī, this process of change and transformation of the human psyche and personality was akin to alchemy, in which low-quality metals are transformed into precious metals such as gold and silver. Similarly, he believed that a sound ethical system based on praxis—the combination of knowledge and practice—must invariably produce a cognizant and self-conscious soul. Human beings fully deserve this elevated consciousness as carriers of the divine breath. In short, he held that there was a way in which the unrestrained human faculties could be trained. A spirit that exclusively gravitates toward the material pleasures of the lower self has the potential to be elevated to another state. In a transformed state, it can appreciate the delight that faculties endowed with angelic faculties may begin to enjoy.

Mysticism and Ethics

Ethicists before Ghazālī, whether ṣūfīs or humanists—ethicists like Junayd, Iṣfahānī, Muḥāsibī, and Miskawayh—would have agreed with him that ethics transforms human character, for if it fails to do so the very purpose of ethics is defeated. What is remarkable about Ghazālī is that he skillfully synthesized several interrelated issues, from questions of epistemology to insights derived from the mystical path (*taṣawwuf*) and the law (*fiqh*), and gracefully inserted these into his ethical project. In the *Balance of Deeds*, this was masterfully accomplished. At first, the reader is under the impression that this may just be another work on ethics, but then the plot is fully revealed, and the reader realizes that this is an ethics with a difference. In many respects, it is a continuation of the method established by Iṣfahānī in *The Means to the Noble Virtues of the Revelation* (*Al-dharīʿaila makārim al-sharīʿa*) or by Muḥāsibī in his *Counsels* (*Al-waṣāya*). The difference is, of course, that Ghazālī established extensive theoretical grounds for the adoption of an ethics that was informed by ṣūfī practices.

Most theologians and jurists who may have otherwise disagreed with Ghazāli on issues related to the mystical path would have agreed with him about the desirability of making believers perform good deeds and practices (*ʿamal*, pl. *aʿmāl*). Orthopraxy, the necessity of performing deeds as a manifestation of faith, is something most sects within Islam agree upon. They disagree, however, about the status of acts and how these impact the definition of who is a believer. Ghazālī suggested that his method of self-realization was that of ṣūfīs. However, he simultaneously maintained that there were also other approaches to self-transformation, such as those held by speculative thinkers (*al-nuẓẓār min ahl al-ʿilm*), by which he meant the methods adopted by the theologians and the jurists—and perhaps even the philosophers. His dual approach to ethics and self-transformation was consistent with what he wrote in the *Resuscitation*: that knowledge can be acquired by means of either revelatory disclosures or repeated and consistent moral practices.

A purposive reading of the *Balance of Deeds* suggests that while Ghazālī preferred the method of the ṣūfīs, he was also cautious. That led him to prevaricate at first, but it was not the first time that he did so. His hesitation may well have been in anticipation of a hostile social reception of his ideas. He responded by saying that asking which method was preferable, that of the ṣūfīs or that of the speculative thinkers, was the wrong question. Speaking personally by prefacing his comment with the phrase, "the truth as it appears to me," Ghazālī proceeded to say that a simple yes or no answer was unsatisfactory, since every response has to take account of the context of the questioner.[52] A firm grounding in discursive knowledge, he says, is clearly preferable, especially for novices, for it equips them with the tools of demonstrative proof and rational knowledge, which leads to the path of happiness. How many ṣūfīs, Ghazālī asks cynically, get stuck for up to ten years pondering a single idea or question that could have easily been resolved if the ṣūfī had been equipped with the discursive sciences?[53]

Most people, however, should busy themselves with the regular practices of religion and the knowledge required to perform these. Only those who have the requisite intellectual capital should proceed to study the discursive sciences, he says, suggesting that only a few need them.[54] Very few people, he adds, have the predisposition to be inducted into the path of the ṣūfīs. He was acutely aware that some people who adopted the ṣūfī path of self-transformation became physically ill and mentally unstable. Hence, he did not recommend it as an appropriate course for everyone. However, Ghazālī noted these qualifications after he had waxed lyrical about the advantages of the ṣūfī path, making it difficult for one to choose any other path. This path was only recommended when the novice engaged in a serious effort to purify the heart and strived to eliminate the negative properties of the soul by means of acts of self-mortification (*mujāhada*) and the renunciation of worldly ties in order to exclusively focus on the divine. With such genuine aspiration in place, combined with a thirst for, and a patient waiting for, the divine mercy, the chances that the essence of all reality would unfold on the heart of the aspirant increased greatly. Just as the true realities of things are unveiled to prophets and saints once their souls reach perfection, without any tuition and teachings, so similar experiences—albeit at lesser intensities—may be had by those seeking out the spiritual path.[55]

Just as his notion of the self was heart-centered, Ghazālī's ethics, too, was centered on the cleansing of the heart. Two groups of artists, he tells us, one Byzantine and one Chinese, were once debating the merits of their respective art forms.[56] A king asked them to compete with each other in order that he might assess the merit of their work. Each team was asked to paint on a canvas. While they worked, a divider separated them so each group could not see the work of the other. The Byzantine artists daily entered their quarter with a variety of paints and brushes. Their Chinese counterparts, surprisingly, used neither paints nor brushes. While the Byzantine artists painted their picture, the Chinese artists spent the time cleaning, scrubbing, and polishing their canvas until it achieved a ravishing brilliance and luster. When the deadline arrived, everyone who had observed the work of the two teams was astonished when the Chinese artists announced that they had completed their assignment.[57]

Upon unveiling their work, the Byzantine artists displayed a beautiful painting composed of dazzling colors on their canvas. When the veil was lifted on the Chinese side, the clarity of the surface was so brilliant that it at once reflected and shone, like a mirror. While it had no visible picture on it, it nevertheless had an extraordinary beauty that impressed the observers. The Chinese artists acquired such an extraordinary level of clarity on their canvas that it spontaneously captured the silhouette and artistic effects of the Byzantine artists' picture in unimaginable and superior ways. The moral of the story is that, like the highly cleansed Chinese canvas, the soul can become a locus to capture the reflections of divine knowledge, says Ghazālī. By way of acquired discursive knowledge, one can attain the divine imprint on the heart in the manner that the Byzantine artists did. Or, by way of a divine imprint of gnostic knowledge, one can have it reflected on the self, as the Chinese artists did. If the surface of the heart is purified sufficiently, it can become a receptacle of every kind of imaginable beauty. Ghazālī favored the Chinese method of creating presence through an absence. His examples suggest his familiarity with different kinds of mystical traditions, but he may also have been saying something innovative. Viewing something as tangible as a picture is no guarantee that one understands what one sees. What is required is a receptacle, a discerning eye, and an interpretive apparatus that can discover the substance of any meaning.

Individual versus Communitarian Authority

In the previous chapter, I discussed individuality and aesthetic autonomy. Now I want to pursue the question: How did Ghazālī imagine autonomy in matters of knowledge, or epistemology? In Ghazālī's moral economy of ethical formation, it is the duty of the moral subject to make knowledge-based decisions. Ghazālī was certainly aware of the compelling psychological and sociological effect that community and group authority can exercise on the individual as a moral subject. The term he invoked for "discursive tradition," I believe, is *madhhab*; he used the plural form, *madhāhib*, to describe those persons affiliated to a discursive tradition and whose corporate authority authenticates knowledge and practices. This is effectively what the classical law schools, and to a lesser extent the theological affiliations in the past, were: corporate discursive traditions with power and authority. At the end of *Balance of Deeds*, Ghazālī anticipates a question that may arise in the mind of his reader. A critic could object, he says, that in this book he presented arguments derived from a plurality of discursive traditions, drawing from the ṣūfīs, the Ashʿarīs, and the dialectical theologians (*mutakallimūn*). Are all these discursive traditions true, Ghazālī's interlocutor asks, or is only one of them true?

The term "discursive tradition" (*madhhab*), Ghazālī argues, is saturated in a spectrum of polysemy. The dominant character of a discursive tradition is shaped by several sets of factors. One set of factors is the social conditioning, socialized prejudice, or bias (*taʿaṣṣub*) that it develops due to acculturation, changing social conditions, the education of its members, and the influence of ideology.[58] A second set of factors relates to educational formation and the predisposition of the recipients on the grounds of capacity, individual potential, ethnic affiliation, and cultural orientation.[59] And a third set of factors is based on the state of the heart and a person's predisposition to gnostic knowledge and spiritual unveilings, in which the subject is freed from any preexisting beliefs and becomes a receptacle, a tabula rasa.

Ghazālī argued that prejudices in favor of a specific discursive tradition or sect become a double-edged sword. Of course, he admits, people are often motivated by rivalry and competition. And, on other occasions, bias serves as a propaganda tool to ensnare unthinking people in order to further the nefarious political ends of the advocates of a given viewpoint.[60] His reading of social contexts will please many modern discourse analysts and political observers of social conflict, for it is as stunning as it is insightful. Ghazālī astutely observes:

> In some parts of the world, whenever there is cohesion in the sect or discursive tradition [*madhhab*] and those who vie for political office fear that they will fail to engender subservience, they proceed to invent issues! They then create the impression that it is necessary to create division and promote prejudice. So some people will dispute whether the official flag should be black or red. One group will say: "The true flag is black." Another will say: "No, it's the red one!" And so the goals of the leaders are accomplished in making the masses subservient to the extent of getting them entangled in a false conflict. While the masses mistakenly believe it to be a vital matter, the leadership knows fully what the real purpose was in fabricating this matter.[61]

Ghazālī was aware that there is a tension, even at times a conflict, between the authority of tradition and the authority and autonomy of an individual to make choices. Though he was skeptical about the factors influencing the shape of discursive traditions (but not about esoteric knowledge), he finally favored the autonomy of the individual subject. This was the only way that he could make the individual subject morally accountable. Ghazālī was certainly single-minded in his insistence that a certain amount of individual independence is not only desirable but necessary in matters of ethics and self-transformation. This concept ties in neatly with his ideas of self-production. Toward the close of the *Balance of Deeds*, he declares himself to be opposed to the slavish adherence to a discursive tradition, but he does not clarify whether he wishes for tradition to disappear entirely, which would be inconsistent with what he wrote elsewhere. His goal was to make the discursive tradition more robust and self-critical. In this context, he pointed out that self-awareness must ideally lead to a certain amount of independence that enables an individual to be morally and ethically accountable. For it often happens that ethical and moral violations occur under the pretext that they are in accord with the views and prejudices attributed to a sect or to the majority of members belonging to a discursive tradition. Just as an informed patient is preferable to an uninformed one, an ethical person must ideally be able to demonstrate a modicum of self-awareness, independence, and self-intelligibility.

Only knowledge of religion can ultimately empower the individual to engage with the process of self-reform. This process is not something Ghazālī arbitrarily recommended to people totally unfamiliar with religion or to nominal believers. Trying to explain the intricacies of faith and the subtle verities of truth to uninformed audiences, in his view, can be damaging, and it can have the effect of alienating people from religion. Most people may prefer to understand the verities of religion in a conventional, even literal, sense. Here, Ghazālī, even though he was not speaking to a specific doctrine, nevertheless used the same structure of argument that the philosophers presented. As discussed in an earlier chapter, the philosophers argued that different audiences—laypersons and the learned elite—understand doctrines in incommensurably different registers of meaning, an idea that so infuriated Ghazālī that he accused them of saying that God engaged in doublespeak. Ghazālī, nevertheless, made a most insightful observation of enduring importance about the necessity to be a reflective individual, one whose opinions about self-realization count:

> Avoid relying on the authority of discursive tradition or collectivities [*madhāhib*]. Seek instead the truth by way of inquiry so that you become a person who holds an authoritative viewpoint [*ṣāḥib madhhab*]. And do not allow yourself to be in position where you follow a guide like a blind person. The guide ostensibly directs you along a path, whereas you are [actually] surrounded by a thousand guides similar to yours; each warns that your guide will lead you to peril and mislead you! Only when you act on your decision to follow your guide, then you come to realize the tyranny of your guide. Therefore, there is no salvation except in independence [*istiqlāl*] of thought.
>
> Forget all you've heard and clutch what you see
> At sunrise what use is Saturn to thee?[62]
>
> If writing these words yields no other outcome save to make you doubt your inherited beliefs, compelling you to inquire, then it was worth it—leave alone profiting you. Doubt transports [you] to the truth. Who does not doubt fails to inquire. Who does not inquire fails to gain insight. Without insight, you remain blind and perplexed. So we seek God's protection from such an outcome.[63]

This is, by all accounts, an extraordinary statement. Who is Ghazālī addressing in this statement? Lay audiences or scholars? He may well have had in mind all types of people. In any case, it remains a radical position. In Ghazālī's view, skepticism is a healthy aid to intellectual inquiry. Based on personal experience, he truly believed that doubt results in healthy ends that will ultimately lead to the self-transformation of the subject. More importantly, in my view, Ghazālī was discounting, if not criticizing, the authority and power of discursive traditions.

Ghazālī's criticism of the authority of discursive traditions may have been indirectly targeted at the authoritarian character of some Ashʿarī theologians for their lack of intellectual rigor and their dogmatic reliance on authority. Dogmatism, as opposed to discursive certainty, was, in his view, the enemy. Bias and prejudice are among the chief characteristics of dogmatism. It was conventional in his time to follow the views of an established and recognized "school" in order to follow the truth. However, when such conventions do not serve honorable goals, he suggests, affiliation to a school prevents the individual from attaining the truth and obstructs enlightenment and emancipation. Ghazālī's final remarks in *Balance of Deeds* were clearly directed at efforts that frustrate critical inquiry and impede the exploration of new frontiers to understand the self and nature.

Ghazālī's contribution to ethics negotiated the distance between forms of juridical and Muʿtazilī objectivism on one end of the spectrum and the mystical and Ashʿarī forms of subjectivism, or antiessentialism, on the other end of the spectrum. In the Muʿtazilī view, the object is nothing but the manifestation of the abstract law of nature. Thus, the Muʿtazilīs posited a strong individual free will and tacit freedom percolated with notions of justice on the one hand and an impenetrable, law-bound object on the other hand. What Ghazālī did was bridge that distance of subject versus object, self versus other, heteronomy versus autonomy. He did so by creating a dialogical relationship between the various dimensions and aspects of phenomena. This is most evident in Ghazālī's notion of the self, as manifest in his treatment of pectoral psychology. Meanings of different components of the self constantly interact with each other and form part of a greater whole. Ghazālī's mutable and intensely dialogic notions of self and consciousness were achieved by this dialogism.

The heteronomous polarity of the law is undoubtedly a very pronounced aspect of Muslim thought in general and of Ghazālian thought in particular. But he also subtly created counterpolarities to heteronomy. Heteronomy is counterbalanced by, or kept in tension with, the autonomy of self-intelligibility, self-production, and aesthetic sensibility. In this way, the law remains under the surveillance of conscience, while the law of the external body and the law of the self remain dialogically engaged.

Given the intermediate (*dihlīz*) position that Ghazālī carved out for himself in the dialogic of the external law (*fiqh al-ẓāhir*) with the inner law (*fiqh al-bāṭin*, or *fiqh al-nafs*), it is not surprising that epistemology and ontology constantly interacted in his work. Whenever Ghazālī, especially the ṣūfī Ghazālī, spoke about epistemology, ontology was not very far from his mind, and vice versa. History and subjectivity, for him, were simply the continuations of a single dialogical process. In the shadow of historical consciousness, the self in the most comprehensive sense transforms reality. It is certainly not a Panglossian self that becomes an obedient reflection of reality, demanding optimism regardless of the circumstances. Nor can one obtain objectivity by means of the disinterested contemplation of reality. Rather, the truth is the product of the interaction between the self and the world—not the banishment of the subject from the object, but an engagement so that the self might come to view the truth more accurately. For Ghazālī, truth was achieved if the individual believer became aware of himself or herself as the universal subject of history. The truth of history, in his narrative, is the prophetic spirit becoming conscious of itself. One can thus hope to historicize while avoiding relativism.

What one consistently encounters in Ghazālī's writings is a recognition that there is a category that mediates between subject and object, namely, self-knowledge, similar to the mediation of the Delphic oracle. The significance of such self-knowledge is that in knowing oneself one simultaneously becomes subject and object. More importantly, the dichotomy between thought and action, or fact and value, is dismantled by this construction of self-knowledge. For, indeed, to know myself is to alter myself. And in engaging myself in the truth of my condition and the subsequent self-transformation, I also come to know what I would need to do in order to become free. The objective of Ghazālian subjectivity is to attain freedom, the pinnacle of which is liberation from the gravitational pull of the lower self so that the subject might experience divine self-disclosure. The purpose of ethical practice is to inevitably lead the subject to some proximity so that the subject may experience the possibility of divine unveilings and intuitive knowledge. But this possibility does not even arise without becoming the subject of ethical practice, namely, following the requirements of the knowledge of transactions (*ʿilm al-muʿāmala*). It is only through the perfection of social practices with an ethical content that the process culminates in mystical unveilings and divine intuitions in the subject—the knowledge of unveilings (*ʿilm al-mukāshafa*).[64]

A relationship of words, carefully spun words, as well as spontaneous outpourings, evasions and confessions. Silent tears, for neither of them could bear to cry openly, and silences, silences that were the most intimate of all the unspoken intimacies. He understood my loneliness, the terror of unbelonging.
—Achmat Dangor, *Kafka's Curse*

I felt, on the last page, that my story was a symbol of the man I had been as I was writing it, and that in order to write that story I had to be that man, and that in order to be that man I had had to write that story, and so on, *ad infinitum*. (And just when I stop believing in him, "Averroës" disappears.)—Jorge Borges, "Averroës' Search"

Conclusion: Knowledge of the Strangers

Sometime between the years 1174 and 1180, the great jurist and philosopher Abū al-Walīd Ibn Rushd (Averroës) wrote a refutation of some of Ghazālī's views in a comprehensive volume called *Incoherence of Incoherence* (*Tahāfut al-tahāfut*). Ibn Rushd defended the Muslim philosophers, whom Ghazālī had mauled in his book *Incoherence of the Philosophers*. Ghazālī had charged that in their fascination with philosophical reasoning the Muslim philosophers knowingly or in error subscribed to certain beliefs that he thought clashed with settled issues of dogma.

As the one who linked Muslim rationalist philosophy to theological piety, Ibn Rushd complained bitterly about Ghazālī's multiple intellectual personas. He was especially bewildered by the flux of ideas in Ghazālī's corpus, a venture of kaleidoscopic proportions that held together in delicate tension Ashʿarite onto-theology and Neoplatonic mysticism laced with subtle iterations of Aristotelian philosophy.

Yet, even in his biting critique, Ibn Rushd was also deferent to Ghazālī. He never doubted the latter's quest for certainty and piety, and he displayed such respect for Ghazālī's insights in legal theory that he abridged Ghazālī's influential text on that subject.[1] It would not be an exaggeration to say that Ibn Rushd's own intellectual agenda, shaped though it was by his debt to Aristotle, was also shaped by his response to Ghazālī.[2]

As the indomitable Abū Muḥammad Ibn Sabʿīn (d. ca. 668–69/1269–71) observed, Ibn Rushd might have been far too placid and uncritical a follower of Aristotle, which would explain his formalism—a trait that stifled his own inventiveness and creativity, culminating in his allergy to Ghazālī's omnivorous intellectual appetite.[3] While Ibn Rushd charged that Ghazālī's intellectual project had serious shortcomings, his student and successor as court physician, Abū al-Ḥajjāj Yūsuf ibn Ṭumlūs (d. 620/1223), welcomed the complexity of Ghazālī's project. It was Ghazālī's intellectual diversity and cosmopolitanism that appealed to Ibn Ṭumlūs, despite his own teacher's deep-seated ambivalence toward the scholar from Ṭūs.[4] Even the limited sample of Ibn Rushd and his student Ibn Ṭumlūs represents the spectrum of rejection, acceptance, and ambivalence toward Ghazālī. While very few people would categorically reject Ghazālī's entire intellectual output, even his staunchest acolytes seem always to have a few reservations about some of his views. This is neither a weakness nor a criticism of Ghazālī, for he had a mind so fine that even if it was violated by a few errant ideas it still retained its luster.

The positive yet uneven reception of Ghazālī and his legacy has in large part to do with his very diverse intellectual repertoire. He stood at the *dihlīz*, the threshold and intersection of many currents of thought and ideas. It was his very location at the *dihlīz* that made it possible for him to theorize and give coherence to the heterogeneity of human thought and experiences. It is, of course, this aspect of his intellectual persona that has caused some people to view his epistemology as anti-reason while causing others to see him as providing a different narrative of reason altogether.

The refreshing complexity and robust manner in which ideas were crafted during Islam's middle period compared to what passes as intellectual creativity today makes one nostalgic. Often, the predilection in the present is to merely dust off Ghazālī or Ibn Rushd or any other prominent figure as a quintessential plastic figure who is expected to provide answers in an oracular manner—often from the grave. More condemnable is the way in which scriptural resources and tradition are violently colonized by certain groups in order to further the construction of the most noxious ideological edifices imaginable. Needless to say, often the methodologies of Islamic reform are mechanistic and random, torturously utilitarian, and lacking in sophistication while almost invariably providing nonsolutions. A more helpful path to reform might require entering into a dialogical engagement with past thinkers and traditions of thought in order to struggle intellectually and arrive at coherent responses to our own dilemmas.

This book is to a large extent an adventure in exploring the creativity and texture of thought that made Ghazālī such an extraordinary figure in Muslim history. Far more significant and worthy of inquiry than recounting his fame is the project of configuring the archeology of his thought—the creativity of his mind and the way he sutured so many different tapestries of thought onto his self in such an effortless manner that he became canonized in Muslim tradition. My purpose has been to grasp the architectonic lines that marked Ghazālī's genius and to ask: What was so unique about his ideas that they enjoyed such longevity? More importantly, how can Ghazālī's intellectual legacy and ideas be a bridge, an exemplar, or an inspiration for contemporary Muslims? It goes without saying that the way Ghazālī will serve as an exemplar will be mediated by a host of issues arising from the diversity of contemporary Muslim discourses, ranging from varieties of traditionalism, modernism, and maximalism (fundamentalism) in the confluence of modernity to liberalism and capitalism, among other hegemonic and globalizing discourses.

Hegemonic modes of knowledge, Walter Mignolo informs us, often erode local forms of knowledge.[5] In other words, one of the major challenges that Muslim societies and cultures—like other cultures overshadowed by the forces of globalization—experience is the erosion of values and lifestyles that reflect their historical subjectivities. Given the differential in power between the colonized and the colonizers, the coloniality of power renders the knowledge of the colonized into subaltern modes. Over time, Boaventura de Sousa Santos points out, placing the knowledge of the other in an inferior position results in "epistemicide," the destruction or murder of the knowledge of a particular social group. Imperialism and epistemicide, observes de Sousa Santos, are part of the ineluctable trajectory of Western modernity.[6] The need to stem this epistemicide is self-evident, as is the necessity to rehabilitate and articulate subaltern modes of knowledge with integrity and coherence without resorting to orientalist modes of knowledge.

At a crucial moment in his encounter with the constitution of modernity, John Locke provided creative answers to his own questions. Similarly, at a crucial stage of his life, while consolidating the paradigmatic transition for Muslim discursivity in the eleventh-century Arabo-Persianate world, Ghazālī too asked many provocative questions and provided equally creative answers. More important than questions and answers, however, is the archeology of the questions and answers. If anything, this book has been an attempt to plot the outlines of the archeology of knowledge that Ghazālī, as a paradigmatic and creative thinker, offered us.

Ghazālī as Exemplar for Critical Traditionalism

Our context differs from that of Ghazālī in several crucial ways. An Islamic empire drove the dominant paradigm in his day. In our time, the dominant paradigm is the imperium of modernity, in which liberal capitalism predominates, a capitalism that marginalizes traditions other than the one from which it emerged in unprecedented ways. However, we are better at knowing what we do not want than we are at fully knowing what we want. However, we do know that we desire a paradigm shift and seek emergent knowledge, both of which will facilitate transitions to alternative futures. While the awaited paradigmatic transition in its messianic calling—teleiopoiesis—is as yet barely discernable, we have a hunch about which direction we wish to go. What we do know is that dominant paradigms within the world system that continue to reproduce themselves have to be contested and countered with alternative ways of knowledge and knowing, as well as with models of society-building and models of living, as part of the strategy for ending epistemicide.

During his time, Ghazālī asked what kind of subjectivity was required for and capable of creating new knowledge for the myriad of challenges in his society. That subjectivity could potentially have had several possibilities and iterations. Ultimately, it took unique shape and form, the contours that were outlined in this book. We might call it a Ghazālian subjectivity. After all, it was embodied in a unique self, one that was also competing at both the epistemological and societal levels with other forms of knowledge that posed as alternative sources for the formation of the Muslim self. Ghazālī, as I have shown, opted for those sources of the self that were heterogeneous. For him, the subjectivity of the self in relation with the divine, nature, and society was the centerpiece and touchstone for the paradigmatic transitions and emergent knowledge of which he was part. A crucial difference, though, was that it was not an ego-centered notion of the self, but one that was related to tradition, revelation, knowledge, and society.

As Muslims explore ways to energize their knowledge traditions, in addition to being critical, robust, and cutting-edge, they will also have to take into account the kind of subjectivity that the paradigmatic tradition aspires to produce, for that is the challenge underlying the search for emergent knowledge. How do Muslims look at their own past while concurrently exploring experiences and resources of knowledge in other non-European experiences, forging partnerships in order to form alternative societies? As de Sousa Santos so poignantly reminds us, the future has dramatically become a personal question for us, one of life and death. "The past is a metonymy of all that we were and were not," he says. "And the past that never was demands a special reflection on the conditions that prevented it from ever being. The more suppressed, the more present. The emergent subjectivity is so radically contemporary with itself that, by dealing with the past as if it were present, it even gains an anachronistic dimension." In a most astute observation that echoes perfectly with the productive and wholesome meaning of tradition discussed earlier in this book, de Sousa Santos adds: "The past is, however, made present, not as a ready-made solution, as in reactionary subjectivity, but rather as a creative problem susceptible of opening up new possibilities."[7] Ghazālī did exactly that. He was courageous and dared to explore new possibilities, while Ibn Rushd and others preferred the comfort zone of the customary methodological puritanism.

The critical work of any project seeking a paradigmatic change is to defamiliarize the canonical tradition, to interrogate it, literally to deconstruct it, in other words, to undertake close readings. But it must not imitate certain forms of postmodernism that only deconstruct, as if deconstruction in itself were an end—where certain forms of postmodernism become victims of Nietzschean extremes, since Nietzsche believed that a true subject is by nature ahistorical.[8] For, together with de Sousa Santos, we must insist that it is only in an archeology that the past becomes present; in other words, it is only in the encounter with the historical that a paradigmatic transition can engage in a radical critique of the politics of the possible without yielding to an impossible politics.[9] "Ontologies of the present," Fredric Jameson reminds us, "demand archeologies of the future, not forecasts of the past."[10]

In my examination of the archeology of the thought of Ghazālī, I have identified several topoi that may be useful signposts in the exploration of an emergent Muslim subjectivity that coincides with a search for a paradigmatic transition in knowledge. At least three broad topoi are forcefully present in Ghazālī's thought and may be useful areas for further exploration. They are poiesis and ethos; the creativity of the threshold, or *dihlīz*, position; and the hope to be found in exile.

Poiesis and Ethos

Philosophy, Seth Bernadette points out, has a certain debt to poetry, despite the ancient quarrel that exists between the two forms of knowledge.[11] Ibn Rushd charged Ghazālī with using poetics, which is a subset of rhetorical discourse, in his analysis, along with philosophy. His main complaint was that Ghazālī introduced an unwelcome heterogeneity of knowledge into his repertoire. He would have preferred if Ghazālī had painstakingly pursued more foundational (apodictic) forms of knowledge, called *burhān*. This, Ibn Rushd believed, would have advanced the magisterial serenity of homogeneous knowledge in philosophical discourse, which might have been salient in many respects.

Poets, on the other hand, know well that one cannot tell a lie unless one knows the truth. In other words, one cannot know the moral without knowing the immoral, the good without the bad. Inherent to poetic discourse is the project of putting what "never happened," says Bernadette, in close proximity to "what never happens." This is what is called the "plot of poetic dialectic," and it is not limited to poetry. We employ this plot anytime we impersonate someone, quote another, or speak nonliterally. Through speech and action, the plot discovers that it conceals two in one or one in two, an inevitable consequence of representation.[12]

The poetical plot is the disclosure, says Bernadette, of impossibilities or apparent impossibilities. In this disclosure lies the critical aspect of poetics. It holds together heterogeneous knowledge—knowledge of the ends of human life, knowledge of the soul. While philosophers are disdainful of the occasional vulgarity of poetics, Ghazālī understood better than some of his contemporaries the value of this mode of discourse. And he put it to effective use in order to mediate complex notions of truth located in the essential heterogeneity of knowledge. For this reason, he had little hesitation in mixing different grammars of thought in order to persuade and cajole his audiences. Therefore, his narrative could simultaneously sustain divine interventions in nature through miracles and also admit to the role of reason and a conception of order in nature that remains open to unpredictability because he does not subscribe to necessary causation. Thus, different kinds of discourse can coexist within a paradigm in a truly heterologous fashion.

Ghazālī also understood that knowledge must be emancipatory. Therefore, he protested the professionalization of knowledge—not that he was opposed to the idea of salaried scholars—as stripping knowledge of its liberatory potential. This was the main reason for his jeremiads against the jurists, who he believed had turned knowledge of the law into a form of legal scientism. Moreover, some academic scholars of religious sciences, in his view, only saw knowledge as a form of cognitive instrumental rationality. He viewed both camps to be oblivious of the mandate that knowledge must of necessity lead to an emancipatory ethics of salvation.

True knowledge, for Ghazālī, is that which leads to the ethical. Knowledge has to lead to the path of the afterlife, to the ultimate salvation and the fulcrum of liberation. The emancipated subject is thus one who is truly liberated from all material dependencies. A truly free subject does not behave like a pseudodivinity on earth, one that perpetrates genocide and epistemicide—two notorious crimes often perpetrated by humans in spiritual and mental bondage. Indeed, in his interpretation, which is consistent with the Muslim tradition, the imperative of knowledge is to act. And an index of freedom is ethical action in the world. For a Muslim, a double emancipation inheres in a moral act: emancipation in this world and salvation in the hereafter. The paradigmatic transition that Muslims seek includes dimensions that are significant in terms of epistemology and society as well as those related to the order of eschatology.

Ghazālī was not only a bricoleur who stood at the threshold of multiple disciplines and currents of thought, as I have cast him: he was also an adventurer and explorer in his thinking. He realized that all the answers to life's complex realities do not reside in a single culture, intellectual tradition, or historical epoch. For that reason, he ventured outside the mainline currents, raiding archives of knowledge in order to see how he could reinforce the positive aspects of the traditions that he had inherited. Not only did he defamiliarize the canonical tradition, but he also supplemented it and refamiliarized it, adding a new narrative gloss, in order to make the luster and vibrancy of tradition more pronounced. By his own admission, he attempted to give life to, or resuscitate (*iḥyā'*), the discursive tradition. Now, by any account, this is an enormous claim for Ghazālī to have made, courageously taking it upon himself to breathe life into the knowledge traditions. For he implied that according to his critical diagnosis there was a problem in the way the tradition—meaning the sciences of religion—was being interpreted.

This critical reconstructionist approach to tradition would resonate well with those whose intellectual temper was predisposed to critical thinking and the intellectual renewal of tradition, but it would certainly offend many formalists as too presumptuous an approach. Perhaps, as some of Ghazālī's critics have pointed out, the problem lay with his personal deficiencies in knowledge rather than in the incompleteness of tradition. Some critics went further, charging that Ghazālī subverted the intellectual tradition for his own ideological ends and intellectual tastes; echoes of these charges still reverberate to this day. If today a few bold insiders to traditional discourses were to make a similar critical analysis about the way tradition is being interpreted, and if they were to make a case for its reconstruction in order to give it new coherence, the response from some doctrinaire traditionalists would most likely be visceral, if recent experiences are anything to go by. Pronouncements of heresy by many *ʿulamāʾ* groups and the use of secular courts to coerce compliance with narrow versions of orthodoxy have increasingly become a pattern in parts of the Muslim world.[13] Therefore, the politics of knowledge construction and the contestation of power centered on knowledge deserve particular attention, attention equal to that we give to the mapping and production of ideas.

Pursuing his goal of resuscitating the sciences of religion, Ghazālī as a bricoleur took a multidisciplinary approach: he drew inspiration from a variety of discourses and sources. Some of his adversaries preferred to describe his approach as an exasperating eclecticism and an intellectual promiscuity, charging that he mixed the good with the bad and that, like a dilettante, he ventured into terrains in which he lacked competence. But history, it turns out, has found the legacy of the amateur and eclectic more worthy of preservation than that of his professional adversaries, and Ghazālī's enriched voice and narrative has held sway for centuries.

His intellectual passion was driven by an insatiable desire to give depth and intellectual legs to the paradigmatic transitions occurring in his society. For this reason, he did not hesitate to use whatever intellectual artifact he thought would be beneficial to the advancement of his cause, without giving undue attention to its provenance or the formalities of its use. This enabled him to rearticulate, amplify, and supplement what he perceived to be the core narratives and topoi of Muslim discursivity, namely, notions of transcendence, law, ethics, history, and piety, among others. One should note that Ghazālī addressed these issues as they appeared to him and as he mediated the confluence of Persian and Arabicate cultures in the eleventh and twelfth centuries. Whatever improved the expression of Islam as a discursive tradition, within his altering and changing experiences, Ghazālī absorbed and internalized into his subjectivity. But it is also equally important to keep in mind that Ghazālī's intellectual project was a work in progress, one that unfolded with the rhythms of his own dilemmas and crises, whether personal or social.

When I began this study of Ghazālī, my concern was to configure why it was that so many Muslim thinkers like him in the past effortlessly engaged with an assortment of knowledge and ideas stemming from different origins without being rejected by tradition, even though they were from time to time greeted with opposition. What became clear to me was that Ghazālī successfully adapted knowledge according to the needs of his own subjectivity. In other words, knowledge to him was intimately related to the needs of the self and his subjectivity, and therefore he did not allow any verdict of authority to veto his quest. In addition, he instilled those paradigmatic transitions in his knowledge into the fabric of the self—irrespective of whether they were radical or subtle—by way of grafting or instilling those concerns into the knowledge tradition. He did not accomplish his goal by an instantaneous act of will, as Pierre Bourdieu would say, but rather by struggling to make the new knowledge part of "the state of the body."[14]

The contemporary relevance of Ghazālī to Muslim thought lies precisely in his critical engagement with tradition, but more specifically in the way in which he modified, adjusted, recalibrated, amended, and supplemented the intellectual tradition. Unlike many of his contemporaries who either uncritically romanticized tradition or, in an apocalyptic spasm, took refuge in it, he took critical thought seriously. It was important for him, just as it is for us, to critically engage with the canonical tradition, a process that must culminate in radical questioning and defamiliarizing of the canonical tradition. This process required Ghazālī to explore the rules of the game that constitute the canon by learning which moves destroy the game and how the canon arranges knowledge and practices so that in the end it secures a reasonable compliance with the fundamental presuppositions of the tradition. Often, reconstructing and refamiliarizing the canonical tradition follows when one adheres to the rules of the game as to how one adds, subtracts, and rearranges within a knowledge tradition. The approach should be at once respectful of the past and not beholden to it. To be critical means to be open to the spirit of the present but not to be overwhelmed by it.

The Muslim intellectual tradition is neither static nor inert. It has its own rhythms of continuity and discontinuity, always recalibrating itself to the imperatives of ethical, moral, and spiritual integrity. For if we wish not to see the ethical imagination lapse into a censorious puritanism that rapidly hurtles toward self-destruction, and if we wish not to degenerate into nostalgic lamentation, then the ethical must be taken seriously not only in its discursive guise but also in its poetical manifestation. What impresses and captivates any reader of Ghazālī is how impressively he recovered poiesis—inventive making and creating—by disseminating into the reading and interpretation of texts, broadly conceived, the extravagant heterogeneity of knowledge.

Where others hesitate to bring art and aesthetics to ethics, Ghazālī unapologetically brought the power of narrative (*ḥikāya*) to the study of the ethical. In his view, the purest of art resides in the heart—the receptacle of subjectivity. "Subjectivity" here means the capacity of the soul or self to submit to all ethical possibilities with the aid of a variety of disciplines and practices that empower it.

A prolonged meditation on Ghazālī also helps us to pose some questions for our time. Why does tradition today no longer demonstrate that vitality, dynamism, and legitimacy that it so consistently demonstrated in previous eras of Muslim society? Why has tradition increasingly become equated to anachronism and associated with forms of physical and symbolic violence? We know, of course, that the discourses of modernity have often helped to caricature tradition, but is that the only reason? To what degree are persons working within traditional worldviews also responsible for the decline of tradition? Should not the rules of the game, the strategies for organizing knowledge and forging authority within tradition, also undergo revision from time to time? For if not, then tradition becomes inert and fossilized. How can the inner transformation of tradition occur with a modicum of legitimacy? For, indeed, the contemporary crisis of Muslim thought can at least be associated with a crisis of legitimacy. One of the insights gained from this study of Ghazālī is that in the past the dialogic of ethos and poiesis continuously nourished the tradition in imaginative ways. In my view, the need to promote a formative bond between ethos and poiesis has never been so dire as it is in contemporary iterations of Muslim thought.

The poetical-ethical imagination that we intuit in Ghazālī's work has the potential to promote an alternative societal project. It is an imagination that straddles the line between two narratives internal to Muslim thought: it touches the highly mystical humanist project of willful self-mastery, as advanced by the ṣūfīs, as well as the onto-theological project of the jurists and theologians. Self-mastery brings one to the precipice of the desire for the Other by requiring one to undertake the regimen required in the science of unveiling (*ʿilm al-mukāshafa*) in order to behold the face of God (*wajh Allāh*). Within the unconscious, this quest stimulates the desire for the Other.

A poetics of desire, of course, also has its limitations. For it is impossible for the poetical to encounter the Other in its otherness. It can only simulate otherness through the reenactment of ritual (mimesis) in a dialogical proximity to the ethical imagination. If the sacrifice of Abraham represents anything, then it demonstrates how different kinds of knowledge coalesce in one instant—poetic and ethical, exoteric and esoteric. The Abrahamic episode in itself closes with a lesson to neither sacrifice the poetical in favor of the ethical nor the ethical in pursuit of the poetic. The obligation is to fathom the ethical from the confounding connotations of poetics and vice versa. Thus, it is always helpful to retain the productive tension between the ethical and the poetic and to struggle with their consequent aporias. Ghazālī, of course, discovered that the poetics of ethics was the artistic impulse traced on the heart and expressed it as self-discernment, an essential sensibility that requires cognitive cultivation in order to interiorize the ethical pedagogy. It is this ethical pedagogy that is at the center of emancipatory knowledge.

The point where the poetic imagination defers to the ethical imagination is the domain of the more mundane but necessary science of transaction (*ʿilm al-muʿāmala*): it presents the rules for the ethical and legal governance of the self, especially in relation to the Other. This is an action that must always be dialogical, going back and forth between the multiple ethical subjects within a network of interdependent moral relations.

The life-form and ethics that Ghazālī conceived is mingled with spirituality and piety. This means that he treated ethics as a personal question and then pursued the worldly realm, or the secular, as a personal question. In this form of ethics, one takes personal responsibility—a responsibility that invests actions and consequences with a new and different order of intensity. It involves making choices and courageous decisions, which Ghazālī was prepared to make while also inviting others to do the same.

Ethics remains the substrate; it is the nexus in which the disciplinary boundaries are neither erased nor bounded. Conceived from such an organic and intensely active spectrum, ethics and law do not morph into a positivist and scientistic account of dos and don'ts. Ethics becomes a comprehensive life-form, one that includes both ambiguities and certainties, contingencies and absolutes. It is a life-form in which polarities are neither resolved nor dissolved but instead remain suspended in an agonistic, contestable, and ultimately productive tension. In ethics, the discourses of epistemology and ontology meet in new conjunctures shaped by temporality/history, personal biography, and tradition. If ethics is the discursive nexus, then it also requires a subject that serves as the point of conjunction of such knowledge, a subject with a capacity to be receptive to the heterogeneity of ethical discourse as Ghazālī conceived it.

Dihlīz / *Threshold*

Often, the position and location of articulation is just as important as the substance of what is said. From what location did Ghazālī speak, and how did his location shape the way he gave coherence to the heterogeneity of knowledge? At an early period in his career, he very much saw himself as being in the mainstream, close to power. However, as his own personal development advanced, he identified and implicitly endorsed an interstitial location, the *dihlīz*. In my view, this in-between space makes eminent sense as a metaphor to explain Ghazālī's location. Indeed, it translates into a larger and complex dialogic between the inner and the outer, the esoteric and the exoteric, and the indigenous and the foreign as polarities. I would argue that while these are binary formulations, they do not strictly play out as rigid polarities, but rather direct our attention to what is produced in the space between the polarities.

The *dihlīz*-ian position is where Ghazālī as subject found himself, struggling between the polarities without committing himself to some intangible middle road. Thus, the *dihlīz*-ian position depends entirely on the force field of the discourse. For it often happened that in one context Ghazālī found himself at one end of the polarity and in a somewhat different and variant setting he found himself at the other end of the spectrum. Here, far from coercing one into adopting one of the polar positions as the correct position, the polarities serve as a spectrum of variabilities.

I am therefore uncomfortable with the view that casts Ghazālī as the one who brought about a synthesis between antinomies. I think it is a misreading of his work. One very popular argument is that he synthesized or reconciled law with mysticism, or that he reconciled logic with theology. But it would be more helpful to say that he demonstrated that there was no contradiction between two apparently antithetical disciplines or sets of ideas, and that he therefore believed they could coherently coexist within a set of beliefs or practices. The apparent contradiction between polarities is neutralized by the work and struggles that take place in the threshold, or the *dihlīz*-ian space, that spans the gap between disciplines and ideas.

Like Ghazālī, we may also wish to shatter the classical equipoise and the self-assured composure of the settled disciplines, interrogating them from new vantage points. In the process, we can forge new and different conversations between the historical tradition and the altered subjectivities of those who engage tradition and attempt to live it. Thus, when Ghazālī did indeed engage the tradition in its temporality, he did so by keeping alive the tension and aporia between the mythic and the rational, the poetic and the exoteric. The outcome was a dynamic narrative capable of keeping the despotically normative predilection of consensus in check by forcing settled dispositions and opinion to be constantly under review. It was also this *dihlīz*-ian subjectivity that allowed Ghazālī to festoon his narrative with insights from philosophy, logic, ethics, theology, metaphysics, cosmology, and spirituality in a carnival of intellectual passion and erudition, insight and creativity. Sometimes, he became so exuberant that the sheer diversity of thought caused occasional lapses in his scrupulousness.

Often, he was caught between the antinomies of equally appealing positions, such as the clarity of logic and philosophy on the one hand and the perplexing onto-theology of divine grace on the other. He was serious in his commitment to the sobriety of law and ethics, while he was equally intoxicated by the delirium of mystical inrushes. Like Ghazālī, those of us who seek an emergent knowledge may find a *dihlīz*-ian subjectivity attractive. In the force field of the threshold position, one is required to negotiate the varieties of knowledge and experiences not only dialogically but also with vigilance in order to guard against a monologue and complacency.

Ghazālī provides a model of discourse that constitutes forms of actual social interaction and practice. His notion of discourse has echoes in the work of Michel de Certeau. Michel de Certeau recognizes discursive activity as a form of social activity and agency, whereas for Michel Foucault a discourse has a modality of existence independent of an agent as something that was always and already historical.[15] Tradition—more specifically a discursive tradition—in Ghazālī's view, has both continuities and discontinuities with the past. And even though Ghazālī was deeply impressed by mysticism, he did not actually naturalize history into a gnostic form as the inexorable trajectory of the spirit. To the contrary, he made no attempt to remove humans from the sphere of history as practice; rather, he constantly sought out the theater of action and the prospects for self-generation in order to confront the bewilderment of the self.

What makes Ghazālī such a phenomenal and axial figure, in my view, is the fact that he discovered the normativity of the liminal. For that discovery is precisely what the spatial metaphor of the *dihlīz* provided him, and it was a discovery that he capitalized on. Without simplifying or reducing Ghazālī's intellectual project, there can be very little disagreement that his genius and creativity rested on his ability to be a bricoleur whose paradigm not only achieved a certain coherence and integrity but also enjoyed a welcome reception for a long time among Muslim communities over the centuries. This coherence was achieved despite the fact that there is a perpetual aggiornamento in his thought, proving that dynamism is not antithetical to coherence.

What we learn from Ghazālī is that his *dihlīz*-ian subjectivity was one that zigzagged and freely oscillated between the dominant, juristic discourses like law and theology while also effortlessly crossing over to the heterological discourses of mysticism. And along the way, he also decided to raid the archives of philosophy for good measure. It was clearly his location that offered him multiple speaking positions. The constant state of flux of his self, in turn, created a real paradox, but it was one that he navigated to his own advantage, playing the role of both insider and outsider in his multiple personal and public roles as public intellectual, scholar, and seeker after spiritual tranquility. The psychic restlessness that he exhibited in his mental and physical crisscrossing over the threshold (*dihlīz*) offers salient lessons for the postcolonial and postmodern Muslim subject in search of emancipatory knowledge and resources to address her many dilemmas. Admittedly, when located at the *dihlīz*, one acknowledges the gray areas, intermediate zones, and degrees of uncertainty that are not unequivocally resolved. Despite Ghazālī's most wrenching desire for personal certainty in matters of faith, in the realm of the ethical he was aware that there is always a penumbra of uncertainty.[16]

Ghazālī's success can be measured by the subtlety with which he decentered and undermined the hegemonies and colonizing practices of several discursive traditions within Muslim discourse. One thinks particularly of how he undermined the dominance of legal scientism. Simultaneously, he engendered his texts not only in the mental space that constitutes the gap between body and corpus but also in bridging the two major cultural traditions that formed the matrix of middle Islam, namely, the Arabicate and Persianate milieus.

The conflict between discursive traditions was not unlike the searing dilemmas that the cosmopolitan, postcolonial Muslim subject faces today. By dint of location and circumstance, today's cosmopolitan subject has to traverse multiple matrices of cultures and politics on almost a daily basis. Ghazālī played no insignificant role in suturing the fabric of Arabicate and Persianate modes of thought into a seamless patchwork of ideas. It was the production of that heterogeneous formative texture that was needed in his time and is equally in demand in our time. Unfortunately, heterogeneity remains anathema to certain proponents of Islamic maximalism and, ironically, even to those who claim to be bearers of tradition and orthodoxy yet who, in practice, have by and large subverted orthodoxies into authoritarian modes of thought.

What is indeed remarkable is the role Ghazālī had in facilitating the translation of Muslim practices and intellectual traditions into a cosmopolitanism and an openness to the Other at a time of extraordinary Muslim political power and cultural ascendancy. It appears that he saw a certain value in cultivating an open epistemology in order to sustain a vibrant intellectual apparatus with which he could interpret the sources and ancillary disciplines related to religion. He risked such openness—notwithstanding the multiple challenges produced by a period that was also not short of political instability and anxiety caused by the Crusades—as he entered the last decade of his life.

Exile

Naturalizing the *dihlīz*-ian position, or espousing a subjectivity that celebrates a threshold position, shares certain features with life in exile. It is about being out of place, being neither insider nor outsider, but rather occupying a permanent in between-ness. Paradoxically, this spatial location also inspires a rare confidence, for it is not a stationary position but one that is dynamic. From this location, one is witness to the movement of endless crisscrossing and connexity between the divergent geographical spaces that in more than one way also simulate life and existence. To inhabit the uniqueness of a threshold position also has a certain strangeness (*ghurba*) attached to it. Did Ghazālī consciously espouse the *dihlīz* in order to accent the notion of an in-between space as well as that of an internal exile (*gharīb*)? I believe he did.

One of the great joys of this attempt to engage Ghazālī in friendship—teleiopoiesis—is produced by my project of exploring a paradigmatic transition based on emergent as well as emancipatory knowledge within the Muslim tradition in partnership with persons in other knowledge traditions. Like Ghazālī, we also recognize that all knowledge can be subverted if it is decoupled from its ethical imperative. Drawing from Ghazālī's writings, one can deduce that exile (*ghurba*) is not only a physical state of removal from one's ancestral land, place of birth, kinship, or nationality. It is also a psychological condition that produces a certain estrangement, even marginalization, in which one experiences denial of liberty, unrequited love, and physical distance. Estrangement is nothing new to the Arabo-Islamic literary tradition, in which the motif of being exiled or estranged (*gharīb*) from that which is familiar and regular is frequently invoked through different forms. To be an exile is to occupy a liminal space, whether it is a prolonged ascetic isolation and monasticism or the intermediate space between two locations. Things viewed from a liminal space or a different location often appear different from when they are viewed from a regular space.

The classic Muslim writing on exile was, of course, by that man of rare genius ʿAyn al-Quḍāt al-Hamadhānī, a jurist, mystic, and martyr. He was put to death by an edict of the Saljūq rulers in 525/1131 at the age of thirty-three for his courageous stand in speaking truth to power. From prison, ʿAyn al-Quḍāt wrote a passionate treatise, "Complaint of a Stranger Exiled from Home" ("*Shakwā al-gharīb min al-awṭān*"). The content of the treatise was addressed to the scholars of his day, few of whom had the courage to respond to his plea for solidarity. ʿAyn al-Quḍāt invoked the notion of exile in the following words:

> What, prison bars and iron chains,
> And yearning's flames, and exile pains,
> And sundering far from those I love?
> What mighty anguish these must prove![17]

Hamadhānī continued to stake out the solidarity among exiles. He cited a verse from the legendary pre-Islamic poet Imraʾ al-Qays, who, addressing a neighbor, says: "Is it not true, that every exile [for one person] is to another a kinsman? . . . But if you reject me, the exile is exile again."

Given the way estrangement, exile, and friendship are used as tropes in Arabo-Islamic literature, the notion of exile is not only limited to poetry. In the prophetic moral tradition, the notion of exile, or being a stranger, is also embedded in at least two senses. In a religious sense, to be an exile or stranger is to be counted among a group of people who suffer in their witness of the moral depravity of their society. Exile occurs when society at large becomes estranged from right living and there is an absence of an ethical spirit and voice, when an era lacks a great moral figure or soul.

A well-known prophetic report (*ḥadīth*) that Ghazālī invoked in his discussion of knowledge reinforces the importance of the notion of exile and the idea of being a stranger. "Islam began as a stranger," the Prophet Muḥammad stated, "and [Islam] will once again return to a state of strangeness the way it began; so, blessed are the exiles."[18] This tradition underscores the pathos of beginning for a social movement or for the making of a community in history. It follows the standard plot: humble beginnings, opposition to the new message, social ostracism, and suffering like that which the early community of Muslims endured in Arabia, all of which leads to success through divine help and the making of a renewed community.

Assuming the events of the plot as given, the prophetic report gives the plot a cyclical twist by predicting that the recurrence of estrangement was a harbinger of emancipation. Hence, the promised estrangement is also measured proleptically against the liberation that the exiles will bring. For the prophetic teaching concludes with the words, "Blessed are the exiles." When asked to identify the characteristics of the exiles, or strangers, the Prophet states: "They are those who will restore [*yuṣliḥūna*] my tradition [*Sunnatī*] that people had corrupted; and they will resuscitate [*yuḥyūna*] that part of my tradition that had been destroyed [*amātūhu*, literally 'that tradition that was killed,' or epistemicide]."[19] In another report that Ghazālī also cites, the Prophet said: "The exiles are those very few people among the large group. Those who detest them among creation will be [numerically] more than those who love them."[20]

These reports are enormously significant, for they provide the map to the heart of Ghazālī's project of resuscitation. But this narrative is also important in terms of the anticipated paradigmatic shift and transition desired by contemporary Muslims and others. Cumulatively, the key words include *iṣlāḥ*, which means "reform," "renewal," and "restoration"; *Sunna*, which means the established normative tradition that is derived from the practice of the Prophet and inspired by his person; *iḥyā'*, which connotes "resuscitating," "giving life," "reviving," and "animating"; and *amāta*, which signifies "to kill" or "to cause to die." The reports appear in a passage in which Ghazālī reflects on the meaning of knowledge, wisdom, and the revival of tradition.

Concealed in Ghazālī's project to resuscitate the sciences of religion was the implicit assumption that tradition had been subjected to a conscious elimination, or epistemicide. His project was to stem the deliberate exclusion of those aspects of tradition that are essential to moral well-being. Therefore, he vehemently opposed legal scientism but fostered juridical ethics. It is no coincidence that the title of Ghazālī's most important book and the mandate given to the exiles (*ghurabā'*) are identical: the duty to resuscitate tradition (*iḥyā' al-sunna*), or engage in discursive resuscitation. The exiles, according to the prophetic tradition, we will recall, are charged with the duty of reviving tradition and knowledge.

Interestingly, Ghazālī understood "the revival of tradition [*sunna*]" not to literally mean the revival of the prophetic tradition, which many of his contemporaries were interested in. The task of the technical scholarly recording of prophetic reports—the job undertaken by experts known as the *ḥadīth* scholars—was one at which he was admittedly unsuccessful, and he has often been chastised for his lack of knowledge of prophetic reports.

However, to his mind, the concept of resuscitation of tradition (*sunna*) meant to discern and understand (*tafaqquh*) the ethical imperatives and practices as they cohere in tradition. In order to grasp these meanings, Ghazālī provided us an innovative hermeneutic, or canonical tradition, one that maps the contours of the discursivity of tradition. This is a task that Ghazālī admirably accomplished, leaving behind an unparalleled legacy.

Indeed, he understood his task to be akin to what botanists understand to be the process of palingenesis. "Palingenesis" in this context literally means regeneration, reanimation, or resuscitation of tradition. It is therefore not surprising that Ghazālī's magnum opus, *Resuscitation*, is not a mere literal restatement and rehearsal of prophetic reports. Rather, he reanimates these reports by juxtaposing his own experiences and those of countless notable predecessors with the narrative of tradition. Burdened by the ethical responsibility of the *gharīb*, the exile, Ghazālī creatively gave life to the prophetic tradition (*Sunna*). Ghazālī understood "the regeneration of tradition" to mean something very specific. He understood tradition the way botanists understand kenogenesis: as a process where the organism, in this case tradition, is modified by the environment in which it finds itself. In other words, tradition is like an organism, alive and organically responsive to the environment. Therefore, Ghazālī did not think of tradition as merely the re-production of a collection of prophetic reports into a manual. In fact, to think of tradition in synthetic terms is to map the modification of tradition, changes caused by the accumulated lived experiences and practices of Muslim communities over time. What is most instructive about Ghazālī's project and his understanding of tradition is that his discourse was flooded with the light of tradition and ventilated with the air of his temporality.

Critical renewal requires exile. Like Abraham, whom Ghazālī imitated, exile involves leaving home, visiting other peoples and climes in order to see the world through the lenses of new experiences. Empowered by the new experiences and insights, the subject becomes capable of speaking truth to power in the way that Abraham challenged his society and the Prophet Muḥammad experienced Makka upon returning there after he had been forced into exile to Madīna.

To be ostracized and marginalized by most people, who refuse to hear the voice of dissent, is only one consequence of exile. Exclusion itself does not represent the essence of exile. Behind alienation and exclusion are the effects that embody exile. Irrespective of if one voluntarily or coercively embraces physical exile or if exile is experienced merely as mental estrangement from society or community, it is the experience of exile that counts. That experience allows one to see things—to view things in a way that a domesticated and complacent gaze may fail to observe. In fact, a prophetic report counsels that one ought to live like an exile, or stranger: "Live in the world as if you are a stranger, or like one crossing a street."[21] It is another way of describing the habits of a traveler.

Cognizant of prophetic wisdom, Ghazālī put into play the uncanny similarities common to the gaze of a stranger or exile and that of a traveler. The traveler, unlike a potentate, does not rely on power, as Edward Said so eloquently reminds us. A traveler depends on motion. It is the traveler who demonstrates an unusual willingness, Said continues, "to go into different worlds, use different idioms, understand a variety of disguises, masks, [and] rhetorics. Travelers must suspend the claim of customary routine in order to live in new rhythms and rituals. . . . the traveler crosses over, traverses territory, abandons fixed positions, all the time."[22] It is the continuous motion, the restlessness of the traveler and the exile that also make them anticipate a return from exile, relishing the liberation.

There is little doubt in my mind that Ghazālī was indeed inspired by the idea of exile (*ghurba*). If this journey with Ghazālī has taught us anything, then hopefully it has made us understand that voyaging through life as an exile or traveler is a desirable goal, a status that enables us to act in our diverse and productive ways to fulfill the promise of that coveted return to new subjectivities and emergent knowledge in our unending transitions to embrace new paradigms and futures.

To break with old habits is difficult, and not everyone welcomes change and motion unless they are justified, especially given modernity's endless desire for motion. There comes a time, ʿAyn al-Quḍāt al-Hamadhānī reminds us in the quotation above, when going against the reluctance of human nature—going against the grain in order to explore the new and unfamiliar—becomes a necessity. He states his rhetorical plea in these words: "But when, then, will the object of disdain ever become the object of desire?"[23] Clearly, Hamadhānī was inviting his audience to embrace motion, movement, and dynamism within the fabric of tradition, even though most people find such a shift challenging, and many often make such an invitation the object of disdain. The necessity for change is what Hamadhānī believed needed to be addressed in his day but was not. For him, the need for change was a matter of having to choose between life and death.

Paradoxically, in Hamadhānī's philosophical and ecstatic meditation there is an implicit suggestion that the poetics of a context on occasion demand that we entertain even that which seemingly appears to be undesirable. In embracing the loathsome, the poetics of imagination as well as the necessity of the context together transform it into an object of desire. In our time, there are indeed few serious Muslim thinkers who need to be convinced of the desideratum of courageous thinking within tradition; in other words, the object of desire is hardly contested. Determining how and when that desire will be fulfilled and, more importantly, what the content of such an "object of desire" will be is a judgment, a contestation, and a responsibility that rests on the shoulders of those who take the Ghazālian tradition, and other Muslim discursive traditions, seriously.

Notes

Abbreviations

EI 2	*Encyclopaedia of Islam*, 2nd ed.
FaAn.	Ghazālī, *Faḍā'il al-anām min rasā'il ḥujjat al-Islām*
Fad.	Ghazālī, *Faḍā'iḥ al-bāṭinīya*
Fay.	Ghazālī, *Faysal al-tafriqa bayna al-Islām wa al-zandaqa*
Ih.	Ghazālī, *Iḥyā' ʿulūm al-dīn*
Ilj.	Ghazālī, *Iljām al-ʿawām ʿan ilm al-kalām*
Jaw.	Ghazālī, *Jawāhir al-Qur'ān*
Kash.	Tahānawī, *Kashshāf iṣṭilāḥāt al-funūn*
Mad.	Ghazālī, *Al-maḍnūn bihi ʿalā ghayr ahlihi*
Maq.	Ghazālī, *Al-maqṣad al-asnā fī asmā' Allāh al-ḥusnā*
Maqasid	Ghazālī, *Maqāṣid al-falāsifa*
Mish.	Ghazālī, *Mishkāt al-anwār*
Miz.	Ghazālī, *Mīzān al-ʿamal*
Mu.	Ghazālī, *Al-munqidh min al-ḍalāl*
Mus.	Ghazālī, *Al-mustasfā fī ʿilm al-uṣūl*
Q.	Qur'ān
Qaw.	Ghazālī, *Qawāʿid al-aqāʿid*
Qi.	Ghazālī, *Al-qisṭās al-mustaqīm*
Ta.	Ghazālī, *Tahāfut al-falāsifa*

Introduction

1. For Arabic transliteration style, I have followed an amended version of the Library of Congress style by omitting the "h" of the ta ة marbūṭa. Also, translations, except where noted, are mine.

2. Information provided in one of Ghazālī's letters. *FaAn.*, 34.

3. Yāfī, "Sīrat," 11. See also Shams al-Dīn, "Muqaddima," 5. Tāmir, *Al-Ghazālī*, 41, misidentifies this teacher as Abū Naṣr al-Ismāʿīlī, or Ismāʿīl b. Saʿda, who he claims was a missionary of the Ismāʿīlī sect; he should be Ibn Masʿada, as stated by Yāfī and Aḥmad Shams al-Dīn.

4. Frye, *Heritage of Central Asia*, 227. Frye says that much of the countryside of Iran remained Zoroastrian until the end of the tenth century and that the impetus to spread Islam into the villages of Iran came from Shīʿa Ismāʿīlī missionaries sent from Egypt.

5. Ibn Khaldūn, *Muqaddima*, 541.

6. Auerbach, *Mimesis*, 10.

7. Khuri, along with several other scholars, makes this claim. *Freedom, Modernity, and Islam*, 214.

8. Sijistānī, *Sunan Abī Dāwūd*, 3:317.

9. Ghazālī here uses the term *fatwā ḥukūmatin*, literally meaning "juridical response" or "opinion of authority." It is an uncommon occurrence for a government to be issuing a juridical response (*fatwā*). We must assume that Ghazālī used the term *fatwā* loosely. His real intent was to say that scholars slavishly follow official government decrees, or that they try to satisfy those in power by issuing rulings favorable to the interests of the rulers instead of being the keepers of the social conscience.

10. "Khuṭbat al-kitāb," *Iḥ.*, 1:8.

11. *Miz.*, 241.

12. Ibid., 241–42.

13. Quoted in Rosenthal, "State and Religion," 48; Q. 107:4–7.

14. Nicholson, *Studies in Islamic Poetry*, 110.

15. "Kitāb al-ʿilm," *Iḥ.*, 1:37–38.

16. Ibid., 38, 45–46.

17. Ibid., 37.

18. Ibn al-Athīr, *Al-Kāmil*, 10:328.

19. Mez, *Renaissance of Islam*.

20. Khalidi, *Arabic Historical Thought*, 214.

21. The noted Iranian reformist thinker Soroush makes frequent reference to Kāshānī's text and demonstrates the impact of both Ghazālī and Kāshānī in modern Muslim thought. *Reason, Freedom and Democracy*, 47–48.

22. *EI* 2, s.v. "Muḥsin-i Fayḍ-i Kāshānī."

23. Abul Hasan Ali Nadwi, *Saviours of Islamic Spirit*, 129.

24. Johnston, *Spiritual Logic*, 1.

25. Lohr, "Arabic Background."

26. Johnston, *Spiritual Logic*, 31.

27. Ibid., 2.

28. Hanley, "St. Thomas' Use."

29. Zaqzūq, *Al-manhaj al-falsafī*, 43.

30. Macdonald, "Life of al-Ghazzālī."

31. Macdonald, *Religious Attitude*, 7.

32. Ibid., 6.

33. Macdonald, "Life of al-Ghazzālī," 115.

34. Macdonald, *Religious Attitude*, 6.

35. Macdonald, "Life of al-Ghazzālī," 71.

36. Said, *The World*, 288.

37. Zwemer, *Moslem Seeker*, 12.
38. Ibid., 12–13.
39. Jabre, *Notion de certitude*, 25.
40. Wensinck, *Pensée de Ghazzālī*, i.
41. Ibid., 199.
42. Hodgson, *Venture*, 1:28.
43. Ibid.
44. Ibid., 1:29.
45. See Jabre, *Lexique de Ghazali*; Gosche, *Ghazzālis Leben und Werke*; Bouyges, *Essai de chronologie*; Watt, "Authenticity"; Nakamura, "Bibliography"; Hourani, "Revised Chronology"; Pourjawadi, *Du mujaddid*.
46. Obermann, *Philosophische und religiöse Subjektivismus*; Laoust, *Politique de Gazali*; Lazarus-Yafeh, *Studies in al-Ghazzali*.
47. Ormsby, *Theodicy in Islamic Thought*; Bello, *Medieval Islamic Controversy*; Reinhart, *Before Revelation*; Frank, *Ashʿarite School*; Burrell, *Faith in Divine Unity*; Burrell and Daher, *Al-Ghazālī*; Burrell, *Friendship*; Abu Sway, *Al-Ghazali*; Hogga, *Orthodoxie, subversion et reforme*; Mitha, *Al-Ghazālī and the Ismāʿīlīs*; Gianotti, *Al-Ghazālī's Unspeakable Doctrine*; Shaw, "City of Garden."
48. Muḥammad Ḥanīf Nadwī, *Taʿlīmāt-e Ghazālī*; see also "Gazālī Özel Sayisi."
49. Nuʿmānī, *Al-Ghazzālī*; Mubārak, *Al-akhlāq ʿinda al-Ghazālī*; Dunyā, *Al-ḥaqīqa fī naẓar al-Ghazālī*; Zarrinkūb, *Al-firār min al-madrasa*; Pourjawadi, *Majmūʿah-ye falsafī-e Marāghah*. This last work, a facsimile collection, consists of treatises by Ghazālī that were found in a codex possibly belonging to a student of one Majd al-Dīn al-Jīlī. For more details, see Pourjawadi's introduction. A closer study of this codex may shed greater light on scholarly disagreements about certain works attributed to Ghazālī; see also Pourjawadi, "ʿAqīda-e Abū Ḥamid al-Ghazālī."
50. In "Kitāb al-ʿilm" (*Iḥ.*, 1:42), Ghazālī urges people to follow the pious ancestors, or *salaf*, as he refers to them elsewhere.
51. Sālim, *Muqārana bayna al-Ghazālī*.
52. For those *salafī*-type traditionalists who are hostile to institutionalized practices of mysticism, Ghazālī does not rank high among historical figures. Practices of piety take different forms in more puritan and anti-*taṣawwuf* versions of Muslim orthodoxy.
53. Bamba, *Masālik al-jinān*; ʿAbd al-Ḥalīm Maḥmūd, "Taqdīm."
54. Jābirī, *Takwīn al-ʿaql al-ʿarabī*, 276, 341.
55. Jābirī, *Al-turāth wa al-ḥadātha*, 171; see also Jābirī, "Al-ṣirāʿ al-madhhabī," 20–21.
56. Jābirī, *Al-turāth wa al-ḥadātha*, 170.
57. Ibid., 169.
58. Ibid., 174.
59. Ḥanafī, "Al-juzūr al-ta'rīkhīya," 187–88; see Khuri, *Freedom, Modernity, and Islam*, 14.
60. Ḥanafī, "Al-juzūr al-ta'rīkhīya," 187–88.
61. Khuri, *Freedom, Modernity, and Islam*, 14.
62. Tawḥīdī, *Kitāb al-imtāʿ*, 1:17.
63. See Lawrence, *Defenders of God*; Abou el-Fadl, *Speaking in God's Name*.

64. The idea of "complex space" I borrow from Millbank, "Resignations of the Age," 19; Asad, *Formations of the Secular*, 179.

65. Foucault, *Discipline and Punish*, 31.

Chapter One: Agonistics of the Self

1. Adūnīs, *Al-masraḥ wa al-marāyā*, 119–54.
2. Brodsky, *Less Than One*, 59. (My thanks to Farouk Mitha for introducing me to the work of Brodsky.)
3. Khuri, *Freedom, Modernity, and Islam*, 215.
4. Brodsky, *Less Than One*, 58.
5. Hazo, *Blood of Adonis*, xvii.
6. Mignolo, *Local Histories*, 115–26.
7. Lévi-Strauss, *Savage Mind*, 19.
8. Ibid., 16.
9. De Certeau, *Heterologies*, 178.
10. Q. 16:68.
11. Lévi-Strauss, *Savage Mind*, 21.
12. Davis, *Aristotle's Poetics*, 123.
13. Vico, *New Science*, 135–43.
14. Ibn Rushd, *Faṣl al-maqāl*, sec. 17, par. 54.
15. Aristotle, *Nicomachean Ethics*, 173.
16. Iqbal, *Reconstruction of Religious Thought*, 97.
17. Dabashi, *Truth and Narrative*.
18. See ʿUlawī, *Shakhṣiyāt*.
19. Ibn Ṭumlūs, *Kitāb al-madkhal*, 16.
20. Derrida, *Politics of Friendship*, 79.
21. Derrida, *Specters of Marx*, 86.
22. Ibid., 36.
23. Chakrabarty, *Provincializing Europe*, 243.
24. *Oxford English Dictionary* s.v. "teleiosis."
25. Derrida, *Politics of Friendship*, 32.
26. "Kitāb al-ʿilm," *Iḥ.*, 1:33.
27. Derrida, *Politics of Friendship*, 29.
28. Spivak, "New International," 12.
29. Nietzsche, *Human All Too Human*, 1, 376, 149.
30. Derrida, *Politics of Friendship*, 29.
31. Ibid., 29–32.
32. Ibid., 37.
33. See Baldick, *Imaginary Muslims*.
34. Muslim b. al-Ḥajjāj Nīsābūrī, *Ṣaḥīḥ Muslim*, 1:453.
35. Q. 41:34.
36. Said, *The World*, 286.
37. Q. 50:37.

38. Ibid.
39. Asad, *Genealogies of Religion*, 177; Chakrabarty, *Provincializing Europe*, 239.
40. Derrida, *Ear of the Other*, 32.
41. James, *Varieties*, 377.
42. De Certeau, *Heterologies*, 174–75.
43. Anzaldúa, *Borderlands*, 101.
44. Ozick, "Fourth Sparrow," 297.
45. Geertz, "Pinch of Destiny," 167.
46. *Mu.*, 62.
47. Ghazali, *Deliverance from Error*, 117 n. 182.
48. Ibn Manẓūr, *Lisān al-ʿarab*, 2:1443; Lane, *Arabic-English Lexicon*, 1:924.
49. Brodsky, *Less Than One*, 3.
50. Beeman, *Language, Status and Power*, 72. Beeman finds the spatial and architectural separation of the exterior and interior dimensions of Persian homes to be a homology of the external (*ẓāhir*) and the internal (*bāṭin*) elements of the self.
51. I have slightly modified Mignolo's felicitous phrase "border-gnosis" (*Local Histories*, 12–14) to "*dihlīz*-ian gnosis."
52. Victor Turner, *Ritual to Theatre*, 11.
53. Yafūt points out that Ghazālī was selective, adopting Greek syllogism while rejecting natural causation, and that he deployed the notion of apodictic proof for gnostic ends but not for rational argumentation in philosophy. "Bayna Ibn Ḥazm," 78–79.
54. Bakhtin, *Dialogic Imagination*, 45, 426.
55. Benjamin, *Philosophy of History*.
56. Mignolo, *Darker Side*.
57. See *Fay.*, 145; *Fad.*, 117.
58. Ghazālī was himself aware of the intense proclivity among Muslim sects to anathematize. See *Fay.*, 148.
59. Nasr, *Knowledge and the Sacred*, 67–73.
60. Ibid., 68.
61. Ibid., 78.
62. Ibid., 79–84.
63. Asad, *Anthropology of Islam*, 14.
64. Ibid.; MacIntyre, *After Virtue*, 206.
65. Asad, *Anthropology of Islam*, 14–15.
66. Ibid., 15.
67. Ibid. See also Hodgson, *Venture*, 1:351. Hodgson laments the deficiency of the term "orthodoxy" as being limiting. But, for him, orthodoxy is any instant in which a given position may be regarded as established either officially or socially. Depending on the period the term is used to describe, orthodoxy is not always identical to *sharīʿa*-mindedness, for there were some periods in early Islam when the *sharīʿa* was still being formulated. See also Jackson, *Theological Tolerance in Islam*, especially the very helpful introduction.
68. Foucault, "Pastoral Power."
69. Wehr, *Modern Written Arabic*, 362.
70. LaCapra, *Rethinking Intellectual History*, 18.

71. Victor Turner uses an even more charming term, "liminoid," which describes something that resembles the liminal but is not identical to the liminal. See *Ritual to Theatre*, 32.

72. Brown, *Religion and Society*, 20.

73. Frei, "Literal Reading of Biblical Narrative," 73.

74. Ibid.

75. Arendt, *Human Condition*, 155.

76. Ibid., 160.

77. Ibid., 163–64.

78. Anzaldúa, *Borderlands*, 100.

79. Byatt anticipates the creativity of all reading. "Now and then there are readings," she says, "which make the hairs on the neck, the non-existent pelt, stand on end and tremble, when every wood burns and shines hard and clear and infinite and exact, like stones of fire, like points of stars in the dark—readings when the knowledge that we *shall know* the writing differently or better or satisfactorily, runs ahead of any capacity to say what we know, or how. In these readings, a sense that the text has appeared to be wholly new, never before seen, is followed, almost immediately, by the sense that it was *always there*, that we the readers, knew it was always there, and have *always known* it was as it was, though we have now for the first time recognized, become fully cognisant of, our knowledge." Byatt, *Possession*, 472.

80. Morrison, *Playing in the Dark*, xii. I am grateful to Amina Wadud for referring me to this text.

81. Eliot, "Tradition," 38.

82. Ibid., 44.

83. Baṣrī, "Kitāb al-futyā," 223.

84. Fakhr al-Dīn al-Rāzī, *Al-tafsīr al-kabīr*, 15:283.

85. MacIntyre, *After Virtue*, 206.

86. See Said, *Orientalism*.

87. Said, "Orientalism Reconsidered," 96–97.

88. I was pleased to discover that Abul Hasan Ali Nadwi, one of the leading traditional scholars of the Indian subcontinent, makes a similar point, suggesting that as a living tradition Islam has had the good fortune not to become a museum exhibit. One can infer that he, as well as others, resists those who turn Muslim traditions into unsustainable knowledge and in doing so dispatch it to the museums. See "Khuṭba-e ṣadārat," 52.

89. Berque, "Islam and Innovation," 70. Berque pithily casts the dilemma in Arabic as "*anṣār al-maṣīr bi lā aṣīl wa anṣār al aṣīl bi lā maṣīr.*"

Chapter Two: Narrativity of the Self

1. Kemal, *Alfarabi, Avicenna and Averroes*, 34–36. Though Kemal does not ignore Ghazālī's contribution to philosophical poetics, and though he examines several works, he limits himself to exploring Ghazālī's translated corpus.

2. "In this, behold, there is indeed a reminder for that one who has a heart or lends an ear and is withal a witness." Q. 50:37.

3. Ibid.

4. Said, *The World*, 36.
5. Badiou, *Ethics*, 122–23.
6. Derrida, *Ear of the Other*, 7.
7. Ibid.
8. *Kash.*, 1:692.
9. Quoted in ibid.
10. *Kash.*, 1:692.
11. Ricoeur, "Life in Quest," 20. See also Massignon, *Passion*, 2:442, where Massignon states that the *ḥikāya* is basically a "story-setting" designed for pious reading. In his notion of *ḥikāya*, all kinds of literary relics, maxims, poems, and anecdotes are brought together without much order. However, in my reading of Ghazālī, I found that the materials are very much ordered, almost in the form of a plot, in order to give effect to the narrative.
12. Ricoeur, "Life in Quest," 21; Massignon, *Passion*, 2:442.
13. Abu Deeb, *Al-Jurjānī's Theory*, 26–27. There is some debate regarding whether Jurjānī was Aristotelian or anti-Aristotelian, an issue not relevant to my inquiry. Abu Deeb's defense of Jurjānī's anti-Aristotelian posture may be perfectly valid against the view of some twentieth-century Egyptian literary critics such as Ṭāhā Ḥusayn and Shukrī Muḥammad ʿAyyād. Ibid., 315–16.
14. ʿAbd al-Muṭṭalib, *Jadalīya al-ifrād*, 157.
15. Jurjānī, *Kitāb asrār al-balāgha*, 245.
16. *Kash.*, 1:400.
17. Among the works by early Muslim thinkers whose insights about mimesis have not been incorporated in this study is Qarṭājannī's *Kitāb al-manāhij al-adabīya*.
18. Since Ibn Khaldūn acknowledges his debts to Ghazālī, it is not surprising that the North African thinker places so much emphasis on the narrative of history, just as Ghazālī emphasized the narrative of ethics. See Azmeh, *Ibn Khaldun*, 10, 154.
19. Ricoeur, "Life in Quest," 26.
20. "Revelatory" here means self-disclosure; it is not used in the theological and religious sense of revelation from the divine.
21. *Mu.*, 23.
22. "Kitāb al-ʿilm," *Iḥ.*, 1:39.
23. *Iḥ.*, 1:41.
24. Hermansen, "Interdisciplinary Approaches," 171. See also Bulliet, "Quantitative Approach."
25. Kris, *Psychoanalytic Explorations in Art*, 65.
26. Kinberg, "Legitimation." See also Hermansen, "Interdisciplinary Approaches," 175.
27. Kinberg, "Legitimation," 48; Meier, "Inspiration by Demons."
28. Subkī, *Ṭabaqāt*, 6:227–40; Ibn ʿAsākir, *Tabyīn*, 296–306.
29. Subkī, *Ṭabaqāt*, 6:258–60. A story unrelated to dreams but which nevertheless advanced the status of Ghazālī in the hagiographical pantheon is one recorded by Ibn al-Zayyāt (d. 628/1230–31). He says that a pious man was asked about those jurists (*fuqahā'*) who had issued edicts that Ghazālī's *Resuscitation* should be torched. Zayyāt reports that the pious man was furious and cursed those jurists who issued the shameful verdicts. "So

every time one of those jurists was mentioned to him, he cursed them," Zayyāt says, "followed by the words: 'By God, these wretched ones will not succeed!' And not a month passed before all those jurists died." See Ibn al-Zayyāt, *Al-tashawwuf*, 451.

30. *Mu.*, 75.

31. "Kitāb dhikr al-mawt wa mā baʿdahu," *Ih.*, 4:439. See also "Kitāb al-ʿilm," *Ih.*, 1:86, where Ghazālī hastens to add that there are numerous levels of revelation (*waḥī*) and that merely knowing these levels does not necessarily imply the acquisition of revelation.

32. "Kitāb al-ʿilm," *Ih.*, 1:80.

33. *Mad.*, 124–25.

34. Hirawī, *Kitāb al-gharībayn*, 5:17–19.

35. *Jaw.*, 31.

36. Ibn Sīrīn al-Baṣrī, *Tafsīr al-aḥlām al-kabīr*, 253.

37. *Jaw.*, 29; *Qi.*, 33.

38. *Jaw.*, 31.

39. Freud, *Interpretation of Dreams*, 351.

40. Kearney, *Wake of Imagination*, 368.

41. Ibid., 368–69.

42. Brodsky, *Less Than One*, 99.

43. Aristotle, *Poetics*, 45, 1447a.

44. Davis, *Aristotle's Poetics*, 3.

45. *Ih.*, 1:9. The word *tamthīl* (to be in the likeness of something) is similar to *tamatthul*, which infers similarity, *tashabbuh*; *ta'assī* is derived from *uswa* (to take as a model) and *iqtidā*, derived from *qudwa* (to adopt as exemplary representation). See Zamakhsharī, *Asās al-balāgha*, 420.

46. Johnson, *Moral Imagination*, 2; Lakoff and Johnson, *Metaphors We Live By*, 193.

47. Davis, *Aristotle's Poetics*, 3–4.

48. Ibid., 5.

49. Ibid., 147.

50. Ibid., 3.

51. Darnton, *Great Cat Massacre*, 23.

52. Subkī, *Ṭabaqāt*, 6:199.

53. Ibn al-Jawzī, *Al-Muntaẓam*, 9:170. A dirham was a silver unit of currency in early Islam weighing roughly 3.12 grams; a kerat (*qīrāẓ*) was 0.195 grams, or one-sixteenth of a dirham. See Ibn Qāḍī Shuhba, *Ṭabaqāt al-Shāfiʿīya*, 1:340–41, for details on Ibn al-Razzāz.

54. See Rosenthal, "Die arabische Autobiographie," for an excellent overview of biographies in Muslim history.

55. Smith, *Early Mystic*, 16.

56. Gohlman, *Life of Ibn Sina*.

57. Much later, the Syrian military leader (*amīr*) Usāma b. Munqidh (d. 584/1188) left an autobiography called *The Book of Learning by Example* (*Kitāb al-iʿtibār*). In it, the patrician, who was familiar with the customs and practices of the Crusader Franks from his childhood, gives a rich account of his eventful life as a commander and diplomat, during which he made the acquaintance of kings and courtiers among both Muslims and Franks. His memoir sheds substantial light on the experiences of the Muslims during the sixth-/

twelfth-century crusades in Syria. See Ibn Mounḳidh, *Autobiography*, and Ibn Munqidh, *Kitab al-iʿtibār*. Carole Hillenbrand, commenting on Ibn Munqidh's book, cautions that it would be "dangerously misleading to take the evidence of his book at its face value," adding that it is not an autobiography in the Western sense (*Crusades*, 260). In a surprising generalization that falls just short of impugning the reliability of such sources, she implies that autobiography in Arabic culture falls in the genre of *adab* literature, in which the truth of a story is stretched for the purposes of performance in order to tell a titillating story and to please audiences. It is generally accepted that all autobiography is the subjective view of the individual, and even modern autobiographies are notorious for their exaggerations and embellishments of fact. This is what sets autobiography apart from biography, and the discerning historian will as a rule try to corroborate unsubstantiated claims, especially subjective ones. Of course, Ibn Munqidh had a great deal to say about his own dealing with the Fāṭimid court in Cairo and his later appearances in Saladin's court, in addition to his curious encounters with the Franks. Apart from regaling us with entertaining details, Ibn Munqidh continuously stresses how different his lifestyle was from that of the Franks and the Egyptians he met.

58. Smith, *Early Mystic*, 6.

59. Goodman, *Avicenna*, 12. See also Arberry, *Avicenna on Theology*, 5. Arberry concludes that almost all members of Ibn Sīnā's immediate family were affiliated with the Shīʿa theological sect.

60. Edward Said egregiously misreads the history of Arabo-Islamic cultures when he says that "autobiography as a genre scarcely exists in Arabic literature." See *Beginnings*, 81.

61. Reynolds, *Interpreting the Self*, 20.

62. Bushnell, Introduction to *University Library*; Burckhardt, *Civilization of the Renaissance*, 1:143–46. The development of autobiography in Muslim writing may not have been entirely uniform, but one does observe this individualistic trend at least in the Persianate Islamic universe that Ghazālī lived in.

63. In light of our growing awareness that the self-disclosure of essential data and the creation of lengthy accounts of lives in early Muslim history were not as rare as they may seem, it is difficult to comprehend Carole Hillenbrand's claim that "autobiography as a literary genre was frowned upon in the Islamic world because it was outside the bounds of the verification process." She argues, "The memoirs of a single person would be viewed as an anarchical and individualistic type of literature and thus it [autobiography] occurred only very rarely." See *Crusades*, 262–63. In fact, Reynolds and his coauthors have put paid to the fallacy that the notion of autobiography and the representation of the self were uniquely Western. *Interpreting the Self*, 20–24.

64. Rosenthal, "I Am You."

65. Melchert outlines this development in *Sunni Schools of Law*, while Hallaq tries to puncture Melchert's idea of regional schools and insists in "From Regional to Personal Schools" that individual labors were central to the juridical enterprise anyway. Both Melchert's and Hallaq's assertions underscore and provide the circumstantial evidence for my claim that the notion of individuality began to show up in the literature and in the social memory of Muslim societies, though it is still too early to provide exact dating as to when this trend really began.

66. Kīlīṭu, *Al-ḥikāya wa-al-ta'wīl*, 71.

67. Ibid., 72.

68. Reynolds, *Interpreting the Self*, 20–24.

69. Q. 93:11.

70. Reynolds, *Interpreting the Self*, 20–24.

71. Some authors translate *munqidh* as "confession" or "deliverance." See Field, *Confessions of al-Ghazzali*; Watt, "Deliverance from Error"; and Anṣārī, *Iʿtirāfāt al-Ghazālī*.

72. See Pourjawadi, "Aḥmad et Muḥammad al-Ghazālī," 167, where Pourjawadi makes the point that "Abū Ḥāmid comme ʿAyn al-Quḍāt et bien d'autres mystiques, au nom de l'unitarisme (*tawḥīd*), attribue tous les événements à la grâce divine. [Abū Ḥāmid, like ʿAyn al-Quḍāt and many other mystics, attributed all eventualities to be a product of divine grace in the name of divine unity.]"

73. Q. 3:103 (emphasis mine); *Mu.*, 59.

74. Ghazālī may well have had in mind sections of the *Kitāb al-waṣāya* by the Baṣran-born mystic Ḥārith al-Muḥāsibī when he wrote *Rescuer*, since there is a strong resemblance in the testimonial character of the two accounts. For further comparison, see Arberry, *Sufism*, 47–50.

75. Watt, *Deliverance from Error*, 24.

76. *Mu.*, 62; see also Watt, *Deliverance from Error*, 63.

77. *Mu.*, 59.

78. Ricoeur, "Life in Quest," 21–23.

79. Isnawī, *Ṭabaqāt al-Shāfiʿīya*.

80. Yāfī, "Sīrat," 9, and Subkī, *Ṭabaqāt*, 6:194, both attribute this phrase to Ghazālī. However, it is worded slightly differently in *Miz.*, 343, where Ghazālī attributes it to those scholars who had achieved mystical realization (*muḥaqqiqūn*), saying: "*Taʿallamnā al-ʿilm li ghayr Allāh, fa abā an yakūna illa lillāh* [We acquired knowledge for other than God, but knowledge refused to be but in the service of God]." The episode is also mentioned in "Kitāb al-ʿilm," *Ih.*, 1:58.

81. "The Personal Letters," in Abelard, *Abelard and Heloise*, 115.

82. Ghazālī states: "What is attained is information [*ḥadīth*] and has not become verified knowledge [*ʿilm taḥqīqī*]." *Miz.*, 343.

83. Ibn al-Jawzī, *Al-muntaẓam*, 9:170.

84. See "Kitāb qawāʿid al-ʿaqā'id," *Ih.*, 1:100; "Kitāb al-imla'," *Ih.*, 5:36; and *Jaw.*, 31. See also the excellent article of Pourjawadi, "Zabān-e."

85. Riffaterre, "Prosopopeia."

86. Ernst discusses the *coincidentia oppositorum* and the science of the opposites in Persian thought, which has echoes of metaphysical alterity. *Words of Ecstasy*, 83–84.

Chapter Three: Poetics of Memory and Writing

1. Brodsky, *Less Than One*, 99.

2. For a discussion of *taʿlīqa*, see Rosenthal, *Technique and Approach*, 7.

3. Subkī, *Ṭabaqāt*, 6:195.

4. Ibid.

5. De Man, *Blindness and Insight*, 114.
6. Plato, *Seventh and Eighth Letters*, sec. 344.
7. Plato, *Phaedrus*, 79–80 (emphasis mine).
8. Said, *The World*, 184.
9. Ibid., 192.
10. Ibid.
11. The phrase *ʿan ẓahr al-qalb* literally translates as "from the surface of the heart." Idiomatically, it means "to recite by heart." See Lane, *Arabic-English Lexicon*, 2:1928–29. See also Zamakhsharī, *Asās al-balāgha*, 291, where the author deems the use of the term *ẓahr* for "surface" to be metaphorical. This expression should not be confused with what I will later describe as "heart-writing."
12. ʿUthmānī, *Fatḥ al-mulhim*, 1:78.
13. See Ibn al-Ṣalāḥ al-Shahrazūrī, *Muqaddima*, 130. See also Bahūjiyānī, "Al-muqaddima," 14.
14. Ibn Jamāʿah al-Kinānī, *Tadhkirat al-sāmiʿ*; see also the English translation of this text, *Memoir of the Listener*.
15. Complex questions were asked concerning the protocols of certification. If a student fell asleep during a class, did he qualify for certification, since he was distracted? See ʿUthmānī, *Fatḥ al-mulhim*, 1:78.
16. Rosenthal, *Technique and Approach*, provides a detailed excursus about the protocols of writing in the sixteenth century.
17. Bulliet, *Patricians*, 50–51.
18. Ibn Jamāʿah al-Kinānī, *Tadhkirat al-sāmiʿ*, 169, 178, and *Memoir of the Listener*, 74, 76.
19. *Qaw.*, 91–92.
20. The famous jurist of Madīna, Mālilk b. Anas (d. 179/796), is also said to have resisted the writing of knowledge (*ʿilm*), by which he meant the writing of *fatāwā* (juridical responsa). When asked why he was opposed to writing, he replied: "You should memorize and then understand until your hearts are enlightened; then you will not need a book." See Shāṭibī, *Al-muwāfaqāt*, 4:98.
21. Said, *The World*, 192.
22. "Solitary mental life" is a phrase that Derrida borrows from Edmund Husserl. See Derrida, *Writing and Difference*.
23. De Man, *Blindness and Insight*, 114.
24. For more on logocentrism, see Arkoun, *Unthought*, 176–78, and "Logocentrisme et vérité religieuse," 192–95.
25. Said, *The World*, 190.
26. Derrida, *Of Grammatology*, 49.
27. Bakhtin, *Dialogic Imagination*, 428.
28. Ibid.
29. *Mus.*, 342–46.
30. "Kitāb āfāt al-lisān," *Ih.*, 3:106.
31. The American-based writer E. L. Doctorow, in an essay titled "The Intuitionist," writes: "[The] creative act doesn't fulfill the ego but changes its nature. As you write you are less the person you ordinarily are—the situation confers strength. You learn to trust

what comes to you unbidden. You learn to trust the act of writing itself. An idea, an image, a voice, comes to you as a discovery, and you don't possess what you write any more than the mountain climber possesses the mountain." See *The Nation*, 19 May 2003, 25.

32. "Kitāb al-tawḥid wa al-tawakkul," *Ih.*, 4:219.

33. "Kitāb sharḥ ʿajāʾib al-qalb," *Ih.*, 3:4.

34. *Ih.*, 4:219. Ghazālī's play on the phrase "to walk on water" is in conversation with a fragment of a report attributed to the Prophet Muḥammad in which he comments on Jesus's miracle of walking on water. After sharing the story of Jesus's miraculous feat with his companions, the Prophet comments on the virtues of inner certainty, saying: "If he [Jesus] had grown [more] in certainty, he would have [even] walked on air." It is remarkable to see how Ghazālī, in his quest for ontological certainty, combines rational and imaginative images—certainty and walking on water—in a seamless web of imagination.

35. Q. 96:1–5. See also "By the pen and what it writes," Q. 68:1.

36. "Kitāb sharḥ ʿajāʾib al-qalb," *Ih.*, 3:16–17. "Kitāb al-tawḥīd wa al-tawakkul," *Ih.*, 4:219, describes how knowledge gets imprinted on the "slate of the heart" (*lawḥ al-qalb*). See also *Jaw.*, 30.

37. Quoted in Zabīdī, *Itḥāf*, 8:443.

38. A delightful image of the wisdom of the pen is provided by Tawḥīdī: "Some of the pious ancestors [*salaf*] reported that the pen has two wisdoms: the eloquence of logic and the majesty of silence. In the triumph of pens, the intellects of men are tried, separating the contradictory from the conclusive. And the imprint of the nibs of pens on the desks is more beautiful than the blush on the cheeks of full-bosomed maidens. And in the lash of the pen the viper is disgorged and the object of desire is reached. At times of anger, the nib of the pen is fire, and at moments of satisfaction it is a friend. Writing is a product of the hand, the lamp of remembrance and elucidation, while the tongue is a distinguished intercessor and an eminent envoy. Many a subtlety is more eloquent than a sentence." *Al-baṣāʾir*, 151.

39. See ʿAbd al-Ḥaqq, *Al-kitāba wa al-tajriba*, for an extensive treatment of writing and the mystical encounter.

40. De Certeau, *Heterologies*, 68.

41. Ghazālī says, "*Wa jamīʿ al-alfāẓ al-madhkūra fī al-lughāt la yumkinu an tustaʿmal fī ḥaqq Allāh taʿālā, illā ʿalā nawʿ min al-istiʿāra wa al-tajawwuz* [It is impossible to (literally) employ the words mentioned in languages with reference to God the Sublime, except by way of metaphoric expression or figurative expansion]." "Kitāb al-tawḥīd wa-al-tawakkul," *Ih.*, 4:223.

42. Calasso, *Literature and the Gods*, 147.

43. *Mu.*, 63.

44. Derrida, *Speech and Phenomena*, 99.

45. "God is the name and the element of that which makes possible an absolutely pure and absolutely self-present self-knowledge. From Descartes to Hegel and in spite of all the differences that separate the different places and moments in the structure of that epoch, God's infinite understanding is the other name for the logos as self-presence." Ibid., 98.

46. *Mu.*, 64.

47. Rumi, *Signs of the Unseen*, 203.

48. Ibid.

49. I have slightly adapted Calasso's expression. See *Literature and the Gods*, 147.
50. Said, *The World*, 134.
51. Said, *Beginnings*, 83–84.
52. Said, *The World*, 185.
53. Kermode, *Pieces*, 163.
54. Ibid.
55. "Kitāb al-imlā'," *Ih.*, 5:18.
56. Ibid.
57. Fīrūzābādī, *Al-qāmūs al-muḥīṭ*, 1:15; Derrida, *Dissemination*, 95–128. See also Ibn al-Shajarī, *Mā ittafaqa lafẓuhu*, 116. Ibn al-Shajarī shows that *dawā'* (extended) means "that which is used as a cure" and that *dawā* (shortened) means "stupid" (*aḥmaq*). Another meaning is "the one who is ill" (*marīḍ*). This semantic elucidation reinforces the point that the *d-w-y*, the root word for *dā'* and *dawā'*, can mean both "cure" and "illness."
58. "Kitāb al-ʿilm," *Ih.*, 1:23.
59. Mutation frequently occurs in the "w" and "y" of the second radical of verbs as well as in the "w" and "y" of the third radical of verbs and nouns. The mutation takes place because the union of similar sounds is distasteful. See Bohas, Guillaume, and Kouloughli, *Arabic Linguistic Tradition*, 85.
60. Similarly, the root letters *q-r-'* for the Qur'ān denote both recitation and what is recited: in other words, they signify both the oral and the written. Ibn Manẓūr, *Lisān al-ʿarab*, 5:3563.
61. Kermode, *Pieces*, 179.
62. Ormsby, "Creation in Time," 262. Ormsby eloquently makes the point that Ghazālī was so filled with energetic zeal that he did not hesitate to use a variety of techniques of persuasion to convert and transform his auditors.
63. Q. 6:125, 94:1, and several other Qur'ān references, I believe, inform Ghazālī's interpretive move.
64. *Mu.*, 29.
65. "*Wa hādhihi hiya al-ʿulūm allatī lā tusṭara fī al-kutub.*" "Kitāb al-ʿIlm," *Ih.*, 1:27.
66. *Qaw.*, 97.

Chapter Four: Liminality and Exile

1. Nicholson, *Studies in Islamic Poetry*, 127.
2. Ibid., 253.
3. Freud, *Lectures on Psychoanalysis*, 356–57.
4. The *rites de passage* theory was first stated by van Gennep in *Rites of Passage*. I have drawn on Victor Turner's development of this theory and from several of his works, among them *Ritual Process*; *Ritual to Theatre*, 20–60; and "Religious Paradigms," 157.
5. Victor Turner, *Ritual Process*, 107. See also Zadra, "Victor Turner's Theory."
6. *Mu.*, 61.
7. Voegelin, "Immortality," 277. See also Fraser, *Time, Passion and Knowledge*, 143.
8. Kierkegaard, *Fear and Trembling*, 66–67.

9. Ibid.
10. Ibn al-Jawzī, *Al-muntaẓam*, 9:169; Dhahabī, *Siyar*, 19:342.
11. Ibn al-Jawzī, *Talbīs*, 237.
12. "Kitāb dhamm al-jāh," *Ih.*, 3:255. See also ʿAfīfī, "Al-Malāmatīya wa al-ṣūfīya."
13. *Ih.*, 3:255.
14. Ibid.
15. Ibid.
16. There is some dispute over the name "Ibn al-Kuraytī." While Zabīdī identifies him as one of Junayd's masters by this name, possibly following Ibn al-Jawzī, other sources have identified him as Ibn al-Karanbī and Ibn al-Kurrīnī. See Zabīdī, *Itḥāf*, 1:52; Abdel-Kader, *Al-Junayd*, 26 n. 3.
17. *Ih.*, 3:255.
18. Zabīdī, *Itḥāf*, 1:52.
19. *Ih.*, 3:255.
20. Ibid.
21. Ibn Ḥazm, *Ṭawq al-ḥamāma*, 86. The editor of this text, Iḥsān ʿAbbās, cites another report in which Abū al-Dardāʾ says, "I like to relax my spirit with a modicum of pleasure so that I can be strong to pursue the truth" (86 n. 6).
22. Calasso, *Literature and the Gods*, 87.
23. Ibn al-Jawzī is cited as saying, "Glory be to the One who expelled Abū Ḥāmid from the circle of law with his compilation of *Iḥyāʾ* [*Subḥāna man akhraja Abā Ḥāmid mi dāʾira al-fiqh bi taṣnīf ʿAl-iḥyāʾ*']." Zabīdī, *Itḥāf*, 1:52.
24. Ibn al-Jawzī, *Al-muntaẓam*, 9:169.
25. "Kitāb al-ʿilm," *Ih.*, 1:24. See also Rahman, "Law and Ethics," 4.
26. De Certeau, *Heterologies*, 36.
27. Zabīdī, *Itḥāf*, 1:52.
28. Ibid.
29. Ibn al-Jawzī, *Al-muntaẓam*, 3:48.
30. Ibid., 52.
31. Subkī, *Ṭabaqāt*, 6:212.
32. Ibid.
33. Q. 6:75–79.
34. Ibid., 2:258.
35. *Qi.*, 7; Q. 2:258.
36. *Qi.*, 7.
37. Ibid.
38. *Mu.*, 61.
39. Ibid., 60.
40. Q. 2:124.
41. Ibid., 2:260.
42. I refrain from using Turner's useful but complex and elaborate term "liminoid," since it covers such a wide range of meanings applicable to industrial society. See Victor Turner, *Ritual to Theatre*, 52–54.
43. Dhahabī, *Siyar*, 19:324; Subkī, *Ṭabaqāt*, 6:208–9.

Chapter Five: Grammar of the Self

1. Wittgenstein, *Lectures and Conversations*, 56.
2. Ibid., 72.
3. Dhahabī, *Siyar*, 19:330.
4. "Kitab al-ʿilm," *Ih.*, 1:41.
5. Ibid.
6. Ibn Ṭufayl, *Ḥayy Ibn Yaqẓān*, 33–34; Goodman, *Hayy Ibn Yaqzān*, 101.
7. *Fay.*, 144.
8. *Mu.*, 45; Rāghib al-Iṣfahānī, *Al-dharīʿa*, 112. One version of this saying adapted by Ghazālī reads, "Know, that whoever apprehends the truth on the authority of the men who adhere to it [such truth], then he will stray in the wilderness of error; know the truth, and if you yourself are in search of truth you will recognize those who adhere to it." See "Kitāb al-ʿilm," *Ih.*, 1:29.
9. *Fad.*, 87.
10. *Mu.*, 46.
11. Erich Auerbach talks about de Montaigne's view that to arrive at the absolute essence of something, one has to isolate it from momentary, accidental contingencies. This, for de Montaigne, was an absurd idea, for he believed that the essence of a thing is lost as soon as one detaches it from its momentary accidents. *Mimesis*, 262.
12. Hegel, "Who Thinks Abstractly," 463.
13. *Mu.*, 47.
14. Ibid.
15. Ibid.
16. The concern about the sources of knowledge that inform our understanding of religion and religious phenomena is an age-old one. Though Ghazālī addressed this question several centuries ago and provided a convincing response, the issue is far from resolved in contemporary Muslim intellectual circles. Most traditional Muslim scholars accept as valid only such knowledge that is authorized by fellow Muslims, especially in matters dealing with religion. Sometimes, the circle is drawn even tighter, limiting sources and authorities to a specific sectarian or ideological affiliation. So, for instance, for some Sunnīs, only a fellow Sunnī who follows the Deoband school of interpretation in modern India, or al-Azhar in Egypt, or a Sunnī of Ḥanbalī persuasion is an acceptable authority. See Maḥaṭwarī, *ʿAdāla al-ruwāt wa al-shuhūd*, for an excellent study of how sectarian affiliations affect the transmission of knowledge traditions in Islam.
17. *Mu.*, 44.
18. Ibid.
19. Ibid.
20. Ibid., 44–45.
21. *FaAn.*, 49.
22. Ibid. This is a surprisingly empathetic interpretation of the doctrine of trinity on the part of a leading Muslim thinker. But I do want to underscore the significant implications this has for his theology and the moral gaze through which he judges the Other in contrast to some of the more doctrinaire interpretations of Ashʿarism. The point to pon-

der is Ghazālī's strong polemic against those Muslim philosophers and Ismāʿīlīs whose doctrinal claims, he charges, had effectively resulted in the rejection of Muḥammad's authority, an observation he made after presenting his conciliatory understanding of the doctrine of trinity.

23. Ghazālī used Akhṭal's poetry as proof in an argument. See *Mus.*, 80.

24. Ibid.

25. Ibn Taymīya, *Majmūʿ fatāwā*, 7:139. See also Ibn Taymīya, *Al-īmān*, 131–33, where he suggests that authorities like Abū Muḥammad al-Khashshāb doubt that these verses of poetry belong to Akhṭal. Others allege that Akhṭal used the word *bayān* (conspicuous elucidation) instead of *kalām* (speech), which would make all the difference in the interpretation of the verses of poetry and their signification.

26. Ibn Taymīya, *Majmūʿ fatāwā*, 7:139–40.

27. Ibid., 7:140.

28. Ibid., 6:296.

29. Ibid.

30. See *Darʾ taʿāruḍ*, 1:8, for Ibn Taymīya's critique of Ghazālī's hermeneutic resembling those held by Christians.

31. Ibid.

32. Wensinck says: "Peut-être pourrai-on soutenir que, comme théologies, Ghazzālī est musulman; comme penseur et homme de science, néo-platonicien et, comme moraliste et mystique, chrétien" (*Pensée de Ghazzālī*, 199), echoing Ibn Taymīya's charge of Christian influences on Ghazālī.

33. Ibn Taymīya, *Majmūʿ fatāwā*, 6:296.

34. Berlin, "Herder and the Enlightenment," 405.

35. "Kitāb al-ʿilm," *Iḥ.*, 29.

36. Ibid.

37. Tawḥīdī, *Al-muqābasāt*, 223.

38. Ibid.

39. "Bayān martaba hādha al-ʿilm wa nisbatuhu ilā al-ʿulūm," *Mus.*, 6–7.

40. Ibid., 10.

41. Tawḥīdī, *Kitāb al-imtāʿ*, 2:18. The word he uses for "religion" is *sharīʿa*, which again shows how polyvalent this term is and how slippery its use has been throughout the history of Islam.

42. Tawḥīdī, "Al-layla al-sābiʿa ʿashara," *Kitāb al-imtāʿ*, 2:11.

43. *Ilj.*, 87.

44. Ibn Ḥazm, *Al-fiṣal fī al-milal*, 1:94.

45. Ibn Rushd argued that the goal of revelation is to produce true knowledge and genuine practice. With knowledge, one can learn how to procure happiness (*saʿāda*) in the hereafter, and with practice one can realize the fulfillment of such desired felicity. Shahrastānī (d. 548/1153) also understood that philosophers advocate two types of wisdom, or philosophy (*ḥikma*): a cognitive type and a practical type. See Sharastānī, *Al-milal wa al-niḥal*, 2:117.

46. See Jackson, *Theological Tolerance in Islam*, for an excellent translation and introduction; my references are to the Arabic text.

47. *Fay.*, 115. There has been an extensive discussion among scholars exploring Gha-

zālī's fidelity to Ashʿarism; see especially Frank, *Ashʿarite School*. Dallal has argued that Ghazālī was consistently committed to traditional Ashʿarism not only at the ideological level but in terms of theoretical conceptions and objections; see "Perils of Interpretation," 78.

48. This is a common expression found in several classical texts, but Ghazālī uses it in *Resuscitation* in a poem. See "Kitāb ādāb al-ulfa wa al-ukhuwwa," *Ih.*, 2:153.

49. Following Massignon, I prefer to use the English term "anathema" for the Arabic word *takfīr*. See *Passion*, 1:375–78.

50. Nayfar, Introduction in *Al-muʿallim bi fawāʾid Muslim*, 100.

51. Ibn al-Jawzī, *Al-muntaẓam*, 9:592. Abū ʿAlī ibn al-Walīd's proper name was Muḥammad b. Aḥmad b. ʿAbd Allāh b. Aḥmad b. al-Walīd Abū ʿAlī al-Muʿtazilī.

52. Martin, Woodward, and Atmaja, *Defenders of Reason*, 25–45.

53. Ibn al-Jawzī, *Al-muntaẓam*, 9:592.

54. Makdisi, *Ibn ʿAqil*, 4.

55. *Fay.*, 117.

56. Ibid., 118.

57. "*Fa isʾalhu: min ayna thabata lahu an yakūna al-ḥaqq wafqan alayhi ḥatta qaḍā bi kufr al-Bāqillānī.*" Ibid.

58. *Maq.*, 160; Burrell and Daher, *Al-Ghazālī*, 147. See also note 95, p. 192, which correctly points out that Ghazālī was warning against the Ashʿarī temptation to overreact to polemics about divine attributes and then hypostatize the attributes.

59. *Maq.*, 160.

60. Ṭāsh Kubrā Zāda, *Muwsūʿa muṣtalaḥat miftāḥ*, 666.

61. *Kash.*, 2:1452.

62. *Fay.*, 118.

63. Ibid., 119.

64. Ibid.

65. Ibid.

66. It is what Tawḥīdī's character describes as the unquestioning confidence and self-satisfaction of religious discourse that makes it different from, say, philosophical discourse. See *Kitāb al-imtāʿ*, 2:10.

Chapter Six: Metaphysics of Belief

1. The discussion that follows is taken from "Kitāb al-tawḥīd wa-al-tawakkul," *Ih.*, 4:215–16.

2. Ghazālī says that such a person is "a monotheist merely by virtue of his tongue; and in this world it protects the claimant from the sword [*sayf*] and spear [*sinān*]." Ibid.

3. "Kitāb al-maḥabba wa al-shawq wa al-uns wa al-riḍā," *Ih.*, 4:307.

4. "Kitāb al-maḥabba," Ih., 4:313. "*Al-ʿajz ʿan dark al-idrāk idrāk.*" *Ilj.*, 68.

5. "Kitāb al-tawḥīd wa al-tawakkul," *Ih.*, 4:216.

6. Ibid.

7. Ibid.

8. Ibid., 217.

9. Ibid., 232.

10. Dhahabī, *Siyar*, 19:334.

11. Ibid.

12. See Tawḥīdī's entertaining discussion concerning the views of the Brethren of Purity in *Kitāb al-imtāʿ*, 2:149.

13. Dhahabī, *Siyar*, 19:327. Ibn Taymīya has a similar anecdote attributed to Ibn al-ʿArabī in which he says that Ghazālī entered the belly of the philosophers and then tried to exit it but failed. See *Darʾ taʿāruḍ*, 1:8.

14. Wittgenstein, *Philosophical Investigations*, 255.

15. "Kitāb al-ʿilm," *Ih.*, 1:28–29.

16. *Ta.*, 3.

17. "*Wa gharaḍuhum al-aqṣā ibṭāl as-sharāʾiʿ.*" *Fad.*, 12.

18. Later Ismāʿīlīs may of course deny this charge, since we know of the flowering of rationality in Ismāʿīlī philosophy, but we are here dealing with Ghazālī's perception of this group.

19. *Mu.*, 25.

20. "Kitāb sharḥ ʿajāʾib al-qalb," *Ih.*, 3:14.

21. *Kash.*, 1:833–34.

22. Vico, *New Science*, 317–18.

23. *Mu.*, 29.

24. Ibid. I disagree with Richard J. McCarthy, who interprets Ghazālī's malady, which lasted two months, as one of his youthful turbulences, viewing it to be different from the illness that led to his depression and inability to teach in Baghdād and subsequently precipitated his departure from the Niẓāmīya College. See Ghazali, *Deliverance from Error*, 104 n. 43. When Ghazālī refers to discarding his adherence to authority and mentions his unslakeable thirst to understand the meaning of things earlier in the text of *Munqidh*, it makes better sense that this could have been an expression of his youthful inquisitiveness. But even about this we have to be tentative, since one does not get much help from Ghazālī in terms of the chronology of the various events in his life.

25. *Mu.*, 27. The idea of wonder, as we know from the Aristotelian tradition, is also the beginning of philosophy.

26. "Kitāb ādāb al-ulfa wa al-ukhuwwa," *Ih.*, 2:153. The summary is derived from two stanzas:

A foe's intelligence is comfort
  A friend's madness is dread
Reason's walk is one, follow it
  Before lunacy's varieties you may tread

27. *Mu.*, 29.

28. See Halevi, "Theologian's Doubts," for an excellent argument as to how Ghazālī steers natural philosophy away from theology.

29. Tawḥīdī, *Kitāb al-imtāʿ*, 2:18.

30. *Ta.*, 4.

31. Ibid.

32. *Mu.*, 49.
33. See *Ta.*, 6, and *Mu.*, 39, for the same argument made by Ghazālī.
34. *Ta.*, 6.
35. Ibid.
36. Ibid., 7.
37. Ibid., 6.
38. "Kitāb ādāb al-ulfa wa al-ukhuwwa," *Ih.*, 2:153.
39. *Qi.*, 30.
40. Ibid.
41. *Ta.*, 170.
42. Ibid., 171.
43. Ibid.
44. Ibid., 172.
45. Ibid., 173.
46. Ormsby, *Theodicy*.
47. *Ta.*, 174.
48. Ibid. (emphasis mine).
49. Ibid.
50. Ibid.
51. *Mish.*, 52.
52. "Kitāb al-ʿilm," *Ih.*, 1:69.
53. "*Al-ʿilm thalātha: kitāb nāṭiq, sunna qāʾima wa lā adrī.*" Ibid.
54. *Ta.*, 178, 226; *Mu.*, 26, 36.
55. Goodman, "Did Al-Ghazālī Deny Causality?"
56. Ḥaqq, "Al-Ghazālī on Causality."

Chapter Seven: Dilemmas of Anathema and Heresy

1. Vajda, "Zindiqs."
2. See *EI* 2, *s.v.* "Bashshār b. Burd."
3. *Fay.*, 134.
4. Ibid., 136.
5. Ibid., 133.
6. Ibid.
7. Indirectly related to this issue, Ibn Qayyim al-Jawzīya interestingly encourages restraint in enforcing the legal process against apostates. He believes the legal process, particularly the penalties for apostasy, act as a disincentive for accused apostates to retract their apostasy, adding: "The goal is to use every means to win their hearts back to Islam." See Ibn Qayyim al-Jawzīya, *Aḥkām ahl al-dhimma*, 1:253.
8. *Fay.*, 136.
9. Ibid., 120.
10. Ibid., 135.
11. Wilde, *Picture of Dorian Gray*, 37.
12. *Fay.*, 120.

13. Q. 42:11.
14. The discussion that follows is drawn from *Fay.*, 121–36.
15. Nuʿmānī, *ʿIlm al-kalām*, 290.
16. *Fay.*, 132.
17. Nuʿmānī, *ʿIlm al-kalām*, 290.
18. Ibid., 291.
19. "Kitāb al-imlāʾ," *Ih.*, 5:22.
20. "Kitāb al-ʿilm," *Ih.*, 1:51.
21. Ibid.; *Ih.*, 5:22–23.
22. *Ih.*, 5:22–23.
23. Ibid., 1:52.
24. *Ta.*, 218.

Chapter Eight: Hermeneutics of the Self and Subjectivity

1. *Kash.*, 1:127–28.
2. See Sherif, *Ghazali's Theory of Virtue*, and Gianotti, *Al-Ghazālī's Unspeakable Doctrine.*
3. I am grateful to Professor Sherman A. Jackson for his assistance in solving the riddle of *fatwā ḥukūma*. He believes that in this context it means a legal opinion in difficult and controversial court cases. Thanks to his help, I have a variant translation that approximates his gloss.
4. The Arabic phrase *ʿinda tahāwush al-ṭaghām* can be rendered in several ways. The word *tahāwush* means "to incite," and *ṭaghām* means "the ignoble and inferior ones." Ghazālī's real intent behind this phrase is difficult to decipher. Is he saying that the scholars are following ordinances of those who are inferior to them in status and that in doing so they are lacking independence in thought? Or is he alleging that the scholars are following government edicts as part of a strategy to pacify the anger of the rioting mobs?
5. "Khuṭba al-kitāb," *Ih.*, 1:8.
6. "Kitāb al-imlāʾ," *Ih.*, 5:18.
7. The word *ḥajāj*, or *ḥijāj*, interestingly, means the bone that surrounds the eye and thus protects it.
8. "Kitāb al-imlāʾ," *Ih.*, 5:18.
9. "Khuṭba al-kitāb," *Ih.*, 1:8.
10. *Miz.*, 67.
11. Sviri, "Self and Its Transformation."
12. *Miz.*, 216.
13. Ibid., 214–215.
14. Arzanjānī, *Minhāj al-yaqīn*, 4.
15. *Miz.*, 237.
16. Ibid., 235.
17. Ibid., 231–32. Human sensory faculties, limbs, and organs that serve the body are like the skills and currency any government requires in order to function properly. So the rational reflective faculty, or the faculty of practical reason, is like the king's intelligence

minister and chief advisor; lust and passions are like an incorrigible slave who pilfers supplies and food from his master; and the virtue of abstention is represented by the deterrent role that the chief of police plays in the public space. As long as police are visible, one can be certain that the criminals and miscreants will not violate the peace. Like the police, the human faculties need to show vigilance over the runaway urges of the body.

18. Ibid., 213. At the front of the brain lies the imaginative faculty, in the same way that communication and postal services play a high-visibility role in government. Communications, Ghazālī observes, take priority among all the branches of government. The reason why the minister of communication and postal services (*ṣāḥib al-barīd*) is important in that he has a pivotal role in ordering intelligence sweeps that relate to matters of state security. The distribution of information, in addition, makes all branches of government function effectively. Memory, he says, is located at the back of the brain, like the servant who is always on call behind the scenes. The expressive faculties he views as translation services; the faculties of action are like scribes and secretaries; and the senses are like spies and intelligence agencies, for they are crucial in vetting and sifting through true and false information. As each faculty performs its specific function, the minister of communication not only scours through it but also presents a concise and accurate report to the monarch.

19. "Kitāb sharḥ ʿajā'ib al-qalb," *Iḥ.*, 3:7.

20. Ibid.

21. *Miz.*, 232.

22. Ibid.

23. See Boyarin, *Carnal Israel*, 1, for an excellent discussion of this topic.

24. *Iḥ.*, 1:52.

25. "Kitāb al-imlā'," *Iḥ.*, 5:22; *Mish.*, 33.

26. Taftāzānī, *Sharḥ*, 192–93.

27. Brown, "Late Antiquity and Islam," esp. 29.

28. Lapidus, "Knowledge, Virtue, and Action," 50.

29. Foucault, *Care of the Self*, 55.

30. Zabīdī, *Itḥāf*, 8:382, points out that what is described as the *sirr*, or *sarīra* (pl. *sarā'ir*), means "the concealed, pure core," a fact that is unclear in the general literature. He provides a valuable insight into the relationship of the *sirr* to the heart, soul, and spirit. What is sure, says Zabīdī, is that the *sirr* is not an independent entity like the spirit and the soul. However, when the soul (*nafs*) becomes highly purified and cleansed, in so doing it unshackles the spirit (*ruḥ*) from the gloom of the soul and thereby allows it to rise to the perception of the heart (*qalb*). This procedure, in turn, loosens the heart from its locus, making it gravitate in the direction of spirit. Under these conditions, the heart develops a quality additional to its regular attributes, which is identified as the *sirr*. Interestingly, the *sirr* is a specular quality: only those who can behold the heart, spirit, and soul can detect the *sirr*, so perhaps not even the one who possesses this attribute can behold it. When those who view the spiritual heart see a mark more pure than the heart itself, they name it the *sirr*, the concealed, pure core. Some see it as a stage more advanced than the heart but prior to the spirit, while others deem it to be a stage beyond the spirit. Those who view the *sirr* to be subtler than the spirit imagine it to be a spirit greatly enhanced by additional

attributes than what are customary. On the other hand, those who view the *sirr* to be a stage prior to the spirit view it as a heart that is greatly enhanced by additional attributes. I am inclined to see the quality represented by the *sirr* to be what we call "conscience."

31. "Kitāb ādāb al-maʿīsha wa akhlāq al-nubuwwa," *Ih.*, 2:318.

32. Bynum, "Individual," 106–8. I am grateful to Professor Talal Asad for drawing my attention to this work.

33. Burckhardt, *Civilization of the Renaissance*, 1:143–44; White, *Tropics of Discourse*, 44.

34. Goitein, "Individualism and Conformity"; Banani, "Conversion and Conformity"; Rosenthal, "I Am You"; Hodgson, *Venture*, 1:72 (emphasis mine).

35. "*Fa kam min shakhsin khāḍa fī al-ʿulūm.*" "Kitāb al-ʿilm," *Ih.*, 1:36.

36. "*Idh qāma bihā wāḥidun, kafā wa saqaṭa al-farḍ ʿan a-ākharīn.*" Ibid., 23.

37. *Ta.*, 223.

38. Dallmayr, *Twilight of Subjectivity*, 57.

39. Zink, *Invention of Literary Subjectivity*, 3; see also "Allegorical Poem."

40. Here, I have drawn freely from Hannah Arendt's "What Is Authority," 94.

41. Zāhī has an interesting discussion of the idea of subjectivity related to another notable thinker of middle Islam, Muḥī al-Dīn Ibn ʿArabī. See "Ibn ʿArabī."

42. "Kitāb al-nīya wa al-ikhlāṣ wa al-ṣidq," *Ih.*, 4:318.

43. Q. 2:165, 16:102, 20:25, 39:22, 94:1.

44. See Jager, "Book of the Heart," for an interesting account of pectoral psychology as a phenomenon in medieval Christendom.

45. "Kitāb sharḥ ʿajāʾib al-qalb," *Ih.*, 3:5.

46. Ibid., 4–5.

47. *Mus.*, 45.

48. "Kitāb sharḥ ʿajāʾib al-qalb," *Ih.*, 3:4.

49. *Mish.*, 5.

50. Ghazālī's subtle definition of the self without a shadow of a doubt incorporates the ṣūfī meaning, where *nafs* is assigned a negative polarity as an earthbound appetitive entity that requires continuous monitoring and control. Control over this self is only possible by controlling the various sensory appetites of the corporeal body. But his second definition places the stress on the psychological meaning, where *nafs* signifies a subtle and transcendent substance.

51. "Kitāb sharḥ ʿajāʾib al-qalb," *Ih.*, 3:4–5.

52. *EI* 2, s.v. "*nafs.*"

53. "Kitāb sharḥ ʿajāʾib al-qalb," *Ih.*, 3:5.

54. In *Al-Ghazālī's Unspeakable Doctrine*, 133, Gianotti translates the word *nafs* in the definiens as "soul."

55. Zabīdī, *Itḥāf*, 8:375.

56. Ibid., 376.

57. "Kitāb sharḥ ʿajāʾib al-qalb," *Ih.*, 3:5.

58. In *Arguing Sainthood*, 258, Ewing brings Ghazālian notions of the subject into dialogue with Lacanian understandings of the subject.

59. Some scholars, especially Montgomery Watt, have cast suspicion that the last part of the *Mishkāt al-anwār* is inconsistent with Ghazālī's other writings, arguing that it may

be the fabrication of a pseudo-Ghazālī. I disagree with this view, for I believe that the section in question is very much consistent with some of Ghazālī's other writings.

60. *Mish.*, 36.

61. Cleary, *Essential Koran*, 82, with some minor changes and italics added for emphasis.

62. In *Marxism and Literature*, 105, Williams usefully describes a homology as a correspondence in origin and development, while an analogy is a correspondence in appearance and function.

63. Given the hybrid nature of the self as Ghazālī construed it, giving equal emphasis to ontology and epistemology, it is difficult to countenance the highly generalized claim made by Ahmet Davutoglu that an Islamic Weltanschauung privileges an ontologically driven epistemology, whereas in the West one encounters an epistemology-driven ontology. The distinction made anticipates a predictable binary relationship between ontology and epistempology; nor is this claim exhaustive of the entire Muslim tradition. Davutoglu, *Alternative Paradigms*, 5. See also Kassim, "Existentialist Tendencies."

64. "Kitāb sharḥ ʿajā'ib al-qalb," *Ih.*, 3:4.

65. *Al-nafs al-lawwāma* (a blaming self); *al-nafs al-ammāra* (a self that enjoins vice); *al-nafs al-muṭma'inna* (a contented self).

66. See Johansen, *Sacred Law*, 57–62, for his observations on the neglect of the religious dimensions of Islamic law in the work of some modern Arab scholars of law.

67. *Miz.*, 232.

68. Kant, *Metaphysic of Morals*, 108.

69. Ghazālī's definition of unbelief is *takdhīb*, to declare the message of the Prophet or revelation as a lie or to reject it. Faith is the opposite of *takdhīb*, namely *taṣdīq*, to assent or to declare as true, derived from *ṣ-d-q*.

70. Levinas, *Entre Nous*, 111.

71. De Certeau, *Heterologies*, 177.

72. Q. 51:56.

73. Levinas, *Entre Nous*, 111.

74. Q. 51:20–21.

75. *Miz.*, 221.

76. *Mish.*, 29–30.

77. Ibid., 38.

78. See Āmulī's commentary on and definition of *dhawq*, which cites Qayṣarī, the commentator on Ibn ʿArabī's *Fuṣūṣ al-ḥikam*, who explicitly differentiates between discursive knowledge and aesthetic knowledge (*dhawq*) and mystical unveilings (*kashf*). Sabzavāri, *Sharḥ al-manẓūma*, 1:188.

79. Dostoevsky, *Crime and Punishment*, 20.

80. Ibid., 21.

81. Ibid.

Chapter Nine: Technologies of the Self and Self-Knowledge

1. See "Kitāb al-ʿilm," *Ih.*, especially the subsection titled "Bayān mā buddila min al-alfāẓ al-ʿulūm," 1:37.

2. In *Political Writings*, 80, Fārābī says: "The art of jurisprudence is that by which a human being is able to infer, from the things the lawgiver declared specifically and determinately, the determination of each of the things he did not specifically declare. And he is able to aspire to verification of that on the basis of the purpose of the lawgiver in the religion he legislated with respect to the nation for which it was legislation. Every religion has opinions and actions. The opinions are like the opinions that are legislated with respect to God, how He is to be described, the world, and other things. The actions are like the actions by which God is praised and the actions by which there are mutual dealings in cities. Therefore the science of jurisprudence has two parts: a part with respect to opinions and a part with respect to actions." Fārābī also talks about the need for jurists to pay attention to questions of language (100).

3. "Kitāb al-ʿilm," *Ih.*, 1:37.

4. *Miz.*, 224.

5. "*Huwa maʿrif al-nafs mā lahā mā ʿalayhā*," the self-cognition of one's rights and duties, where "duties" means "responsibility" rather than anything akin to the Kantian idea of duty. *Kash.*, 1:40.

6. Ibid., 42.

7. Ibn Khaldūn, *Shifāʾ al-sāʾil*, 103.

8. *Kash.*, 1:171.

9. *Miz.*, 224.

10. See, for example, "Kitāb al-ʿilm," *Ih.*, 1:55.

11. *Miz.*, 253.

12. "Kitāb riyāḍat al-nafs," *Ih.*, 3:55.

13. *Miz.*, 256.; *Ih.*, 3:55.

14. Among the twentieth-century scholars who took Ghazālī's notion of *fiqh al-nafs* seriously were the Indian scholars associated with the school of Deoband, especially Anwar Shāh Kashmīrī (d. 1352/1933) and his students. See Ḥasanī, *Nuzhat al-khawaṭir*, 7:90–94, where Ḥasanī not only cites the phrase but also cites a poem of Kashmīrī's using this idea. Among Kashmīrī's students, Yūsuf Binnawrī used this phrase frequently. See Binnawrī, "Yatīma al-bayān."

15. "Say: '[Our life takes its] takes its color [naturalness] from God!' And who could better decorate a life than God, if only we truly adore Him." Q. 2:138. See also Hirawī, *Kitāb al-gharībayn*, 3:324, for my interpolations, where *ṣibgha* is also interpolated as "naturalness" or the "primordial predisposition" (*fiṭra*).

16. Q. 2:138.

17. "Kitāb riyāḍa al-nafs," *Ih.*, 3:55.

18. Koselleck, *Critique and Crisis*, 26.

19. For Derrida's notion of the law, see his "Force of Law."

20. Ghazālī was, of course, not the first to talk about *fiqh* in this way, as T. J. Winter points out. However, he deserves credit for refining the idea and giving it wider currency than any of his predecessors. See Ghazālī, *Disciplining the Soul*, 36 n. A.

21. To describe what essentially amounts to the *in foro interno* of the moral subject, he used different terms like *bāṭin* (interior or esoteric), *sirr* or *sarāʾir* (purified dimensions of the heart or conscience), and *qalb* (heart) to signify interiority.

22. Qaraḍāwī, *Al-Imām al-Ghazālī.*
23. Eagleton, *After Theory*, 129.
24. *Miz.*, 232.
25. Ibid., 232–33.
26. Q. 2:269.
27. *Miz.*, 234.
28. Rāghib al-Iṣfahānī, *Al-dharīʿa*, 183.
29. Ibid.
30. Q. 42:17, 55:7.
31. Rāghib al-Iṣfahānī, *Al-dharīʿa*, 183.
32. This sensibility of justice is strongly felt even in modern times. We have to consider, says a modern Egyptian *muftī* (jurist), "that which is more convenient and better for people, as long as God had commanded us to act with justice and equity [*ʿadl*] without limiting us to the means of achieving this justice and equity." See *Fatāwā al-Islāmīya*, 8:3032.
33. Ibn Qayyim al-Jawzīya, *Iʿlām al-muwaqqiʿīn*, 3:3. See also Maḥmaṣānī, *Falsafa al-tashrīʿ*, 220, and the same book translated by Ziadeh, *Philosophy of Jurisprudence*, 106. Ibn Qayyim states: "God had sent His Prophets and revealed His books so that people could establish justice. It is the truth on which the firmament of the heavens and earth rests. When the indices of truth are established, when the proofs of reason are decided and become clear by whatever means, then surely that is the Law of God, His religion, His consent and His command. And God the sublime has not limited the methods and sources of justice and its indices in one genus [of methods] and invalidated it in other methods, which are more clear, more explicit and self-evident. In fact, He demonstrated in His methods as contained in His legislation that His goal was to establish truth and justice and ground people in equity. So by whatever means truth is discovered and justice is known, then it is obligatory to rule by the dictates and compulsion of these two [notions]. Methods are but causes and means that are not desired in themselves but for their ends, which are the objectives [*maqāṣid*] [of the law]." *Iʿlām al-mawaqqiʿīn*, 4:373.
34. *Miz.*, 358.
35. Ibid.
36. See ibid., 342, where Ghazālī says, "*Al-ʿilm ʿibāda al-nafs, wa fī lisān al-sharʿ ʿibāda al-qalb.*"
37. Ibid., 359.
38. Ibid.
39. Ibid., 191.
40. Ibid.
41. Ibid., 195.
42. *Mus.*, 47.
43. Ibid. For a discussion of some of the metaphysical dimensions of ethics, see Moosa, "Allegory of the Rule."
44. *Mus.*, 45–46.
45. Ibid., 47.
46. Ibid., 46.
47. *Miz.*, 347. Ghazālī says that one of the reasons for the prohibition of pork was to

ensure that Muslims did not become complacent in their interactions with non-Muslims, especially when Muslims were not strong in their commitment to faith.

48. *Mus.*, 46.

49. Ibid.

50. Ibid.

51. *Miz.*, 179.

52. Ibid., 226.

53. Ibid., 224.

54. Ibid., 227.

55. Ibid., 222.

56. "Kitāb sharḥ ʿajā'ib al-qalb," *Ih.*, 3:21.

57. A vague reference to this tale is found in some Buddhist traditions. See Yampolsky, *Platform Sutra*, 129–31, in which one of the monks writes a mind verse. (Actually, he paints it on a wall.) It is mentioned in the Diamond Sutra that "all forms everywhere are unreal and false."

58. *Miz.*, 406.

59. Even in pedagogical matters, Ghazālī argues, one has to adopt flexible criteria and assess every context. One does not have to impose a uniform curriculum in all instances in order to generate rigid conformism. "The question of discursive tradition [*madhhab*] from this point of view changes and differs according to each person and his ability to comprehend," he argues (ibid., 407). While he does advise that one should exercise discretion according to the temperament and ability of the audience, he also warns against allowing a dogmatic adherence to existing orientations to become the pretext for prejudice, tribalism, regionalism, and parochialism.

60. Ibid., 406. Ghazālī's insights about the abuse of school affiliation confirm modern readings of the ideological function and excesses of group formations and communitarian projects.

61. *Miz.*, 407. Karl Marx would have been delighted to know about Ghazālī's insight as an addition to his idea of false consciousness!

62. The idiomatic expression has to do with travelers and their use of Saturn as a navigational point at night, the utility of which is diminished by the radiance of the sun. Here, I have used Lenn Goodman's excellent poetic rendition. See Goodman, *Hayy Ibn Yaqzān*, 101.

63. *Miz.*, 409.

64. What Ghazālī accomplished in Islamdom is perhaps not unlike what Origen did in Christendom. There are many parallels between Ghazālī and Origen (d. ca. 254–55). The latter was the foremost member of the Catechetical School at Alexandria; he subsequently founded a school in Caesarea in Palestine. While Origen had every intention of remaining an orthodox Christian, he also had an equally compulsive desire to reconcile Neoplatonism with Christianity. His enthusiasm for the allegorical interpretation of the Scriptures in particular led him at times to hold heterodox opinions. Ghazālī too had the desire to remain within the dominant consensus in the intellectual politics of religion and religious discourse. Since he was contesting interpretations as well as disputing the positions of

others, he was both contesting orthodoxies and simultaneously constructing alternative ones. But the interpretive moves that he made in order to realize a new ethical subjectivity are obviously controversial ones; he was at times inclined to allegorize certain statements that had previously been interpreted in their literal sense. This is where his acquaintance with the philosophy of Aristotle, Plato, and Plotinus made the most significant impact on his writings.

Conclusion: Knowledge of the Strangers

1. ʿAlawī, "Al-Ghazālī wa tashakkul." See also Ibn Rushd, *Al-ḍarūrī fī uṣūl.*
2. ʿAlawī, "Al-Ghazālī wa tashakkul," 136.
3. Urvoy, *Ibn Rushd*, 118.
4. Ṣughayyir, "Ishkāliyya istimrār," esp. 84.
5. Mignolo, *Local Histories.*
6. De Sousa Santos, *New Common Sense*, 345.
7. Ibid.
8. Nietzsche, *Genealogy of Morals*, essay 1, sec. 2, 25.
9. De Sousa Santos, *New Common Sense*, 491.
10. Jameson, *Singular Modernity*, 215.
11. Bernadette, *Bow and the Lyre*, xii.
12. Ibid., xiii.
13. Insiders like Muḥammad ʿAbduh, the Egyptian reformer, and his student Rashīd Riḍā, or figures like Aḥmad Amīn, Amīn al-Khūlī, and ʿAlī ʿAbd al-Rāziq, especially the latter two, have been on the receiving end of opprobrium from their peers for treating the tradition as a living organism. Recently, Cairo University professor Naṣr Ḥāmid Abū Zayd, a person not belonging to the ranks of the *ʿulamāʾ*, was tried in an Egyptian secular court for allegedly questioning doctrines that should be accepted as theologically a priori true, and he was thus declared an apostate. See Dupret and Ferrié, "Inner Self." On several blasphemy trials pending in Pakistan, where accused Muslim and non-Muslims languish in jail for alleged violations while others have been sentenced, see Shakir, "Blasphemy Law."
14. Bourdieu, "Belief and the Body," 68.
15. De Certeau, *Heterologies*, xx; Foucault, *Archaeology of Knowledge*, 116–17.
16. Even in his most aggressive ethical and political judgments, when he deemed it legitimate to execute Ismāʿīlī leaders whom he believed were incorrigible liars and thus, in his view, beyond rehabilitation, he still showed uncertainty. When pressed if there could be a counter viewpoint to his darker judgment, he readily admitted that his opinion was based on independent judgment (*ijtihād*) and was therefore subject to the vagaries of uncertainty and error.
17. Hamadhānī, *Sufi Martyr*, 21, and "Šakwa-Ġarīb," 25.
18. "Kitāb al-ʿilm," *Iḥ.*, 1:42–43.
19. Ibid., 42.
20. Ibid., 42–43.

21. "Kitāb dhikr al-mawt wa mā baʿdahu," *Iḥ.*, 4:394. In some editions of *Iḥyāʾ*, the first part of this *ḥadīth* recording the words of the Prophet addressed to ʿAbd Allāh ibn ʿUmar, namely, "*Kun fī al-dunyā ka annaka gharīb aw ʿābir sabīl*," are elided. An edition edited by ʿAbd Allāh al-Khālidī (Beirut: Sharika Dār al-Arqam Bin Abi al-Arqam, 1419/1998) includes the first part. For the full *ḥadīth* reference, see Kashmīrī, *Fayḍ al-bārī*, 4:424.

22. Said, "Identity, Authority and Freedom," 18.

23. Hamadhānī, *Sufi Martyr*, 29. See also Hamadhānī, "Šakwa-L-Ġarīb," 31.

Glossary

ʿabd, pl. *ʿibād*. Slave, servant
ʿabra. Tear
ʿāda. Habit, custom
adab, pl. *ādāb*. Civility, etiquette, virtues, ethical pedagogy
ʿadāla. Justice
adīb. Belles lettrist
ʿadl. Justice
afwāh. Mouths
akhlāq. Behavior, character traits, ethics
ʿālam al-malakūt. Angelic universe
ʿālim, pl. *ʿulamāʾ*. Learned person, scholar
alqā al-samʿ. Lit. throw the ear; fig. listen attentively
ʿamal, pl. *aʿmāl*. Action, deed, practice
amīr. Leader
ʿaqīda, pl. *ʿaqāʾid*. Dogma, beliefs
ʿaql. Intellect, reason
ʿaqlī. Rational, abstract
ʿarḍ, pl. *aʿrāḍ*. Accident
ʿasabīya. Social cohesion
awḥā. Inspire
awṣāf, sing. *waṣf*. Attributes, predicates
awwal. First

bāb. Door
baqāʾ. Duration
basharīya. Humanity
bāṭil. Falsehood, distraction
bāṭin. Inner, esoteric
bayān. Conspicuous elucidation, explanation
bidʿa. Heretical belief
burhān. Proof, apodictic knowledge

dāʾ. Disease, illness
dalīl. Proof
dawāʾ. Remedy, medicine
dawām. Permanent
dhāt. Essence
dhātīya. Essential, subjectivity
dhawq. Taste, aesthetic sensibility
dhikr. Remembrance
dihlīz. Threshold position, intermediate space, portal, passage
dīn. Religion, tradition
dunyā. World, secular, temporal

faḍīla. Virtue
faḥwa. Implicit sense
fanāʾ. Annihilation
faqīh, pl. *fuqahāʾ*. Jurist, discerner
faqīr. Ascetic
farḍ. Obligatory, mandatory
fatwā, pl. *fatāwā*. Legal opinion, juridical response
fiqh. Understanding, comprehension, law, positive law
fiqh al-bāṭin. Subjectivity
fiqh al-nafs. Self-understanding, self-intelligibility
fiqh al-ẓāhir. Outward form of the law
fiṭra. Natural state, innate disposition

fuqahā', sing. *faqīh*. Jurists
furūj, sing. *farj*. Pudenda

ghaḍab. Anger
gharīb. Stranger, exiled one
ghumūdh. Obscurity
ghurba. Strangeness, banishment

ḥadīth, pl. *aḥādīth*. Prophetic report
ḥajāj. Protector
ḥajj. Pilgrimage to Makka
halakha. Law
ḥanīfīya. Primitive monotheism
ḥaqīqa. Sense of reality, ultimate truth
ḥaqq. Truth, right, true reality
ḥarām. Forbidden, prohibited
ḥarīr. Silk
ḥawādith, sing. *ḥadith*. Events, happenings, episodes
ḥawzīya. Traditional religious schools in Iran and Iraq
hay'a. Disposition
ḥijāj. Protector
Ḥijāz. Early name for the region of Western Arabia on the Red Sea coast referring to the area of Makka and Madīna in the Arabian peninsula
hijra. Exile, migration
ḥikāya, pl. *ḥikāyāt*. Narrative, stories
ḥikma. Wisdom, philosophy
ḥilm. Temperance
ḥujja. Proof, testimony
ḥukm. Judgment, ruling, law
ḥulūl. Incarnation, inherence
ḥuqūq al-ʿibād. Duties toward fellow humans
ḥuqūq Allāh. Duties toward God

ʿibād, sing. *ʿabd*. Human beings, servants, slaves
ʿibāra, pl. *ʿibārāt*. Expression, text
ʿibra. Edificatory admonition
ibtakara. Invent, fabricate
iḍāfīya. Relational
ʿiffa. Abstinence
iḥyā'. Resuscitation, to give life, revive
ijāza. Certification, authorization
ijmāʿ. Consensus
ijmāl. Synopsis
ijtihād. Personal intellectual effort
ikhlāṣ. Sincerity, intentionality
ʿilm. Knowledge, science
ʿilm al-muʿāmala. Knowledge of moral practices
ʿilm al-mukāshafa. Revelatory knowledge
ʿilm al-sulūk. Science of proper conduct, mysticism
ʿilm al-taṣawwuf. Science of mysticism
imām. Leader
īmān. Faith
intiẓām. Harmony, order
ʿirfān. Intuitive knowledge, gnosis
iṣlāḥ. Reform, improve, rehabilitate
islām. Surrender, submission
isnād. Chain of narrators, authority
istiʿāra. Metaphor
iṣṭilā'. To seek warmth
istimrār. Continuation
istiqāma. Integrity, consistency
istiqlāl. Independence
istishhād. Proof citation
iʿtibār, pl. *iʿtibārāt*. Perspective, to be edified
iʿtiqād. Doctrine, belief, doctrinal rectitude
ittibāʿ. To reenact, to follow, to imitate
ittiḥād. Identification, union

jadalīya. Dialectical polemics
jāh. Egotism, status
jawhar. Substance, attribute
jummāʿ. Aggregate, totality

kāfir. Infidel
kalām. Speech, dialectical theology
kashf. Unveiling

khabar, pl. *akhbār*. News, information, historical narrative
khalīfa. Vicegerent, steward
khalīl. Bosom friend
khāṣṣ. Particular
khātam. Seal
khiṭāb. Address, discourse
khiṭāb al-sharʿ. Nomothetic discourse, revelatory address
khiṭābīya. Discursive strategy
kitāb. Book
kufr. Unbelief, heresy, ingratitude

laṭīfa. Subtlety
lawḥ. Slate, tablet
lawḥ al-qalb. Tablet of the heart
lisān al-ḥal. Prosopopeia

maʿānī, sing. *maʿnā*. Ideas, meanings
madhhab, pl. *madhāhib*. Law school, adopted policy or procedure, discursive tradition
madīna. City
madrasa. School, seminary
mafhūm. Implicit sense
maḥjūj. Defeated or overcome by argument
makrūh. Disapproved, abominable
malak. Angel
malaka. Habitus
mālik. King, sovereign, owner
mandūb. Recommended
manṭiq. Logic
maṣlaḥa, pl. *maṣāliḥ*. Expediency, interest
muʿāmala. Interactive action, transaction
mubāḥ. Indifferent
mubayyan. Univocal
mufassir. Expert in Qur'ān exegesis
muftī. Jurisconsult, one who is expert in giving *fatwā*
muḥaddith. Traditionist, expert in prophetic reports
muḥākāt. Mimesis
muḥāll. Impossible
mujaddid. Renewer
mujāhada. Self struggle
mujmal. Equivocal
mujtahid. Master jurist, one who is qualified to do independent intellectual labor in law
mukāshafa. Mutual unveiling
mulk. Kingdom, polis
munāsaba. Appropriate, adequate
munqidh. Rescuer
muqaddima. Preamble, introduction
muqallid. Follower, journeyman
muqayyad. Precise, unqualified, determined
murābiṭ. Warrior-ascetic
musammā. Denotation
mushāhada, pl. *mushāhadāt*. Contemplative vision, testamentary contemplation
mustaḥabb. Recommended
mustanṭaq. Oracle
muṭāʿ. Obeyed one
mutakallim. Dialectical theologian
mutaṣawwif. One who practices mysticism
muṭlaq. Unqualified
muwaḥḥid. Confessional monotheist
muwallad. Postclassical poet

nafs. Spirit, person
naṣṣ, pl. *nuṣūṣ*. Scriptural authority
naẓar. Investigation
naẓm. Construction, coherence
nifāq. Hypocrisy
nīya. Intention
nūr. Light, illumination
nūrānīya. Luminous
nuẓẓār. Speculative thinker

qabas. Burning brand
qāḍī. Judge
qalam. Pen
qalb. Heart, mutation
qānūn. Principle, law
qāṣṣ, pl. *quṣṣāṣ*. Storyteller, raconteur
qaṭʿī. Apodictic

qibla. Direction of prayer toward Makka
qishr. Peel, shell
qiṣṣa. Story
qubḥ. Detestable
quwwa, pl. *quwwāt*. Strength

rabbānīya. Divine
rajā'. Hope
ri'āya. Administration
ribāṭ. Fortress
risāla. Proclamation, letter
rububīya. Divinity
rūḥ, pl. *arwāḥ*. Soul
rūḥānī. Spiritual, immaterial

sa'āda. Happiness
ṣadr. Bosom
ṣāḥib. Companion, possessor, owner
salaf. Pious ancestor
sālik. Seeker
samā'. Listening, listening to music
sarīr. Concealed core, conscience
shadīd. Strong, witness
shahwa. Appetite
shakhṣ. Person, individual
shar'. Revelation, revealed law, religion
sharī'a. Revealed law
shi'ār. Symbol
shi'r. Poetry
shi'rīya. Poiesis
shirk. Associationism, polytheism
shujā'a. Bravery, courage
shu'ūr. Inner feeling, conscious feeling
ṣibgha. Color
ṣifa. Attribute
sirr. Secret
siyāsa. Governance, politics
ṣūfī. Mystic, seeker
sulṭān. Sultan
sulūk. Conduct
Sunna. Body of prophetic traditions and practices
sūq. Market
ṣūra, pl. *ṣuwar*. Form

ta'addub. Moral cultivation
ta'ajjub. Wonder
ta'assī. Imitation
ta'bīr. Edificatory meaning, interpretation of dreams
ta'dīb. Disciplinary education
tafaqquh. Enlightened discernment
tafhīm. Instruct
tahdhīb. Disciplining
tajawwuz. Figurative expansion
takdhīb. Falsification
takfīr. Anathematize
taklīf. Moral responsibility, capacity concept, moral accountability
talbīs. Deception
ta'līf. Composition
ta'līqa. Dissertation
tamatthul. Simulacrum, simulate
tamthīl. Simile, simulation
taqlīd. Imitation
ṭarīq. Path, road
tarjama. Translate
tarjama nafsahu. Explaining oneself, autobiography
ṭarrār. Scoundrel, rogue
taṣawwuf. Mysticism
taṣdīq. Willing assent, verification
tashbīh. Simile
taṣnīf. Script
tatabbu'. To expound sequentially, to follow
ta'thīr. Efficiency
tawakkul. Absolute reliance and trust in God
tawḥīd. Confessing to the unity of the divine, monotheism
ta'wīl. Interpretation
thamanīya. Monetary character
ṭūr. Mountain

'ubūr. Crossing
'ulamā', sing. *'ālim*. Learned persons, scholars
umma. Community

uqnūmīya. Hypostasis
uṣūl, sing. *aṣl*. Roots, principles, foundations
ʿuwaysī. Long-distance friend

wādī. Riverbed
waḥī. Revelation
wahib. Giver, provider
wāḥid. One person
wajh, pl. *wujūh* or *awjuh*. Face
wājib. Obligatory
waṣāyā. Counsels
wasf mūma' ilayhi. Allusive quality
wazīr. Prime minister, minister, vizier
wijdān. Discovery through experience, ecstasy, emotion, sentiment
wujūd. Existence
wuṣūl. Mystical attainment, connection

yaqīn. Certainty
yudrik. Grasp
yulabbī. To announce one's readiness to serve God
yutarjimu. Translating

zāhid. Ascetic
ẓāhir. Outer, exoteric
zandaqa, pl. *zanādiq* or *zanādiqa*. Religious and doctrinal subversives
zaytūn. Olive

Bibliography

ʿAbd al-Ḥaqq, Munṣif. *Al-kitāba wa al-tajriba al-ṣūfīya: Namūdhaj Muḥī al-Dīn Ibn ʿArabī.* Rabat: Maṭbaʿa ʿUkāẓ, 1988.

ʿAbd al-Muṭṭalib, Muḥammad. *Jadlīya al-ifrād wa al-tarkīb.* Cairo: Longman, 1995.

ʿAbd al-Rāziq, ʿAlī. *Al-Islām wa uṣūl al-ḥukm.* Beirut: Dār Maktaba al-Ḥayāt, 1966.

Abdel-Kader, Ali Hassen. *The Life, Personality and Writings of al-Junayd.* London: Luzac, 1962.

Abelard, Peter. *The Letters of Abelard and Heloise.* Translated by Betty Radice. London: Penguin, 1974.

Abou el-Fadl, Khaled. *Speaking in God's Name.* Oxford: Oneworld, 2001.

Abū al-Fidāʾ, ʿImād al-Dīn Ismāʿīl. *Al-mukhtaṣar fī akhbār al-bashar: Taʾrīkh Abī al-Fidāʾ.* 4 vols. Cairo: Maktaba al-Mutanabbī, n.d.

Abu Deeb, Kamal. *Al-Jurjānī's Theory of Poetic Imagery.* Guildford, U.K.: Arris and Phillips, 1979.

Abū Saʿīd Ibn Abi al-Khayr, Muḥammad b. al-Munawwar Abī Saʿīd b. Abī Ṭāhir b. *Asrār al-tawḥīd.* Tehran, 1313. Costa Mesa, Calif.: Mazda Publishers in association with Bibliotheca Persica, 1992.

Abu Sway, Mustafa. *Al-Ghazali: A Study in Islamic Epistemology.* Kuala Lumpur: Dewan Bahasa Dan Pustaka, 1996.

Abū Zahra, Muḥammad. "Al-Ghazālī al-faqih." In *Abū Ḥāmid al-Ghazālī fī al-dhikrā al-miʾawīya li mīlādihi*, edited by Zakī Najīb Maḥmūd, 525–85. Damascus: Al-Majlis al-Aʿlā li Riʿāyat al-Funūn wa al-Ādāb wa al-ʿUlūm al-Ijtimāʿīya, 1380/1961.

Adonis/Adūnīs (ʿAli Aḥmad Saʿīd). *Al-masraḥ wa al-marāyā.* Beirut: Manshūrāt Dar al-Ādāb, 1988.

ʿAfīfī, Abū al-ʿAlā. "Al-Malāmatīya wa al-ṣūfīya wa ahl al-futuwwa." *Majalla kullīya al-ādāb jāmiʿa fuʾād al-awwal* 1 (May 1943): 10–67.

Al-ʿAlawī, Jamāl al-Dīn. "Al-Ghazālī wa tashakkul al-khiṭāb al-falsafī li Ibn Rushd." In *Ghazālī la raison et le miracle*, edited by A. M. Turki, 135–60. Paris: Maisonneuve et Larose, 1987.

Amīn, Aḥmad. *Ḍuḥā al-Islām.* Cairo: Maktaba al-Nahḍa al-Miṣrīya, 1964.

Amīn, Ḥusayn. *Ghazālī faqīhan, wa faylasūfan wa mutaṣawwifan.* Baghdad: Maṭbaʿa al-Irshād, 1963.

Al-Anṣārī, ʿAbd al-Dāʾim Abū al-ʿAṭā al-Baqarī. *Iʿtirāfāt al-Ghazālī aw kayfa arrakha Ghazālī nafsahu*. Cairo: Maktaba al-Angelo-Miṣrīya, 1985.

Anzaldúa, Gloria. *Borderlands / La Frontera*. 2nd ed. San Francisco: Aunt Lute Books, 1999.

Arberry, Arthur J. *Avicenna on Theology*. London: Murray, 1951.

———. *Sufism: An Account of the Mystics of Islam*. 1950. New York: Harper and Row, 1970.

Arendt, Hannah. *Between Past and Future: Eight Exercises in Political Thought*. New York: Viking, 1968.

———. *The Human Condition*. New York: Anchor, 1958.

———. "What Is Authority?" In *Between Past and Future: Eight Exercises in Political Thought*, 91–141. New York: Penguin, 1968.

Aristotle. *Nicomachean Ethics, Book VI*. Edited by Louise Ropes Loomis. New York: Walter J. Black, 1943.

———. *Poetics*. Translated by James Hutton. New York: W. W. Norton, 1982.

Arkoun, Mohammed. "Logocentrisme et vérité religieuse dans la pensée Islamique." In *Essais sur la pensée Islamique*, 185–231. Paris: Maisonneuve et Larose, 1984.

———. *The Unthought in Contemporary Islamic Thought*. London: Saqi Books / The Institute of Ismaili Studies, 2002.

Arsalān, Amīr Shakīb. *Our Decline and Its Causes*. Translated by M. A. Shakoor. Lahore: Shaikh Muhammad Ashraf, 1962.

Arzanjānī, ʿUways Wafā Khānzāda. *Minhāj al-yaqīn: Sharḥ adab al-dunyā wa al-dīn*. Istanbul: Mahmud Bey Matbaʿsi, 1910.

Asad, Talal. *Formations of the Secular*. Stanford: Stanford University Press, 2003.

———. *Genealogies of Religion: Discipline and Reasons of Power in Christianity and Islam*. Baltimore: Johns Hopkins University Press, 1993.

———. *The Idea of an Anthropology of Islam*. Occasional Paper Series. Washington, D.C.: Center for Contemporary Arab Studies, Georgetown University, 1986.

Al-Aʿsam, ʿAbd al-Amīr. *Al-faylasūf al-Ghazālī*. Tunis: Al-Dār al-Tūnisīya li al-Nashr, 1988.

Ashtor, E. *A Social and Economic History of the Near East in the Middle Ages*. London: Collins, 1976.

Asín Palacios, Miguel. *La espiritualidad de Algazel y su sentido Cristiano* (*Al-Ghazālī's Spirituality and Its Christian Meaning*). Madrid: Imprenta de Estanislao Maestre, 1934.

Auerbach, Erich. *Mimesis: The Representation of Reality in Western Literature*. Translated by Willard Trask. New York: Doubleday Anchor, 1957.

Al-Azmeh, Aziz. *Ibn Khaldun*. London: Routledge, 1990.

ʿAzzām, Idrīs. "Al-Sulṭa al-siyāsīya wa waẓīfatuhā al-ijtimāʿīya: Qirāʾa jadīda li baʿḍi jawānib al-fikr al-siyāsī li ḥujja al-Islām Abī Ḥāmid al-Ghazālī." *Majallā al-ʿulūm al-ijtimāʿīya* 14, no. 4 (Winter 1986): 15–38.

Badawī, ʿAbd al-Raḥmān. *Muʾallafāt al-Ghazālī*. 2nd ed. Kuwait: Wakālat al-Matbūʿāt, 1977.

Badiou, Alain. *Ethics: An Essay on the Understanding of Evil*. London: Verso, 2002.

Bahūjiyānī, Muḥammad ʿAṭāʾ Allāh Ḥanīf. "Al-muqaddima fī farāʾid al-fawāʾid al-muhimma." In Shāh Aḥmad Walī Allāh al-Dihlāwī, *Itḥāf al-nabīh fī mā yaḥtāju ilayhi al-muḥaddith wa al-faqīh*, 13–36. Lahore: Al-Maktaba al-Salafīya, 1386/1969.

Bakhtin, M. M. *The Dialogic Imagination*. Edited by Michael Holquist. Translated by Caryl Emerson and Michael Holquist. Austin: University of Texas Press, 1981.

Baldick, Julian. *Imaginary Muslims: The Uwaysi Sufis of Central Asia*. New York: New York University Press, 1993.

Bāmbā, Aḥmad. *Masālik al-jinān: Ḥaqq al-bukā'*. Translated by Serigne Same M'Baye. Touba, Senegal: Imprimiere Al Azhar Editions, 2000.

Banani, Amin. "Conversion and Conformity in a Self-Conscious Elite." In *Individualism and Conformity in Classical Islam*, edited by Amin Banani and Speros Vryonis Jr., 19–31. Wiesbaden: Otto Harrassowitz, 1977.

Barthold, V. V. *Four Studies on the History of Central Asia*. Vol. 3 of *Mīr ʿAlī Shīr: A History of the Turkman People*. Translated by V. Minorsky and T. Minorsky. Leiden: E. J. Brill, 1962.

———. *Turkestan Down to the Mongol Invasion*. London: Luzac, 1968.

Al-Baṣrī, Abū ʿUthmān ʿAmr b. Baḥr b. Maḥbūb. "Kitāb al-futyā." In *Rasāʾil al-Jāḥiẓ*, edited by Muḥammad Bāsil ʿUyūn al-Sūd, 221–26. Vol. 1 of *Rasāʾil al-Jāḥiẓ*. Beirut: Dār al-Kutub al-ʿIlmīya, 1420/2000.

Beeman, William O. *Language, Status and Power in Iran*. Bloomington: Indiana University Press, 1986.

Bello, I. *The Medieval Islamic Controversy between Philosophy and Orthodoxy*. Leiden: E. J. Brill, 1989.

Bernadette, Seth. *The Bow and the Lyre*. Lanham, Md.: Rowman and Littlefield, 1997.

Benjamin, Walter. "Thesis on the Philosophy of History." In *Illuminations: Essays and Reflections*, edited by Hannah Arendt, 253–64. New York: Schocken, 1968.

Berlin, Isaiah. "Herder and the Enlightenment." In *The Proper Study of Mankind: An Anthology of Essays*, edited by Henry Hardy and Roger Hausheer, 359–435. New York: Farrar, Straus and Giroux, 1997.

Berque, Jacques. "Islam and Innovation." In *Islam, Philosophy and Science: Four Public Lectures Organized by Unesco, June 1980*, 69–98. Paris: Unesco Press, 1981.

Binnawrī, Yūsuf. "Yatīma al-bayān li mushkilāt al-Qur'ān." In *Mushkilāt al-Qur'ān*, by Muḥammad Anwar Shāh al-Kashmīrī, 1–84. Multan: Idāra-e Ta'līfāt-e Ashrafīya, ca. 1356/1937.

Bohas, G., J. P. Guillaume, and D. E. Kouloughli. *The Arabic Linguistic Tradition*. London: Routledge, 1990.

Borges, Jorge Luis. "Averroës' Search." In *Collected Fictions*, translated by Andrew Hurley, 235–41. New York: Penguin, 1999.

Bourdieu, Pierre. "Belief and the Body." In *The Logic of Practice*, 66–79. Stanford: Stanford University Press, 1980.

Bouyges, Maurice. *Essai de chronologie des oeuvres de al-Ghazali (Algazel)*. Edited by Michel Allard. Beirut: L'Institut de Lettres Orientales de Beyrouth, 1959.

Boyarin, Daniel. *Carnal Israel: Reading Sex in Talmudic Culture*. Berkeley: University of California Press, 1993.

Brodsky, Joseph. *Less Than One: Selected Essays*. New York: Farrar, Straus and Giroux, 1986.
Brown, Peter. "Late Antiquity and Islam: Parallels and Contrasts." In *Moral Conduct and Authority: The Place of Adab in South Asian Islam*, edited by Barbara D. Metcalf, 23–37. Berkeley: University of California Press, 1984.
———. *Religion and Society in the Age of Saint Augustine*. London: Faber and Faber, 1972.
Bulliet, Richard W. *The Patricians of Nishapur: A Study in Medieval Islamic Social History*. Cambridge, Mass.: Harvard University Press, 1972.
———. "A Quantitative Approach to Medieval Muslim Biographical Dictionaries." *Journal of the Economic and Social History of the Orient* 1 (1970): 195–211.
Burckhardt, Jacob. *The Civilization of the Renaissance in Italy*. 2 vols. New York: Harper, 1958.
Burrell, David B. *Friendship and Ways to Truth*. Notre Dame: University of Notre Dame Press, 2000.
———, trans. *Faith in Divine Unity and Trust in Divine Providence [Kitab al-tawhid wa al-tawakkul]: Book XXXV of the Revival of the Religious Sciences [Ihya' 'ulum al-din] by al-Ghazali*. Louisville: Fons Vitae, 2001.
Burrell, David B., and Nazih Daher, trans. *Al-Ghazālī: The Ninety-Nine Beautiful Names of God*. Cambridge: Islamic Texts Society, 1979.
Bushnell, Charles. Introduction to *University Library of Autobiography*. Vol. 2 of *The Middle Ages and Their Autobiographers*. New York: F. Tyler Daniels, 1918. Reprint, National Alumni, 1927.
Busse, Heribert. *Chalif und Grosskönig: Die Buyiden im Iraq 945–1055*. Beirut and Wiesbaden: Franz Steiner Verlag / Orient-Institut der Deutschen Morgenländischen Gesellschaft, 1969.
Byatt, Antonia S. *Possession*. London: Vintage, 1991.
Bynum, Caroline W. "Did the Twelfth Century Discover the Individual?" In *Jesus as Mother: Studies in the Spirituality of the High Middle Ages*, 82–109. Berkeley: University of California Press, 1982.
Cahen, Claude. "The Turkish Invasion: The Selchükids." In vol. 1 of *A History of the Crusades*, edited by Kenneth M. Setton and Marshall W. Baldwin, 135–76. Philadelphia: University of Pennsylvania Press, 1958.
Calasso, Roberto. *Literature and the Gods*. Translated by Tim Parks. New York: Alfred A. Knopf, 2001.
Chakrabarty, Dipesh. *Provincializing Europe: Postcolonial Thought and Historical Difference*. Princeton: Princeton University Press, 2000.
Cleary, Thomas. *The Essential Koran*. San Francisco: HarperSanFrancisco, 1993.
Cook, Michael. *Commanding Right and Forbidding Wrong in Islamic Thought*. Cambridge: Cambridge University Press, 2000.
Crone, Patricia. "Did al-Ghazālī Write a Mirror for Princes? On the Authorship of *Naṣīḥat al-mulūk*." *Jerusalem Studies in Arabic and Islam* 10 (1987): 167–91.
Dabashi, Hamid. *Truth and Narrative: The Untimely Thoughts of 'Ayn al-Quḍāt al-Hamadhānī*. London: Curzon, 1999.

Dallal, Ahmad. "Ghazālī and the Perils of Interpretation." *Journal of the American Oriental Society* 122, no. 4 (Oct.–Dec. 2002): 773–87.

Dallmayr, Fred A. *Twilight of Subjectivity: Contributions to a Post-individualist Theory of Politics.* Amherst: University of Massachusetts Press, 1981.

Dankoff, Robert. Introduction to *Wisdom of Royal Glory [Kutadgu Bilig]: A Turko-Islamic Mirror for Princes*, by Yūsuf Khāṣṣ Ḥājib. Chicago: University of Chicago Press, 1983.

Al-Darīnī, Muḥammad Fatḥī. "Al-fikr al-siyāsī ʿinda al-Ghazālī, wa al-Māwardī wa-Ibn Khaldūn." *Al-Turāth al-ʿarabī* 22 (1986): 23–67.

Darnton, Robert. *The Great Cat Massacre and Other Episodes in French Cultural History.* New York: Vintage, 1984.

———. "Looking the Devil in the Face." *New York Review of Books*, 12 February 2000, 14–17.

Davis, Michael. *Aristotle's Poetics: The Poetry of Philosophy.* Lanham, Md.: Rowman and Littlefield, 1992.

Davutoglu, Ahmet. *Alternative Paradigms: The Impact of Islamic and Western Weltanschauungs on Political Theory.* Lanham, Md.: University Press of America, 1994.

De Certeau, Michel. *Heterologies: Discourse on the Other.* Translated by Brian Massumi. Minneapolis: University of Minnesota Press, 2000.

De Man, Paul. *Blindness and Insight.* New York: Oxford University Press, 1971.

Derrida, Jacques. *Dissemination.* Translated by Barbara Johnson. Chicago: University of Chicago Press, 1981.

———. *The Ear of the Other: Otobiography, Transference, Translation.* Edited by Christie V. McDonald. Translated by Peggy Kamuf and Avita Ronell. New York: Schocken, 1985.

———. "Force of Law: The Mystical Foundation of Authority." In *Deconstruction and the Possibility of Justice*, edited by Drucilla Cornell, 3–67. New York: Routledge, 1992.

———. *Of Grammatology.* Translated by Gayatri Chakravorty Spivak. Baltimore: Johns Hopkins University Press, 1976.

———. *Politics of Friendship.* Translated by George Collins. London: Verso, 1997.

———. *Specters of Marx: The State of the Debt, the Work of Mourning and the New International.* Translated by Peggy Kamuf. New York: Routledge, 1994.

———. *Speech and Phenomena and Other Essays on Husserl's Theory of Signs.* Translated by David B. Allison. Evanston, Ill.: Northwestern University Press, 1973.

———. *Writing and Difference.* Translated by Alan Bass. Chicago: University of Chicago Press, 1978.

De Slane, Le Baron. *Histoire des Berbres.* Paris: Librairie Orientaliste, 1969.

De Sousa Santos, Boaventura. *Toward a New Common Sense: Law, Globalization and Emancipation.* London: Butterworths LexisNexis, 2002.

Al-Dhahabī, Shams al-Dīn Muḥammad b. Aḥmad b. ʿUthmān. *Siyar aʿlām al-nubalāʾ.* Edited by Shuʿayb al-Arnaʾūṭ. 25 vols. Beirut: Muʾassasa al-Risāla, 1410/1990.

Al-Dīnawarī, Abū Muḥammad ʿAbd Allāh b. Muslim b. Quṭayba. *ʿAyūn al-akhbār.* Edited by Yūsuf ʿAlī Ṭawīl. 4 vols. Beirut: Dār al-Kutub al-ʿIlmīya, 1986.

Diyab, Adib Nayif. "Al-Ghazālī." In *Religion, Learning and Science in the Abbassid Period*, edited by M. J. L. Young, J. D. Latham, and R. B. Serjeant, 424–45. Cambridge: Cambridge University Press, 1990.

Dostoevsky, Fyodor. *Crime and Punishment*. Translated by Jessie Coulson. Oxford: Oxford University Press, 1998.

Dunyā, Sulaymān. *Al-ḥaqīqa fī naẓar al-Ghazālī*. Cairo: Dār al-Maʿārif, 1965.

Dupret, Baudouin, and Jean-Noël Ferrié. "The Inner Self and Public Order." In *Muslim Traditions and Modern Techniques of Power*, edited by Armando Salvatore, 141–62. Münster, Ger.: Lit; Piscataway, N.J.: Transaction Publishers, 2001.

Eagleton, Terry. *After Theory*. New York: Basic Books, 2003.

Eliot, T. S. "Tradition and the Individual Talent." In *Selected Prose of T. S. Eliot*, edited by Frank Kermode, 37–44. London: Faber and Faber, 1975.

Encyclopaedia of Islam. 2nd ed. Leiden: E. J. Brill, 1999.

Engineer, Asghar Ali. "The Ismaʿilis: Harbingers of Protest and Rationalist Movement in Islam." In *Reason and Tradition in Islamic Thought*, edited by Mahmudul Haq, 75–97. Aligarh: Institute of Islamic Studies, Aligarh Muslim University, 1992.

Ernst, Carl W. *Words of Ecstasy in Islam*. Albany: State University of New York Press, 1985.

Ewing, Katherine Pratt. *Arguing Sainthood: Modernity, Psychoanalysis and Islam*. Durham: Duke University Press, 1997.

Al-Farabi. *The Political Writings: Selected Aphorisms and Other Texts*. Translated by Charles E. Butterworth. Ithaca: Cornell University Press, 2001.

Faris, Nabih Amin. *The Book of Knowledge, Being a Translation with Notes of the Kitāb al-ʿIlm of al-Ghazzālī's "Iḥyāʾ ʿUlūm al-Dīn."* Lahore: Shaykh Muhammad Ashraf, 1970.

Farrūkh, ʿUmar. *Taʾrīkh al-fikr al-ʿarabī ilā ayyām Ibn Khaldūn*. Beirut: Dār al-ʿIlm li al-Milāyīn, 1983.

Al-Fāsī, Muḥammad b. Ḥasan al-Ḥujawī al-Thaʿālabī. *Al-fikr al-sāmī fī taʾrīkh al-fiqh al-Islāmī*. Edited by ʿAbd al-ʿAzīz b. ʿAbd al-Fattāḥ al-Qārī. 2 vols. Cairo: Maktaba Dār al-Turāth, 1397/1976.

Al-fatāwā al-Islāmīya min dār al-iftāʾ al-miṣrīya. 16 vols. Cairo: Al-Majlis al-Aʿlā li ʾl-Shuʾūn al-Islāmīya, 1403/1983–84.

Field, Claud. *The Confessions of al-Ghazzali*. 1909. Reprint, Lahore: Shaikh Muhammad Ashraf, 1978.

Al-Fīrūzābādī, Majd al-Dīn Muḥammad b. Yaʿqūb. *Al-qāmūs al-muḥīṭ*. 4 vols. Beirut: Dār al-Jīl, n.d.

Foucault, Michel. *The Archaeology of Knowledge*. Translated by A. M. Sheridan Smith. New York: Pantheon, 1972.

———. *The Care of the Self*. Vol. 3 of *The History of Sexuality*. Translated by Robert Hurly. New York: Vintage, 1988.

———. *"Discipline and Punish" and "The Birth of the Prison."* Translated by Alan Sheridan. New York: Vintage, 1995.

———. "Pastoral Power and Political Reason." In *Religion and Culture*, edited by Jeremy R. Carette, 135–52. New York: Routledge, 1999.

Frank, Richard M. *Al-Ghazālī and the Ashʿarite School*. Durham: Duke University Press, 1994.

Fraser, J. T. *Of Time, Passion and Knowledge: Reflections on the Strategy of Existence*. Rev. ed. Princeton: Princeton University Press, 1990.

Frei, Hans. "Literal Reading of Biblical Narrative in Christian Tradition: Does It Stretch or Will It Break?" In *The Bible and Narrative Tradition*, edited by Frank McConnell, 36–77. Oxford: Oxford University Press, 1986.

Freud, Sigmund. *The Interpretation of Dreams*. Translated by James Strachey. New York: Avon, 1965.

———. *Introductory Lectures on Psychoanalysis*. Edited and translated by James Strachey. New York: W. W. Norton, 1966.

Frye, Richard N. *The Heritage of Central Asia: From Antiquity to the Turkish Expansion*. Princeton, N.J.: Markus Wiener, 1996.

"Gazālī Özel Sayisi." Special issue, *Islāmī araştirmalar* (Journal of Islamic Research) 13, no. 3–4 (2000).

Geertz, Clifford. "The Pinch of Destiny: Religion as Experience, Meaning, Identity, Power." In *Available Light: Anthropological Reflections on Philosophical Topics*, 167–86. Princeton: Princeton University Press, 2000.

Al-Ghazali. *Deliverance from Error: Five Key Texts Including His Spiritual Autobiography, Al-Munqidh mir al-Dalal*. Translated and annotated by R. J. McCarthy. Louisville: Fons Vitae, 1980.

———. *Ghazali's Book of Counsel for Kings*. Edited and translated by F. R. C. Bagley. London: Oxford University Press, 1971.

Al-Ghazālī. *"On Disciplining the Soul" and "On Breaking the Two Desires."* Translated by T. J. Winter. Cambridge: Islamic Texts Society, 1995.

Al-Ghazālī, Abū Ḥāmid Muḥammad b. Muḥammad. *Faḍā'iḥ al-bāṭinīya*. Beirut: Maktaba al-ʿaṣrīya, 2001.

———. *Faḍā'il al-anām min rasā'il ḥujjat al-Islām*. Edited by ʿAlī Nūr al-Dīn. Tunis: Al-Dār al-Tūnisīya li al-Nashr, 1972.

———. *Fayṣal al-tafriqa bayna al-Islām wa al-zandaqa*. Vol. 3 of *Majmūʿa rasā'il al-Imām al-Ghazālī*. Edited by Aḥmad Shams al-Dīn. Beirut: Dar al-Kutub al-ʿIlmīyah, 1406/1986.

———. *Iḥyā' ʿulūm al-dīn*. 5 vols. Beirut: Dar al-Kutub al-ʿIlmīya, 2001.

———. *Iljām al-ʿawām ʿan ilm al-kalām*. Vol. 4 of *Majmūʿa rasā'il al-Imām al-Ghazālī*. Edited by Aḥmad Shams al-Dīn. Beirut: Dār al-Kutub al-ʿIlmīya, 1406/1986.

———. *Al-iqtiṣād fī al-iʿtiqād*. Cairo: Maktaba wa Maṭbaʿa Muḥammad ʿAli Subayḥ wa Awlāduhu, 1390/1971.

———. *Jawāhir al-Qur'ān*. Beirut: Dar al-Āfāq al-Jadīda, 1990.

———. *Kīmyā' al-saʿāda*. Vol. 5 of *majmūʿa rasā'il al-Imām al-Ghazālī*. Edited by Aḥmad Shams al-Dīn. Beirut: Dār al-Kutub al-ʿIlmīya, 1409/1988.

———. *Kitāb al-imlā' fī ishkāliyāt "al-Iḥyā'."* In vol. 5 of *Iḥyā' ʿulūm al-dīn*, 13–41. Beirut: Dar al-Kutub al-ʿIlmīya, 2001.

———. *Kitāb miḥakk al-naẓar*. Edited by Rafīq ʿAjam. Beirut: Dār al-Fikr al-Lubnānī, 1994.

———. *Al-madnūn bihi ʿalā ghayr ahlihi*. Vol. 4 of *Majmūʿa rasā'il al-Imām al-Ghazālī*. Edited by Aḥmad Shams al-Dīn. Beirut: Dar al-Kutub al-ʿIlmīya, 1406/1986.

———. *Al-mankhūl*. Beirut: Dar al-Fikr Muʿaṣir; Damascus: Dar al-Fikr, 1998.

———. *Al-mankhūl min taʿlīqāt al-uṣūl*. Edited by Muḥammad Ḥasan Haytū. Damascus: Dār al-Fikr, 1980.
———. *Maqāṣid al-falāsifa*. Egypt: Dar al-Maʿarif, n.d.
———. *Al-maqṣad al-asnā fī asmāʾ Allāh al-ḥusnā*. Beirut: Dar al-Mashriq, 1971.
———. *Mishkāt al-anwār*. Translated by David Buchman. Provo, Utah: Brigham Young University Press, 1998.
———. *Mīzān al-ʿamal*. Edited by Sulaymān Dunyā. Cairo: Dar al-Maʿarif, 1964.
———. *Mūʿīd al-ʿilm fī al-manṭiq*. Beirut: Dar al-Kutub al-ʿIlmīya, 1990.
———. *Al-munqidh min al-ḍalāl*. Vol. 5 of *Majmūʿa al-rasāʾil al-Imām al-Ghazālī*. Edited by Aḥmad Shams al-Dīn. Beirut: Dar al-Kutub al-ʿIlmīya, 1409/1988.
———. *Al-mustasfā fī ʿilm al-uṣūl*. Beirut: Dar al-Kutub al-ʿIlmīya, 1413/1993.
———. *Qawāʿid al-aqāʾid*. In vol. 1 of *Iḥyāʾ ʿulūm al-dīn*, 88–120. Beirut: Dar al-Kutub al-ʿIlmīya, 2001.
———. *Al-qisṭās al-mustaqīm*. Vol. 3 of *Majmūʿa al-rasāʾil al-Imām al-Ghazālī*. Edited by Aḥmad Shams al-Dīn. Beirut: Dar al-Kutub al-ʿIlmīya, 1406/1986.
———. *Tahāfut al-falāsifa*. Cairo: Dar al-Maʿarif, 1980.
———. *Al-tibr al-masbūk fī naṣīḥat al-mulūk*. Edited by Sāmī Khiḍr. Beirut: Dār Ibn Zaydūn, 1407/1987.
Al-Ghazzālī, Aḥmad. *Aphorismen ueber die Liebe*. Edited by Hellmut Ritter. Istanbul: Staatsdruckerei, 1942.
Gianotti, Timothy J. *Al-Ghazālī's Unspeakable Doctrine of the Soul: Unveiling the Esoteric Psychology and Eschatology of the "Iḥyā'."* Leiden: E. J. Brill, 2001.
Gibb, Sir Hamilton A. R. "The Caliphate and the Arab States." In vol. 1 of *A History of the Crusades*, edited by Kenneth Setton and Marshall W. Baldwin, 81–98. Philadelphia: University of Pennsylvania Press, 1955.
Gibb, Sir Hamilton A. R., and J. H. Kramers. *Shorter Encyclopaedia of Islam*. Ithaca: Cornell University Press, 1965.
Ginzburg, Carlo. *The Judge and the Historian*. Translated by Anthony Shugaar. London: Verso, 1999.
Gohlman, William E. *The Life of Ibn Sina*. Albany: State University of New York Press, 1974.
Goitein, Shlomo D. "Individualism and Conformity in Classical Islam." In *Individualism and Conformity in Classical Islam*, edited by Amin Banani and Speros Vryonis Jr., 3–17. Wiesbaden: Otto Harrassowitz, 1977.
———. *Le livere de Mohammed Ibn Toumert*. Algiers: Imprimerie Orientale Pierre Fontana, 1903.
———. "The Rise of the Middle-Eastern Bourgeoisie in Early Islamic Times." In *Studies in Islamic History and Institutions*, 217–41. Leiden: E. J. Brill, 1966.
———. "Tod und Andeken des Chalifen Jezīd I." *Zeitschrift des Deutschen Morgenländischen Gesellschaft* 66 (1912): 139–42.
Goodman, Lenn. *Avicenna*. London: Routledge, 1992.
———. "Did Al-Ghazālī Deny Causality?" *Studia Islamica* 47 (1978): 83–120.
———. *Ibn Tufayl's "Hayy Ibn Yaqzān": A Philosophical Tale*. Translated by Lenn E. Goodman. Los Angeles: Gee Tee Bee, 1996.

———. *Islamic Humanism*. New York: Oxford University Press, 2003.
Gosche, R. *Uber Ghazzālis Leben und Werke*. Berlin: Königl. Akademie der Wissenschaften, 1858.
Ḥājib, Yūsuf Khāṣṣ. *Wisdom of Royal Glory [Kutadgu Bilig]: A Turko-Islamic Mirror for Princes*. Translated by Robert Dankoff. Chicago: University of Chicago Press, 1983.
Halevi, Leor. "The Theologian's Doubts: Natural Philosophy and the Skeptical Games of Ghazālī." *Journal of the History of Ideas* 63, no. 1 (January 2002): 19–39.
Hallaq, Wael B. "From Regional to Personal Schools of Law: A Reevaluation." *Islamic Law and Society* 8, no. 1 (2001): 1–26.
Al-Hamadhānī, ʿAyn al-Quḍāt. "Šakwā-ġarīb ʿani L-ʿawṭān ʾilā ʿulamāʾ-Buldān." Edited by Mohammed Ben Abd el-Jalil. *Journal Asiatique* 216 (January–March 1930): 1–76.
———. *A Sufi Martyr: The "Apologia" of ʿAin al-Quḍāt al-Hamadhānī*. Translated by A. J. Arberry. London: Allen and Unwin, 1969.
Hammad, Ahmad Zaki. "Ghazālī's Juristic Treatment of the Shariʿah Rules in al-Mustaṣfa." *American Journal of Islamic Social Sciences* 4, no. 2 (1987): 159–77.
Ḥanafī, Ḥasan. "Al-Juẓūr al-Taʾrīkhīya li ʿazmat al-ḥurrīya wa al-dīmuqrāṭīya fī wijdānninā al-muʿāṣir." In *Al-dīmuqrāṭīya wa ḥuqūq al-insān fī al-waṭan al-ʿarabī*, 170–88. Cairo: Dār al-Mustaqbal al-ʿArabī / Markaz al-Waḥda al-ʿArabīya, 1984.
Hanley, Thomas. "St. Thomas' Use of Al-Ghazali's Maqasid al-Falasifa." *Medieval Studies* 44 (1982): 243–70.
Al-Ḥaqq, Jalāl. "Al-Ghazālī on Causality, Induction, and Miracles." *Al-tawḥid* 3, no. 3 (Rajab–Ramaḍān 1406/1986): 55–62.
Al-Ḥasanī, ʿAbd al-Ḥayy b. Fakhr al-Dīn. *Nuzhat al-khawāṭir*. 8 vols. Rae Bareli, India: Dār ʿIrfān, 1413/1933.
Hazo, Samuel. *The Blood of Adonis*. Pittsburgh: University of Pittsburgh Press, 1971.
Hegel, G. W. "Who Thinks Abstractly." In *Hegel: Reinterpretation, Texts and Commentary*, edited by Walter Kaufmann, 113–18. New York: Doubleday, 1965.
Hermansen, Marcia K. "Interdisciplinary Approaches to Islamic Biographical Materials." *Religion* 18 (1988): 163–82.
Hillenbrand, Carole. *The Crusades: Islamic Perspectives*. Edinburgh: Edinburgh University Press, 1999.
Al-Hirawī, Abū ʿUbayd Aḥmad b. Muḥammad b. Muḥammad. *Kitāb al-gharībayn*. Edited by M. A. Aḥmad. 6 vols. Hyderabad: Maṭbaʿa Majlis Dāʾirat al-Maʿārif al-ʿUthmānīya, 1408/1988.
Hitti, Philip K. *Capital Cities of Arab Islam*. Minneapolis: University of Minnesota Press, 1973.
Hodgson, Marshall G. S. *The Order of Assassins: The Struggle of the Early Nizārī Ismāʿīlīs against the Islamic World*. The Hague: Mouton, 1955.
———. *The Venture of Islam: Conscience and History in a World Civilization; The Classical Age of Islam*. 3 vols. Chicago: University of Chicago Press, 1977.
Hogga, Mustapha. *Orthodoxie, subversion et réforme en Islam*. Paris: Libraire Philosophique J. Vrin, 1993.
Hourani, George F. "A Revised Chronology of Ghazālī's Writings." *Journal of the American Oriental Society* 104 (1984): 289–302.

Houtsma, M. Th. "The Death of Niẓām al-Mulk and Its Consequences." *Journal of Indian History* 3, no. 8 (September 1924): 147–60.

Hughes, Aaron. "Imagining the Divine: Ghazali on Imagination, Dreams, and Dreaming." *Journal of the American Academy of Religion* 70, no. 1 (March 2002): 33–53.

Al-Ḥusaynī, Ṣadr al-Dīn Abu al-Ḥasan ʿAlī b. Nāṣ. *Zubdat al-tawārīkh: Akhbār al-umaraʾ wa al-mulūk al-Saljūqīya*. Edited by Muḥammad Nūr al-Dīn. Beirut: Dār Iqraʾ, 1405/1985.

Ibn al-Athīr, ʿIzz al-Dīn. *Al-kāmil fī al-taʾrīkh*. 10 vols. Beirut: Dār Ṣādir, 1386/1966.

Ibn al-ʿImād, ʿAbd al-Hayy ibn Ahmad. *Shadharāt al-dhahab fī akhbār man dhahab*. Edited by ʿAbd al-Qādir Arnaʾūṭ and Maḥmūd Arnaʾūṭ. Beirut: Dār Ibn Kathīr, 1986.

Ibn al-Jawzī, ʿAbū al-Faraj ʿAbd al-Raḥmān b. ʿAlī. *Al-muntaẓam fī tawārīkh al-mulūk wa al-umam*. Edited by Suhayl Zukkār. 10 vols. Beirut: Dār al-Fikr, 1415/1995.

———. *Naqd al-ʿilm wa-al-ʿulamāʾ aw talbīs iblīs*. Edited by Muḥammad Munīr al-Dimashqī. Cairo: Idāra al-Ṭibāʿa al-Munīrīya, 1966.

Ibn al-Shajarī, Hibat Allāh b. ʿAlī b. Muḥammad b. ʿAlī al-Ḥusaynī. *Mā ittafaqa lafẓuhu wa ikhtalafa maʿnāh*. Edited by ʿAṭīya Rizq. Stuttgart: Frantz Steiner, 1992.

Ibn al-Zayyāt, Yūsuf b. Yaḥyā. *Al-tashawwuf ilā al-rijāl al-taṣawwuf*. Edited by Aḥmad al-Tawfīq. Rabat: Kulliya al-Ādāb, 1984.

Ibn ʿAsākir, ʿAlī b. al-Ḥasan. *Tabyīn kadhib al-muftarī*. Damascus: Maṭbaʿa al-Tawfīq, 1928.

Ibn Ḥazm, ʿAlī b. Aḥmad. *Al-fiṣal fī al-milal wa-al-niḥal*. 3 vols. Cairo: Dār al-Kutub al-ʿIlmīya, 1996.

———. *Ṭawq al-ḥamāma fī al-ulfa wa al-ullāf*. Edited by Iḥsān ʿAbbās. Beirut: Muʾassasa al-ʿArabīya li al-Dirāsāt wa al-Nashr, 1993.

Ibn Jamāʿah al-Kinānī, Badr al-Dīn b. Abī Isḥāq Ibrāhīm. *The Memoir of the Listener and the Speaker in the Training of Teacher and Student*. Translated by Noor Muhammad Ghifari. Islamabad: Pakistan Hijra Council, 1412/1992.

———. *Tadhkirat al-sāmiʿ wa-al-mutakallim fī adab al-ʿālim wa-al-mutaʿallim*. Edited by al-Sayyid Muḥammad Hāshim al-Nadawī. Amman: Dār al-Maʿālī, 1419/1998.

Ibn Kathīr. *Al-bidāya wa al-nihāya*. Edited by Aḥmad Abū Hakīm, ʿAlī Najīb ʿAṭwī, Fuʾād al-Sayyid, Mahdī Nāṣir al-Dīn, and ʿAli ʿAbd al-Sattār. 15 vols. Beirut: Dār al-Kutub al-ʿIlmīya, 1404/1985.

Ibn Khaldūn, ʿAbd al-Raḥmān b. Muḥammad. *Muqaddima*. Edited by Darwīsh Juwaydī. Sayda, Leb.: al-Maktaba al-Aṣrīya, 1420/2000.

———. *Shifāʾ al-sāʾil wa tahdhīb al-masāʾil*. Edited by Muḥammad Muṭīʿ al-Ḥāfiẓ. Beirut: Dār al-Fikr, 1996.

———. *Tarīkh Ibn Khaldūn: Al-musammā bi-kitāb al-ʿibar wa dīwān al-mubtadāʾ wa-al-khabar fī ayyām al-ʿarab wa-al-ʿajam wa al-barbar wa man ʿāṣarahum min dhawī al-sulṭan al-akbar*. 7 vols. 1867. Beirut: Muʾassasat al-ʿĀlamī li al-Maṭbūʿāt, 1971.

Ibn Khallikān, Abū al-ʿAbbās Shams al-Dīn Aḥmad b. Muḥammad b. Abī Bakr. *Wafayāt al-aʿyān wa anbāʾ abnāʾ al-zamān*. Edited by Iḥsān ʿAbbās. Beirut: Dār Ṣādir, n.d.

Ibn Manẓūr, Jamāl al-Dīn Muḥammad Ibn Mukarram. *Lisān al-ʿarab*. Edited by ʿAbd Allāh ʿAlī al-Kabīr. 6 vols. Cairo: Dār al-Maʿārif, n.d.

Ibn Mounkidh, Ousāma. *The Autobiography of Ousama*. Translated by George Richard Potter. New York: Harcourt, Brace, 1929.

Ibn Munqidh, Usāma. *Kitāb al-iʿtibār*. Cairo: Maktaba al-Thaqāfa al-Dīnīya, 2001.

Ibn Qāḍī Shuhba, Abū Bakr b. Aḥmad b. Muḥammad b. ʿUmar b. Muḥammad Taqī al-Dīn. *Ṭabaqāt al-shāfiʿīya*. Edited by ʿAbd al-ʿAlīm Khān. 4 vols. Hyderabad: Maṭbaʿa Majlis Dāʾirat al-Maʿārif al-ʿUthmānīya, 1398/1978.

Ibn Qayyim al-Jawzīya. *Aḥkām ahl al-dhimma*. Edited by Ṭāhā ʿAbd al-Raʾūf Saʿd. 2 vols. Beirut: Dār al-Kutub al-ʿIlmīya, 1423/2002.

———. *Iʿlām al-muwaqqiʿīn ʿan rabb al-ʿālamīn*. Edited by Ṭāhā ʿAbd al-Raʾūf Saʿd. 3 vols. Beirut: Dār al-Jīl, n.d.

Ibn Rushd, Abū al-Walīd. *Al-ḍarūrī fī uṣūl al-fiqh aw mukhtaṣar al-Mustaṣfā*. Edited by Jamāl al-Dīn al-Alawī. Beirut: Dār al-Gharb al-Islāmī, 1994.

———. *Faṣl al-maqāl fī taqrīr mā bayna al-sharīʿa wa al-ḥikma min al-ittiṣāl aw wujūb al-naẓar al-ʿaqalī wa ḥudūd al-wa, wīl al-dīn wa al-mujtamaʿ*. Edited by Muḥammad ʿĀbid al-Jābirī. 3rd ed. Beirut: Markaz Dirāsāt al-Waḥda al-ʿArabīya, 2002.

———. *Tahāfut al-tahāfut*. Introduction and commentary by Muḥammad ʿĀbid al-Jābirī. Beirut: Markaz Dirāsāt al-Waḥda al-ʿArabīya, 2001.

Ibn Sīrīn al-Baṣrī, Muḥammad. *Tafsīr al-aḥlām al-kabīr*. Beirut: Dār al-Kutub al-ʿIlmīya, 1424/2002.

Ibn Taymīya, Taqī al-Dīn. *Darʾ taʿāruḍ al-ʿaql wa al-naql*. Edited by ʿAbd al-Laṭīf ʿAbd al-Raḥmān. 5 vols. Beirut: Dār al-Kutub al-ʿIlmīya, 1417/1997.

———. *Al-īmān*. Beirut: al-Maktab al-Islāmī, 1399/1978.

———. *Majmūʿ fatāwā*. 20 vols. Riyadh: Dār al-wafāʾ, 1998.

Ibn Ṭufayl. *"Ḥayy Ibn Yaqẓān" fī: "Ḥayy bin Yaqẓān" lī Ibn Sīnā wa Ibn Tufayl wa al-Suhrawardī*. Edited by Aḥmad Amīn. Cairo: Dār al-Maʿarif, 1959.

Ibn Ṭumlūs, Abū al-Ḥajjāj b. Muḥammad. *Kitāb al-madkhal li ṣināʿa al-manṭiq*. Madrid: Al-Maṭbaʿa al-Ibīrqa, 1916.

Iqbal, Muhammad. *The Reconstruction of Religious Thought in Islam*. Lahore: Shaikh Muhammad Ashraf, 1960.

Irwin, Robert. "The Emergence of the Islamic World System, 1000–1500." In *The Cambridge Illustrated History of the Islamic World*, edited by Francis Robinson, 32–61. Cambridge: Cambridge University Press, 1996.

Al-Isnawī, Abd al-Raḥīm b. al-Ḥasan. *Ṭabaqāt al-Shāfiʿīya*. Edited by Kamāl Yūsuf Ḥūt. 2 vols. Beirut: Dār al-Kutub al-ʿIlmīya, 1987.

Al-Jābirī, Muḥammad ʿĀbid. "Al-ṣirāʿ al-madhhabī, wa laysa al-dīn warāʾ 'Tahāfut al-falāsifa' li al-Ghazālī." Introduction to Ibn Rushd, *Tahāfut al-falāsifa*. 2nd ed. Beirut: Markaz Dirāsāt al-Waḥda al-ʿArabīya, 2001.

———. *Takwīn al-ʿaql al-ʿarabī*. Beirut: Markaz Dirāsāt al-Waḥda al-ʿArabīya, 2002.

———. *Al-turāth wa al-ḥadātha: Dirāsāt wa munāqashāt*. Beirut: Markaz al-Dirāsāt al-Waḥda al-ʿArabiyya, 1991.

Jabre, Farid. *Essai sur le lexique de Ghazali*. Beirut: Publications de L'Universite Libanaise, 1985.

———. *La notion de certitude selon Ghazali: Dan ses origines psychologiques et historiques*. Paris: Librairie Philosophique J. Vrin, 1958.

Jackson, Sherman A. *On the Boundaries of Theological Tolerance in Islam: Abū Ḥāmid*

al-Ghazālī's "Faysal al-tafriqa bayna al-Islam wa al-zandaqa." Karachi: Oxford University Press, 2002.
Jager, Eric. "The Book of the Heart: Reading and Writing the Medieval Subject." *Speculum* 71, no. 1 (January 1996): 1–26.
Al-Jāḥiz. *See* al-Baṣrī.
Jalabi [Chelebi] Kātib, [Hājī Khalīfa]. *Kashf al-ẓunūn ʿan asāmī al-kutub wa al-funūn*. 6 vols. Edited by Muḥammad Sharaf al-Dīn Yaltaqāyā. Istanbul: Wakālat al-Maʿārif al-Jalīla, 1360/1941.
James, William. *The Varieties of Religious Experience*. New York: Triumph Books, 1991.
Jameson, Fredric. *A Singular Modernity: An Essay on the Ontology of the Present*. New York: Verso, 2002.
Jawād, Muṣṭafā. "ʿAṣr al-Imām al-Ghazālī." *Al-turāth al-ʿarabī* 22 (1986): 109–19.
Jay, Aḥmad Muḥammad. "Al-Ghazālī wa atharuhu fī al-taṣawwuf." *Al-Islām al-yawm* 4 (Rajab 1406/April 1986): 47–52.
———. "The Impact of al-Ghazzali's Work on Sufism." *Islam Today / L'Islam Aujourd'hui* 4 (Rajab 1406/April 1986): 35–43.
Johansen, Baber. *Contingency in a Sacred Law: Legal and Ethical Norms in the Muslim Fiqh*. Leiden: E. J. Brill, 1999.
Johnson, Mark. *Moral Imagination: Implications of Cognitive Science for Ethics*. Chicago: University of Chicago Press, 1993.
Johnston, Mark D. *The Spiritual Logic of Ramon Lull*. Oxford: Clarendon Press, 1987.
Al-Jurjānī, ʿAbd al-Qāhir. *Kitāb asrār al-balāgha*. Edited by H. Ritter. Beirut: Dār al-Masīra, 1403/1983.
Kafesoglu, İbrahim. *A History of the Seljuks: İbrahim Kafesoğlu's Interpretation and the Resulting Controversy*. Edited and translated by Gary Leiser. Carbondale: Southern Illinois University Press, 1988.
Kant, Immanuel. *Groundwork of the Metaphysic of Morals*. Translated by H. J. Paton. New York: Harper, 1964.
Al-Kāshānī, Muḥammad al-Murtaḍā al-Muḥsin. *Al-maḥajja al-bayḍāʾ fī tahdhīb Al-iḥyāʾ*. Edited by ʿAlī Akbar al-Ghaffārī. 8 vols. Qom: Daftar Intishārāt Islāmī, ca. 1383/1963.
Al-Kashmīrī, Muḥammad Anwar al-Diyawbandī. *Fayḍ al-bārī ʿalā Ṣaḥīḥ al-Bukhārī*. 4 vols. Peshawar: Maktaba Ḥaqqānīya, n.d.
Kassim, Husain. "Existentialist Tendencies in Ghazali and Kierkegaard." *Islamic Studies* 10 (1971): 103–28.
Kearney, Richard. *The Wake of Imagination: Toward a Postmodern Culture*. Minneapolis: University of Minnesota Press, 1988.
Kemal, Salim. *The Philosophical Poetics of Alfarabi, Avicenna and Averroes*. London: Routledge Curzon, 2003.
Kermode, Frank. *Pieces of My Mind*. New York: Farrar, Straus and Giroux, 2003.
Al-Khāl, Ibrāhīm. "Al-Ghazālī." *Al-aqlām: Majalla fikriyya ʿāmma* 1, no. 10 (Ṣafar 1385 / Ḥazīrān 1965): 60–84.
Khalidi, Tarif. *Arabic Historical Thought in the Classical Period*. Cambridge: Cambridge University Press, 1994.

Khuri, Richard K. *Freedom, Modernity, and Islam: Toward a Creative Synthesis*. Albany: Syracuse University Press, 1998.

Khusraw, Naṣir-i. *Naser-e Khosraw's Book of Travels—Safarnāma*. Albany, N.Y.: Bibliotheca Persica, 1986.

Kierkegaard, Søren. *Fear and Trembling*. Translated by Walter Lowrie. Princeton: Princeton University Press, 1968.

Kīlīṭu, ʿAbd al-Fattāḥ (Abdelfattah Kilito). *Al-ḥikāya wa-al-taʾwīl*. Casablanca: Dār Tūbqāl li al-Nashr, 1988.

Kinberg, Leah. "The Legitimation of the Madhāhib through Dreams." *Arabica* 32 (1985): 47–79.

King, Richard. *Orientalism and Religion*. London: Routledge, 1999.

Kisāʾī, Nūr Allāh. *Madāris-i niẓāmīya wa taʾthīrāt ʿilmī va ijtimāʿī-ian*. Tehran: Muʾassasa Intishārāt Amīr Kabīr, 1363/1984.

Koselleck, Reinhart. *Critique and Crisis: Enlightenment and the Pathogenesis of Modern Society*. Cambridge, Mass.: MIT Press, 1988.

Kris, Ernst. *Psychoanalytic Explorations in Art*. New York: International Universities Press, 1952.

LaCapra, Dominick. *Rethinking Intellectual History: Texts, Contexts, Language*. Ithaca: Cornell University Press, 1983.

Lakoff, George, and Mark Johnson. *Metaphors We Live By*. Chicago: University of Chicago Press, 1980.

Lambton, Anne K. "Aspects of Saljūq-Ghuzz Settlement." *Islamic Civilization*, edited by D. S. Richards, 105–25. Oxford: Bruno Cassirer, 1973.

Landau-Tasseron, Ella. "The 'Cyclical Reform': A Study of the Mujaddid Tradition." *Studia Islamica* 70 (1989): 77–117.

Lane, E. W. *Arabic-English Lexicon*. 2 vols. London: Williams and Norgate, 1863.

Laoust, Henri. "Les agitations religieuses a Baghdad aux IVe et Ve siecles de l'hegire." In *Islamic Civilization*, edited by D. S. Richards, 169–85. Oxford: Bruno Cassirer, 1973.

———. *La politique de Gazali*. Paris: Librairie Orientaliste Paul Geuthner, 1970.

Lapidus, Ira. "Knowledge, Virtue, and Action: The Classical Muslim Conception of Adab and the Nature of Religious Fulfillment in Islam." In *Moral Conduct and Authority: The Place of Adab in South Asian Islam*, edited by Barbara D. Metcalf, 38–61. Berkeley: University of California Press, 1984.

Lawrence, Bruce B. *Defenders of God*. San Francisco: Harper and Row, 1989.

Lazarus-Yafeh, Hava. *Studies in al-Ghazzali*. Jerusalem: Magnes Press, 1970.

Le Goff, Jacques. "Head or Heart? The Political Use of Body Metaphors in the Middle Ages." In *Fragments for a History of the Human Body*, part 3, edited by Michel Feher, 13–26. New York: Zone, 1989.

Le Strange, Guy. *Baghdad during the Abbasid Caliphate*. 1900. London: Oxford University Press, 1924.

Levinas, Emmanuel. *Entre Nous: On Thinking-of-the-Other*. Translated by Michael B. Smith and Barbara Harshav. New York: Columbia University Press, 1998.

Lévi-Strauss, Claude. *The Savage Mind*. Chicago: University of Chicago Press, 1966.

Lewis, Bernard. *The Origins of Ismaʿīlism: A Study of the Historical Background of the Fāṭimid Caliphate*. Cambridge: W. Heffer, 1940.

Lohr, Charles. "The Arabic Background to Ramon Lull's *Liber Chaos* (ca. 1285)." *Tradition* 5 (2000): 159–70.

———. "'Art' and Possibility: The Rule Concerning Possibility in *Ars lulliana*." In *Potentialität und Possibilität: Modalaussagen in der Geschichte der Metaphysik*, edited by Thomas Bucheim, Corneille Henri Kneepkens, and Kuno Lorenz, 165–73. Stuttgart: Frommann-Holzboog, 2001.

Macdonald, Duncan B. "The Life of al-Ghazzālī, with Special Reference to His Religious Experiences and Opinions." *Journal of the American Oriental Society* 20 (1899): 71–132.

———. *The Religious Attitude and Life in Islam*. 1909. Beirut: Khayats, 1965.

MacIntyre, Alisdair. *After Virtue: A Study in Moral Theory*. Notre Dame: University of Notre Dame Press, 1984.

Al-Mahaṭwarī, al-Murtaḍā bin Zayd. *ʿAdāla al-ruwāt wa al-shuhūd wa taṭbīqātuhā fi al-ḥayāt al-muʿāṣira*. Sana, Yemen: Maktaba Badar, 1417/1997.

Maḥmaṣānī, Ṣubḥī. *Falsafa al-tashrīʿ fī al-Islām*. 5th ed. Beirut: Dār al-ʿIlm, 1980.

Maḥmūd, ʿAbd al-Ḥalīm. "Taqdīm." In *Qawāʿid al-ʿaqāʾid*, by Abū Ḥāmid al-Ghazālī, edited by Raʾūf Shalabī and Mūsā Muḥammad ʿAlī, 1–21. Cairo: Majmaʿ al-Buhūth al-Islāmīya, 1390/1970.

Maḥmūd, Fawqīya Ḥusayn. *Al-Juwaynī: Imām al-ḥaramayn*. 2nd ed. Cairo: Al-Hayʾa al-Miṣrīya al-ʿĀmmā li al-Taʾlīf wa al-Nashr, 1970.

Makdisi, George. *Ibn ʿAqil: Religion and Culture in Classical Islam*. Edinburgh: Edinburgh University Press, 1997.

———. *Rise of Colleges: Institutions of Learning in Islam and the West*. Edinburgh: Edinburgh University Press, 1981.

———. "The Sunni Revival in Islamic Civilization." In *Islamic Civilization*, edited by D. S. Richards, 155–69. Oxford: Bruno Cassirer, 1973.

Martin, Richard C., Mark R. Woodward, and Dwi S. Atmaja. *Defenders of Reason in Islam: Muʿtazilism from Medieval School to Modern Symbol*. Oxford: Oneworld, 1997.

Massignon, Louis. *The Passion of al-Hallāj: Mystic and Martyr of Islam*. Translated by Herbert Mason. 4 vols. Princeton: Princeton University Press, 1982.

Mayer, Tobias. "Al-Ghazâlī and the Ashʿarite School." *Journal of Qurʿanic Studies* 1, no. 1 (2001): 170–82.

Meier, Fritz. "Some Aspects of Inspiration by Demons in Islam." In *The Dream and Human Societies*, edited by Gustave E. von Grunebaum and Roger Caillois, 421–29. Berkeley: University of California Press, 1966.

Meisami, Julie Scott. *Persian Historiography*. Edinburgh: Edinburgh University Press, 1999.

Melchert, Christopher. *The Formation of the Sunni Schools of Law, 9th–10th Centuries CE*. Leiden: E. J. Brill, 1997.

Mez, Adam. *The Renaissance of Islam*. Translated by Salahuddin Khuda Baksh and D. S. Margoliouth. London: Luzac, 1937.

Mignolo, Walter D. *The Darker Side of the Renaissance: Literacy, Territoriality and Colonization.* Ann Arbor: University of Michigan Press, 2001.

———. *Local Histories / Global Designs: Coloniality, Subaltern Knowledges and Border Thinking.* Princeton: Princeton University Press, 2000.

Millbank, John. "Against the Resignations of the Age." In *Things Old and New: Catholic Social Teaching Revisited*, edited by F. P. McHugh and S. M. Natale, 1–39. New York: University Press of America, 1993.

Mitha, Farouk. *Al-Ghazālī and the Ismāʿīlīs: A Debate on Reason and Authority in Medieval Islam.* London: I. B. Tauris, 2001.

Moosa, Ebrahim. "Allegory of the Rule (*Ḥukm*): Law as Simulacrum in Islam." *History of Religions* 38, no. 1 (August 1998): 1–24.

Morrison, Toni. *Playing in the Dark: Whiteness and the Literary Imagination.* New York: Vintage, 1992.

Mubārak, Zakī. *Al-akhlāq ʿinda al-Ghazālī.* Beirut: Dār al-Jīl, 1408/1988.

———. *Nathr al-fannī.* Cairo: Al-Maktaba al-Tijārīya al-Kubrā, 1957.

Al-Muḥāsibī, Ḥārith b. Asad. *Kitāb al-waṣāyā.* Edited by ʿAbd al-Qadir Aḥmad ʿAṭā. Beirut: Dār al-Kutub al-ʿIlmīya, 1406/1986.

Nadwi, Abul Hasan Ali. "Khuṭbā-e ṣadārat." In *Jadīd Fiqhī Mabāḥith*, edited by Mawlānā Mujāhidul Islām Qāsimī, 1:48–65. Karachi: Idārat al-Qur'ān wa al-ʿUlūm al-Islāmīya, n.d.

———. *Saviours of Islamic Spirit.* Translated by Mohiuddin Ahmad. Lucknow: Academy of Islamic Research and Publications, 1976.

Nadwī, Muḥammad Ḥanīf. *Taʿlīmāt-e Ghazālī.* Lahore: Idāra-e Thaqāfat-e Islāmīya, 1962.

Nakamura, Kojiro. "A Bibliography on Imām al-Ghazzālī." *Orient* 13 (1977): 119–34.

Naṣr, Muḥammad ʿAbd al-ʿAzīz. "Falsafa al-siyāsīya ʿinda al-Ghazālī." In *Abū Ḥāmid al-Ghazālī fī al-Dhikrā al-Miʾawīya al-Tāsiʿa li Mīlādihi*, edited by Zakī Najīb Maḥmūd. Damascus: Al-Majlis al-Aʿlā li Riʿāya al-Funūn wa al-Ādāb wa al-ʿUlūm al-Ijtimāʿīya, 1961.

Nasr, Seyyed Hossein. *Knowledge and the Sacred.* Edinburgh: Edinburgh University Press, 1981.

Al-Nayfar, Muḥammad al-Shādhilī. "Al-Māzarī." Introduction to Muḥammad b. ʿAlī b. ʿUmar al-Māzarī in vol. 1 of *Al-muʿallim bi fawāʾid Muslim*, edited by Muḥammad al-Shādhilī al-Nayfar. 3 vols. 2nd ed. Beirut: Dār al-Gharb al-Islāmī, 1992.

Nicholson, Reynold A. *Studies in Islamic Poetry, with Arabic Selections from the Luzūmiyyāt.* 1921. Reprint, Cambridge: Cambridge University Press, 1969.

Nietzsche, Friedrich. *Human All Too Human.* Translated by R. Hollingdale. Cambridge: Cambridge University Press, 1986.

———. *On the Genealogy of Morals.* Edited and translated by Walter Kaufmann. New York: Vintage, 1989.

Al-Nīsābūrī, Abū al-Ḥasan Muslim b. al-Ḥajjāj al-Qushayrī. *Ṣaḥīḥ Muslim bi sharḥ al-Nawawī.* Edited by ʿIṣām al-Ṣabābiṭī, Ḥāzim Muḥammad, and ʿImād ʿĀmir. 9 vols. Cairo: Dār Abī Ḥayyān, 1415/1995.

Al-Nīsābūrī, al-Ḥākim Mḥammad b. ʿAbd Allāh. *Al-mustadrak ʿalā ṣaḥīḥayn al-ḥadīth.* 4 vols. Riyadh: Maktaba wa al-Maṭābiʿ al-Naṣr al-Ḥadītha, 1968.

Nuʿmānī, Shiblī. *Al-Ghazzālī.* Delhi: Rangīn Press, 1923.

———. *ʿIlm al-kalām awr kalām.* 3rd ed. Karachi: Nafīs Akademi, 1979.

Obermann, Julian. *Der philosophische und religiöse Subjektivismus Ghazalis: Ein Beitrag zum Problem der Religion.* Vienna: W. Braumüller, 1921.

Obeyesekere, Ganath. *The Work of Culture.* Chicago: University of Chicago Press, 1990.

Ormsby, Eric L. "Creation in Time in Islamic Thought, with Special Reference to Al-Ghazālī." In *God and Creation: An Ecumenical Symposium*, edited by David B. Burrell and Bernard McGinn, 246–64. Notre Dame: University of Notre Dame Press, 1990.

———. "The Taste of Truth: The Structure of Experience in Al-Ghazālī's al-Munqidh min al-Ḍalāl." In *Islamic Studies Presented to Charles J. Adams*, edited by Wael B. Hallaq and Donald P. Little, 133–52. Leiden: E. J. Brill, 1991.

———. *Theodicy in Islamic Thought: The Dispute over al-Ghazālī's "Best of all Possible Worlds."* Princeton: Princeton University Press, 1984.

Ozick, Cynthia. "The Fourth Sparrow: The Magisterial Reach of Gershom Scholem." In *What Henry James Knew and Other Essays*, 288–304. London: Jonathan Cape, 1993.

Plato. *Phaedrus.* Translated by Alexander Nehemas and Paul Woodruff. Indianapolis: Hacket, 1995.

———. *Phaedrus and the Seventh and Eighth Letters.* Translated by Walter Hamilton. New York: Penguin, 1973.

Pourjawadi, Nasrullah. "Aḥmad et Muḥammad al-Ghazālī: Influence réciproque." In *Ghazālī: La raison et le miracle*, edited by A. M. Turki, 163–68. Paris: Editions Maisonneuve et Larose, 1987.

———. "ʿAqīda-e Abū Ḥamid al-Ghazālī va kāye-gāh-e tārīkhi-ān." *Maʿārif* 7, no. 2 (November 1990): 3–28.

———. *Du mujaddid: Pizhuhishhāyī dar bārah-i Muḥammad Ghazzālī va Fakhr Rāzī.* Tehran: Markaz-i Nashr-i Danishgāhī, 2002.

———. "Zabān-e ḥāl dar adabiyāt-e fārisī." *Nashr-e dānish* 17, no. 2 (Summer 2000): 25–42.

———, ed. *Majmūʿah-ye falsafī-e Marāgha* (*A Philosophical Anthology from Marāghah*). Tehran: Iran University Press, 2002.

Al-Qaradāghī, ʿAli Muḥī al-Dīn. "Aṣr al-Ghazālī." Introduction to *Al-wasīt fī al-madhhab*, by Abū Ḥāmid al-Ghazālī, 21–293. Cairo: Dar al-Ansār, 1983.

Al-Qaraḍāwī, Yūsuf. *Al-Imām al-Ghazālī: Bayna mādiḥīhi wa nāqidīh.* El Mansûra: Dār al-Wafāʾ, 1988.

Al-Qarṭājannī, Abū ʿUbayd Allāh b. Ḥāzim. *Kitāb al-manāhij al-adabīya.* In *Ḥāzim al-Qarṭājannī: Wa naẓariyāt arisṭū fī al-shiʿr wa al-balāgha*, edited by ʿAbd al-Rahmān Badawī, 7–62. Cairo: n.p., 1961.

Rāghib al-Iṣfahānī, Abū al Qāsim Ḥusayn b. Muḥammad. *Al-dharīʿa ilā makārim al-sharīʿa.* Edited by Saʿad Ṭāhā ʿAbd al-Raʿūf. Cairo: Maktabat al-Kullīya al-Azharīya, 1973.

Rahman, Fazlur. "Law and Ethics in Islam." In *Ethics in Islam*, edited by Richard G. Hovannisian, 3–15. Malibu: Undena Publications, 1985.

Al-Rāzī, Fakhr al-Dīn. *Al-tafsīr al-kabīr aw mafātīh al-ghayb*. 2nd ed. 16 vols. Beirut: Dār al-Fikr, 1983.

Al-Rāzī, Muḥammad b. Abī Bakr b. ʿAbd al-Qādir. *Mukhtār al-ṣiḥāḥ*. Edited by Maḥmūd Khāṭir Bikk. Cairo: Maṭbaʿa al-Amīrīya bi-Bulāq, 1355/1937.

Reinhart, A. Kevin. *Before Revelation: The Boundaries of Muslim Moral Thought*. Albany: State University of New York Press, 1995.

Reynolds, Dwight F., ed. *Interpreting the Self: Autobiography in the Arabic Literary Tradition*. Berkeley: University of California Press, 2001.

Rice, Tamara Talbot. *The Seljuks in Asia Minor*. New York: Praeger, 1961.

Ricoeur, Paul. "Life in Quest of Narrative." In *On Paul Ricoeur: Narrative and Interpretation*, edited by David Wood, 20–33. London: Routledge, 1991.

Riffaterre, Michael. "Prosopopeia." *Yale French Studies* 69 (1985): 107–23.

Rosenthal, Franz. "Die arabische Autobiographie." 1937. Reprinted in *Muslim Intellectual and Social History: A Collection of Essays*, 3–40. London: Variorum, 1990.

———. "'I Am You'—Individual Piety and Society in Islam." In *Individuality and Conformity in Classical Islam*, edited by Amin Banani and Speros Vryonis Jr., 33–60. Wiesbaden: Otto Harrassowitz, 1977.

———. "State and Religion according to Abū al-Ḥasan al-ʿĀmirī." In *Muslim Intellectuals and Social History: A Collection of Essays*, 42–52. London: Variorum, 1990.

———. *The Technique and Approach of Muslim Scholarship*. Rome: Pontificum Institutum Biblicum, 1947.

Rumi, Jalaluddin. *Signs of the Unseen: The Discourses of Jalaluddin Rumi*. Translated by Wheeler M. Thackston. Boston: Shambhala, 1999.

Sabzavāri, Mulla Hādī. *"Sharḥ al-manẓūma," with Commentary by Āyāt Allāh Ḥasan Zādeh al-Āmulī*. Edited by Masʿūd Ṭālibī. 5 vols. Tehran: Kutub Khāna Millī, 1380/1960.

Safi, Omid. "Power and the Politics of Knowledge: Negotiating Political Ideology and Religious Orthodoxy in Saljūq Iran." Ph.D. diss., Duke University, 2000.

Al-Ṣaḥrāwī, ʿAbd al-Qādir. "Jawānib min shakhṣīya Yūsuf b. Tāshfīn." *Daʿwat al-ḥaqq* 2, no. 10 (Muḥarram 1379/July 1959): 48–58.

Said, Edward W. *Beginnings: Intention and Method*. New York: Columbia University Press, 1985.

———. "Identity, Authority and Freedom: The Potentate and the Traveller." Thirty-first T. B. Davie Memorial Lecture. Cape Town: University of Cape Town, 1991.

———. *Orientalism*. London: Routledge and Kegan Paul, 1978.

———. "Orientalism Reconsidered." *Cultural Critique* (Fall 2005): 89–105.

———. *The World, the Text and the Critic*. London: Vintage, 1991.

Sālim, Muḥammad Rashād. *Muqārana bayna al-Ghazālī wa Ibn Taymīya*. Kuwait: Dār al-Qalam, 1975.

Schmitt, Carl. *Political Theology*. Cambridge, Mass.: MIT Press, 1985.

Al-Shahrazūrī, Ibn al-Ṣalāh Abū ʿUmar ʿUthmān b. ʿAbd al-Raḥmān. *Muqaddima Ibn al-Ṣalāḥ*. Edited by Nūr al-Dīn ʿItr. Damascus: Dār al-Fikr, 1406/1986.

Shāh Walī Allāh, Aḥmad ibn ʿAbd al-Raḥīm. *Ḥujja Allāh al-Bāligha*. Edited by Muḥammad Aḥsan al-Nānotwī, al-Sayyid Sābiq, and Muḥammad Sharīf Sukkar. 2 vols. Karachi: Qadīmī Kutub Khāna, n.d.

Shakir, Naeem. "Pakistan: The Blasphemy Law in Pakistan and Its Impact." *Human Rights Solidarity* 9, no. 8 (August 1999), <http://www.ahrchk.net/hrsolid/mainfile.php/1999vol09no08/1230/>.
Shalaby, Aḥmad. *History of Muslim Education*. Beirut: Dār al-Kashshaf, 1954.
Shams al-Dīn, Aḥmad. "Muqaddima." In vol. 7 of *Mujmūʿa rasāʾil al-Imām al-Ghazālī*, edited by Aḥmad Shams al-Dīn, 3–22. Beirut: Dār al-Kutub al-ʿIlmīya, 1409/1988.
Al-Sharastānī, Abū al-Fatḥ ʿAbd al-Karīm. *Al-Milal wa al-niḥal*. Edited by ʿAbd al-Azīz Muḥammad al-Wakīl. 3 vols. Cairo: Muʾassasa al-Ḥalabī, n.d.
Al-Shāṭibī, Abū Isḥāq. *Al-muwāfaqāt*. Edited by Abd Allāh Darāz. 4 vols. Beirut: Dār al-Maʿrifa, n.d.
Shaw, Daniel G. "City of Garden: St. Augustine and al-Ghazālī on the Final Estate of the Blessed." Ph.D. diss., Northwestern University, 1987.
Shehadi, Fadlou. *Ghazali's Unique Unknowable God*. Leiden: E. J. Brill, 1964.
Sherif, Mohamed Ahmed. *Ghazali's Theory of Virtue*. Albany: State University of New York Press, 1975.
Sibṭ ibn al-Jawzī, Yūsuf Ibn Qizughlī. *Mirʾāt al-zamān*. 2 vols. Hyderabad: Maṭbaʿa Dāʾirat al-Maʿārif al-ʿUthmānīya, 1951–52.
Al-Sijistānī, Abū Dāwūd Sulaymān al-Ashʿath al-Azdī. Vol. 3 of *Sunan Abī Dāwūd*, edited by Muḥammad Muḥī al-Dīn ʿAbd al-Ḥamīd. Cairo: Maṭbaʿa Muṣṭafā Muḥammad, n.d.
Smith, Margaret. *An Early Mystic of Baghdad*. 1935. London: Sheldon Press, 1973.
Soroush, Abdolkarim. *Reason, Freedom and Democracy in Islam*. Edited and translated by Mahmoud Sadri and Ahmad Sadri. New York: Oxford University Press, 2000.
Spivak, Gayatri Chakravorty. "A Note on the New International." *Parallax* 7, no. 3 (2001): 12–16.
Al-Subkī, Tāj al-Dīn. *Muʿīd al-niʿam wa mubīd al-niqam*. Edited by M. A. Najjār. Cairo: Maktaba al-Kangī, 1948.
———. *Ṭabaqāt al-shāfiʿīya al-kubrā*. 10 vols. Cairo: Dār Iḥyāʾ Kutub al-ʿArabīya / ʿĪsā Bābī al-Ḥalabī, 1396/1976.
Al-Ṣughayyir, ʿAbd al-Majīd. "Al-buʿd al-siyāsī fī naqd al-qāḍī Ibn al-ʿArabī li taṣawwuf al-Ghazālī." In *Abū Ḥāmid al-Ghazzālī: Dirāsāt fī fikrihi wa ʿaṣrihi wa taʾthīrihi*, edited by Saʿīd bin Saʿīd al-ʿAlawī, 178–93. Rabat: Manshūrāt kullīya al-ādāb wa al-ʿulūm al-insānīya, 1988.
———. "Ishkālīya istimrār al-dars al-falsafī al-rushdī ḥawl athar al-Ghazālī fī al-madrasa al-rushdīya bi-al-maghrib." *Alif* 16 (1996): 77–88.
Sviri, Sara. "The Self and Its Transformation in Ṣūfīsm." In *Self and Self-Transformation in the History of Religions*, edited by David Shulman and Guy G. Strousma, 195–215. Oxford: Oxford University Press, 2002.
Al-Taftāzānī, Saʿd al-Dīn Masʿūd b. ʿUmar. *Sharḥ al-ʿaqāʾid al-nasafīya fī uṣūl al-dīn wa ʿilm al-kalām*. Edited by Claude Salāma. Damascus: Manshūrāt wazāra al-Thaqāfa wa al-Irshād al-Qawmī, 1974.
Tahānawī, ʿAbd al-Aʿlā. *Kashshāf iṣṭilāḥāt al-funūn*. 2 vols. Beirut: Maktaba Lubnān, 1997.
Tāmir, ʿĀrif. *Al-Ghazālī bayna al-falsafa wa al-dīn*. London: Riad el-Rayyes, 1987.
Ṭāsh Kubrā Zāda, Aḥmad b. Muṣṭafā. *Muwsūʿa muṣṭalaḥat miftaḥ al-saʿāda wa miṣbāḥ*

al-siyāda fī mawḍū'āt al-'ulūm. Edited by Rafīq al-'Ajam and 'Alī Daḥrūj. Beirut: Maktaba Lubnān, 1998.

Al-Tawḥīdī, Abū Ḥayyān 'Alī b. Muḥammad b. al-'Abbās. *Kitāb al-imtā' wa al-mu'ānasa*. Edited by Aḥmad Amīn and Aḥmad al-Zayn. 3 vols. Beirut: Manshūrāt Dār Maktaba al-Ḥayāt, n.d.

———. *Al-muqābasāt*. Beirut: Dār al-Ādāb, 1989.

———. Vol. 3 of *Al-baṣā'ir wa-al-dhakhā'ir*, edited by Wadād al-Qāḍī. Beirut: Dār Ṣādir, 1408/1988.

Tibawi, A. L. "Al-Ghazālī's Sojourn in Damascus and Jerusalem" (part 1); "Al-Risālah al-Qudsiyyah: Edited Arabic Text" (part 2); "The Jerusalem Tract: Annotated English Translation" (part 3). In "Al-Ghazālī's Tract on Dogmatic Theology," edited and translated by A. L. Tibawi, *Islamic Quarterly* 9 (July-December 1965): 65–122.

Turner, Bryan S. *Weber and Islam*. London: Routledge, 1974.

Turner, Victor. *From Ritual to Theatre: The Human Seriousness of Play*. New York: Performing Arts Journal Publications, 1982.

———. "Religious Paradigms and Political Action: The Murder in the Cathedral of Thomas Becket." In *The Biographical Process*, edited by Frank Reynolds and Donald Capps, 153–86. The Hague: Mouton, 1976.

———. *The Ritual Process*. Chicago: Aldine, 1969.

Al-'Ulawī, Hādī. *Shakhṣiyāt ghayr qaliqa fī al-Islām*. Beirut: Dār al-Kunūz al-Adabīya, 1995.

Al-'Uthmānī, Shabbīr Aḥmad al-Dewbandī. *Fatḥ al-mulhim: Sharḥ ṣaḥīḥ Muslim*. 3 vols. Karachi: Maktaba Rashidīya, n.d.

Urvoy, Dominique. *Ibn Rushd*. Translated by Olivia Stewart. London: Routledge, 1991.

Vajda, Georges. "The Zindiqs in the Muslim World during the Early 'Abbasid Period." In *Studies on the History of Sects in Medieval Islam*, edited by Farwaq Omar Fawzi, 85–138. Al-Mafraq: Al al-Bayt University, 2001.

Van den Berg, Simon. "Ghazali on 'Gratitude Towards God' and Its Greek Sources." *Studia Islamica* 7 (1957): 77–98.

Van Ess, Josef. "Quelques remarques sur le Munqid min Aḍ-Ḍalāl." In *Ghazālī: La raison et le miracle*, edited by A. M. Turki, 57–68. Paris: Maisonneuve et Larose, 1987.

Van Gennep, Arnold. *The Rites of Passage*. Translated by Monika B. Vizedom and Gabrielle L. Caffee. 1909. London: Routledge and Kegan Paul, 1960.

Vico, Giambattista. *New Science*. 1744. Translated by David Marsh. Reprint, London: Penguin, 2001.

Voegelin, Eric. "Immortality: Experience and Symbol." *Harvard Theological Review* 60 (1967): 235–79.

Watt, W. Montgomery. "The Authenticity of the Works Attributed to al-Ghazālī." *Journal of the Royal Asiatic Society* (April 1952): 24–45.

———. "Deliverance from Error and Attachment to the Lord of Might and Majesty." In *The Faith and Practice of al-Ghazālī*, 17–92. 1953. Reprint, Oxford: Oneworld 1998.

———. *A History of Islamic Spain*. Edinburgh: Edinburgh University Press, 1965.

———. *Muslim Intellectual: A Study of al-Ghazali*. Edinburgh: Edinburgh University Press, 1963.

———. "Reflections on al-Ghazālī's Political Theory." *Transactions—Glasgow University Oriental Society* 21 (1965–66): 12–24.

Wehr, Hans. *A Dictionary of Modern Written Arabic*. Edited by J. M. Cowan. Wiesbaden: Harassowitz, 1979; Ithaca: Spoken Languages Services, 1994.

Wensinck, A. J. *La Pensée de Ghazzālī*. Paris: Adrien-Maisonneuve, 1940.

———. "On the Relationship between Ghazālī's Cosmology and His Mysticism." *Verhandelingen der Koninklijke Nederlandse Akademie van Wetenschappen, afd. Letterkunde* 75, no. 6 (1933): 183–209.

Wensinck, A. J., and J. H. Kramers, eds. *Handworterbuch des Islam*. Leiden: E. J. Brill, 1941.

White, Hayden. *Tropics of Discourse: Essays in Cultural Criticism*. Baltimore: Johns Hopkins University Press, 1985.

Wilde, Oscar. *The Picture of Dorian Gray*. In *The Complete Oscar Wilde*, 11–161. New York: Crescent Books, 1990.

Williams, Raymond. *Marxism and Literature*. Oxford: Oxford University Press, 1977.

Wittgenstein, Ludwig. *Lectures and Conversations on Aesthetics, Psychology and Religious Belief*. Edited by Cyril Barrett. Berkeley: University of California Press, 1972.

———. *Philosophical Investigations*. Translated by G. E. M. Anscombe. Oxford: Basil Blackwell, 1968.

Al-Yāfī, ʿAbd al-Karīm. "Sīrat al-Imām Abī Ḥāmid al-Ghazālī wa makānatuhu." *Al-turāth al-ʿarabī* 22 (January 1986): 7–22.

Yafūt, Sālim. "Bayna Ibn Ḥazm wa al-Ghazālī: Al-manṭiq al-arasṭī." In *Abū Ḥāmid al-Ghazzālī: Dirāsāt fī fikrihi wa ʿaṣrihi wa taʾthīrihi*, edited by Saʿīd bin Saʿīd al-ʿAlawī, 69–83. Rabat: Manshūrāt kullīya al-ādāb wa al-ʿulūm al-insānīya, 1988.

Yampolsky, Philip B. *The Platform Sutra of the Sixth Patriarch*. New York: Columbia University Press, 1967.

Yavari, Neguin. "Niẓām al-Mulk Remembered: A Study in Historical Representation." Ph.D. diss., Columbia University, 1992.

Al-Zabīdī, Murtāḍā. *Itḥāf as-sādāt al-muttaqīn bi sharḥ "Iḥyāʾ ʿulūm al-dīn."* 14 vols. Beirut: Dār al-Kutub al-ʿIlmīya, n.d.

Zadra, Dario. "Victor Turner's Theory of Religion: Towards an Analysis of Symbolic Time." In *Anthropology and the Study of Religion*, edited by Robert L. Moore and Frank E. Reynolds, 77–104. Chicago: Center for the Scientific Study of Religion, 1984.

Al-Zāhī, Farīd. "Ibn ʿArabī: Al-ṣūra wa al-ākhar." *Nizwa: Majalla faslīya Thaqāfīya* 23 (Rajab 1423/October 2002): 40–45.

Al-Zamakhsharī, Jār Allāh Abūʾ al-Qāsim Maḥmūd b. ʿUmar. *Asās al-balāgha*. Edited by ʿAbd al-Raḥīm Maḥmūd. Cairo: Maṭbaʿa Awlād Awrqānd, 1372/1953.

Zaqzūq, Maḥmūd Ḥamdī. *Al-manhaj al-falsafī bayna al-Ghazālī wa Dīkārt*. Cairo: Maktaba al-Angelo al-Miṣrīya, 1973.

Zarrinkūb, ʿAbd al-Ḥusayn. *Al-firār min al-madrasa: Dirāsa fī ḥayāt wa fikr Abī Ḥāmid al-Ghazālī*. Beirut: Dār al-Rawḍa, 1412/1992.

Zaydān, Jirji. *Taʾrīkh al-tamaddun al-Islāmī*. 5 vols. Cairo: Kitāb al-Adab, 1968.

Ziadeh, Farhat J., trans. *The Philosophy of Jurisprudence in Islam*, by S. Mahmasani. Leiden: E. J. Brill, 1961.

Zink, Michel. "The Allegorical Poem as Interior Memoir." *Yale French Studies* 70 (1986): 100–126.

———. *The Invention of Literary Subjectivity*. Translated by Davis Sices. Baltimore: Johns Hopkins University Press, 1999.

Al-Zuḥaylī, Muḥammad. "Ghazālī al-faqīh wa kitābuhu *Al-wajīz*." *Al-turāth al-ʿarabī* 22 (1986): 79–108.

Zwemer, Samuel M. *A Moslem Seeker after God*. New York: Fleming H. Revell, 1920.

Index